FENWAY PARK

Christian Elias, right, a 17-year veteran of the inner workings of the Green Monster, manned the left-field scoreboard with the help of Nate Moulter in May 2007. Players and scoreboard operators have left their mark on the walls for decades.

"Fenway is the essence of baseball."

—Tom Seaver, Hall of Fame pitcher

FENWAY PARK

A SALUTE TO THE COOLEST, CRUELEST,
LONGEST-RUNNING MAJOR LEAGUE BALLPARK IN AMERICA

BY JOHN POWERS
AND RON DRISCOLL
FOREWORD BY
JIM LONBORG
SPECIAL INTRODUCTION BY
BENJAMIN TAYLOR

Running Press
PHILADELPHIA · LONDON

© 2012 by the *Boston Globe*
Published by Running Press,
A Member of the Perseus Books Group

Books published by Running Press are available at special discounts for
bulk purchases in the United States by corporations, institutions, and
other organizations. For more information, please contact the Special
Markets Department at the Perseus Books Group, 2300 Chestnut
Street, Suite 200, Philadelphia, PA 19103, or call (800) 810-4145, ext.
5000, or e-mail special.markets@perseusbooks.com.

ISBN 978-0-7624-4204-1
Library of Congress Control Number: 2011925148

E-book ISBN 978-0-7624-4490-8

9 8 7 6 5 4 3 2 1
Digit on the right indicates the number of this printing

Cover and Interior Design: Joshua McDonnell
Timelines Design: *Boston Globe*
Editor (Running Press): Greg Jones
Editor (*Globe*): Janice Page
Photo Director (*Globe*): Susan Vermazen
Research (*Globe*): Stephanie Schorow

Running Press Book Publishers
2300 Chestnut Street
Philadelphia, PA 19103-4371

Visit us on the Web!
www.runningpress.com

www.bostonglobe.com and www.boston.com

"The game opens in other stadiums in the country, in those giant modern saucers, and the day is a joyous, modern, klieg-light event. The game opens here, and it is a continuation. It is a pleasant click on the calendar. It is a celebration of the past, the present and everything in between. It is newly painted history."

—Leigh Montville, *Boston Globe*, Opening Day 1982

DEDICATION

To George, who knows every inch of the lyric little bandbox and who preceded me at the typewriter.

—John Powers

To Kathi, Molly, and Meg; and to our first Fenway forays: doubleheader Sundays in the mid-1960s, when the ballpark truly was the star.

—Ron Driscoll

ACKNOWLEDGMENTS

The histories of Fenway Park and the Boston Red Sox have been intertwined with the *Boston Globe* from the outset, and also with the Taylor family, which owned the *Globe* for much of the newspaper's first 125 years, and which played a key role with the team and its ballpark at various times. Thus we would like to especially thank the Red Sox, present and former staff members of the *Globe*, and the Taylor family for their involvement in helping to create 100 years of Fenway Park history, and in making it come alive for readers and sports fans in New England, and increasingly, around the world.

A huge thank you as well to Janice Page, the *Globe*'s book development editor, who masterfully guided the project from start to fruition; to *Globe* editor Martin Baron, publisher Christopher Mayer, deputy managing editor Mark Morrow, and the entire Sports staff, especially columnists Dan Shaughnessy and Bob Ryan and editor Joe Sullivan. Our appreciation also goes to the book's keen-eyed photo director, Susan Vermazen, as well as Jim Wilson, Leanne Burden, David Ryan, Jim Davis, Stan Grossfeld, and all members of the photo department, along with graphics staffers Daigo Fujiwara, Javier Zarracina, and David Schutz. Thanks as well to the indefatigable Lisa Tuite and the library staff for their research efforts, and Stephanie Schorow (research and fact checking), Alan Wirzbicki (fact checking), Richard Kassirer, Paul Colton, William Herzog, Jim Matte (proofreading), and Ray Marsden and John Ioven (imaging).

At Running Press, special thanks to editor Greg Jones, designer Joshua McDonnell, and every exacting copy editor who had a hand in these pages.

Cheers to Ben Taylor, for sharing both memories and memorabilia, and to Jim Lonborg, who's just as classy off the field as he was on it.

As always, we are grateful for the support of Lane Zachary and Todd Shuster at Zachary, Shuster, Harmsworth Literary Agency. We also thank the good people at the Boston Public Library (Jane Winton, Tom Blake, Catherine Wood), Tim Wiles of the National Baseball Hall of Fame, and our friends at Dorian Color Lab in Arlington, Massachusetts. And we especially appreciate the generosity of Dan Rea, Susan Goodenow, David Friedman, and everyone in the Fenway Park front office.

"The ballpark is the star. In the age of Tris Speaker and Babe Ruth, the era of Jimmie Foxx and Ted Williams, through the empty-seats epoch of Don Buddin and Willie Tasby and unto the decades of Carl Yastrzemski and Jim Rice, the ballpark is the star. A crazy-quilt violation of city planning principles, an irregular pile of architecture, a menace to marketing consultants, Fenway Park works. It works as a symbol of New England's pride, as a repository of evergreen hopes, as a tabernacle of lost innocence. It works as a place to watch baseball."

—**Martin F. Nolan, former *Boston Globe* editorial page editor**

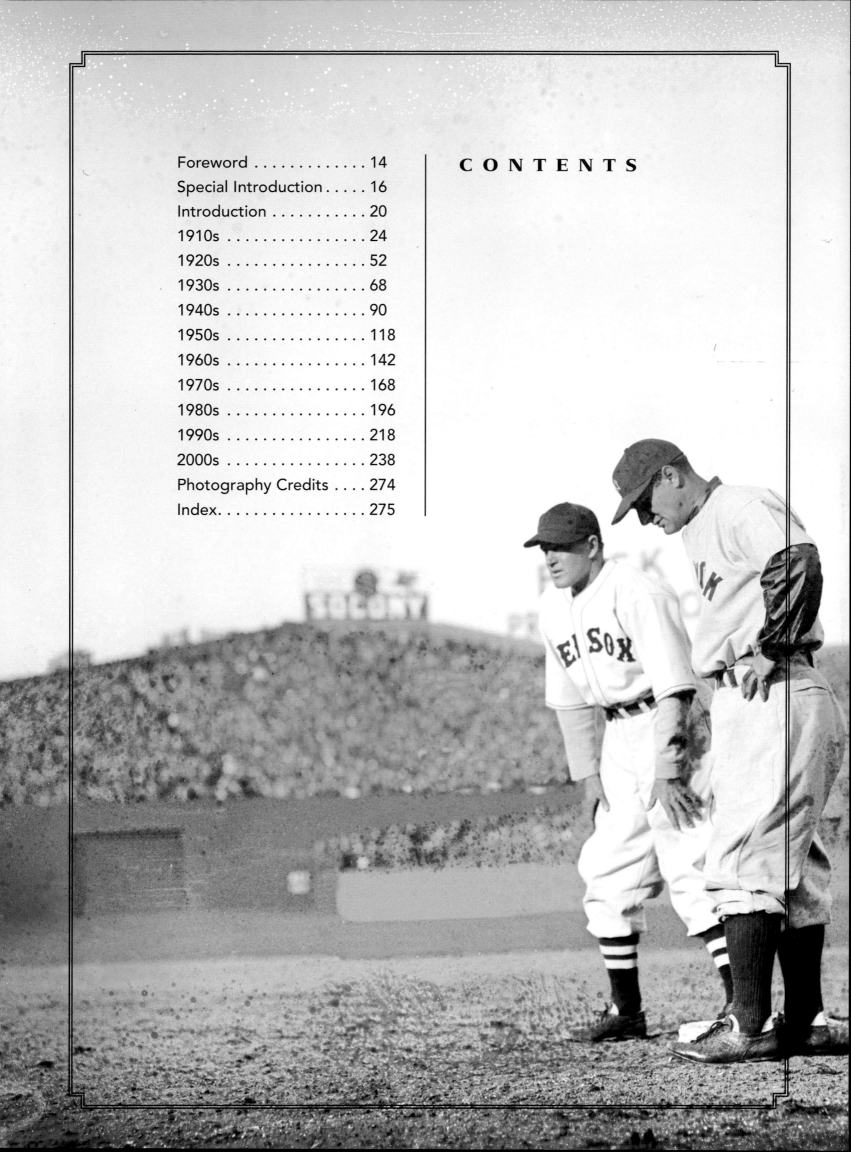

CONTENTS

FOREWORD

BY

JIM LONBORG

first saw Fenway Park in 1965 when I was a rookie pitcher for the Red Sox. We had played a couple of exhibitions on the way home from spring training in Scottsdale, Arizona, and had flown into Boston on Saturday night. We were staying at the Kenmore Hotel and we walked over for a workout on Sunday. I was used to ballparks like Candlestick Park and Dodger Stadium in California, so it was unique to be in a city setting and enter through a beautiful brick facade.

I remember coming through the tunnel on the first-base side and the first thing I saw was the Wall. I thought, this is where I have to work? I stepped off the distance from home plate to the Wall to see whether the posted distance of 315 feet was an accurate reading and it wasn't. But our coaching staff did a really good job of preparing us mentally to pitch in Fenway. The Wall can help you as much as it hurts you because a lot of line drives are knocked down by it. Since I was a sinkerball pitcher, if balls were up in the sky I wasn't making very good pitches.

My first major-league victory came in Fenway against the Yankees on May 10. It was a thrill to pitch against Mickey Mantle, who'd been one of my boyhood heroes, and I struck him out in his first at-bat. After that, though, he had a single and a homer, and when Mickey hit a double with two out in the ninth Billy Herman, our manager, came out and said, "I think it's time to bring in the Big Guy." So Dick Radatz came in for the save and we won 3-2.

There weren't many fans at our games during my first two years and sounds travel very well at Fenway so you could hear what players and fans were yelling. But in 1967 after we won 10 in a row and returned from that road trip, we came back to packed seats. People still tell me that it was the greatest summer of their lives. None of us ever had been in a pennant race before. That year we had four teams involved—the Twins, White Sox, Tigers, and us—and you couldn't help but scoreboard-watch. At Fenway we had the best way of keeping score—the guy in the Wall. You would see that number disappear and wait for the next one to come up. It wasn't like it was being blurted out on a Jumbotron. You'd be in a situation where you wouldn't be expecting a cheer and you'd turn around and look at the scoreboard.

That final game against Minnesota was so tense all the way through. To make the comeback we did, to be on the field at the end and celebrate with all the players and then to turn around and see thousands of fans coming onto the field was the most exciting moment of my life. It was something a little kid would think about when he was a make-believe pitcher.

But as the fans were carrying me on their shoulders, the feeling went from jubilation to a little bit of fear. I was going places where I didn't want to go, out by Pesky's Pole. Finally the police got me to where I wanted to go, which was the clubhouse, where we still had to wait for the Angels-Tigers game to end in Detroit. For us to be sitting around a radio instead of a TV, it reminded me of an old-time movie where you were listening for news of some important event.

After the Angels beat the Tigers and we'd won the pennant, I went upstairs to see Mr. Yawkey to give him the game ball that my teammates had given to me. I knew that it was such a long time since he'd had anything good like that happen for him that I thought he should have it. It was almost like the owner's office in *The Natural*, with the dark hallway and the dark-paneled room. Mr. Yawkey was there and I gave him the ball. He cried a lot that day. That was a special chapter of a fabled story. The beauty of the Red Sox is that every year is a different chapter—and there's still more to this book.

Whenever I come back to Fenway I try to go in through the same ramp that I did that first time in 1965, and it's the same feeling. It has so many great memories for me. The greenness, the majesty of the Wall. That image never goes away.

Jim Lonborg was the first Red Sox pitcher to win the Cy Young Award (1967)

LEFT: On the final day of the 1967 season, teammates and fans rushed Jim Lonborg after he pitched the Red Sox to victory over the Minnesota Twins to gain at least a tie for the American League pennant.

SPECIAL INTRODUCTION

BY

BENJAMIN TAYLOR

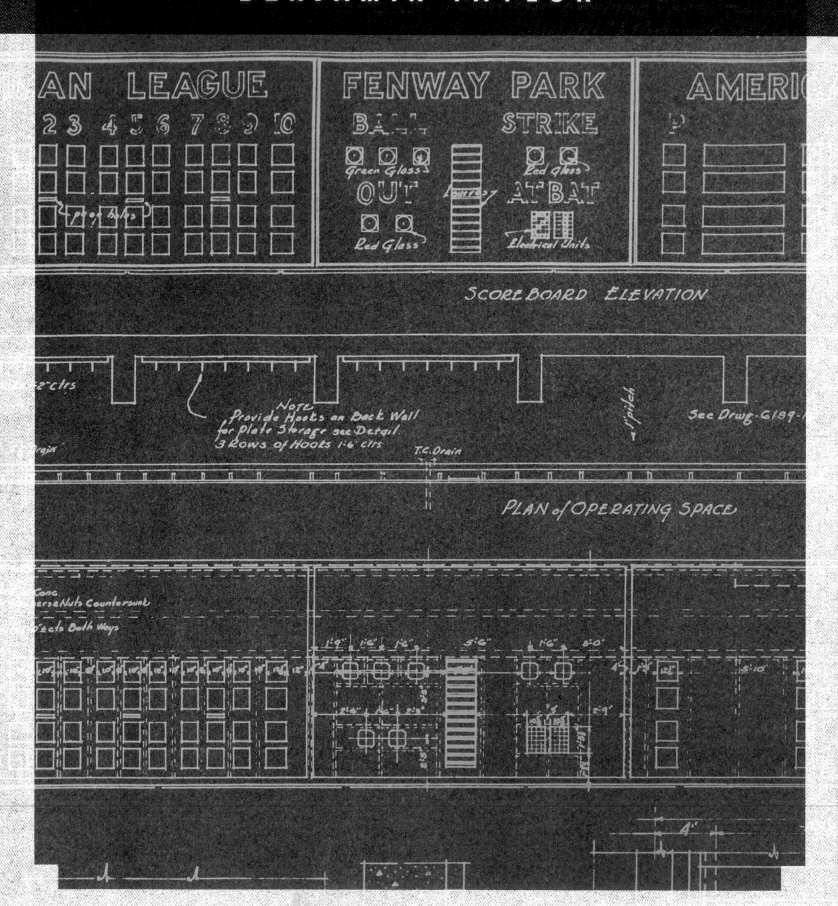

After the death of my father, John I. Taylor, in June of 1987, I had to clean out his office at the *Boston Globe*, where he had spent more than five decades as a newspaperman. Most of what I found was unremarkable, with one exception. In the dark recesses of a closet, I discovered a couple of blueprints. One was of Fenway Park and the other a detailed sketch of the hand-operated scoreboard still extant on the park's left-field wall. Upon closer inspection, I realized that the blueprints were of the renovation of the park in 1933 by then-owner Thomas A. Yawkey. I assumed that they were given to my father because his father, also named John I. Taylor, is credited with having built Fenway Park.

I never met my grandfather. He died in 1938, ten years before I was born. I was vaguely aware—no doubt from reading the great Peter Gammons—that he was the president of Boston's American League franchise from 1904 to 1911, that he changed the name of the team from the Boston Americans to the Boston Red Sox, and that he built Fenway Park. Other than this, I knew very little about him. Conversations with my older brothers confirm that our father rarely talked about his father. I cannot deny feeling a bit of family pride around his connection to Fenway Park, but I am also aware that my grandfather was thoroughly trashed as a meddlesome owner and dilettante by Glenn Stout and Richard A. Johnson in their book *Red Sox Century*.

I hung the blueprints in my office at the *Globe* and then at home after I left the paper in late 1999. When I discovered they were fading because of exposure to the light, I took them off the wall and stored them in our attic where they now reside, gathering dust. (You can see them, restored to their original blue, at left and on the next page.)

As a fan, my experience is not unlike thousands of others in New England. In the first game I can remember attending at Fenway, the Red Sox played the great 1954 Cleveland Indians team that won 111 games during the 154-game regular season. I was seven years old. That same decade, I remember my parents telling me I couldn't go to a game with the rest of the family because of the polio scare. Like many Red Sox fans of a certain age, I was thrilled by the magical seasons of 1967, 1975, and 1986, when the Sox came within one game of winning the World Series and breaking the Curse of the Bambino. I became addicted to reading newspapers when I was young because of the Red Sox coverage. To this day, Sox stories in the *Globe* remain one of the first staples I turn to each morning.

On my office wall now, I have a picture of Ted Williams and his beautiful swing during the All-Star Game in 1946. On the same wall, near the *Globe* front page of August 9, 1974 announcing Nixon's resignation, is a framed reproduction of the *Globe*'s front page of October 28, 2004 chronicling the Sox victory in the World Series for the first time since 1918. Like many Red Sox fans, I feel we are extremely fortunate that the current ownership chose to improve Fenway rather than build a new park. They have preserved a national treasure. That choice seems to have been a good business decision too, as the Sox continue to draw extraordinary crowds for home games.

My mother was a consummate Red Sox fan. She used to listen to games on the radio. Curt Gowdy's mellifluous tones and then Ned Martin's were familiar sounds in my house growing up. Born in 1915, which made her too young to remember the championship seasons of that year, 1916, and 1918, my mother used to say her one wish was that the Red Sox win a World Series before she died. She died in 1990, missing the championships of 2004 and 2007 that finally ended the club's long stretch of futility.

There is no way to predict the future, or how long Fenway will survive into the 21st century. It is important not to stay stuck in the past. Fenway, though vastly improved in recent years, is not without flaws. The right-field grandstand seats have lousy sightlines that apparently are very difficult to improve. Legroom is not the park's strongest suit. Many of the best seats have become financially prohibitive. Nevertheless, as it celebrates its 100th anniversary, the park still works remarkably well as a place where fans can enjoy professional baseball at the highest level. Those of us who love the game can only hope that Fenway Park remains an essential part of the soul of New England and of the national pastime for a long time to come.

Benjamin Taylor is a former publisher of the Boston Globe

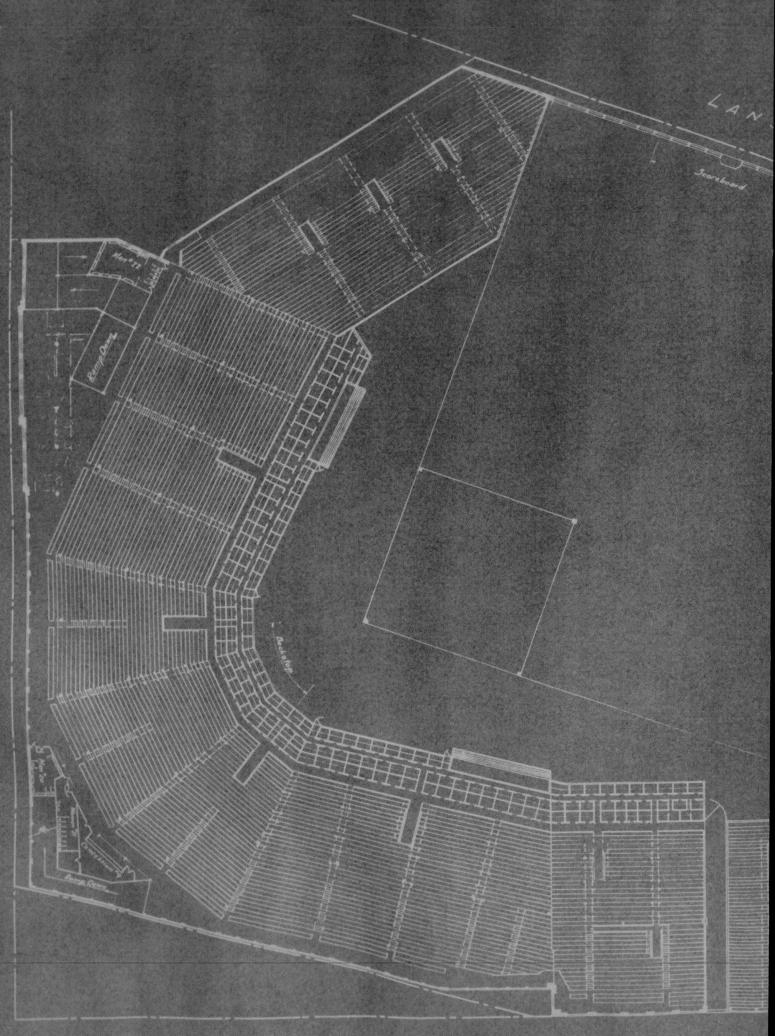

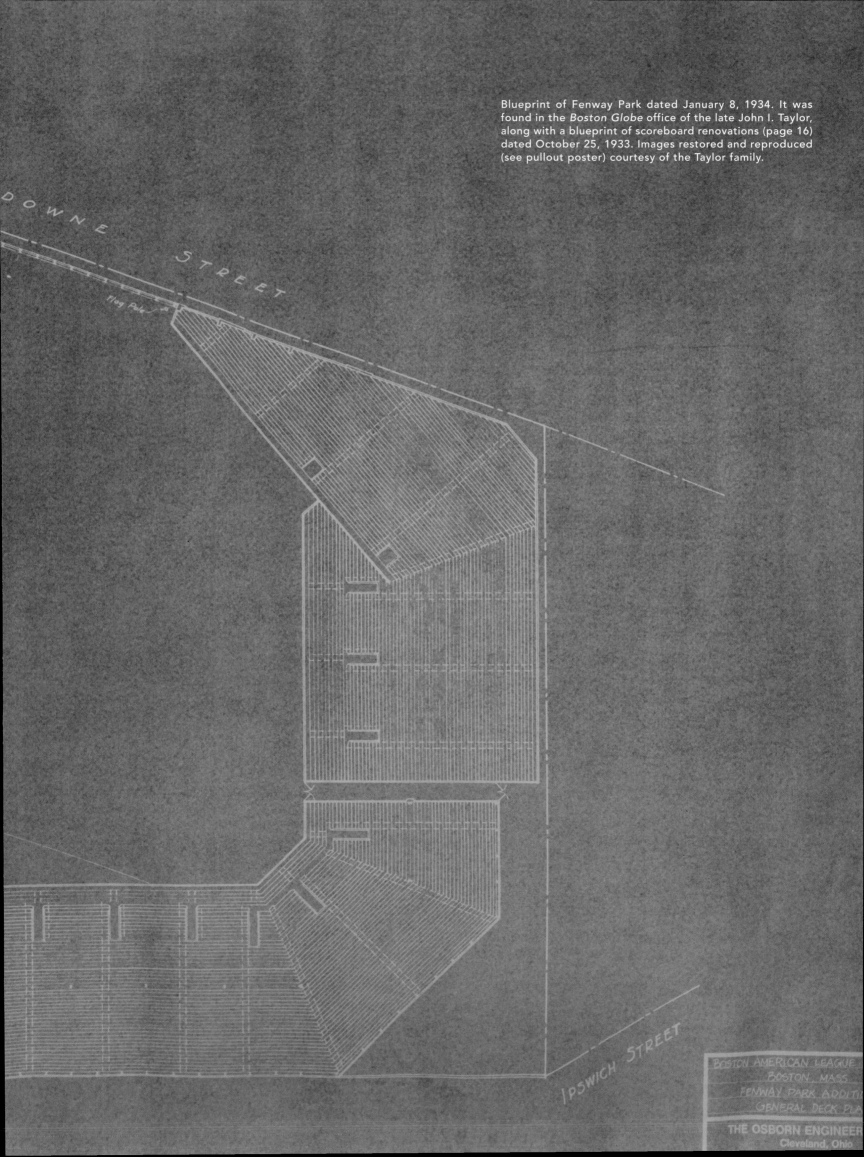

Blueprint of Fenway Park dated January 8, 1934. It was found in the *Boston Globe* office of the late John I. Taylor, along with a blueprint of scoreboard renovations (page 16) dated October 25, 1933. Images restored and reproduced (see pullout poster) courtesy of the Taylor family.

INTRODUCTION

The storied home of the Red Sox for a century, "America's Most Beloved Ballpark" also is the oldest in the major leagues, and the most famous. From the classic brick entrance on Yawkey Way, to the unique left-field wall with its manual scoreboard, to Pesky's Pole in right field, its timeless features are recognized from the Bronx to the Dominican Republic to Japan.

John Updike's "lyric little bandbox," which he likened to "an old-fashioned peeping-type Easter egg," is so linked with Boston and baseball history that it is a destination in itself, equal to the Freedom Trail and the swan boats, with visitors taking guided ballpark tours even during winter. In *Cheers*, the long-running situation comedy based in a Back Bay tavern, bartender Sam "Mayday" Malone was a former Red Sox relief pitcher. The fan film *Fever Pitch* is based around Fenway. It is also where Kevin Costner took James Earl Jones for an inspirational outing in *Field of Dreams*.

Fenway's field is like no other. Because the park was jammed into a city lot bounded by narrow streets, its dimensions are a crazy confluence of oblique angles—like the three-sided oddity in center field that can turn the game into Pachinko, with the ball bouncing and rattling about. There is so little playable foul territory that dozens of balls end up in the stands, which are so close to the diamond that fans can hear the players' chatter.

Fenway is a charmingly auditory experience, from the scalpers on Brookline Avenue ("Who needs tickets?"), to the fans singing "Sweet Caroline" during the eighth inning, to the playing of "Dirty Water" over the public address system after victories.

Fenway's endearing quirkiness is the key to much of its allure. Except for some increased seating and creature comforts, the park has remained largely unchanged since it opened in 1912 in the same week that the Titanic sank.

"When I brought my kids to Fenway, they never complained about the inconveniences of the ancient ballpark," wrote *Boston Globe* columnist Dan Shaughnessy, who confessed that he still took "some weird comfort in the knowledge that the poles that occasionally obscured our vision of the pitcher are the same green beams that blocked the vision of my dad and his dad when they would take the trolley from Cambridge to watch the Red Sox in the 1920s."

Babe Ruth threw his first pitch and Ted Williams hit his last home run at Fenway. From Christy Mathewson, to Ty Cobb, to Satchel Paige, to Joe DiMaggio, to Hank Aaron, most of baseball's greatest names have appeared on Fenway's stage, which also has accommodated an extraordinary variety of other athletes, politicians, and entertainers.

Three of Boston's professional football teams—the Redskins, the Yanks, and the Patriots—performed at Fenway. The Bruins and Flyers, two of hockey's fiercest rivals, played in the Winter Classic there on New Year's Day. Franklin Delano Roosevelt gave his final campaign address at Fenway. The Rolling Stones, Stevie Wonder, Paul McCartney, and Bruce Springsteen all sang there.

Through it all the *Boston Globe* has been the consistent, respected chronicler—both in words and in pictures—of every important event in Fenway's history. The Taylor family, the newspaper's founders and longtime stewards, owned and named both the team and the park. So it's appropriate that the *Globe* has produced the definitive book celebrating 100 years of Fenway Park, a collector's item featuring exceptional writing and unforgettable images from the *Globe*'s incomparable archive of photographs, illustrations, and front pages.

Every significant moment from every year is here, and then some. The dramatic World Series victory over the Giants in 1912. The 1934 fire that scorched Tom Yawkey's renovated park. Ted Williams's "Great Expectoration" of 1956. Jim Lonborg's "hero's ride" after putting the Sox in position to secure the Impossible Dream pennant in 1967. Carlton Fisk's dramatic, "is-it-fair?" homer in the 12th inning of Game 6 of the 1975 World Series against the Reds. Bucky "Bleeping" Dent's heartbreaking screen shot in the 1978 divisional playoff game with New York. Roger Clemens's record 20 strikeouts against the Mariners in 1986. Dave Roberts' stolen base against the Yankees in 2004 that was the beginning of the end of 86 years of October frustration.

Fenway is all about lore. The Royal Rooters torturing visiting ballplayers with incessant renditions of "Tessie." Williams's monster bleacher shot knocking a hole in a fan's straw hat. Manny Ramirez's mystery disappearance inside the belly of the Monster. Jimmy Piersall oinking like a pig on the base paths. Luis Tiant's rhumba windup that the *New Yorker*'s Roger Angell dubbed "Call the Osteopath." Pedro Martinez playing matador to former skipper Don Zimmer's enraged bull during a brawl with the Yankees. A midget coming out of the stands to cover third when the Indians used the "Williams Shift."

This is the story of 100 years of Fenway Park, in chapter and verse, by the people who lived it.

1910s

A member of the Royal Rooters, a group of passionate Red Sox fans, sounded the drumbeat during a 1903 World Series game with the Pittsburgh Pirates at Huntington Avenue Grounds. The Rooters continued their antics for several years after the Sox moved to Fenway.

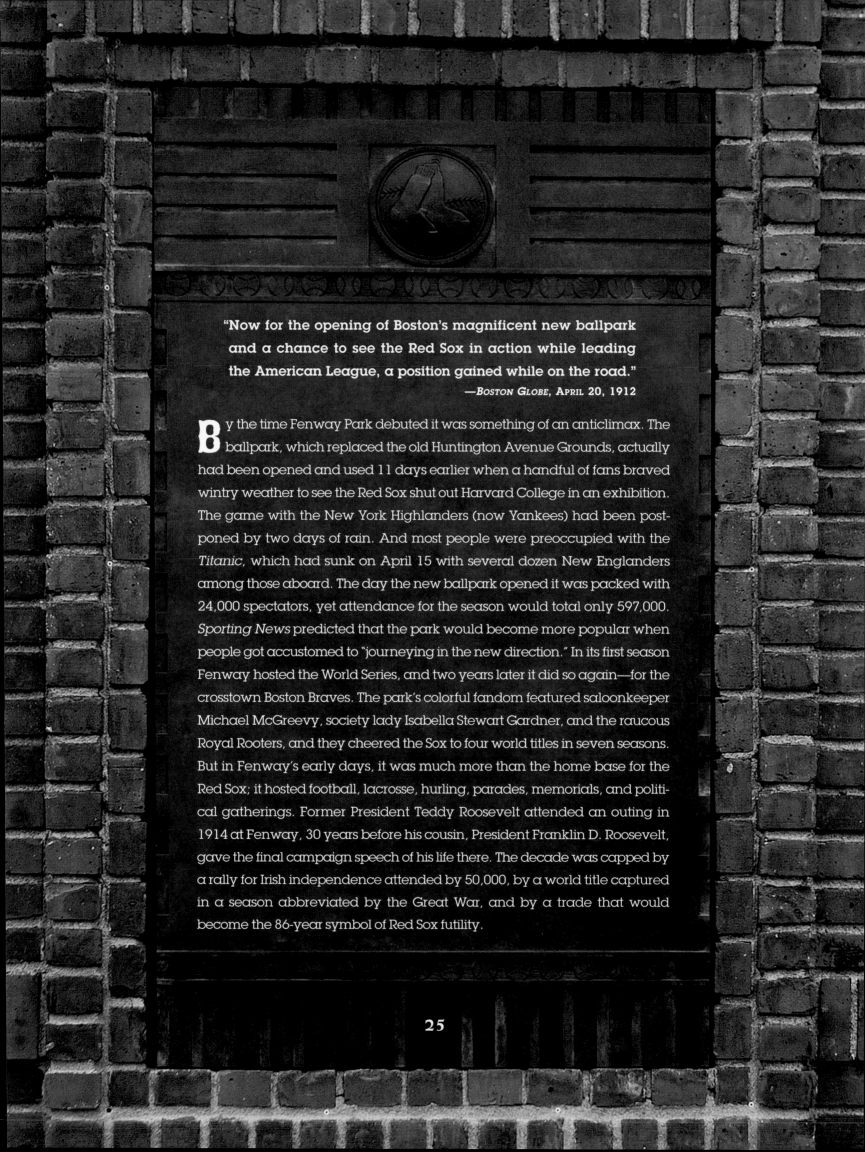

> "Now for the opening of Boston's magnificent new ballpark and a chance to see the Red Sox in action while leading the American League, a position gained while on the road."
> —*Boston Globe*, April 20, 1912

By the time Fenway Park debuted it was something of an anticlimax. The ballpark, which replaced the old Huntington Avenue Grounds, actually had been opened and used 11 days earlier when a handful of fans braved wintry weather to see the Red Sox shut out Harvard College in an exhibition. The game with the New York Highlanders (now Yankees) had been postponed by two days of rain. And most people were preoccupied with the *Titanic*, which had sunk on April 15 with several dozen New Englanders among those aboard. The day the new ballpark opened it was packed with 24,000 spectators, yet attendance for the season would total only 597,000. *Sporting News* predicted that the park would become more popular when people got accustomed to "journeying in the new direction." In its first season Fenway hosted the World Series, and two years later it did so again—for the crosstown Boston Braves. The park's colorful fandom featured saloonkeeper Michael McGreevy, society lady Isabella Stewart Gardner, and the raucous Royal Rooters, and they cheered the Sox to four world titles in seven seasons. But in Fenway's early days, it was much more than the home base for the Red Sox; it hosted football, lacrosse, hurling, parades, memorials, and political gatherings. Former President Teddy Roosevelt attended an outing in 1914 at Fenway, 30 years before his cousin, President Franklin D. Roosevelt, gave the final campaign speech of his life there. The decade was capped by a rally for Irish independence attended by 50,000, by a world title captured in a season abbreviated by the Great War, and by a trade that would become the 86-year symbol of Red Sox futility.

NEW HOME OF THE RED SOX; PLANT IDEAL IN EQUIPMENT AND LOCATION.

Baseball Park Will Contain 365,308 Square Feet of Land With Stands of the Most Approved Type, Providing Seating Accommodations for 28,000—
Completed Product, It Is Understood, Will Represent an Outlay of $1,000,000.

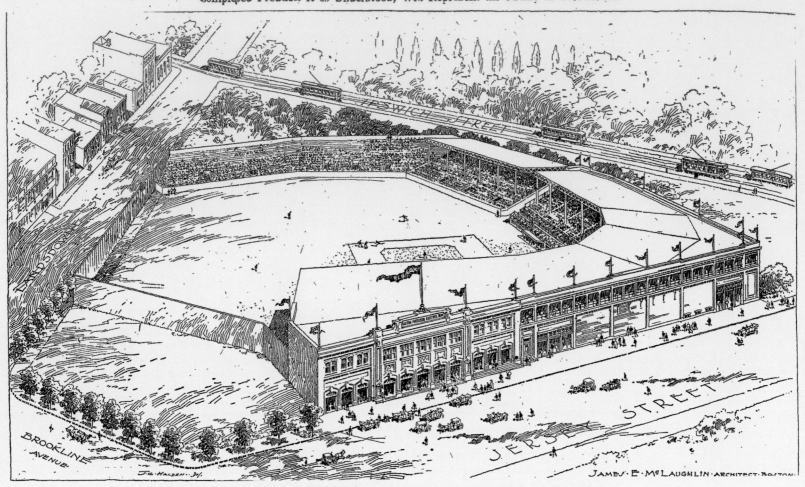

NEW BASEBALL PARK FOR THE BOSTON AMERICAN LEAGUE TEAM AS IT WILL APPEAR WHEN COMPLETED

From the very beginning, the cherished and cursed home of the Boston Red Sox was the most misshapen and quirky collection of angles and corners in baseball. It was, John Updike wrote, "a compromise between Man's Euclidean determinations and Nature's beguiling irregularities." Even the much-beloved name started as a simple tribute to geography. "It's in the Fenway section, isn't it?" the team's owner said at the time.

The very genesis of Fenway Park was a matter of straightforward commerce. John I. Taylor was the owner of a ball club that played in a rented park. What he wanted was to own half of a club playing in a ballpark that he fully controlled, preferably in the embryonic neighborhood where his real estate company owned a large chunk of the reclaimed swampland that he and his partners hoped to develop into one of Boston's desirable districts.

So he bought more than 365,000 square feet from his company, had architect James McLaughlin draw up plans and sold half of the Red Sox to former Washington Senators manager Jimmy McAleer for $150,000. Taylor then set about building what the *Boston Globe* promised would be a "magnificent baseball plant" between Lansdowne and Ipswich Streets. The new facility would be

A rendering of the new ballpark from architect James E. McLaughlin was published in the *Boston Globe*, which estimated the cost of the park at $1 million.

made of concrete and steel with a brick exterior that was a cross between a South End bowfront and a New England cotton mill and it would accommodate 28,000 spectators, twice as many as did the wooden Huntington Avenue Grounds in which the team had played since 1901.

Taylor, whose father Charles was publisher of the *Globe*, opted for the obvious and commercially convenient name of Fenway Park. The constraints of the site, cost, calendar, and concern for squinting batsmen led to Fenway's endearing and infuriating dimensions.

Since Taylor didn't want hitters blinded by the setting sun in an era when games began at 3:30 p.m., he had the diamond oriented with home plate looking out toward Lansdowne.

He didn't want freeloaders sneaking into the standing areas in the outfield or peering down from nearby rooftops, so he erected a 25-foot wooden wall that he could cover with paid advertisements and that was buttressed by

FOR DEVELOPMENT.

Fenway Park, New Home of Red
Sox, Transferred to Three
Trustees for Improvement.

As a first move in the changes in the
Boston American league baseball club
matters, papers were passed yesterday
transferring the Fenway park grounds
on Ipswich and Lansdowne sts to Chas.
H. Taylor of Boston, Ashton L. Carr of
Melrose and Arthur C. Wise or lling-
ham, as trustees, to develop the property, build grandstand, pavilions and
otherwise grade and improve the
grounds so that for capacity and character the accommodations will be second to none in this country.

Of the trustees, Gen Taylor is the
head of the Globe newspaper company;
his son, John I. Taylor, is president of
the Boston Americans; Mr Carr is vice
president and treasurer of the State-st
trust company and Mr Wise is a member of the firm of Millett, Roe & Hagen,
which firm has bought the bonds issued
in financing the operation.

For convenience in developing and
improving, the Fenway realty trust, of
which the above named men are trustees, is created with a capital of $300,000,
divided into 3000 shares of $100 each,
practically all held by the owners of
the club, this form being advised as the
most convenient way to carry out the
new development. A mortgage securing
$275,000 5 per cent nontaxable bonds has
been recorded with the trust deed.

The Charles Logue building company,
which has the contract for the erection
of the grandstand, etc, has begun work
on the foundation. The architect is
James E. McLaughlin of Boston.

The baseball public will look forward
with interest to the development of the
new grounds, situated as they are, convenient of access, with ample room and
accommodation for the largest crowd
on any holiday or day of special features.

The bonds will be offered shortly by
Millett, Roe & Hagen.

ABOVE: Red Sox team president John I. Taylor, whose
father was principal owner of the *Globe*, sold half of the
Red Sox and built Fenway Park on land that he owned in
the newly developed Fenway section of the city.

RIGHT: The first ball put into play in the first game at
Fenway Park, with an inscription by umpire Tom Connolly.

How Boston's New Baseball Park Looked at the Opening Game

The pictures reproduced below, taken specially for the Sunday Post, give the public a good idea of how the new American league grounds look. The upper picture shows the general arrangement of the stands. These have a much larger seating capacity than those at the old grounds. Other pictures show a closer view of some sections of the stands.

GENERAL VIEW SHOWING ARRANGEMENT OF STANDS

ENTRANCE TO THE NEW PARK.

FIRST BASE BLEACHES SHOWING ROOF CONSTRUCTION

CLOSE VIEW OF ONE OF THE MAIN GRAND STANDS

a 10-foot incline that made fielding fly balls something between art and accident.

Although the foundation was designed to support an upper deck, Taylor wanted his $650,000 playpen finished in time for the 1912 season, which left only seven months from the September groundbreaking. So a grandstand was built to hold 15,000 ticket holders with additional seating along the lines. Quartets of box seats were offered at $250 for the season, with pavilion seats going for 50 cents a game and bleacher spaces for 25 cents.

Fenway Park was such a novelty and the April weather so inhospitable that what the *Globe* called "the real down-to-the-book official dedication with the music stuff, the flowers and the flags" did not occur until May 17, when the Sox lost to Chicago, 5-2, after leading 2-1 until the ninth, before 17,000 fans. Only 3,000 witnesses had turned out for the dress rehearsal on April 9, a 2-0 exhibition game victory over Harvard that was played amid snow flurries. "It was no day for baseball," the *Globe* concluded. Nor were April 18 and Patriots Day, when the scheduled league opener and rescheduled doubleheader were rained out.

When the sun finally appeared on April 20, more than 24,000 fans were on hand for the first official game and what would, in later decades, become a celebrated rarity—a victory over New York, this one achieved in 11 innings by a 7-6 count.

It took another four games for a ball to be knocked over the left-field wall, which then was more of a barrier than a monster. The man who did it, reserve first baseman Hugh Bradley, had hit only one other homer in his career and never managed another. But after sitting on one of southpaw Lefty Russell's corkscrew curves, Bradley lashed "a terrific smash" over the fence for a three-run shot that gave the Sox a 7-6 victory over the Athletics. "The scene that followed was indescribable," Tim Murnane wrote in the *Globe.* "Spectators jumped onto their seats and threw their hats in the air and howled like Indians until Bradley had ducked out of sight, with the Boston players offering congratulations." The Sox quickly proved themselves capable of running up dizzying numbers. "SWAT! SWAT! SWAT!" read the *Globe* headline after the "Speed Boys" outgunned Washington, 33-19, in a May 29 home doubleheader, with the scorers for both clubs covering over three-and-a-half miles ("Hitting and Run-Getting on Wholesale Basis at Fenway Park"). On June 29, rain washed out the game with New York with Boston leading, 10-0, with two out in the first inning. But the hosts won, 8-0, the next day.

By July 20, when the club was in first place by seven games over the Senators, the *Globe* essentially awarded it the pennant with this headline: "Keen Head Work Combined With Acutely Schemed Team Play; Excellent Pitching, Catching, Infield and Outfield Action; Timely Hitting and Shrewd Base Running Have Shined Gloriously Bright the Outlook for Winning the 1912 Championship."

Howard "Smoky Joe" Wood, the game's best "twirler,"

"The game was full of interest, the crowd holding its seats to the end, figuring that the Red Sox would eventually nose out the Broadway swells."

—T. H. Murnane, *Boston Globe,* April 21, 1912, in a story headlined "Sox Open to Packed Park"

BACK IN THE DAY

BY JOHN POWERS

The Red Sox began the 1912 season with a new brick-and-steel ball yard ("the mammoth plant with the commodious fittings") and no ghosts. Their fifth-place finish in 1911 had been forgotten. By the time they hosted the New York Highlanders on April 20, a sunny Saturday afternoon, they were already sitting in first place in the eight-team American League, well on the way to the finest year in club history (105-47 and the world championship over the New York Giants).

J. Garland "Jake" Stahl, the new player-manager who worked as a Chicago banker in the off-season, had promised no less. The Red Sox, he said, would give the Boston public "only the best of baseball this season, barring accidents."

"It will be good to play some baseball," Stahl said. "We have come out of Hot Springs [Arkansas] ready to go. We started well and we do not need any more postponements."

The Red Sox were 4-1 after wins in New York and Philadelphia on the way north. The visiting Highlanders had not liked sitting around in their hotel—the Copley Plaza—for extra, wasteful days.

Opening Day was perhaps something of an anticlimax. Fenway Park, which replaced the old Huntington Avenue Grounds, actually had been opened and used 11 days earlier when 3,000 customers shivered amid snow flurries while the Red Sox shut out Harvard in an exhibition. The game with the Highlanders (now Yankees) had been postponed by two days of rain, from Thursday to Saturday. And most people were preoccupied with the *Titanic*, which had sunk on Monday morning with several dozen New Englanders aboard.

The Boston-New York game was listed on the amusements page of the newspaper, merely one of several urban attractions that day. Billie Burke was playing in *The Runaway* at the Hollis Street Theatre. There was a Taft rally at Faneuil Hall, the Textile and Power Show at the Mechanics Building (admission 25 cents), the BSO at Symphony Hall. And at the Park Theatre, *Hoopla! Father Doesn't Care!!*

If you wanted to attend Opening Day, you could buy a reserved seat in the grandstands for 75 cents or a bleacher seat for a quarter. Tickets were available at Wright and Ditson at 344 Washington Street or at the gate. The ballpark was packed with 24,000 spectators, with hundreds of them standing behind a rope in the outfield. Yet attendance for the season would total only 597,000. *The Sporting News* predicted that the park would become more popular when people got accustomed to "journeying in the new direction."

If you owned a car in 1912, you could park it almost anywhere you pleased near the ballpark. The only two buildings near the park were a riding school and a garage out beyond right field. The West Fens was terra nova at the time. Artists, students, musicians, and assorted bohemians lived there, out beyond the water and marsh. Speculators owned the land, looking to sell it to developers who would erect apartment buildings near the trolley lines.

Most of the Opening Day crowd arrived by public transit, taking the Ipswich Street, Beacon Street or Commonwealth Avenue cars and walking past open lots to the park. A cadre of "big, fine-looking officers" from Division 16 preserved order. Inside the park customers drank Pureoxia ginger ale, Dr. Swett's Original Root Beer, and cold lager. If Fenway Franks were available, it was not recorded.

Mayor John "Honey Fitz" Fitzgerald (the future maternal grandfather of President John F. Kennedy) tossed out the first ball, with Governor Eugene Foss at his side, and Buck O'Brien threw the first pitch at 3:10 p.m. "There was no time wasted in childish parades," *Globe* writer T.H. Murnane observed. The boisterous Royal Rooters, led by South End saloonkeeper Michael T. "Nuf Ced" McGreevy, serenaded the assemblage with their theme song, "Tessie."

The Red Sox, also called the Speed Boys, climbed out of a 5-1 hole and won, 7-6, in 11 innings, helped by five hits, including a pair of doubles, by second baseman Steve Yerkes. Murnane wrote, "Tristram Speaker, the Texas sharpshooter, with two down in the 11th inning and Yerkes on third, smashed the ball too fast for the shortstop to handle and the winning run came over the plate . . . the immense crowd leaving for home for a cold supper but wreathed in smiles." The size of the crowd may have hindered the Red Sox cause, said Murnane. "Before the game, the crowd broke into the outfield and remained behind the ropes, forcing the teams to make ground rules, all hits going for two bases. This ruling was a big disadvantage to the home team, for the Highland laddies never hit for more than a single, while three of Boston's hits went into the crowd, whereas with a clear field they would have gone for three-base drives and possibly home runs, and would have landed the home team a winner before the ninth inning."

The writers finished up their scorecards promptly at 6:20 and went back to Newspaper Row. Nobody bothered entering the clubhouse to talk to the players.

ABOVE: Boston Mayor John "Honey Fitz" Fitzgerald tipped his hat after throwing out the first pitch on April 20, 1912, the first official game in Fenway Park history.

BELOW: A view from the stands in 1912.

ABOVE: Even if you didn't have a ticket, you could view the 1912 World Series through gaps in a fence at the new Fenway Park, where the Red Sox took on the New York Giants.

BELOW: Mayor John Fitzgerald (standing) and star pitcher "Smoky Joe" Wood (in the back, with bow tie) took part in Boston's victory parade after the 1912 World Series.

went an astounding 34-5 for the Sox in 1912, while his teammates Buck O'Brien and Hugh Bedient each won 20 games. Tris Speaker batted .383 and Duffy Lewis knocked in 109 runs. The Sox didn't even have to clinch the pennant on their own. When they were being rained out in Cleveland on September 18, the White Sox beat the Athletics to give Boston its first American League title since 1904. By then management had already begun expanding Fenway's capacity to 32,000, adding 900 box seats and new stands in left and right field.

When the team returned from Detroit on September 23, a crowd of 200,000 jammed Summer Street for a parade as the players rode in cars from South Station to the Common. "No general and his army, returning victorious from war, were ever received with wilder or more enthusiastic acclaim," James O'Leary observed in the *Globe*. Pennant fever was contagious. Women wore scarlet hose and carried dolls dressed in Boston uniforms while men sported oversized neckties with large red stockings woven in.

After the Sox took the World Series opener from the Giants in New York, more than 1,000 fans were in line at dawn when bleacher seats went on sale for the first home date. "Many had attendants with them who did their bid-

"Smoky Joe" Wood dominated the American League in 1912 with a 34-5 record, including 10 shutouts. He also contributed three World Series victories as the Red Sox vanquished the New York Giants.

ding, such as running errands to procure cigars, eatables, and wraps when the night air was biting," the *Globe* reported.

Not since the Sox defeated Pittsburgh for the 1903 championship had they played in the Series and it was the social event of the year. "Staid citizens of conservative Boston danced in their boxes," remarked the *Globe*. "They shouted, they hugged their neighbors and punched perfect strangers in the ribs, inquiring opinions they could not hear and didn't care about."

More than 6,000 supporters who couldn't acquire tickets stood 25 deep on Washington Street, watching the game unfold on a scoreboard in front of the *Globe* offices downtown with "the stentorian tones of Frank J. Flynn announcing play after play."

The game was called for darkness after 11 innings with the score deadlocked at 6-6 and after the visitors won the replay a day later, the stage was set for a Series where

HOLY SMOKY: WOOD'S SEASON FOR THE AGES

BY BOB RYAN

If you could be one Boston athlete for one year of the 20th century, who would it be? Bobby Orr in 1970? Larry Bird in 1986? Ted Williams in 1941? Doug Flutie in 1984? These are all worthy choices.

But my choice is a 22-year-old young man having the ultimate career year playing baseball in a baseball-mad town. There was an aura of freshness and spontaneity because the team had opened a new ballpark. Imagine being 34-5 and dominant enough to have two official nicknames. Imagine being able to help yourself continually with both the bat and the glove. Imagine staring down the immortal Walter Johnson in the most ballyhooed regular-season game ever played in Fenway Park. Imagine winning three games in the World Series. Imagine being that young, that intelligent, that handsome, that gracious, that talented, and that idolized. Imagine being Smoky Joe Wood in 1912. I can't think of anything better.

Joe Wood had been with the team since the late stages of 1908. He had come out of the West, the true "Wild West," in his own words—born in the southwestern Colorado town of Ouray on October 25, 1889, and raised in Ness City, Kansas.

He was a sturdy 5-11 and 180 pounds, and Joe Wood had such a fastball that sometimes batters only saw the vapors; hence the nickname "Smoky Joe."

"Can I throw harder than Joe Wood? Listen, my friend, there's no man alive who can throw harder than Smoky Joe Wood." So said Walter "Big Train" Johnson, who had a pretty good heater himself.

Smoky Joe, who was also known as the "Kansas Cyclone," had 35 complete games in 38 starts, and in the opening game in New York, he beat the Highlanders with a seven-hitter while driving in two runs and fielding his position like a circus acrobat. By the end of May, word was out that the great Johnson had a major pitching rival in this young Mr. Wood. A tremendous crowd turned out at Griffith Stadium to see the two compete on June 26, and Smoky Joe sent them home with newfound respect after dispatching the Washington Senators with a three-hit shutout in the second game of a doubleheader. That made him 15-3 and gave him at least two victories over every opposing club in the eight-team league.

Wood entered August with a 21-4 record. He came out 28-4, and now thoughts were turning to an upcoming visit by the Senators, for Johnson was not relinquishing his title as Mound King easily. He was en route to a record-tying 16-game winning streak. It was becoming clear that a showdown was in order, and it happened on September 6 at Fenway.

It was the custom in those days to allow overflow fans to spill onto the outfield. Ropes were put up, and balls bounding into the crowd were ground-rule doubles. But such was the interest in this game that spectators were also permitted to line the foul lines, which no one had ever seen and would never see again. For the era, it was a massive crowd, estimated at 29,000.

Johnson was 28-10 and had just had a 16-game winning streak snapped. Wood was 29-4, with a 13-game winning streak. "One of the greatest pitching duels that has been fought should result," said the *Globe* in a front-page story.

With such hype, there was scant chance of the game living up to its billing, except that it did. On a glorious late-summer afternoon, the Red Sox scored the game's only run in the sixth when Tris Speaker doubled into the crowd in left and Duffy Lewis delivered him with a fly ball to right that ticked off Danny Moeller's glove for another double.

Wood gave up six hits and walked three, but in the ninth, with a man on second base with one away, he got two strikeouts to end the game and give himself victory No. 30.

The Red Sox clinched the pennant with two weeks to spare and were honored with a parade from South Station to the Common. And guess who rode in the spot of honor?

The Red Sox expected to win the Series for one very simple reason. Sure, John McGraw's Giants had the great Christy Mathewson, but in 1912, the premier pitcher in the land was Smoky Joe Wood. He beat the Giants, 4-3, in Game 1, finishing the game by striking out Otis Crandall to leave the tying run on second.

Wood pitched again in Game 4, with the Series tied at 1-1-1, Game 2 having ended at 6-6 when darkness prevailed. He mixed his pitches well and beat the Giants, 3-1, prompting Mathewson, in his ghostwritten newspaper column, to say, "His was the work of an artist." Wood also drove in the third run in the ninth inning.

But given a chance to conclude the Series with Boston ahead, 3-2-1 in Game 7, Joe Wood could not tie the ribbon on the package. He was removed after one horrible inning in which he gave up six hits and was reached for a double steal.

It looked as if Wood's storybook season would have a very inappropriate ending. The following day, Jake Stahl brought him out of the bullpen in the eighth inning of a 1-1 game. Wood threw two shutout innings before New York pushed across a run in the top of the 10th and would have scored another one if Joe hadn't made a tremendous barehanded stop of a Chief Meyers line drive to the box. At any rate, he was the losing pitcher of record until his team came to bat. But the Red Sox, aided by some storied Giants misplays (the Fred Snodgrass muff of a routine fly ball and a Speaker pop foul that fell among three Giants), scored twice in the bottom of the inning. Joe Wood had his third Series win and the Red Sox had the 1912 world championship.

It is all in the books. In 1912, Wood had a league-leading 10 shutouts. He won 16 straight games. He threw 344 innings. He hit .290 and slugged .435. He won games with his glove. He won three games in the World Series.

Mayor John Fitzgerald (the celebrated "Honey Fitz") orchestrated a massive civic celebration for the Red Sox. Joe Wood simply got up and said, "I did all I could, and I just want to thank you."

"When I brought my kids to Fenway, they never complained about the inconveniences of the ancient ballpark. . . . I still take some weird comfort in the knowledge that the poles that occasionally obscured our view of the pitcher are the same green beams that blocked the vision of my dad and his dad when they would take the trolley from Cambridge to watch the Red Sox in the 1920s."

—Dan Shaughnessy, Boston Globe sports columnist

Fans filled the third-base grandstand, as well as the temporary stands erected against the left-field wall, for the 1912 World Series against the New York Giants.

winning at home was a challenge. After New York battered Wood with six first-inning runs and went on to win by an 11-4 count to knot the Series at three games each, the season came down to one game at Fenway, and one historic blunder—the "$30,000 Muff" of pinch hitter Clyde Engle's routine fly by New York outfielder Fred Snodgrass that put the tying run on second in the 10th inning.

"I didn't seem to be able to hold the ball," he later told the *New York Times,* saying that the error "froze him to the marrow." The ball "just dropped out of the glove and that's all there was to it." Snodgrass immediately made amends by snagging Harry Hooper's shot to deep center. The real killer miscue was a miscall by New York pitcher Christy Mathewson on Speaker's foul pop-up, which fell uncaught. Speaker then knocked in the tying run and Larry Gardner's sacrifice fly scored Boston's Steve Yerkes with the winner, setting off what the *Globe*'s Murnane

called an "outburst of insane enthusiasm."

There was another celebratory parade the next day, this one from Park Square to Faneuil Hall, where Mayor John F. "Honey Fitz" Fitzgerald proclaimed the Sox victory "an epoch in the history of this city."

The euphoria continued throughout the winter, with a reprise assumed all around. "The more I think it over, the more convinced I am that we will be stronger next season than we were last," McAleer said in February. So the 10-9 loss to Philadelphia in the home opener was shrugged off. "What's One Lost Game to a Team That Can Win 105 in a Year?" asked the *Globe* headline.

But by April 20 the Sox found themselves in seventh place, and there was "shock over the Red Sox start." Injuries didn't help. Wood hurt his thumb while slipping as he was fielding a bunt and left fielder Duffy Lewis, shortstop Heinie Wagner, and the team's player-manager Jake Stahl were all sidelined. "Having had their spring vacation, it is to be hoped that the Red Sox are now going to work with renewed vigor," the *Globe* observed on May 11, when the club was in sixth.

Babe Ruth in 1915, age 20, when he won 18 games for the Red Sox and helped them win the first of three world championships in four years, before his infamous trade to the Yankees.

PEOPLE OF THE PARK

"MRS. JACK" WAS AN EARLY FANATIC

As the *Globe*'s Jack Thomas wrote in 1988: "There was only one Isabella Stewart Gardner, which is too bad, for nobody was better at shocking Boston society in the late 19th and early 20th centuries, and Boston today could use another like her. She is remembered not only for the Gardner Museum that she built with her husband's money, but also for her impact on Boston's cultural and social history from her arrival in 1860 as Jack's 20-year-old bride until her burial in Mount Auburn Cemetery in July 1924.

"She was not even born in Boston, as her biographer pointed out. Jack met her in New York, married her two days before the Civil War began, brought her to Boston and moved into the Boylston Hotel, later the Touraine, until their house at 152 Beacon Street was built. She was aristocratic, eccentric, and scandalous. Her husband had money and patience and, being married to her, needed both. She demonstrated contempt for propriety by walking down Beacon Street with pet lions, and posed in a low-cut dress with pearls around her hips for a John Singer Sargent portrait considered so risqué that when it was displayed at the St. Botolph Club in the winter of 1888, Jack ordered it taken down, and it was never again shown in his lifetime."

Mrs. Jack, as she was known, once caused another huge commotion at Symphony Hall. In December 1912, two months after the Red Sox beat the New York Giants in the World Series, she appeared at a concert wearing "a white band around her head and on it the words, 'Oh you Red Sox' in red letters," as a Boston gossip columnist put it. "It looked as if the woman had gone crazy . . . almost causing a panic among those in the audience who discovered the ornamentation, and even for a moment upsetting [the musicians] so that their startled eyes wandered from their music stands."

Why the hubbub? "'Oh you Red Sox' was a song popular with the Royal Rooters, a group of Boston baseball fans known for rowdyism," Patrick McMahon, a Museum of Fine Arts curatorial project manager, told the *Globe* in 2005. "Symphony-goers must have thought for a moment that one of those raucous drunks had slipped into the building."

Mrs. Jack wasn't just jumping on the bandwagon, insisted Gardner Museum archivist Kristin Parker. While perusing Gardner's scrapbooks in 2005, Parker found numerous Red Sox news items, photos, and notations of scores dating to the Boston Americans' triumph in the first World Series in 1903. In 1912, the 72-year-old Gardner purchased season tickets to the newly built Fenway Park, a stone's throw from her palazzo. "One of the only things that kept [humorist] Robert Benchley from going 'crazy with boredom' in Boston in the summer of 1912, I've read, was meeting Gardner," Parker said. "She took Benchley to Fenway, where she 'loudly encouraged all the Boston players by name.'"

She was once called Boston's most famous "insider outsider," and some wondered about the death of her infant son, her only child, and whether the magnificent palazzo in the Fenway was a memorial to him. In one of the museum's paintings, a Madonna and child by the Spanish artist Francisco de Zurbaran, she must have seen, as others have, that the child in the painting looked remarkably like one of the photographs of her little son. A *Globe* story about a museum renovation in 1928 said: "Everything was put back in its place, so the museum looks exactly as it did when Mrs. Gardner died. Nothing has been added, nothing removed. That is as she wished—and willed—it should be."

More recently, in a nod to Mrs. Jack's baseball allegiance, anyone wearing a Red Sox-branded item receives $2 off admission to the Gardner. If you're named Isabella, you get in free—for life.

Portrait of Isabella Stewart Gardner by John Singer Sargent, 1888.

IT WAS HIS CLIFF

He was a member of the Red Sox outfield that many consider to be the best in baseball history. He saw the first home run Babe Ruth hit and the last, No. 714. He is also one of the few players to ever pinch-hit for the legendary slugger.

They even named a cliff after him.

He was the venerable George "Duffy" Lewis, a Red Sox outfielder in the early glory days of World Series victories and later a traveling secretary for the Boston Braves. He was one-third of the famed Lewis-Speaker-Hooper outfield that sparked the Red Sox to World Series triumphs in 1912 and 1915.

After an outstanding career as a player that started with the Red Sox in 1910, Lewis was also a coach, manager, owner, and, finally, traveling secretary for the Boston and Milwaukee Braves, before retiring in 1961.

Born April 18, 1888, in San Francisco, George Edward Lewis was one of three children. His mother's maiden name was Duffy and somehow that became his nickname. Along with his lifelong friend and fellow outfielder, Harry Hooper, Lewis attended St. Mary's College in Oakland, California. In 1908, the pair played in the so-called "Outlaw League" in California and then jumped to the state's City League.

Lewis came to the Red Sox from Oakland in 1910, joining Hooper, who had been brought up the year before. Lewis had been spotted and signed by John I. Taylor, owner of the Red Sox, for a $200 bonus. His first year's salary was $3,000 and his biggest contract as a Red Sox outfielder was for $5,000.

When Lewis came up, the Red Sox had Tris Speaker in center, Harry Niles in right, and Harry Hooper in left. The Sox lost the first three games. Lewis was put in left and Hooper moved to right. Lewis's hitting won the first game he played in for the Sox and he remained in left for the next 151 games. That established the Red Sox outfield for the next six seasons.

As the Red Sox left fielder, Lewis patrolled the most unusual parcel of real estate of any ballpark in America. Fenway's left field then included a precarious grassy slope ris-

ing about 10 feet to the base of the wall. A player had to be part mountain goat to scale it, catch an outfield fly, and then stride downhill to throw the ball into the infield.

"The first time I saw it," Lewis recalled in an April 21, 1978 Globe story by Joe Dinneen, "I said to myself, 'Holy cow! What have we got here?' It looked pretty awesome."

Lewis would go out to the park early and have somebody hit the ball again and again out to the wall. He experimented with every angle of approach up the "cliff." He mastered the slope so well that it was referred to as "Duffy's Cliff."

Bulldozers knocked the cliff down to just about level when Tom Yawkey remodeled Fenway Park in 1934.

The Red Sox enjoyed their most successful seasons during the stewardship of their mighty outfield trio. In 1912, they beat the New York Giants in seven games in the World Series, but Lewis's real starring roles were to come in Boston's 1915 and 1916 Series wins.

In 1915, the Red Sox faced the Philadelphia Phillies, led by the great pitcher Grover Cleveland Alexander. But Boston clobbered the Phillies, winning four of five games, losing only the

"They taught me how to go up the hill, but they didn't teach me how to go down."

—A visiting left fielder in the days of "Duffy's Cliff"

first to Alexander. Duffy led all the regulars with a .444 average.

T.H. Murnane of the *Globe* wrote, "Duffy Lewis was the real hero of this Series, or any other. I have witnessed all of the contests for the game's highest honors in the last 30 years and I want to say that the all-around work of the modest Californian never has been equaled in a big series."

In 1916, the Red Sox had to defend their championship without Speaker, who was traded to Cleveland just before the season. After securing the pennant, they faced Brooklyn in the World Series, and again the Sox prevailed by a 4-1 margin as Lewis batted .353. Lewis played with the Red Sox through 1917, spent some time in the Navy during World War I, and then was with the Yankees for two seasons before winding up his playing career with one season in Washington.

Lewis was an established player when Babe Ruth came up to the Red Sox as a pitcher in 1914. Ruth had a terrible memory for names and always greeted everyone with, "Hi, kid." For some reason, Duffy recalled, Ruth remembered him and always saluted him with, "Hi, Duff."

The Babe, Lewis said, was a pretty fair hitter in his early days, but had a habit of striking out a lot. And that's how Lewis came to pinch-hit for the Sultan of Swat.

"I was on the bench nursing a bad ankle," Lewis recalled. "Bill Carrigan, our manager, asked me if I could hit. I said sure.

So he sent me to pinch-hit for Ruth. I got a hit, too. I used to think it won the game, but someone told me a few years ago that it didn't."

In 1947, Lewis received a testimonial dinner at the Hotel Statler, with more than 1,000 friends and fans turning out. He was reunited for the evening with old outfield compatriots Speaker and Hooper.

Lewis threw out the first pitch to open the 1975 World Series at Fenway Park. Perhaps the only sad note in his long baseball career is that it did not end with a place in the Hall of Fame.

Speaker had been part of the Hall's second group in 1937. Hooper was inducted in 1971 and spent the remaining years of his life plugging for Duffy to make it.

Frank Frisch, a member of the Hall of Fame Veterans Committee, once told Lewis: "You, Speaker and Hooper all should have gone into the Hall of Fame at the same time. As the best outfield of your day, it would have been right."

Lewis shrugged it off. "A lot of people have said I should have gone in with the others. But I have no regrets. I'm doing all right."

Duffy Lewis died in Salem, New Hampshire, in 1979 at the age of 91. He was inducted into the Red Sox Hall of Fame in 2002.

The 10-foot-high incline in left field that abutted the wall (visible behind players) was named for Duffy Lewis (opposite page), the Red Sox left fielder who mastered its vagaries.

LENDING AN EAR TO DE VALERA

Eamon de Valera, president of the Irish Republic, came to America in 1919 to plead the cause of independence for the fledgling Irish state, and his visit to Boston brought a massive crowd of 50,000 to Fenway Park.

The *Globe*'s A.J. Philpott wrote, "It was an inspiring assemblage—one in which the spirit of the Irish people rose above the spirit of faction, of group or party." Of the Irish president, he wrote, "The very mystery which attaches to this man, who was comparatively unheard of until recently, somehow fulfilled the dreams of the race—that some great figure would arise at the crucial moment and lead Ireland to freedom. In the thoughtful, militant, clean-cut face and gaunt personality of de Valera there is somehow also personified that new spirit which has come to Irishmen in which the demand has superseded the appeal for justice to Ireland. In that vast audience, you sensed this new dignity that has sunk into their consciousness."

A large audience was expected, according to the *Globe*. But instead of 25,000, some 50,000 descended on the grounds. They filled the grandstand first, and then the wings on the right and left, and then they poured into the field and filled the space between the platform and grandstand—jammed it—then flowed around and backward in all directions, and there were thousands on the streets outside.

It was an ideal day for a great outdoor meeting—clear, sunny, and not too warm—and the location could not have been much improved. When a series of resolutions demanding the recognition of the Irish Republic were read, the unanimous "Ayes" could be heard over in Dorchester, and the silence that followed when the call came for the "Nays" led to a shout of laughter.

Some excitement was caused when three mounted policemen forced a passageway through the crowd to enable the committee, with President de Valera, to reach the speaker's platform, which had been erected near home plate of the baseball diamond. On the whole, however, it was an orderly and patient audience. More than 20,000 members of the crowd stood from about 2 o'clock until after 5 o'clock, when "The Star-Spangled Banner" was sung and the audience dispersed quietly.

Two days later, as Eamon de Valera left New England for New York, he issued a message thanking the people of the region: "I did not need to come to Boston or to America to know that Americans would not lend themselves to an act of injustice against an ancient nation that clung to its traditions and maintained its spirit of independence through seven centuries of blood and tears. In the name of Ireland, I thank you."

By June 25, when the pennant finally was raised before a chilled crowd of only 6,500, the Sox were only in fifth. In mid-July, McAleer replaced Stahl, who'd played only two games due to a foot injury, with catcher Bill Carrigan. A player-manager who couldn't play wasn't much good, especially one who was rumored to want his job, McAleer reckoned. But the burly Carrigan, known as "Rough" for his rugged play behind the plate, couldn't pull his mates out of their hole and they finished fourth, more than 15 games behind Philadelphia. With no world championship to contend for, the Sox challenged the Braves to a best-of-seven series. But their crosstown neighbors begged off because a couple of their key players were hurt.

There would be another World Series at Fenway in 1914, but it would be the Braves acting as hosts after they staged the greatest comeback in the sport's young history. The threadbare neighbors hadn't had a winning season since 1902, when they were the Beaneaters, and had since changed their name three times. On July 18 they were in last place, 11 games behind the Giants. Then, guided by Manager George "Miracle Man" Stallings, the Braves went on a relentless hot streak, winning 59 of their final 75 to claim the pennant by 10½ games.

By early August, their revival had attracted so much attention that their home, South End Grounds, which seated only 5,000, was being overrun. So Sox owner Joseph Lannin, who'd bought the franchise during the pre-ceding winter, offered the Braves the use of Fenway for the rest of the season. His own club was a distant second to the Athletics by then, but its renaissance already was underway in the form of pitcher George Herman Ruth, a 19-year-old son of a Baltimore saloon owner the *Globe* described as "one of the most sensational moundsmen who ever toed a slab in the International League."

Lannin, who'd emigrated from Quebec and started as a hotel bellboy, had made his fortune in real estate and commodities. He saw rare potential in the raw and untutored Ruth, bought him from the minor-league Orioles with Ben Egan and Ernie Shore for a reported $25,000 (give or take several thousand, depending on your source), and promptly put him in uniform. But the Sox couldn't catch the Athletics, who went on to play the Braves in the World Series.

By then even the Royal Rooters had switched allegiances. The town was entranced—73,000 people had turned out for a separate-admission Labor Day doubleheader between the Braves and the Giants, with another 10,000 turned away. And nearly 70,000 showed up for the final two games of the Series as the Braves sealed the first sweep in World Series history with 5-4 and 3-1 victories. "There was joy last night in Boston," said the *Globe* editorial, "the land of the free and home of the Braves."

The Braves' days as a glorified Twilight League team, playing in a sandlot at the corner of Walpole Street and Columbus Avenue, were over. Owner James Gaffney was

PERFECT RELIEF FOR RUTH

Ernie Shore was acquired by the Red Sox in the same deal that brought them Babe Ruth in 1914. Shore became an outstanding pitcher for the Red Sox, going 19-8 with a 1.64 ERA in the 1915 world championship season, and winning 16 more games the following year when the Sox repeated as world champs. He even pitched a three-hitter in the title-clinching victory. However, Shore is forever linked with Ruth and best known for his performance in one of the oddest games in baseball history.

Shore was in the dugout on June 23, 1917, two days removed from a pitching outing when Ruth started on the mound at Fenway against the Washington Senators. Ruth walked the leadoff hitter, Ray Morgan, but his gripes with the strike zone were immediate and forceful. He complained to plate umpire Brick Owens repeatedly, and after the ball four call, Ruth and Owens met in front of the plate, where Ruth apparently threw a punch at Owens. Along with Sox catcher Chet Walker, Ruth was ejected and later received a 10-game suspension, and the Red Sox were now short a pitcher.

Shore came on in relief, getting only five warm-up throws according to the rules of the time. No matter, Shore thought, he would be replaced once another pitcher had sufficient time to warm up. Morgan was quickly caught attempting to steal second by new catcher Sam Agnew, and Shore went on to retire batter after batter after batter—26 in a row after the man was caught stealing, to complete a Red Sox no-hitter. In fact, Shore got credit for a perfect game for more than 70 years, before a baseball committee ruled in 1991 that it couldn't be regarded as a perfect game, since Shore hadn't started it.

Shore, who retired with 65 victories in seven seasons, went on to become a county sheriff in North Carolina, and he enjoyed the notoriety of his distinctive performance. He died in 1980, before his status as a perfect-game pitcher was downgraded to a combined no-hitter.

"Practically everyone has heard of me," Shore told *Sports Illustrated* in 1962. "People are always asking me about that game. I can't say I really mind."

Real estate tycoon Joseph Lannin became sole owner of the Red Sox in 1914. He brought Babe Ruth to Boston, which helped the club capture World Series wins in 1915, 1916, and 1918. Lannin sold the team to Harry Frazee in 1917, setting the stage for The Curse.

building a capacious new park between Commonwealth Avenue and the Charles River that had foul lines of more than 400 feet and a distance of 440 to dead center and that seated better than 40,000.

That was considerably more than Fenway could accommodate, so the Sox were content to accept the Braves' offer to use their new playpen for the 1915 World Series. In case Carrigan and his teammates needed an added incentive, they had to stand and watch the Athletics raise the 1914 pennant on Opening Day at Shibe Park. Though injuries hobbled them early—the Sox were in fourth place at the end of May—their superior pitching eventually came into play. "I still believe, as do most of the other players in the circuit, that Boston is the really dangerous club," Tigers star Ty Cobb said in the *Globe* on June 27.

After sweeping three home doubleheaders in three days from the Senators in early July, the Sox were on the move and by July 19 had taken over the lead from Chicago. By then the Braves were making another surge up from the cellar and for a couple of months the city was daydreaming about a Trolleycar Series, but the defending champions couldn't catch the Phillies.

The Sox essentially had wrapped things up by September 20 after taking three straight at home from the Tigers to go up by four games. "Goodby, Ty Cobb. You failed to show," taunted the *Globe*. Before they went on the road for the final seven games of the season, the Sox practiced for three days at Braves Field to get a feel for its supersized dimensions and found them suitable, if initially strange.

By the time the club faced the Phillies in the Series, it found its temporary autumnal home quite comfortable. Sox pitchers Dutch Leonard and Ernie Shore each baffled the visitors by 2-1 counts to give the Sox a 3-1 Series advantage. As it turned out, the Fens would have been overrun by the crowds, which numbered 42,300 and 41,096 for the two games at Braves Field, with thousands still outside when the gates were locked. When Boston closed out the

Series in Philadelphia, it marked the beginning of a mini-dynasty, with three championships in four years.

Though he could have raised ticket prices in the wake of the championship, as most clubs do, Lannin actually lowered them for 1916, reducing a box seat from $1.50 to $1 and all but the first five rows of the grandstand to 75 cents. But even with Wood sitting out the season and Speaker dealt to the Indians, the Sox managed to repeat behind an extraordinary pitching staff. Ruth, who out-dueled Washington legend Walter Johnson four times, posted a 23-12 mark, followed by Leonard (18-12), Carl Mays (18-13), Shore (16-10), and Rube Foster (14-7).

For the only time in franchise history, two Sox pitchers threw no-hitters at Fenway in the same season. "The Broadway tribe had about as much chance of getting a base knock off the Oklahoma farmer as they have of changing the situation in Mexico," the *Globe* reckoned after Foster blanked New York, 2-0, on June 21. By the time Leonard squelched St. Louis, 4-0, on August 30, Boston was firmly in first place. "Their specialty for two years now has been beating pennant rivals in the pinch," Grantland Rice wrote in the *Globe*. "Their favorite dish is Crucial Series, frapped."

After the Sox held off Chicago by two games for the pennant, they returned to Braves Field for a World Series date with the Brooklyn Robins (as the Dodgers then were known). After Ruth stifled the visitors for 14 innings before 41,373 in the second game, it was clear that Boston had a bird in hand. "Only a Miracle Can Stop Sox," the *Globe* declared after a 2-1 victory put them up two games going back to Brooklyn. When the Sox split there, it was left to Shore to stifle the Robins, 4-1, for the crown at home. Boston, Rice proclaimed, was "the unconquered citadel of the game."

With consecutive titles on his résumé and a world war on the boil, Lannin figured it was a propitious time to cash out, so he sold the club and the ballpark for $675,000 a few weeks after the season ended to theatrical men Harry Frazee and Hugh Ward. "I think I have turned over to the new owners the best team in the world," Lannin said, "and it is now up to them to keep the champions at the top."

With the same team back and Ruth coming into dominance, that seemed likely in 1917. While Ruth already was a gifted hitter—he hit two doubles and a triple to beat New York on Opening Day and also earned a win on the mound—his pitching was at least as notable. He won his

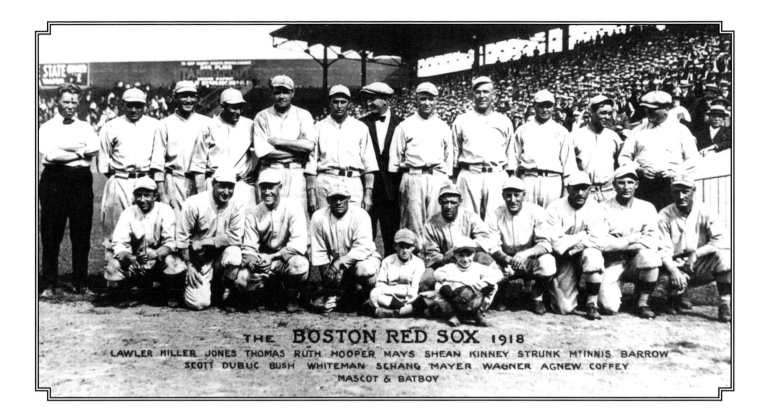

THE BOSTON RED SOX 1918

LAWLER MILLER JONES THOMAS RUTH HOOPER MAYS SHEAN KINNEY STRUNK McINNIS BARROW
SCOTT DUBUC BUSH WHITEMAN SCHANG MAYER WAGNER AGNEW COFFEY
MASCOT & BATBOY

first seven games with what the *Globe* called "Ruthless warfare." Then on June 23, he provided the unwitting prelude to Shore's "perfect game" against Washington.

After walking the first batter on four pitches, Ruth accused umpire Brick Owens of missing two of them. "Open your eyes and keep them open," Ruth shouted. "Get in and pitch or I will run you out of there," Owens replied. "You run me out and I will come in and bust you on the nose," threatened Ruth, who proceeded to clock Owens and had to be dragged off by Jack Barry, the club's new player-manager, and several policemen. On came Shore, who didn't allow a Senator to reach base. "I don't think I could have worked easier if I'd been sitting in a rocking chair," he later recalled.

As expected, Boston's pitching was superb, with Ruth winning 24 games and Mays winning 22. The club was in first place at the end of July. But punchless hitting did in the Sox down the stretch. "There is no use bewailing the fact that we cannot win this year," Frazee concluded just before the Tigers swept his club at home in September.

So he sent a congratulatory telegram to counterpart Charles Comiskey after the White Sox won the pennant by nine games, and then turned down the sixth-place Braves' offer of a consolation city series. "What Boston wants is a World Series and that is what the Red Sox are going after next season," Frazee stated.

The Sox indeed were back in the Series in 1918, but amid dramatically altered circumstances. With America at war and "Work or Fight" the popular antislacker slogan, baseball was regarded as a frivolous pastime. Fenway atten-

The 1918 Red Sox were led by Babe Ruth (back row, fifth from left), who won 13 games as a pitcher in his final season with the club and hit 11 home runs in a season abridged by World War I. The team defeated the Chicago Cubs in six games in the World Series.

dance dropped from 387,856 to a record-low 249,513 in a season that was chopped to 126 games and ended on Labor Day. But after Frazee acquired first baseman John "Stuffy" McInnis, pitcher Joe Bush, catcher Wally Schang, and outfielder Amos Strunk from the penniless Athletics, his club was the class of a league that had been depleted by military enlistments. And Ruth, the game's top slugger and an overpowering pitcher, undeniably was at the head of the class.

He was in fine shape after spending the winter chopping wood at his North Sudbury cottage. Ruth was an imposing woodsman at the plate that season also, hitting .300 and leading the league in homers and slugging percentage. "Just bust 'em," he told the *Globe,* adding, "a base on balls is an obstacle on the path of progress. Take a good cut and bang that apple on the nose."

When Ruth jumped the club in July after a clash with Ed Barrow, the new manager who was hired after Barry went off to the Navy, the issue was hitting—specifically, Ruth's refusal to follow Barrow's orders. "I got as mad as a March hare and told Barrow, then and there, that I was through with him and his team," Ruth said. But he was back a few days later and it was his pitching that made the difference in the Series against Chicago.

"TESSIE" AND THE ROYAL ROOTERS

"Tessie," a Broadway show tune written by William R. Anderson, became the theme song of the Boston fans known as the Royal Rooters when they followed the Red Sox to Pittsburgh in the first World Series in 1903. The Red Sox were seen as huge underdogs to the Pirates, and though the song had nothing to do with baseball, it seemed to provide luck to the Red Sox in important games. Perhaps it didn't hurt Boston's chances that the song was frequently reworded to cast aspersions on the talents, manliness, and parentage of their opponents.

The Red Sox won that first World Series, and in 1904 the Royal Rooters accompanied the team to New York for the final two games of the season. The Red Sox needed but one victory in the two games to capture the AL pennant, a situation that would recur in 1949. The Rooters, led by "Chief" Johnny Keenan, along with Michael "Nuf Ced" McGreevy and Jerry Watson, hired a band to accompany them, and they wrapped up the 1904 AL championship in the first game with the help of a wild pitch by the Highlanders' ace, Jack Chesbro. Since the National League champion New York Giants refused to play the American League champion Red Sox, the Sox were declared unofficial world champions.

The song was reprised in the championship season of 1912, when the Red Sox christened Fenway Park with a World Series victory over the New York Giants. In 1914, the "Miracle Braves" borrowed Fenway for their home World Series games, and they swept the Philadelphia Athletics with the song as background. Over three more Series victories—in 1915, 1916, and 1918—Red Sox fans belted out "Tessie."

Before the 1915 World Series, the Philadelphia "Nationals" stated their opposition to the Royal Rooters "assembling as one body" at the Series games hosted by Philadelphia. On October 2, Red Sox president Joseph Lannin traveled to New York on the midnight train to confer with American League President Ban Johnson.

Lannin said, "I will move heaven and earth to see that they are accorded the treatment to which they are entitled. . . . The Boston Royal Rooters are known all over the country for their loyalty and gameness, and are considered as much a part of a World's Series in which a Boston team figures as are the players themselves. Whatever happens, the Royal Rooters and "Tessie" will have their accustomed places in the World's Series setting."

As a result of the negotiations, the Rooters received 400 seats for the Series games in Philadelphia.

As it turned out, the Red Sox hosted their own World Series games at Braves Field in 1915 and 1916 because the brand new park accommodated thousands more fans, and the more spacious playing field also played more to the Red Sox strengths of speed, pitching, and defense. The Red Sox drew more than 40,000 fans to four of their five home games in the two World Series and won all five games.

Late in the 1915 pennant race with the Detroit Tigers, a *Globe* story headlined "Old 'Tessie' Still on Job" began: "Maybe the presence of the Royal Rooters had nothing to do with the ultimate result, and maybe 'Tessie' did not figure at all in the Red Sox victory, but it is a matter of history nevertheless that the Rooters and their beloved 'Tessie' were there just the same—very much there— and that the Rooters and 'Tessie' have yet to trail with a losing Boston team."

The story went on: "Three hundred loyal, lusty fans congregated on Commonwealth Ave. at the exit of the tunnel at 2:20, and at a word from Chief Johnny Keenan wended their way through the thousands of prospective spectators and again rendezvoused on Lansdowne Street, where the Royal Rooters' band was ready to take up the strains of the wonderful baseball campaign song."

They then marched to their customary position in the right-field bleachers, where they typically heckled the visiting teams while sunning themselves.

In April 1916, a *Globe* article noted that demand for Fenway box seats had more than doubled from any previous season, perhaps a testament to the team's world championship the previous year. The Red Sox offered a 25-game ticket book for women at $12.50. Any number of the tickets could be used at any single game, and "the management expects that women will be more numerous at the games this season than ever before."

Indeed, when the Red Sox made the 1916 World Series, the Royal Rooters under chairman John M. Killeen announced that for World Series games at the home of the Brooklyn team (then called the Robins, but soon to be the Dodgers), "special transportation arrangements for women with escorts" would be included, a feature not part of the planning since 1912. The rate for traveling fans for that World Series was $37, which included round-trip train transportation (parlor cars $2 extra), automobile transport to the park and back to the Elks' Home at 43rd Street, pennants, souvenirs, and grandstand seats for five games, two in Brooklyn and three at home.

The Royal Rooters' band of the time featured 30 pieces, though it was augmented for the World Series by 20 jubilee singers in Red Sox uniforms.

Michael "Nuf Ced" McGreevy's 3rd Base Saloon, at Tremont and Ruggles Streets in Roxbury, opened in 1894. It was the principal

Rooter's Souvenir
BOSTON - PITTSBURG
Oct., 1903.   M. T. McGreevy

TESSIE,
You Are The Only, Only, Only.

CHORUS.

Tessie, you make me feel so badly;
  Why don't you turn around.
Tessie, you know I love you madly;
  Babe, my heart weighs about a
  pound.
Don't blame me if I ever doubt you,
  You know, I wouldn't live with-
  out you;
Tessie, you are the only, only,
  only, -ly.

3d Base.   Nuf Ced.
Who Kidnapped the Pittsburg Band
Nuf Ced—McGreevy.

gathering spot for the Royal Rooters and is generally considered the first sports bar in the country, with both the South End Grounds and the soon-to-be-built Huntington Avenue Grounds a few blocks away. The saloon closed in 1921, shortly after Prohibition had outlawed the sale of alcohol in 1920. McGreevy's bar got its name because it was the last stop before home for its patrons, and his own nickname reflected his habit of pounding his fist on the bar and announcing, "Nuf said," when he decided that an argument between patrons need not escalate any further.

In 2008, Ken Casey of the Boston band the Dropkick Murphys (which reworked and reprised "Tessie" in 2004) and baseball historian Peter Nash opened McGreevy's on Boylston Street, a tribute to the original bar and to Boston sports history.

ABOVE: The Royal Rooters temporarily ceded the megaphone to Red Sox bat boy Jerry McCarthy during the 1912 World Series.

BELOW: Baseball didn't provide the only action on the field in 1912. Police had their hands full trying to push back Royal Rooters in the area known as Duffy's Cliff, where temporary seats were a coveted World Series vantage point.

A REGIONAL MEETING PLACE

Not long after Fenway Park opened for baseball in 1912, it became the venue of choice for all kinds of activities—from baseball and other organized sports to civic and religious meetings, including a massive turnout of 50,000 on June 29, 1919, for Irish political leader Eamon de Valera and the adoption of resolutions in favor of Ireland's independence.

In subsequent decades, Fenway was rarely opened for non-Red Sox events, which makes the first decade's schedule unusual. Among the hundreds of events held there in its first decade:

- In 1913, the Boston Braves were allowed to play several games at Fenway when the Red Sox were out of town. The holiday twin bills—featuring the Braves against the New York Giants on Patriots Day, and the Braves versus the Brooklyn Robins on Memorial Day—were expected to draw much larger crowds than their South End Grounds could accommodate. More than 22,000 fans watched each of the separate-admission holiday doubleheaders. Braves Field opened in 1915.

- In 1914, the Boston Lacrosse Club played the University of Toronto on June 1, immediately after the Red Sox played a game against the Washington Senators. It was noted that Red Sox President Joseph John Lannin, "an old lacrosse player himself," approved the use of the field, with baseball fans allowed to stay after the game to watch the lacrosse match free of charge.

- Later in June 1914, Boston College held a "baseball carnival" at Fenway, with the BC baseball squad dropping an 8-0 decision to Holy Cross, after Boston College High School had beaten Rindge Technical, 2-1, in the first game. The games were featured as part of BC Commencement Week, and two bands entertained some 3,500 fans between games and between innings.

- In July 1914, Fenway Park was the scene of dancing, acrobatics, band and orchestra music, and a parade, all put on, according to the *Globe* story, "of the children, by the children and for the children." The hope was that some 30,000 children in the Boston area would spend 10 cents each in order to attend, thus raising $3,000 to benefit children in Salem, Massachusetts, left destitute by a massive fire there on June 25. Boston vaudeville theaters and "moving picture houses" were expected to provide several acrobatic displays and other acts.

- On August 17, 1914, the Progressive political party held a Fenway Park outing at which former U.S. President Theodore Roosevelt was to speak. More than 10,000 tickets were sold for the event, and Boston Mayor James M. Curley was to attend. The outing included track events and a baseball game, but partway through the ball game in the late afternoon, rain forced the cancellation of the rest of the athletic program, and Roosevelt's address was hastily moved to Boston Arena. About 4,000 people assembled for the address, which required "a great scurrying for trolley cars, taxis, and other means of conveyance from the baseball grounds to the arena," where Roosevelt spoke for an hour.

- In November 1914, the Dartmouth College football team thumped Syracuse, 40-0, before some 13,000 fans, in what the *Globe* story called "a display of versatility in modern football which has never been surpassed by any eleven which the Boston public has had opportunity to see in action." The Syracuse team had earlier in the season defeated football powers Michigan and Carlisle, but was no match for Dartmouth, which went on to outscore its remaining nine opponents for the season by 359-25.

- Just one week later, on November 29, 1914, a combination of local All-Star football players, most from Harvard, defeated the Carlisle Indians, 13-6, before a crowd of 5,000 in a game to benefit the Children's Island Sanitarium. The game was called the last important game of the local season.

- In July 1915, it was "Natick Day" at Fenway Park, where the Red Sox played the Chicago White Sox, and the town of Natick, Massachusetts, feted one of its own—veteran American League umpire Tommy Connolly. Nearly 5,000 residents of Natick attended the game, which required "39 special electric cars to bring the greater part of the throng," along with autos and railroad trains. Practically all business in Natick was suspended for the afternoon, and umpire Connolly was honored in a pregame ceremony. A Natick representative "told umpire Connolly what a great umpire he is and how beloved he is by his fellow citizens," and Connolly was presented with a silver loving cup.

- In November 1915, Everett High defeated Waltham High, 6-0, before 12,000 fans at Fenway in "one of the very best played school football games ever seen in Greater Boston," thus winning the right to play Central High School of Detroit for the national scholastic football championship.

- On Memorial Day, 1916, about 5,000 Spanish-American war veterans formed in line at Copley Square and marched to Fenway Park for a memorial service featuring bands and drum corps. Two years later, on May 26, 1918, about 35,000 attended a memorial service presided over by Boston's Cardinal O'Connell for departed U.S. soldiers and sailors.

- On September 4, 1916, the Galway Men's Association hosted a field day at Fenway Park with several thousand in attendance. The event featured Irish football, foot races, and step dancing. The highlight was a hurling match between the Shamrocks of South Boston and the Cork Club of New York, which the hosts won handily.

- Some 10 days later, the Bay State Odd Fellows held a parade through the streets of Boston, followed by religious and patriotic services at Fenway Park, with some 14,000 in attendance. The story noted that, "it was neither too warm nor too cool. . . . This and the splendid music made the parade enjoyable for even the women, about 400 of them."

Ruth had spent much of the season playing in the outfield so that his bat could be in the lineup every day. After blanking the Cubs, 1-0, on September 5 in the road opener of the Series, he held them scoreless until the eighth inning of the fourth game, running his postseason scoreless streak (including his 1916 appearance) to 29⅔ innings, breaking Christy Mathewson's record.

Since attendance had tumbled, the Series was back at Fenway instead of Braves Field and the fifth game almost wasn't played after both teams initially refused to take the field as a protest against their reduced shares. "The players have agreed to play for the sake of the public and the wounded soldiers in the stands," Mayor Fitzgerald told the crowd after a settlement was reached. Although the Cubs prevailed, 3-0, the Sox took the championship a day later as Mays, who'd won both ends of the August 30 doubleheader against the Athletics that all but clinched the pennant, mastered the visitors, 2-1, on three hits.

The victory left a bitter aftertaste. "With many minds wandering in serious channels, it can plainly be seen that it was a fatal mistake for baseball men to argue over dollars," the Globe observed, "creating a situation that should have been diplomatically squelched in its infancy." In retribution the national commission that oversaw the sport deprived the players of the diamond lapel pin that was the precursor to the championship ring.

It also was the last hurrah for the Sox, who didn't reach the Series again until 1946 and didn't win it again until 2004. It wasn't until 1934 that Boston even finished in the first division again. The 1919 season was a dismal downer. Mays, who'd won 72 games for the Sox in five seasons, left the club in mid-July and was dealt to New York just before the August trading deadline. Ruth, whose rambunctious roistering had become a clubhouse problem, squabbled with both Frazee and Barrow. But if he frequently acted as if he was above the team, it may have been because he was its colossus. Even as the club tumbled into the second division, eventually finishing fifth with its worst record (66-71) in a dozen years, the Big Fellow was its top drawing card.

It was clear to Ruth, if not his employer, that he was worth twice as much as the $10,000 per year he was earning. "Frazee knows what I want," Ruth declared as he flew off to Los Angeles to make a movie called *Headin' Home*. "And unless he meets my demands I will not play with the Boston club next year." But the thought of paying $20,000 to an ungovernable, if inimitable, man-child was anathema to the owner, who decided that he could make a far better deal with a certain gentleman in New York.

Boston Evening Globe

Evening 1c Edition

VOL. XCIV—NO. 73   BOSTON, WEDNESDAY EVENING, SEPTEMBER 11, 1918—FOURTEEN PAGES   COPYRIGHT, 1918, BY THE GLOBE NEWSPAPER CO.   CLOSING MARKET PRICES

EVENING EDITION—7:30 LATEST

SOX WIN CHAMPIONSHIP

U. S. TROOPSHIP TORPEDOED, BUT ALL ON BOARD SAVED

LONDON, Tuesday, Sept 10—A troopship with 2800 American soldiers on board has been torpedoed. All hands were saved. The troopship was beached.

GUIDE FOR MEN REGISTERING FOR THE DRAFT TOMORROW

Full Score of the Game:

BOSTON	AB	R	BH	TB	PO	A	E
Hooper rf	3	0	0	0	1	0	0
Shean 2b	3	1	0	0	1	4	0
Strunk cf	4	0	2	2	0	0	0
Whiteman lf	4	0	0	0	1	0	0
Ruth lf	0	0	0	0	0	0	0
McInnis 1b	4	0	1	1	16	1	0
Scott ss	4	0	0	0	2	5	0
Thomas 3b	2	0	0	0	1	2	0
Schang c	1	0	1	1	4	0	0
Mays p	2	1	1	1	0	6	0
Totals	27	2	5	5	27	18	0

CHICAGO	AB	R	BH	TB	PO	A	E
Flack rf	3	1	1	1	0	1	0
Hollocher ss	4	0	0	0	1	3	0
Mann lf	3	0	0	0	2	0	0
Paskert cf	2	0	0	0	1	0	0
Merkle 1b	3	0	1	1	8	2	1
Pick 2b	3	0	1	1	2	1	0
Deal 3b	2	0	0	0	2	1	0
Zeider	0	0	0	0	0	0	0
Barber	1	0	0	0	0	0	0
Killefer c	2	0	0	0	4	1	0
Tyler p	2	0	0	0	0	3	1
Hendrix p	0	0	0	0	0	0	0
O'Farrell	1	0	0	0	0	0	0
McCabe	0	0	0	0	0	0	0
Totals	00	0	3	3	24	12	2

*Barber batted for Deal in 8th.

IN THE NEIGHBORHOOD

BY RON DRISCOLL

When the team's popularity outgrew the Huntington Avenue Grounds (now the site of Northeastern University), the Red Sox built their new ballpark. With the same directness with which he baptized the team, John I. Taylor, whose family also owned the *Globe*, said, "It's in the Fenway section, isn't it? Then name it Fenway Park."

The astute Taylors would not be hurt at all by this choice, as they also controlled the Fenway Realty Trust and were poised to directly benefit from development around the ballpark.

The Fens section of Boston was the centerpiece of the "Emerald Necklace" of parks designed by Frederick Law Olmsted, a planned environment of babbling brooks and green vistas, a design that held out a peaceful vision for urban America. But the stronger influence upon Fenway Park, wrote the *Globe*'s Marty Nolan in 1986, was the unplanned, anti-pastoral engine of haphazard growth that butchered Boston's landscape: the railroad. Lansdowne Street necessitated the improbable left-field wall because the street was squeezed by the multi-lined pathway of the Boston and Albany Railroad.

"In some ways, the Fenway is Boston's secret little neighborhood," said Michael Ross, its longtime city council representative, in 2009. "You might not even notice it if you're not looking for it."

The Fenway begins where the Back Bay leaves off, at Massachusetts Avenue, and contains some of the city's landmark cultural, medical, and academic institutions: Symphony Hall, the Museum of Fine Arts, Harvard Medical School, Children's Hospital, Northeastern University, and the Boston Latin School.

It also has plenty of sports history besides Fenway Park, as the place where the Red Sox, Bruins, and Celtics all played their first home games. About one-and-a-half miles from the ballpark, the first-ever World Series game was played in 1903 at the Huntington Avenue Grounds. Boston Arena, now called Matthews Arena and home to Northeastern athletics, hosted the Bruins from their 1924 inception through 1928, when Boston Garden opened. The Celtics debuted at Boston Arena in 1946.

"Fenway Park, unlike other sports venues, is not an aloof stadium surrounded by a desolate tundra of parking. It's surrounded and hugged by real city streets. People and buildings, lights and signs seem to swirl and crash into one another in a visual metaphor of city vitality. This is the kind of urbanism that feels spontaneous, not like something overly planned."

—Robert Campbell and Peter Vanderwarker, *Globe Magazine*, August 2004

A panoramic view of Fenway Park in 1914.

You can find a statue of baseball's winningest pitcher, Cy Young, in front of Northeastern's Churchill Hall, positioned about where the pitcher's mound was on the old diamond. Young threw the first modern perfect game here for the Red Sox in 1904.

Across Lansdowne Street from the Green Monster is the House of Blues, which inherited the space that was long occupied by Avalon. The latest incarnation of the music club chain got off to a rollicking start in 2009 when the hometown Dropkick Murphys played six sold-out shows around St. Patrick's Day. The venue is but one of several restaurants and nightspots within a long fly ball of the Fenway bleachers.

A short distance from Fenway Park's clamor, you enter an area of three- and four-story walk-ups known as the West Fenway. "There are days when you could be in the West Fenway and not know there's a ball game going on a block away," said Ross. "It's somewhat tucked away, a little bit of an enclave."

At the end of the West Fenway's Kilmarnock Street are Park Drive and the Fens. More than just open space, the area includes the Fenway Victory Gardens, originated in 1942 as part of the war effort, and Roberto Clemente Field for athletics. Across the way is Simmons College, which straddles Avenue Louis Pasteur beside Emmanuel College.

Emmanuel, founded in 1919 as the first Roman Catholic women's college in New England, has benefited from a partnership with Merck, and it's impossible to miss the gleaming 12-story lab building that opened in 2004 on campus. Simmons has also built on its legacy as a women's college founded in 1899. In 2009, it opened one of the first green college buildings in the area, the $17 million, five-story School of Management and Academic Building.

A bit farther down Avenue Louis Pasteur is the Boston Latin School, the oldest school in the United States, having been founded in 1635. The current building dates to 1921, with an addition in 2000. Part of school lore is that Harvard University was founded so that Latin's first graduates would have a college to attend. Alas, Benjamin Franklin was a dropout.

Harvard is represented in impressive fashion at the avenue's end, where it meets Longwood Avenue. Harvard Medical School was founded in 1782, making it the third-oldest in the country, and it moved to the "great white quadrangle" of five marble buildings and a center quad in 1906.

Northeastern had a goal: to crack the top 100 in the *U.S. News & World Report* college ratings, and it embarked on that decade-long quest in the mid-1990s. It became more selective, strengthened its faculty, and spent more than $400 million on buildings and campus enhancements. Nowhere is NU's transformation more striking than in the area of Centennial Common, just off Huntington Avenue.

The Museum of Fine Arts began in 1876 on the site of what is now the Copley Plaza Hotel in the Back Bay, and it moved to Huntington Avenue in 1909. For its centennial, the MFA embarked on a $500 million expansion and renovation that started with the reopening of its entrance on The Fenway.

Long known as one of Boston's most beautiful spots, the Gardner Museum's courtyard remains an idyllic setting for contemplation. The Gardner came into being in 1903 as one of the first buildings on the Fens, the vision of Isabella Stewart Gardner.

Lately, reminders of what is missing—13 priceless works stolen in March 1990 in the largest art heist in history— have overshadowed the 2,500 works that remain. Many of the frames still sit empty, and though dozens of leads have been tracked, the whereabouts of the stolen art, by Rembrandt, Vermeer, Degas, and Manet, remains a mystery.

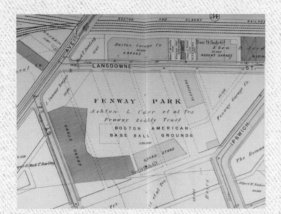

APRIL 9
The Red Sox open the ballpark with a 2-0 victory in an exhibition game against Harvard College.

APRIL 20
The Red Sox beat the New York Highlanders (later known as the Yankees), 7-6, in 11 innings, before 24,000 fans on Opening Day. The opener was delayed by two days of rain.

MARCH 29
The Fenway Garage, designed by architect James McLaughlin, is opened at Ipswich and Lansdowne Streets.

APRIL 13
The Boston Braves are granted the use of Fenway for a doubleheader against the New York Giants; they return for another doubleheader on May 30.

JULY 15
Red Sox Manager J. Garland "Jake" Stahl resigns; Bill Carrigan becomes manager.

MAY 14
Lannin buys out Red Sox stock from Taylor and becomes sole owner of the team.

JULY 9
Lannin buys a promising young pitcher, George Herman Ruth, Jr., better known as Babe Ruth, from the minor league Orioles with catcher Ben Egan and pitcher Eddie Shore, reportedly paying more than $25,000 for the trio.

AUGUST 17
The Progressive Party holds a field day at Fenway with former President Theodore Roosevelt in attendance.

1910   1911   1912   1913   1914

JUNE 24
Red Sox owner John Taylor, son of *Boston Globe* publisher Charles Taylor, announces plans to build a new home for the Red Sox.

SEPTEMBER 24
Ground is broken on the new park, even before developers file a building permit.

SEPTEMBER 29
Papers are signed that transfer Fenway Park grounds on Ipswich and Lansdowne Streets to Charles Taylor and other investors. Construction by the Charles Logue Building Company, overseen by architect James McLaughlin.

MAY 17
Fenway Park is formally dedicated "with the music stuff, the flowers, and the flags" before 17,000 people; the Red Sox go on to lose to the White Sox, 5-2.

OCTOBER 9
The second game of the first World Series held at Fenway ends in a 6-6 tie between the Red Sox and the New York Giants after 11 innings.

OCTOBER 16
In the eighth game of the World Series, the Red Sox score twice in the 11th inning to overcome a 2-1 deficit and claim the title.

DECEMBER 1
Joseph J. Lannin, a real estate developer, buys Red Sox stock owned by James McAleer and Robert McRoy, and becomes the Sox co-owner with Taylor.

OCTOBER 13
The "Miracle" Boston Braves complete a four-game sweep of the favored Philadelphia A's in the World Series with a 3-1 victory in Fenway Park.

Red Sox warming up at Fenway Park, Boston, Mass.

The Bos

SOX OPEN TO PACKED PARK

GARDNER KICK

Congressman Charges

Shakeup in Ta
And Roosevelt

heir Win Over New York
Is Seen by 24,000.

irst Game at New Field Goes

VOL LXXXI—NO 112.   BOSTON. SUN

BABE RUTH
P.—Boston Red Sox

JUNE 21
George "Rube" Foster pitches Fenway's first no-hitter, beating the Yankees.

AUGUST 30
Hubert "Dutch" Leonard pitches a no-hitter against the St. Louis Browns.

OCTOBER 7-12
At Braves Field, the Red Sox again win the World Series, beating the Brooklyn Robins (later the Dodgers) with the help of Babe Ruth, who pitches a 14-inning, complete game for the 2-1 win in Game 2 at Braves Field.

MAY 23
A military service is held for Americans killed in the Spanish-American War. Governor David Walsh and Mayor James Michael Curley attend.

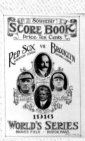

JANUARY 22
Jack Barry resigns as manager to serve in the Naval Reserves.

FEBRUARY 11
Ed Barrow becomes manager.

MAY 26
Memorial Mass in tribute to U.S. military losses held in park, with Cardinal William O'Connell presiding and 30,000 in attendance.

JUNE 29
Before a crowd of 50,000 at Fenway Park, Irish political leader Eamon de Valera asks Boston for support in the effort to form the Irish Republic.

1915   1916   1917   1918   1919

JUNE 25
Babe Ruth hits his first home run at Fenway.

OCTOBER 8-13
Playing their home games at Braves Field to take advantage of its larger seating capacity, the Red Sox win the World Series against Philadelphia.

NOVEMBER 1
New York theater owner and producer Harry H. Frazee and associate Hugh Ward purchase the Boston Red Sox from owner Joseph Lannin. Bill Carrigan, the Sox player-manager, announces his retirement.

JANUARY 5
Jack Barry is hired as player-manager.

DECEMBER 14
In what the Globe called a "sensational trade," the Sox acquire "Bullet Joe" Bush, Amos Strunk, and Wally Schang.

SEPTEMBER 11
The Red Sox defeat the Chicago Cubs, 2-1, in Game 6 at Fenway to win the World Series, the first and only World Series played from start to finish in September because of war restrictions. It was the third Red Sox title in four years, and their last one for 86 years. Babe Ruth extends his pitching streak to 29 2/3 scoreless World Series innings, a record that stood until 1961, and also tied for the league lead with 11 home runs.

Top of page (l-r): Babe Ruth, Bill Carrigan, Jack Barry, and Vean Gregg in 1916; chronicling the team's Fenway debut, 1912; postcard of the Fenway grandstand, 1912. Timeline: map of the Fenway area, 1912; postcard of the park in its opening decade; Babe Ruth's rookie card; World Series scorebook, 1916.

1920s

Fronted by the city's official seal, Boston Mayor James Michael Curley threw out the first pitch at the 1924 home opener. The season was the sixth in a streak of 16 consecutive non-winning years for the Red Sox from 1919 to 1934.

As the Roaring Twenties progressed, those associated with the Red Sox must have kept telling themselves that it couldn't possibly get worse—but it did, again and again. When the Fenway grandstand caught fire in May 1926, destroying a huge swath of seats, a *Globe* story said of team owner Robert Quinn, who had bought the club from Harry Frazee, "The Boston baseball public realizes what a difficult task he has had and has a world of sympathy for him." There was no such sympathy for Frazee, who, upon selling Babe Ruth to the Yankees in January 1920, said of the New Yorkers, "I do not mind saying I think they are taking a gamble." If it was a gamble, the Yanks hit the lottery several times over, as Ruth hit 54 home runs in his first season and led the team to six pennants in the 1920s alone. The trade was really just the first act in a continuous shunting of Boston's talent to the Yankees by Frazee. For Quinn's part, once he bought the club from Frazee in July 1923, he continued where Frazee had left off by making all the wrong moves. By 1923, the Sox didn't have a single player remaining from their 1918 world championship team; and seven of those traded played for the Yankees in the 1923 World Series game that clinched New York's first title. From the start, Boston fans flocked to Ruth's return engagements at Fenway. On his first trip back, 28,000 turned out for a doubleheader; the *Globe* called it "one of the largest crowds . . . ever packed into the park for any game except a World's Championship contest." The story went on to say, "They saw what many of them went to see: the 'Swatting Babe' pole out a home run." One wonders at what point the sight became tiresome.

The decade barely had begun when Harry Frazee made the deal that would be credited—and cursed—for elevating one franchise while eviscerating the other. "You're going to be sore as hell at me for what I'm going to tell you," the owner informed Manager Ed Barrow. "You're going to sell the Big Fellow," Barrow figured. The price for Babe Ruth was massive for the time—$100,000 from the Yankees, plus a $300,000 loan from New York owner Jacob Ruppert with Fenway Park as security. Frazee insisted that he would have preferred getting players in return, "but no club could have given me the equivalent in men without wrecking itself."

While critics then and now claimed that Frazee wrecked his own club for more than a quarter-century, the fact was that the Sox already were headed south in the wake of their worst finish in a dozen years. For all his boisterous brilliance, Ruth hadn't seemed likely to change that. "What the fans want, I take it, and what I want, because they want it, is a winning team," said Frazee, "rather than a one-man team which finishes in sixth place."

Although the reaction from many journalists and fans ranged from shock and depression to anger and betrayal, those feelings weren't universal. "Men who have been in the baseball business generally conceded that Frazee was justified in making the sale," James O'Leary wrote in the *Globe*. The sellee, however, complained he'd been made the goat for his former club's failings. "I am going to return to Boston in the near future," Ruth proclaimed in a telegram printed on the front page of the *Globe*, "and at that time the fireworks will start."

But it was the Sox who provided the pyrotechnics for Ruth's return, bashing New York, 6-0 and 8-3, in their Patriots Day doubleheader at Fenway and going on to win 10 of their first 12 games of the season. "I do not predict a pennant winner, but surprising things have happened in baseball and I may have a 1920 miracle crew in the present Sox," said Barrow, whose club was in first place in late May. "Who knows?"

But when New York returned to sweep their hosts in four games just before Memorial Day, it was the start of a 4-14 slump during which Boston tumbled into fourth place and never recovered. Yet even without the Big Fellow, the Sox still managed a modest upgrade, finishing one place higher than they had the previous year. And Ruth remained immensely popular in the city where he'd made his name. More than 33,000 fans turned up for a "Babe Ruth Day" doubleheader on the Saturday of Labor Day weekend when the Knights of Columbus gave him a set of

diamond cuff links between games, each of which Ruth punctuated with a home run.

The Hope Diamond itself wouldn't have been enough to lure the man back to Boston, though, and his exodus was only the first in a procession of departures for the Bronx. Next was Barrow, who left after three years to become the Yankees' business manager and one of the fiscal architects of what would become the game's greatest dynasty.

Following him out the door before Christmas were pitchers Waite Hoyt and Harry Harper, second baseman Mike McNally, and catcher-outfielder Wally Schang. Thus continued what Boston faithful still call "The Rape of the Red Sox." Then outfielder Harry Hooper, who thought he'd be offered the manager's job instead of Hugh Duffy after wearing the uniform since 1909, departed for the White Sox. Hooper played in Chicago for another five seasons and went on to make the Hall of Fame. "One by one the old stars of the Red Sox leave us," the *Globe* observed ruefully.

By then Boston undeniably was a second-division club. League president Ban Johnson pointedly ignored the Red Sox in his preseason evaluation for 1921 and only 7,500 fans turned up for the Fenway opener on April 21 to see the hosts blank the Senators, 1-0.

One of the season's few home highlights was a mid-June sweep of the Tigers, punctuated by the ejection of the

Herb Pennock won 240 games in the major leagues, and was part of two world championship teams with the Red Sox and four with the Yankees.

The Boston Daily Globe EXTRA

Entered as second class matter at Boston, Mass., under the act of March 3, 1879.

BOSTON, TUESDAY MORNING, JANUARY 6, 1920—SIXTEEN PAGES

COPYRIGHT, 1920, BY THE GLOBE NEWSPAPER CO.

TWO CENTS

RED SOX SELL RUTH FOR $100,000 CASH

Demon Slugger of American League, Who Made 29 Home Runs Last Season, Goes to New York Yankees

"BABE" RUTH.

Premier Slugger of the American League, Sold by the Red Sox to the New York Yankees.

Frazee to Buy New Players

Calls One-Man Team Here a Failure

Star's Demands, He Says, Upset the Local Club

'Babe' Says He Will Play in Boston or Nowhere

By JAMES C. O'LEARY

"Babe" Ruth, home-run hitter extraordinary of the Red Sox, has been sold to the New York American League club for a cash price of probably $100,000 and possibly more.

Pres Frazee in announcing the sale at Red Sox headquarters in the Carney Building late yesterday afternoon declined to state the amount.

"The price was something enormous, but I do not care to name the figures," said Mr Frazee. "It was an amount the club could not afford to refuse.

"I should have preferred to have taken players in exchange for Ruth, but no club could have given me the equivalent in men without wrecking itself, and so the deal had to be made on a cash basis.

"No other club could afford to give the amount the Yankees have paid for him, and I do not mind saying I think they are taking a gamble.

"With this money the Boston club can now go into the market and buy other players and have a stronger and better team in all respects than

Continued on the Fifth Page.

Place a regular order with your newsdealer or newsboy for the Daily and Sunday Globe. Read the Want pages today.

..R MAKERS LOSE IN SUPREME COURT

..ess' Right to Fix Alcoholic Content Under ..Time Dry Act Upheld 5 to 4—Sales of ..2.75" Before Oct 28 Declared Legal

..cutions ..anned

..by Justice Brandeis

..of Wets Killed, ..ry Leaders

..Amendment ..Cases Filed

..N, Jan 5—By a mar- ..the Supreme Court ..he right of Congress ..cating liquors, insofar ..artime prohibition. ..our opinion rendered ..Justice Brandeis the ..the constitutionality ..the Volstead Prohibi-

..the Second Page.

FULLER IN RACE PLEDGED TO WOOD

Announces Candidacy For Delegate-at-Large

Warns Old Guard Plans Trick by Favorite Son Booms

By CHARLES S. GROVES

WASHINGTON, Jan 5—Representative Alvan T. Fuller formally announced this afternoon his candidacy for delegate-at-large to the Republican National convention, pledged to the nomination of Gen Leonard Wood.

Mr Fuller says that he has had assurances from the manager of the Wood campaign that his candidacy would not be repudiated. In other words, that the Wood managers are entirely willing to have him go ahead and test out the sentiment in Massachusetts for the General, regardless of the candidacy of Gov Coolidge and the fact that Senator Lodge, Ex-Senator Crane and other Republican leaders in the State are to be candidates in the primaries pledged to Coolidge.

Sees Plan to Smother Wood

Mr Fuller in conversation with the reporters said that it appears to be the purpose to "smother" the sentiment for Gen Wood in various States by encouraging the candidacies of "favorite sons," the nomination of anyone of whom was admittedly doubtful if not improbable. By this method, he said, the "Old Guard" proposed to defeat Gen Wood in the convention and nominate their own man.

Continued on the Second Page.

HARVARD SQUAD DUE IN BOSTON TONIGHT

Victorious Players Given Great Welcome in Chicago

Graduates and Students Plan to Greet Tourists at Station Upon Arrival Home

Special Dispatch to the Globe

ELKHART, Ind, Jan 5—Harvard's fighting football team rolled into Chicago this morning at 11:30 on the California Limited, right on time. Again the Crimson winners received a great reception, one even greater that that accorded them when they stopped in Chicago on the way west. It was evident beyond doubt, judging by the handshaking and congratulations given the Harvard huskies when they stepped from the taxicabs into the University Club, that all the world loves a winner.

Every one was happy to have a few hours away from the monotony of train riding. The first move made by every member of the party was for the big swimming pool at the University Club and for nearly an hour they made the most of this opportunity to refresh themselves.

Imediately after luncheon the players split up and visited friends around the city, meeting again to catch the 5:15 train headed east. It was evident at the station that many students were traveling east, returning to school or college after their Christmas recess. The train bearing the Harvard team had to be split into three sections, the third section carrying the Harvard party.

Several of the players have found the sudden return to cold weather too much for them, with the result that Dr Paul Withington and Derrick Parmenter have a sizable hospital list of players ailing with colds. There is no serious sickness in the party, however. This morning the thermometer read zero when the group reached Chicago.

Dr Paul Withington left the rest of the team to visit Madison for a couple of days. He probably will arrive in Boston two days after the rest. The two Horween boys welcomed the chance to visit their parents during the after-

Continued on the Fifth Page.

TRAINER HAYWARD IS OREGON'S GOAT

Taught His Players to Hold Rivals Lightly

Insisted on Having Bench in Front of Harvard's Stand

By W. D. SULLIVAN

LOS ANGELES, Calif, Jan 5—Harvard's home coming victorious football players are more than 2000 miles from Los Angeles tonight. They are on the last lap of their long trip, if they left Chicago as their schedule planned, just at the dinner hour this evening.

Although they have been gone since Friday they have left in the Far West a record that still continues to plunge the loyal Californians into spasms of defense for defeated Oregon. The players from the Northwest, who have gone to their own homes, had recovered from the disappointment of defeat before they left town, but they were a sore lot of boys when they pulled out for the North. Their superstitious trainer, Bill Hayward, who boasts some Indian blood, was the goat of their squad. They attribute all their troubles to him.

How differently they felt in the Harvard camp toward their devoted and diplomatic trainer, Pooch Donovan, gives the key to the fundamental difference between the two elevens. It was the difference in policy, too, that just turned the scale in favor of the Crimson.

Pooch and Coach Fisher, from the day the expedition started, never let up a

Continued on the Fifth Page.

EQUALITY IN G. O. P. DEMAND OF WOMEN

Want Member for Member on National Committee

Suggest Ten Planks for Platform at Chicago Conference

CHICAGO, Jan 5—Republican women from 14 States of the mid-West, conferring today on party plans and issues for the 1920 Presidential campaign, demanded equal representation with the men on the National Committee of the party and urged "a fair representation of women delegates from each State" in the National convention in June.

Many of the women professed to see

Continued on the Second Page.

DELAY EXAMINATION OF SUSPECTED REDS

Thirty-Eight More Sent to Deer Island

Deportations May Be Under Way Within 40 Days

Owing to the fact that the steamship Cretic, carrying hundreds of immigrants, is due in Boston today, thus keeping the immigration officials busy with their regular work, the examination of the 400 odd alleged Reds who are confined on Deer Island probably will not begin before tomorrow, according to officials of the Department of Justice last night.

Preliminary questioning of the alleged alien agitators on the island was begun yesterday under the supervision of Immigration Commissioner Henry J. Skeffington, who visited the island, but it was stated later that this was merely for the purpose of listing the political offenders and to facilitate the real work of examination when it is begun.

That the work will be speeded up and completed as quickly as possible was admitted yesterday by Mr Skeffington, and it is expected that the alleged undesirables—or at least those who are found by the officials to be really dangerous to the American Government—will be started on their way across the seas inside of 40 days.

Some Discharges Expected

Some of the officials admit that the examinations likely will show that some of the persons already interned on Deer Island should not have been sent there; that they are not members of organizations which seek to destroy the American Government by violence. Mr Skeffington said yesterday that already two members of the Socialist party, said to be enemies of the Communists, have been found among the Deer Island

Continued on the Third Page.

THE WEATHER

Forecast for Boston and Vicinity: Fair and warmer Tuesday and Wednesday; moderate shifting winds, becoming southerly.

Washington Forecast for New England and Eastern New York: Fair and warmer Tuesday. Wednesday partly cloudy and warmer.

Globe's Forecast—Wednesday fair and warmer. Thursday probably fair; continued moderate temperature; southerly winds.

The Temperature Yesterday at Thompson's Spa—3 a m, 9; 6 a m, 9; 9 a m, 13; 12 m, 23; 3 p m, 27; 6 p m, 27; 9 p m, 19; 12 mid, 18. Average temperature yesterday, 17¾; average one year ago, 20 11-12.

Temperatures at 8 Last Night—San Francisco, 52; Williston, 18; St Louis, 28; Chicago, 22; Nantucket, 24; Portland, 14; Eastport, 10; New York, 18; Washington, 22. Precipitation in Boston, 24 hours, to 8 p m, trace.

MME GALLI-CURCI GIVEN A DIVORCE

Husband Withdraws His Infidelity Charges

CHICAGO, Jan 5—Mme Amelita M. Galli-Curci, noted soprano of the Chicago Grand Opera Company, today won a divorce from Luigi C. Curci after a short hearing before Judge McDonald in Superior Court.

The proceedings, which promised to be lengthy and sensational, were brought to an early close when Curci, in a statement filed with the court, withdrew his answer to his wife's suit.

Curci, replying to charges of infidelity, in which Mme Galli-Curci named Melissa Brown as corespondent, countered with similar accusation, naming Homer Samuels, the singer's accompanist.

The courtroom was crowded with members of the opera company, society women and curiosity-seekers when the trial opened.

Curci's formal statement to the court stated that the charges made in his answer was based on a "misapprehension of the facts," an action that he "profoundly regrets."

"I am now convinced that the information was false and that all charges made in my answer reflecting in any manner on Mme Galli-Curci are untrue and without basis in fact," the statement continued. "I have contested these proceedings for divorce instituted by Mme Galli-Curci in the hope that I might somehow win back her affection and esteem."

He denied charges contained in his wife's bill that he had been guilty of misconduct with Melissa Brown of Fleischmans, N Y, and other women.

SAUGUS MINISTER RESIGNS ON SPOT

Rev Mr MacDougall Says He's No Man's Servant

Special Dispatch to the Globe

SAUGUS, Jan 5—"I will be the servant of no man and immediately after this service I will resign," declared Rev Arthur MacDougall, pastor of the First Congregational Church, yesterday, after he had been interrupted in his sermon by Timothy J. Stackpole, a member of the church board, who stood up to question the pastor.

As soon as he finished his sermon he wrote his resignation on church paper with a pencil and handed it to the church board.

When Mr Stackpole arose from his seat yesterday, the pastor told him to keep his seat and it is said that the latter retorted, "I will when you keep yours." It is claimed that the resignation is really the climax of new amendments which have been introduced into the bylaws of the church by the church board, to which the pastor objected.

No action has been taken to secure a new minister. Rev Mr MacDougall was born in Scotland and is a graduate of the University of Glasgow. He came to the First Congregational Church on Dec 4 from Ludlow, Mass.

WOOD ALCOHOL BAIL FIXED AT $100,000

Three Arraigned Before New York Commissioner

Chauffeur Arrested in Catskills and Garage Keeper Held

NEW YORK, Jan 5—Bail of $100,000 each was demanded by United States Commissioner Reifschneider today when John Romanelli, an undertaker; Samuel K. Saleeby, a druggist; Edward G. Ware, Saleeby's brother-in-law, were arraigned before him on charges of selling alcohol in violation of the law. The trio are alleged to have been responsible for the distribution in New York, New Jersey and New England of wood alcohol which later was colored and sold as whisky, causing more than 100 deaths.

It is understood that the men will be taken to Connecticut and tried on charges of manslaughter.

Cosimo D'Ambrosio, a Brooklyn chauffeur, arrested Saturday in a farmhouse in the Catskills, was arraigned before United States Commission Hitchcock and held in $25,000 bail.

William Woller, a Brooklyn garage keeper, whose arrest also was announced, was turned over to the Federal authorities in Brooklyn. Charges against D'Ambrosio and Woller were not made public. Woller is said to have had a large amount of wood alcohol on his premises and D'Ambrosio is said to have helped transport it.

GRAND JURY CALLED FOR WOOD ALCOHOL INQUIRY

SPRINGFIELD, Jan 5—Call for a special session of the Hampden County Grand Jury to act upon the wood alcohol cases now pending in the Holyoke and Chicopee police courts was received here today from Chief Justice John A. Aiken of Superior Court, acting on the instigation of Dist Atty J. B. Ely, in cooperation with Charles H. Wright of Pittsfield, who takes office Wednesday. The Grand Jury will convene on that day and will take jurisdiction over the 14 cases now pending in Chicopee and two in Holyoke, in all of which the

TODAY'S GLOBE CONTENTS

Page 1.

Babe Ruth sold to the New York Yankees for a cash price of probably $100,000.

Representative Fuller enters race for delegate-at-large to Republican convention pledged to Gen Wood.

Supreme Court, 5 to 4, upholds right of Congress during war time to fix legal alcoholic content of beverages.

Mme Galli-Curci, opera singer, given divorce in Chicago.

Harvard football squad due in Boston tonight.

Soreness in Far West over actions of Oregon trainer, says W. D. Sullivan.

Republican women demand equal representation with men on National committee.

Rev Arthur MacDougall says he's "no man's servant," and resigns Saugus pastorate.

Hearings for alleged Reds at Deer Island to be begun soon.

Bail fixed at $100,000 in cases of three wood alcohol suspects.

Page 2.

Government asks Supreme Court to dismiss suits to test prohibition amendment to the Constitution.

Jack Geraghty declared still legally married to Julia French Geraghty of Newport, R I.

Mysterious firing of volleys near fort magazine at Phoenix Park.

New fight on behalf of 2.75 percent beer planned.

McSweeney speaks at Catholic Union in criticism of "Americanization" methods.

Page 3.

City Council votes $15,000 for use of Mayor's Committee in combatting Red propaganda.

West End woman, charged with having in her possession a private still, held to Jan 20, with man accused.

Democrats in Bay State House in contest for leadership.

Roundup of Reds resumed in New York.

Rev William H. van Allen, in address to Baptist Social Union, says all true Americans will help Government crush Reds here.

Hostetters forgive eloping daughter and receive son-in-law.

Mrs Ellen Conroy, 72, North Dorchester, badly burned.

Frederick Houston Kent, Northampton, speaks on "The Real British Attitude toward America" at the Boston

Two-alarm fire in West Somerville.

Page 4.

Attractions at the theatres.

Mel Trotter at Tremont Temple urges devotion of bodies to service of Christ.

Cathedral five scores its eighth straight win; other results.

Page 5.

Wladek Zbyszko and Jim Londas winners in wrestling bouts in New York.

Alger defeats Sheldon on a foul in Suffolk A. A. bout.

School swimming season opens; Boston E. H. S. defeats Cambridge Latin, 43-19.

Formal opening of the new Ice Pavilion at Cambridge.

Hitchings sets a new record in bowling Boston pins.

Page 6.

Financial news.

Page 7.

Financial and commercial news.

Rogers offers bill to transfer vocational education work to War Risk Bureau.

News of the water front.

Judge Advocate reprimanded at court-martial of Capt Detzer in New York.

Special Commission on Street Railways turns back to State $10,700, or more than half of the appropriation allowed.

Railroad executives will retain some of Government's changes in management of roads.

Charles H. Tenney, Methuen hat manufacturer, left estate of $158,604.

Page 8.

Congress resumes sessions; Mann to support Berger's claim to seat.

Radicals at miners' convention condemn acceptance of President's plan.

Gen Edwards tells of great good to be accomplished by Y-D Club; drive for $200,000 clubhouse fund opens Monday.

Sir George Paish confers with Sec Glass; says Europe asks loan of only half of $25,000,000,000 from United States.

Page 9.

Inauguration of Somerville City Government.

Capt William Hart of Ladder 2, East Boston, probably fatally hurt by fall while rushing to answer alarm.

Supt Crowley says the police have not suppressed news of crime.

Attempted holdup in Charlestown laundry fails.

Page 10.

"They're Off," by Uncle Dudley.

Gallivan and Lufkin introduce resolutions calling for facts on medal awards in both Army and Navy.

President to send "important word of greeting" to Democrats at Jackson Day banquet.

Gov Lowden of Illinois, answering Senator Borah's demand for his position on League of Nations, favors ratification of the peace treaty with the Senate's reservations in substance.

Supreme Council tentatively sets Jan 10 as date for final ratification of peace.

"More Truth Than Poetry," by James J. Montague.

Page 11.

Marriage intentions.

Page 12.

Household Department.

Page 16.

Harry K. Mansfield, former owner of Ferncroft Inn, Middleton, dies.

Information about income tax returns.

Four arrested for Woburn shooting.

THE CURSE IS BORN

BY BOB RYAN

> "Let me tell you this. You're going to ruin yourself and the Red Sox in Boston for a long time to come."
>
> —Ed Barrow, Red Sox manager, when owner Harry Frazee told him he was selling Babe Ruth to the Yankees

The shocking news was delivered in the dead of winter.

The good people of New England awoke on the morning of January 6, 1920, to discover that the most beloved baseball player in town was now a Yankee.

Thus was born "The Curse of the Bambino."

Now, we all know there is no such thing. It is a whimsical hypothesis, the idea being that selling Babe Ruth was the equivalent of an original sin from which there can never be an absolution. Good throwaway line, that, and nothing more.

The truth is that it wasn't just the sale of Ruth to the Yankees that plunged the Red Sox into the abyss (nine last-place finishes, a seventh and a sixth between 1922 and 1933), a situation that wasn't remedied until Tom Yawkey bought the team and began spending tremendous sums of money.

It was the sale of Ruth and the subsequent sales and/or trades of catcher Wally Schang, shortstop Everett Scott, and pitchers Waite Hoyt, "Bullet Joe" Bush, "Sad Sam" Jones, and Herb Pennock to the Yankees that enabled the heretofore impotent team in New York to exchange places with the team that had been a four-time world champion between 1912 and 1918. When the Yankees clinched their first world championship by defeating the Giants in Game 6 of the 1923 Series, all seven played in the game.

That's the crime. It wasn't just the idea that owner Harry Frazee sold Ruth to the Yankees. It's the complete package. What he did was provide New York with the complete foundation of a dynasty. Burt Whitman of the *Boston Herald* called it "The Rape of the Red Sox."

But selling Ruth to New York was the hot-button move for all time. For as big as Ruth was in Boston, over the next 15 years in New York he became more than just a successful baseball player. He became a true American icon.

Sixty-five years after his last game, he remains the biggest baseball star of them all. He was the sports embodiment of the Roaring Twenties, swashbuckling his way through both American League pitching and life itself. No sports reality has galled Bostonians over the past 80 years as much as the fact that We created him and They—and not just any They but the most hated They of them all—reaped the full benefits, both short- and long-term.

People were upset at the time, of course, but the feeling wasn't universal. The soon-to-be 25-year-old Babe was a highly flawed diamond. He was already starting to put on weight, he had a bad knee, and, most of all, he was a thoroughly undisciplined brat whose self-absorption, some said, was running the risk of harming the team. In fact, Frazee employed this last argument as a major rationale for selling his star, pointing out that despite Ruth's individual heroics in 1919 (a record 29 home runs while leading the league in runs batted in with 114, runs with 103, and total bases with 284—all with the dead ball), the team had finished sixth.

Citing Ruth's defiant behavior, which included missing the final game of the season in order to play a lucrative exhibition game in Connecticut, Frazee said, "It would have been impossible for us to have started the next season with Ruth and have a smooth working machine, or one that would have had any chance of being in the running."

Baseball historians have spent the past eight decades debating the incident. Was Frazee in serious debt? Did he really, really need the $450,000 he received from the Yankees (there was also a $350,000 loan involved, with Fenway Park as collateral) in order to finance a Broadway musical called *No, No Nanette*? Or was he to be taken at face value when he said he had made a decision based on what he honestly believed to be in the best interests of the team? One thing is for sure: the musical in question didn't open until 1925, so it wasn't the catalyst for the trade.

Still, Frazee is hard to defend. Ruth was a handful, but rather than spend the Yankee money to acquire more talent, as he promised, all Frazee did was sell, sell, sell. The record is clear. The Red Sox hung on with fifth-place finishes in both 1920 and 1921, but in 1922 they took up what was almost permanent residence in the league basement for the next decade, as the Yankees, utilizing all the aforementioned Red Sox stars, were winning pennants in 1921, 1922, 1923, 1926, 1927, 1928, and 1932.

Despite his future success in New York, Ruth fondly recalled most of his time in Boston, where he first lived in Mrs. Lindbergh's rooming house on Batavia Street (now Symphony Road); where he met his first wife, Helen Woodford, in a Copley Square coffee shop; where he bought an 80-acre farm in Sudbury in 1916; and where he became established as a star and a World Series hero.

As for Frazee, he left town on the midnight train for New York, a gesture of infinite symbolism for millions of Sox fans not yet born.

CHAOTIC KENMORE SQUARE

When the Red Sox play a home game, Kenmore Square is the conduit for the lion's share of the more than 35,000 fans who converge on the ballpark. And like the Fenway neighborhood itself, Kenmore Square didn't exist until the late 19th century.

The land the square sits on was then called Sewall's Point, and it was pretty much surrounded by tidal salt marsh. Sewell's Point was connected to downtown Boston by a narrow road (later to become Beacon Street) that ran atop a dam along the Charles River. When the Back Bay was filled in the late 19th century, the former dam road became Beacon Street, which connected to Brookline Avenue. A short time later, Commonwealth Avenue was constructed, and the three roads converged at what became known as Governor's Square.

Governor's Square (renamed Kenmore Square in 1932) became an important local transportation hub. The Peerless Motor Car Building on the west side of the square now houses Boston University's Barnes and Noble Bookstore, but its main claim to fame is the Citgo sign on its roof; it was born in the 1950s as a Cities Services billboard, and it became the landmark neon beacon in the 1960s.

Because of the local college-student population, Kenmore Square and the streets close to the ballpark feature plenty of restaurants, cafes, and music venues. The most famous jazz club was Storyville, which was located at the Hotel Buckminster starting in 1950. Legends such as Dave Brubeck, Louis Armstrong, Charlie Parker, and Sarah Vaughan played the club, which was in the ground-floor space of the Buckminster now occupied by Pizzeria Uno. The legendary rock club The Rathskeller, a.k.a. "The Rat," played grimy host to some of rock music's great bands in the 1970s and 1980s as they paid their dues, including The Police, the B-52s, R.E.M., U2, the Ramones, Tom Petty, Blondie, and Sonic Youth. It closed in 1997, and its site is now occupied by the Hotel Commonwealth, which opened in 2003.

On Patriots Day, more than 20,000 official runners pass through the square on the home stretch of the Boston Marathon, the world's oldest annual marathon. Hundreds of thousands of spectators root the runners on, and the square offers a convergence of race day and Red Sox fans spilling out of the traditional 11 a.m. holiday game.

The square was once noted for its hotels, including the Buckminster, at the corner of Beacon Street and Brookline Avenue, which was designed by Stanford White. It was the site of the first network radio broadcast, and it also played a part in the infamous "Black Sox" baseball scandal. On Sept. 18, 1919, the same day that the Chicago White Sox defeated the Red Sox, 3-2, at Fenway, bookmaker and gambler Joseph "Sport" Sullivan went to the hotel room of Arnold "Chick" Gandil, White Sox first baseman. There they hatched a plot to fix the 1919 World Series, which was to start 13 days later.

In 1915, the Kenmore Apartments building opened at the corner of Kenmore Street and Commonwealth Avenue. It later became the Hotel Kenmore, an elegant, 400-room operation that was once Boston's baseball headquarters—at one time in the late 1940s when the Braves still played in Boston, all 14 visiting major-league clubs stayed there. Countless trades were made, managers hired and fired, and post-game parties featured celebrities of the day.

> "As I grew up, I knew that [Fenway Park] was on the level of Mount Olympus, the Pyramid at Giza, the nation's Capitol, the czar's Winter Palace, and the Louvre—except, of course, that it is better than all those inconsequential places."
>
> —Former Major League Baseball Commissioner Bart Giamatti

combustible Ty Cobb in the ninth inning of the finale. Cobb, who'd been arguing pitch calls from the on-deck circle, berated the umpire, dropped a bat on the arbiter's foot, and then stepped on the man's heels as he followed him around the plate and, as the *Globe* reported without specifying, "did things for which there was no justification whatever, and which led up to another incident as deplorable and more disgusting than anything that Cobb had done."

After key injuries led to a ruined July, the club rallied with a strong finish and flirted with third place before slipping back to fifth. But that would be the best showing for more than a dozen years as the talent exodus to the Bronx continued during the offseason. Frazee swapped shortstop Everett Scott, who'd played nearly 1,100 games for Boston, plus pitchers "Sad Sam" Jones and "Bullet Joe" Bush for shortstop Roger Peckinpaugh and three hurlers. While critics lambasted the owner for continuing his yard sale, his money had paid for the furnishings. "It is Frazee's team," the *Globe*'s James O'Leary reminded readers, "and if he has goldbricked himself he is the one who will suffer."

By Opening Day in 1922, nobody from the 1918 champions remained on the Red Sox roster. Even the stockings had been changed to ones with a dark stripe. "Picking red socks for the boys must have been left to someone who is color-blind," Mel Webb observed in the *Globe*.

Though the club won four of five from the Yankees at home in late June, Boston couldn't replace Jones and Bush, who won 39 games for New York that year. After their rotation fell apart, the Sox quickly sank from sight in July, dropping six in a row to the Indians and Tigers (the last by a 16-7 count). The club ended up losing 93 games, its most in a season since 1905, and finished in the cellar 33 games behind the Yankees. Since 1915, that had been the residence of the Athletics. Except for one season, Boston would be the new annual tenant there until Tom Yawkey bought the club in 1933.

That was the end for Duffy, who was kept on as a scout and "general all-round man." In came Frank Chance, the "Peerless Leader," who as player-manager had led the Cubs to world championships in 1907 and 1908 and to the National League pennant in 1906 and 1910. Chance, who had no illusions about what he was inheriting in the Hub, reckoned that it would take at least three years to transform the Sox into contenders.

With only a handful of regulars returning, the roster obviously was a reconstruction zone in 1923. And while Frazee predicted that the club "will be the finest, smartest lot of youngsters ever hired by a major-league ball club," Boston essentially had become a minor-league franchise. After losing the first four games in New York, the Sox had dropped to the bottom by May 12 and never inched higher than sixth for the duration. After a brutal 27-3 loss at Cleveland on July 7—when reliever Lefty O'Doul gave up a club-record 13 runs in the sixth inning—Chance knew that the task exceeded his enthusiasm and

Michael William "Leaping Mike" Menosky played left field for the Red Sox after Babe Ruth was sold to the Yankees. He was with the Red Sox for four years, during which time he hit a total of nine home runs.

HARRY FRAZEE: THE MAN BEHIND THE CURSE

BY DAN SHAUGHNESSY

On Monday, January 5, 1920, the Harvard University football team, still celebrating its New Year's Day, 7-6, Rose Bowl victory over Oregon, rolled eastward into Chicago on the California Limited. In Washington, D.C., in a 5-4 decision rendered by Justice Louis D. Brandeis, the Supreme Court upheld the right of Congress to define intoxicating liquors, sustaining the constitutionality of provisions in the Volstead Act. Elsewhere, the last of the U.S. troops in France made their way home across the Atlantic, and a New York Supreme Court justice ruled that it was not immoral for women to smoke cigarettes.

There was one more bit of news that day. Late in the afternoon, Harry Frazee held a press conference and announced that slugger-pitcher George Herman "Babe" Ruth had been sold for cash to the New York Yankees.

"The price was something enormous, but I do not care to name the figures," said Frazee that day. "No other club could afford to give the amount the Yankees have paid for him, and I do not mind saying I think they are taking a gamble."

Prohibition was 11 days away when Frazee made this move, which would drive Sox fans to drink.

There was some outrage when the Ruth transaction was announced but none of the hysteria that would accompany such a transaction in today's age of media overkill. The sale of Babe Ruth to Gotham was front-page news in all the Boston papers. John J. Hallahan of the *Evening Globe* led his story with: "Boston's greatest baseball player has been cast adrift. George H. Ruth, the middle initial apparently standing for 'Hercules,' maker of home runs and the most colorful star in the game today, became the property of the New York Yankees yesterday afternoon." A newspaper cartoon showed Faneuil Hall and the Boston Public Library wearing "For Sale" signs.

In his autobiography, Ruth admitted, "As for my reaction over coming to the big town, at first I was pleased, largely because it meant more money. Then I got the bad feeling we all have when we pull up our roots. My home, all my connections, affiliations and friends were in Boston. The town had been good to me."

Frazee's name was mud in Boston, just as it is now. One night he was out in Boston with character actor Walter Catlett. In an attempt to impress a pair of young ladies, Frazee had a cab driver take the group to Fenway Park. He got out of the cab and proudly displayed his baseball empire. The cab driver overheard the boasts and asked if this passenger was in fact Harry H. Frazee, owner of the Red Sox. Frazee said he was, and the driver decked him with one punch.

On July 11, 1923, Frazee sold the Red Sox to Robert Quinn for $1.25 million. The 1923 Red Sox did not have one player left from the championship season of 1918. The man who did the dirty deed didn't care anymore. While the Sox stumbled through the Roaring Twenties, Frazee finally hit the mother lode in 1925 with *No, No, Nanette.* It had a New York run of 321 performances and was one of the most successful shows of the 1920s, earning more than $2.5 million for Frazee.

But Frazee didn't have much time to enjoy his money. The shows after *Nanette* didn't do as well, and on June 4, 1929, four weeks shy of his 49th birthday, Harry H. Frazee, or "Big Harry" as he is known in family lore, died of kidney problems at his home in New York City. Frazee always said that the best thing about Boston was the train to New York, and New York City Mayor Jimmy Walker was at Frazee's bedside when he died.

Ruth went on to establish himself as his sport's greatest performer. He set a major-league record with 60 home runs in 1927 and was still the idol of millions of Americans when he died of cancer in 1948. His record of 714 career home runs stood until Hank Aaron passed him in 1974. He was one of the original five players enshrined in baseball's Hall of Fame.

Red Sox owner Harry Frazee (left) and manager Frank Chance huddled at Yankee Stadium in 1923. Frazee sold the franchise and park in July of that year.

RUTH'S TRIUMPHANT RETURN

Were Bostonians anxiously awaiting Babe Ruth's return after his trade to the Yankees in January 1920? The day before the Yankees and Red Sox squared off at Fenway, Harry Hooper won a game for the Red Sox against the St. Louis Browns with a home run in the last of the 11th inning. One headline said, "Babe Ruth missed? Not when Harry Hooper decides to settle game with his own bat."

When the Yankees arrived on May 27, Ruth hit a pair of home runs, but was nearly upstaged by a brawl that started with an umpire and a pitcher squaring off. (The headline read: "Player and umpire fight; Ruth hits two home runs.") Obviously, there was nary a dull moment, although surprisingly, only an estimated 11,000 attended.

Those fans witnessed "[Pitcher Bob] Shawkey of the visitors attack umpire [George] Hildebrand, who sideswiped the player on the head with his mask. The fans had then watched with consuming interest a regular football scrimmage in which 10 or 15 would-be peacemakers were trying to restrain the belligerents; they had seen Ruth, the demon home run swatter, knock the ball out of the lot twice . . . and altogether, they had had a great day."

Regarding Ruth, "many in the big crowd had come to see him make a home run, one having been his limit each of the previous three days." In the sixth inning of New York's 6-1 win, Ruth homered into the right-field bleachers, "a mighty drive." In the eighth inning, Ruth "knocked the ball over the left-field fence, an unusual hit for a left-handed batter against a right-handed pitcher. The ball hit the top of the fence and bounded 50 feet beyond, across Lansdowne Street. It was about the same kind of a hit he made on Ruth Day last season." Ruth would go on to hit 54 homers in 1920; the player with the next-highest total in the league only managed to hit 19.

The next day at Fenway, the story was the assembled crowd, though Ruth again played a prominent role, according to the *Globe*'s James C. O'Leary: "Babe Ruth and the Yankees, but mostly Ruth, made a cleanup of the Boston-New York series by winning both games of the doubleheader at Fenway Park in the presence of 28,000 fans, one of the largest crowds—and certainly the biggest money crowd—ever packed into the park for any game except a World's Championship contest. They saw what many of them went to see: the 'Swatting Babe' pole out a home run. With one on, he hit the ball high over the clock which tops the left-field fence."

The Yankees won the games, 4-3 and 8-3, on a day in which the Red Sox fielding "was far below their standard, and altogether they had a decidedly off-day." The large crowd necessitated roping off the field, with any hit going into the crowd that ringed the outfield against the fence being ruled a ground-rule double. "The overflow of 5,000 or 6,000 spread out onto what ordinarily is used as the playing field, stretching from back of third base around by way of the terrace in left field (Duffy's Cliff), across center to and across the right foul line. Many of those in the 50-cent seats hopped the fence and became a part of this mass of humanity, which included many women, who were unable to get even standing room in the grandstand."

Ruth hit his homer in the fourth inning of Game 1: "With a runner on base, two out and himself crippled with two strikes—though that does not appear to be a disability so far as 'Babe' is concerned—Ruth developed two runs in the twinkling of an eye by sloughing the ball over the left-field fence."

The first game ended pitifully for the Red Sox, as they had the bases loaded with none out in the last of the ninth, trailing by one run, but could not push even the tying run across. Yankees' pitcher Jack Quinn induced two force plays at the plate, and the game ended on another force play, this time at second base.

In the second game, Ruth banged out a double, but the story noted, "It looked as if Ruth's double to right was going over into the bleachers, but [Harry] Hooper would easily have captured it if he could have played where he usually sets himself with Ruth at bat."

YES, THAT MONSTER CROWD SAW WHAT IT WENT TO SEE—BABE HOISTED ONE OVER THE BARRIER

endurance. "I have a one-year contract and that is enough," he told a former Cubs director.

After seven years as owner, Frazee wanted out as well. On July 11, he agreed to sell the franchise and the park for a reported $1.25 million to Robert Quinn, the St. Louis Browns business manager who headed a Columbus syndicate and immediately asked fans for a rain check on the rest of the season. "I bespeak patience on the part of the Boston baseball public with my efforts," he said.

League President Ban Johnson, who despised Frazee, was delighted with the change. "Quinn will have a good team here before you know it," he predicted. But the manager knew otherwise. "The new owners of the Boston club have the franchise and the park, but they must get a ball club," Chance said in late August, and then told his players that he'd been misquoted.

The Yankees, who pulverized Boston, 24-4, at Fenway on September 28, with Ruth producing a three-run homer, two doubles, and two singles in six at-bats, now had most of the old club, as more than a dozen former Sox won World Series rings that year with New York. What the Sox had for 1924 was a ball bag full of optimism fueled by Quinn's promise to spend hundreds of thousands of dollars on players, and a new skipper in the person of Lee Fohl, the former catcher for Pittsburgh and Cincinnati who'd produced winning seasons managing the Indians and Browns. "That Quinn and Fohl and time are a winning combination has already been demonstrated," O'Leary wrote, "and there is no reason to anticipate any reversal of form."

The Sox blossomed early that year and found themselves in first place in early June but they went to seed in July, losing nine straight at Fenway, including an 18-1 battering by the Tigers. While the seventh-place showing was a slight upgrade from the basement and attendance doubled to nearly 450,000, the season was an outlier—a misleading prelude to the three worst consecutive years in franchise history.

In the wake of the previous season's fade, Quinn was circumspect about the club's prospects for 1925. "All I can say is that we have hopes," he stated in February. But by the time the Sox played their home opener against Philadelphia, they already had dropped five of their first six games en route to a 2-12 start that essentially interred them. "Once again we hear, 'What's the matter?'" Mel Webb observed in the Globe. "Just now everything is the matter."

The Sox ended up losing 105 games, finishing nearly 50 behind the Senators. They were last on merit. Boston had the worst offense (640 runs scored) and worst defense (921 runs allowed) in the league and absorbed scoreboard-busting home beatings—the Athletics lashed their hosts by 15-4, 15-2, and 12-2 margins.

FIRE SWEEPS THROUGH THE GRANDSTANDS

As if their on-field woes were not enough, the Red Sox were dealt a huge blow in May of 1926 when a fire swept through Fenway's third-base grandstand and briefly threatened the entire ballpark. The fire, on the night of May 8, had followed a spate of small fires under the grandstand during a game the previous day, and caused an estimated $26,705 in damage.

The headline in the Globe of May 10 described the third-base "bleachers" as a mass of ruins and told of plans to put a concrete stand in place later. The team co-owner and president, Robert Quinn, already financially strapped, never implemented the plan, and until Tom Yawkey bought the team in 1933, the park had a gap where the burned stands had been torn out. This meant that for the next several years, the area occupied today roughly by grandstand sections 29 to 33 was an open area that was in play. This made for a huge foul territory, and the left fielder often disappeared from view chasing balls, with the bases umpire scurrying after him to rule on the play.

The Globe story by James O'Leary also said: "The destruction of the bleachers was complete, only charred timbers and boards remaining. The boardwalk on the roof leading to the press box caught fire in two or three places, and a small blaze started under the floor of the press box; only fine work by the fire department saved the grandstand. The burnt section of the bleachers will be roped off today, and when the debris has been cleared away, a concrete stand will be erected. . . .

"Since he bought the club a little more than two years ago, Pres. Quinn has spent between $65,000 and $70,000 in renovating the plant and bringing it up to date. Mr. Quinn appeared yesterday to be more concerned over the poor showing, thus far, of his ball club than he was about the fire loss. . . .

"President Quinn had been tendered the use of Braves Field for as long as he wished to make use of it by the Boston National League club, but finds that he will not have to avail himself of the courtesy."

The story ended: "The Boston baseball public realizes what a difficult task he has had and has a world of sympathy for him."

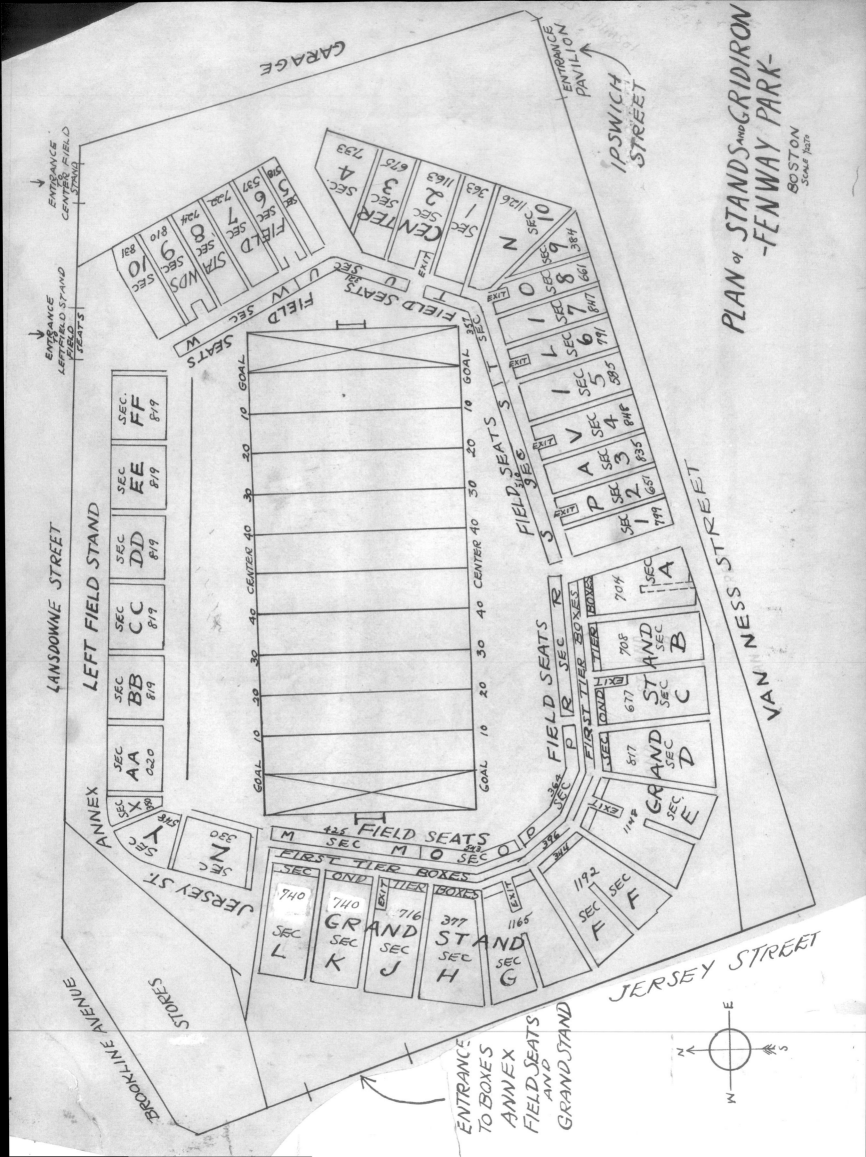

BC DEFEATS HOLY CROSS

More than 30,000 football fans turned out on the last day of November 1929 to watch the archrival Boston College and Holy Cross squads square off in their annual contest, with BC taking the victory, 12-0. The *Globe* stories of the next day described the scene in the ballpark and in the streets around Fenway.

In the game story, Melville E. Webb Jr. wrote: "In freezing weather for player and spectator alike, the Eagle[s], superior on attack, unpassable on defense, twice scored on its Worcester rival. One touchdown, a fierce, unbroken march for more than 25 yards followed the recovery of the ball on a flubbed kick. A second touchdown scored as the shadows were dark upon the flinty field during the closing moments, when Michael Vodoklys seized a Crusader forward pass, hurled from behind the Purple's goal, and tore relentlessly back to a point behind the Worcester posts. . . .

"The chill numbed but did not drive many from the hard-fought game. . . . No more grueling, slashing, desperate football fight ever has been waged between the forces of Boston College and Holy Cross than that on the Fenway battleground yesterday. No game ever was more productive of exciting thrills or more frequently marked by error, for the most part almost instantly redeemed. . . .

"Two hours freezing play, yet in all save less than five minutes of it a Worcester team threatening ever but never coming through. On Boston's door the Crusader was thumping all day long—but the stronghold never once gave way."

The postgame scene was described in another story: "Fewer than 10,000 persons who attended the game parked cars in the nearby streets, and when the flood of shivering fans rolled out after the game there was no long delay or jam. About 200 policemen helped enforce the rules, which prohibited parking on Brookline Avenue, Jersey Street, and Commonwealth Avenue, near Governor Square (known as Kenmore Square starting in 1932). Jersey Street and Brookline Avenue were made one-way streets during the game.

"After the game, about 500 BC students and friends who had secured a parade permit to march from the field to the Common via Commonwealth Avenue started a celebration and snake dance. The lines of cheering students were admirably handled by the police so as not to conflict with traffic, but the victors' enthusiasm wore off quickly and none of the group got much farther than Massachusetts Avenue before seeking shelter.

"Some careless motorists found their radiators had frozen during the game, and nearby garages did a rushing business thawing them out."

"I never believed in 'crying over spilled milk,'" Quinn declared as the campaign was winding down in September with attendance nearly halved. "And there isn't any use in alibiing a team which has finished last in every department of play." Only a rainout of the season's finale with Washington prevented the club from finishing with the worst record in franchise history.

But the bad news didn't end with the season. In November, the state board of appeals ruled that Quinn had to pay an additional $27,575 in taxes on the club's profits from the sale of Ruth and Mays to New York.

Since it didn't seem possible that things could be worse in 1926, even Kenesaw Mountain Landis sensed at least a possibility of improvement. "You seem to have a fine lot of athletes here and I wish you all kinds of luck," the commissioner of baseball told Quinn at the club's New Orleans training camp, saying that he'd wager "a golf stick or two" that Boston would pull itself out of the basement.

When the Sox came from 10 runs down in the fifth inning to nearly catch the Yankees on Opening Day in the Fens, it seemed that they might at least quicken heartbeats. "If you are inclined to apoplexy, heart trouble, shocks or faints don't spend your afternoons at Fenway Park," the *Globe*'s Ford Sawyer cautioned after the riveting 12-11 loss.

But after the hosts went down, 11-2, to the Indians on May 7, the distress signals were unmistakable. "The Sinking of the Ship. A Farce-Comedy in Nine Acts directed by T. Speaker," read the *Globe* headline the next morning. A day later, the theater itself was charred by a three-alarm fire that ravaged the third-base bleachers.

The front office, which had far more seats than it needed for a last-place enterprise, simply roped off the area and continued as before. The owner was more concerned about his ramshackle club, which was a far more extensive and expensive renovation project. "We get players who have been highly recommended, and who were desired by other clubs," said Quinn, "but when we get them they do not seem to hold up for us."

By Memorial Day, all that his club was holding up was the rest of the league. The Sox were 18½ games behind, en route to their poorest campaign ever (46-107). After they lost their final 14 games, all at home, Quinn was looking for a savior who actually had seen a pennant flying over the premises.

The obvious candidate was Bill Carrigan, the former catcher-manager who'd led the club to its 1915 and 1916 championships. Carrigan, however, was content with his life in Maine and had no desire to return to the dugout. "I shall not get back in the game," he declared in October after Fohl had resigned. But by December, after visiting with Quinn, Carrigan found himself back on the payroll. "I got talking baseball," he said, "and before I knew it I was manager of the Red Sox again."

He was, Sawyer wrote, "the Moses who is expected to lead a downcast Boston aggregation out of the wilderness of defeat and disappointment." But Carrigan would have had a better chance of parting the Charles River than of leading the bedraggled Sox to the first division, much less the promised land. His club, a 50-1 long shot to win the 1927 pennant, was dead on arrival by Opening Day.

The Sox dropped the season's first game by four runs at Washington, as the skipper "exhorted, wheedled, commanded, coaxed, bullied, and pleaded." They were swept by the Senators, and then lost three of four games at New York, including a 14-2 blasting. By Labor Day, the only reason to come to the park was to watch Ruth, Lou Gehrig, and the rest of the Yankees' "Murderer's Row" launch baseballs skyward. Nearly 35,000 showed up for the doubleheader with New York, the largest Fenway crowd since 1915, with the *Globe* reporting that "other thousands crashed the barriers, broke them down and swept into the grounds."

So fans were startled to see the Sox outlast the Yankees, 12-11, in the 18-inning opener, with Red Ruffing pitching the first 15 innings for the home side. The game lasted so long—four hours and 20 minutes—that the nightcap had to be shortened to five innings, which were completed in a brisk 55 minutes with New York winning, 5-0. The clubs split another twin bill the next day, with Ruth clouting three homers. The first, which cleared the center-field fence to the right of the flagpole, was deemed the longest hit at Fenway up to that point. "Nobody at the park could tell where it landed," wrote O'Leary, "but when it disappeared it was headed for the Charles River Basin."

The Yankees went on to claim the pennant by a whopping 19 games and swept the Pirates in the World Series, as Boston was buried 40 games behind in the cellar. Still, Carrigan was optimistic about his men's chances for 1928, predicting that they'd be "a better ball club in many ways." Indeed, the Sox climbed out of the basement amid a May blossoming that had them in fourth place after six home victories in a row. "The time-worn theory that there are only eight basic jokes will have to be revised," the *New York Post* suggested. "The Boston Red Sox have climbed into the first division in the American League."

Even Quinn was intrigued by that novelty, announcing

that he would spend a million dollars to double-deck the ballpark and increase capacity to more than 52,000—as soon as his club was good enough to make it necessary. Acrophobia and gravity proved a fatal combination, though, and the Sox soon began free falling. Before the end of July they were back at the bottom of the standings and the *Globe* provided an early obituary ("A Sad Decline") in early September. "On the diamond we produce, instead of a succession of championship teams, a perpetuation of tailenders," the editorial concluded.

After four years of viewing the league from an upside-down perspective, the Sox were justifiably reserved about their prospects for 1929. "I am predicting nothing, but I am hopeful," Carrigan said before the season. An Opening Day triumph over the Yankees at home was a splendid start, but Boston already was sending out distress signals on May Day when the Athletics dispensed a 24-6 drubbing that at the time set a Fenway record for offense—by the visitors. The *Boston Globe* tallied what it described as "a terrific cyclone of bingles of all descriptions"—29 hits, 44 total bases (11 by Jimmie Foxx), three homers, and six doubles, with 10 Philadelphia runs coming in the sixth inning.

By mid-month, the season already was a lost cause for Boston's two baseball teams, which both finished eighth in their respective leagues. "In a postseason series between the Braves and the Red Sox, which would win?" the *Globe* mused in October. "Don't you mean post-mortem series?" retorted the *Brockton Enterprise*. ♣

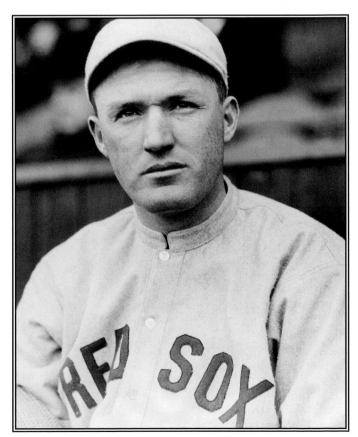

LEFT: No longer a member of the Red Sox, the Babe still went to bat for some Boston causes, including this Girl Scout Day promotion at Fenway in 1923.

RIGHT: Until Terry Francona duplicated the feat in 2007, Bill Carrigan was the only manager to have won two World Series titles with Boston (in 1915 and 1916). He returned to manage the Red Sox in 1927, but couldn't do better than last place in each of his three seasons.

JANUARY 5
Babe Ruth is sold to the Yankees by Red Sox owner Harry Frazee, beginning what many called, "The Curse of the Bambino."

MAY 3
Red Sox owner Harry Frazee and the Taylor family sign a deal that makes Frazee sole owner of Fenway Park.

OCTOBER 28
Ed Barrow leaves as manager to become business manager of the Yankees.

1920 | 1921 | 1922 | 1923 | 1924

NOVEMBER 5
Hugh Duffy is hired as manager.

SEPTEMBER 30
The Red Sox finish in eighth place (and would remain in the basement for much of the next decade).

DECEMBER 11
Hugh Duffy is out as manager and is replaced by Frank Chance.

JULY 11
Harry Frazee sells the club to a group of businessmen from Ohio, led by J.A. Robert Quinn. The new owners finally take possession on August 1.

SEPTEMBER 27
Chance is out as manager.

OCTOBER 23
Lee Fohl is hired as manager.

APRIL 9
The first exhibition city series game between the Red Sox and the Braves takes place. This tradition ended in 1952 when the Braves moved to Milwaukee.

OCTOBER 17
Fenway Park hosts its first professional soccer matches.

Sunday Post
SOX PARK HAS BLEACHER FIRE

FEBRUARY 20
Though granted the right to play Sunday baseball, the Red Sox play at Braves Field instead of Fenway Park because, by law, Fenway is too close to a church

DECEMBER 20
Bill Carrigan retires for good. Charles "Heinie" Wagner becomes the Red Sox new manager.

| 1925 | 1926 | 1927 | 1928 | 1929 |

MAY 8
Fire destroys bleachers along the left-field line. Owner Robert Quinn simply carts out the charred remains due to a lack of funds to rebuild the bleachers.

OCTOBER 22
Lee Fohl resigns as manager.

NOVEMBER 30
Bill Carrigan comes out of retirement to helm the Sox again.

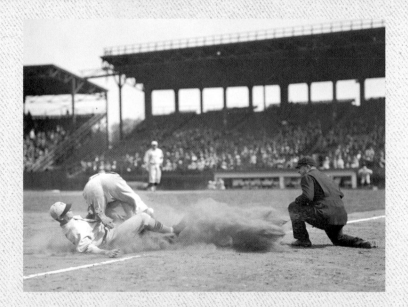

Top of page (l-r): A game-day crowd, 1924; Hugh Duffy as Red Sox manager; acting Mayor of Boston Timothy Donovan and Massachusetts Governor Frank Allen, opening day 1929. Timeline: Red Sox trainer Bits Bierhalter (with shovel) stoking up the hot stove in the Fenway clubhouse; Red Sox manager Lee Fohl; players rallying around the flagpole, 1924; photographer Leslie Jones inside a Fenway tarp, 1928; safe at third base, 1929.

1930s

Lefty Grove, who won 105 games for the Red Sox between 1934 and 1941, watches the action from the dugout.

By the time the 1930s were in the rearview mirror, Fenway Park itself and its major inhabitants had undergone a transformation. The team and the ballpark got a new owner in 1933, and the Red Sox made a slow climb from being cellar dwellers in nine out of 11 seasons through 1932 to a pair of second-place finishes in 1938-39. This effort was no doubt helped along by Tom Yawkey's inclination to spend his considerable wealth on players he thought could help. The park itself also benefited from the infusion of Yawkey's cash and enthusiasm. Although a five-alarm fire undid many of the off-season renovations that had cost nearly $1 million to complete by January 1934, Sox General Manager Eddie Collins vowed that the team would still open the season in a retooled Fenway. It required a massive additional commitment of money and manpower, but Collins was correct. For probably the first time, the Red Sox attempted to tailor their home field to take advantage of the presence of a slugger. Rookie Ted Williams had hit .327 with 31 home runs and an amazing 145 RBI in 1939. So bullpens were constructed in right and right-center field during the next off-season, with the expectation that Williams would be able to reach the seats (or at least the bullpens) more often en route to a potential Triple Crown-winning season. Williams, feeling the weight of expectation, hit fewer homers in 1940, and his on-again, off-again relationship with fans—and his open feud with newspaper writers—hit a significant rough patch. "There were 49 million newspapers in Boston, from the *Globe* to the *Brookline Something-or-Other*, all ready to jump us," said Ted years later. Indeed, it must have seemed that way. The Boston Braves (later Redskins) of the National Football League debuted in this decade, but the NFL failed to rouse enough local support, so the Redskins left for Washington after the 1936 season.

A Red Sox-Yankees doubleheader brought an early-morning crowd to Fenway on August 12, 1937.

As the thirties began, the Depression in the Fens already had been underway for a decade. Defeated and dispirited after three dreary years in the league basement, the skipper, who'd been used to pennants flapping during his days as player-manager, threw up his hands. "After handling three tailenders Bill Carrigan decided that he would not try again to start the Red Sox on an upward journey," Mel Webb wrote in the *Globe*.

That task fell to Charles "Heinie" Wagner, Carrigan's assistant and former teammate who'd seen enough of his players to be realistic. "All we need is a little quiet discipline and a little time," he said after inheriting the job just before Christmas of 1929. "You can't bring a ball team up to the top in a minute."

It should have been an omen when President Herbert Hoover threw out the first pitch for Boston's initial game at Washington and bounced the ball. Before the next day's home opener against the Senators, which the Sox dropped by a 6-1 count before 7,500 chilled fans, Wagner was presented with an enormous floral horseshoe that required three men to shoulder to the plate.

It was intended as a good luck gesture, but it might as well have been a funeral wreath as his club was all but buried by Memorial Day, falling back into the cellar after

dropping 14 straight games. The most fortunate man on the premises was pitcher Charles "Red" Ruffing, who'd led the league in losses for two years. He was dealt to the Yankees that spring and went on to earn a half-dozen World Series rings and make the Hall of Fame.

Despite 102 losses and a sixth consecutive last-place finish, owner Bob Quinn was ebullient about his club's chances for 1931 under new skipper John "Shano" Collins, a Charlestown native who'd already been knocked around enough for a lifetime. He'd been named the victim in the case against the Chicago Black Sox, eight of whom were accused of conspiring to throw the 1919 World Series, which cost Collins $1,784 according to court documents, and then he had been traded to Boston just in time for the Sox downward spiral.

So even though the Red Sox were at the bottom of the standings and 41 games out at the beginning of the Labor Day weekend, Collins was optimistic. "I am confident that some other club will finish in last place," he predicted before his men dropped a doubleheader on September 4 to the

Athletics. By then the only bit of suspense was whether Earl Webb would break the record for most doubles in a season.

Webb, who'd mined coal before he made the majors, was a journeyman outfielder whose erratic glove cost his team nearly as many two-baggers as he produced. But he banged out 67 doubles that year with only three triples while knocking in 103 runs and hitting .333. Though Webb was suspected of deliberately holding up at second, Collins said that "The Earl of Doublin" simply was "too darned slow on the bases to get to third."

The Sox managed to crawl upward to sixth place, their best finish in a decade. But by the middle of the 1932 season Collins had concluded that they were past the point of mending and quit on June 19. "I have worked unusually hard with the Red Sox," he said. "I have learned, however, that I was more or less on a treadmill and not going any place in particular."

So Quinn tapped infielder Marty McManus to take over what he deemed "the most thoroughly demoralized ball club that ever existed." Quinn, who'd been struggling financially even before the Depression, was demoralized as well. His club soon fell back to last place and ended up a whopping 64 games behind the Yankees after losing 111 games, the most in franchise history. Attendance plunged by half to 182,000, roughly a third of what the Braves were drawing on Commonwealth Avenue.

What Quinn needed was either a savior or a sucker who would take the club off his hands for a price, as he put it. The man was Thomas Austin Yawkey, a 30-year-old Yale grad who'd just inherited a fortune from his family's lumber and mining interests. On February 25, four days after his birthday, Yawkey purchased both Fenway Park and the Sox for $1.2 million. Tom's uncle and adoptive father, Bill Yawkey, had owned the Detroit Tigers from 1903 to 1919 and saw them win pennants in 1907, 1908, and 1909. Tom, who had the same aspirations, immediately began a refurbishment of both the park and the club. "Painters, plasterers and carpenters were scattered about the plant and soon everything will be in order," the *Globe* reported a few days before the 1933 opening game of a city series with the Braves on April 8 (which the Sox won, 7-0).

Yawkey's first priority was expanding the bleachers, where he believed the real fans congregated. "I may be mistaken but I think the grandstand fan is a casual—he comes to the game in much the same mood and manner that the theatre-goer goes to a popular hit," he said. Renovating the roster was a more daunting challenge, but Yawkey was quick to start upgrading the Sox from 500-1 long shots to contenders, paying top dollar and over-the-top dollar for anyone he could grab.

SUNDAYS IN THE PARK

The legendary Massachusetts Blue Laws, which set aside Sunday as a day of worship and rest, prohibited Boston's professional baseball teams from hosting Sunday home games from their very beginnings. Boston was not alone in banning Sunday baseball, but by 1918, all but three American League cities—Boston, Baltimore, and Philadelphia—had allowed it. The state law was amended in 1929 to allow for Sunday baseball, but the Red Sox were still stymied from playing at Fenway Park because of its proximity to a church. They played their Sunday contests at Braves Field for the next few seasons, until they caught a break from legislators.

In May 1932, the Massachusetts House of Representatives sponsored a bill that would loosen the restriction and allow the Sox to play at Fenway on Sundays. Specifically, the bill would lower the required church buffer zone from 1,000 feet to 700 feet, and the Church of the Disciples, at Jersey and Peterborough Streets, was about 850 feet away from Fenway. The church raised no objection, and the bill passed the state Senate on May 19, 1932. The Sox hosted their first Sunday game at Fenway on July 3.

If they were hoping to come out winners in their first-ever Fenway game on the Sabbath, the Sox might have chosen a more fortuitous season and a less daunting foe than the Bronx Bombers. In a game that took only 2 hours and 28 minutes to complete before a crowd of 7,000, the Yankees trounced the Sox, 13-2. As a result, the Yankees improved their 1932 record to 50-21, while the Red Sox were comfortably settled in last place at 14-57. Boston would go on to finish 43-111 that season, their worst record ever—64 games behind first-place New York.

The headline of the story said: "Ten Hits in Sixth, in which 14 Hostiles Go to Bat, Convert Game into Parade." Dave "the Colonel" Egan, the *Globe* baseball writer, wrote that the nine-run Yankee inning was filled with "carnage and sabotage and rioting."

Egan went on to write, "Ivy Paul Andrews, late of the Yankees, was the unfortunate youth upon whom the wrath of the New Yor-curs fell. He seen his duty and done it noble for the first five innings, but when the smoke of battle had cleared in the sixth, nine runs had been scored, the Messrs Andrews and Pete Jablonowski were weeping on each other's shoulders in the showers, and Bob Kline was pitching and ducking.

"In that sordid sixth, 14 of the visitors paraded to the plate, assumed a battling posture, and collected 10 hits, thus reaching a new high for the year and convincing the experts that the Depression is over. And George Pipgras upset all the fine traditions of the pitching industry by making two singles in that one stretch. There should be a law against it."

PEOPLE ⁓THE⁓ PARK

LADY WITH A MEGAPHONE

Mrs. Lillian Hopkins was known to thousands of Red Sox fans and players simply as "Lolly." A lifelong resident of Providence, she was awarded a lifetime pass to Fenway Park as the team's No. 1 fan. She made the 100-mile round-trip hundreds of times over 27 seasons between 1932 and shortly before her death in September 1959 at age 69.

Lolly occupied Seat 24 in Row 1 of Section 14, and she always came to Fenway with a megaphone and a scorebook. Many fans never met her but recognized her voice as she hollered advice and encouragement to players, managers, and umpires. According to a 1959 feature story in the *Globe*, "Lolly had become a baseball expert through the years and never hesitated to prove it. Many have felt the good-natured wrath with which she would set them straight."

One woman asked in 1958, "Why doesn't she go over to third base, so Williams can hear her better?"

"It's habit, a habit I developed when I was a little girl and my father used to bring me up from Providence to see games at the Walpole Street and Huntington Avenue Grounds," Lolly explained. "I always tried to get seats in that section if possible."

The late Smoky Kelleher, a sports official and a Red Sox fan to rival Lolly in loyalty, used to sit in a box in front of her, where he became accustomed to her hollering. One day in 1938, he gave her a megaphone, telling her it would save her voice. Lolly hollered as loud as ever; the megaphone merely multiplied her range.

Today, Lolly's passion for the Red Sox is preserved in the Baseball Hall of Fame. A life-size figure of her, megaphone and all, is front and center in an exhibit of some of the game's most beloved fans.

His biggest blockbuster came shortly before Christmas of 1933 when he dispatched two players and $120,000 to the penniless Athletics for pitchers Lefty Grove and Rube Walberg and second baseman Max Bishop. "Yawkey appears to be Boston baseball Santa," a *Globe* headline declared. "Has quite an array of Sox to hang up for local fans."

Yawkey had more than enough cash to fund his horsehide hobby. He owned a massive South Carolina plantation, a New York apartment, and soon acquired a suite at the Ritz in Boston. He also supplied fare for the Yuletide groaning board, sending up duck, quail, and venison that he and a few of his new Sox employees had shot during a hunting trip on his land.

There would be a new manager as well. Though McManus had nudged the Sox up from the cellar, Yawkey and new Sox General Manager Eddie Collins, the future Hall of Famer who'd been one of Yawkey's boyhood heroes at the Irving School in New York, wanted a bigger presence. "If we could find a second edition of Connie Mack, that would be our idea of the perfect manager," Collins remarked.

He hired Stanley "Bucky" Harris, the "Boy Manager" who'd directed the once-woeful Senators to two pennants and a Series championship before he'd turned 30 and

who'd just been cut loose by Detroit. Harris inherited an expensive new lineup for 1934 and an even more expensive playpen that Yawkey had to renovate twice after a January fire turned much of his new handiwork into cinders. Though the construction costs were soaring for what would be the city's biggest private building project of the decade, Yawkey had cash to burn. "Hang the money," he declared in early January. "What is the use of having money unless you do something with it?"

More than 30,000 fans turned up for the home opener against defending champion Washington and marveled at the Fenway improvements, which included an electronic scoreboard at the bottom of the left-field wall that was a baseball version of a traffic signal with its red and green lights. "They did everything in christening the new Fenway but crack a bottle of champagne over the prow of home plate," John Barry remarked in the *Globe*.

When the Yankees came to town five days later, nearly 45,000 people jammed into the park and another 10,000

Park improvements in the early 1930s included a new dugout for the visiting team.

DAVE EGAN: "THE COLONEL" HELD COURT

In 1977, *Boston Globe* columnist Mike Barnicle wrote about Dave Egan, who covered the Red Sox for the *Globe* and later, for the *Boston Record*. Barnicle told the story of a boy who spotted Egan sitting alone at the old Hotel Kenmore bar.

"Excuse me," the boy stuttered as he approached. "Are you Dave Egan?"

"I am," Egan said, looking older and smaller than the boy ever imagined.

"I write you letters all the time. I think you're wrong a lot," the boy said, his knees shaking.

"I probably am, kid," Egan replied. "But I never look back. It takes too much time."

"It must be great, knowing all those ballplayers and everything like you do," the boy said.

"Listen, kid," Egan replied. "They're lucky to know me."

Egan, who apparently awarded himself the "Colonel" nickname, was never shy about displaying his ego in print. "[He] would put these awful things in the paper—these awful, outrageous, untrue, fascinating, interesting things," wrote Barnicle. "Ted Williams was always 'T. W'ms Esq.' in one of The Colonel's pieces. . . . Egan was so irritating that he probably sold 100,000 copies a day on his own."

Ray Flynn, who would go on to become the mayor of Boston, told Leigh Montville, "I used to sell the *Record* at the ballpark when I was a kid. Ted Williams was my idol. Whenever The Colonel would write something bad about him, I'd go through all my papers and rip out the page that had The Colonel's column on it. It was my own little tribute to my hero. I swear on my mother I did this."

When Egan died in 1958 at age 57, Boston's archbishop, Richard J. Cushing, lauded him as a man "blessed with a great natural talent. . . . While all the people who read his columns didn't agree with him, they all appreciated him."

An example of Egan's prose was his story about the 1932 home opener at Fenway Park, in which Senators left fielder Henry "Heinie" Manush hit a game-winning, three-run homer with two outs in the ninth inning. The piece began: "Perhaps he is not a varlet. Probably he is not even a viper. But Henry E. Manush of the Washington Senators (born in Tuscumbia, Ala., in 1901, by actual count) was the ruination of the Red Sox yesterday afternoon at Fenway Park.

"The ninth inning froze the chilled crowd that sat through the harsh April day. Jack Russell, who threw them for the Red Sox, had staggered through the game quite well, viewing everything in a large and statesmanlike manner, and entered the last inning with a comfortable lead of three runs. But woeful events transpired, and Manush lashed out his home run, and so the Red Sox lost their second successive game by the margin of one run.

"The Chowder and Marching Organization, headed by the Messrs Bob Quinn, Nick Altrock and Al Schacht, and accompanied by Jimmy Coughlin's 10th Infantry Band plus the athletes, gave a swank parade to the flagpole in center field, where Walter Johnson and "Shano" Collins raised the American flag on high.

"Hon. James M. Curley, Mayor of Boston, emulated Jimmy Walker, Mayor of New York, by arriving on the scene at a late hour, and it is to his discredit that he sneaked away before the blazing finish of the game. I suppose it proves that Hizzoner has no end of brains, for it was an Antarctic afternoon, more suitable for football than baseball.

"But let us get around to the ball game, if you please . . ."

In an October 9, 1976, op-ed story, the *Globe*'s Robert Taylor lamented departed writers, including the late Egan: "The Colonel was the maestro of sprung syntax ("And this I tell you . . ."), whose prose made you feel that you were in the back room of a dingy smoke shop, with the cops pounding on the door and the proprietor swallowing the betting slips."

A TASTE FOR PIGSKIN

When the Newark Tornadoes of the National Football League folded after the 1930 season, the franchise was sold back to the NFL. The players and the berth in the league would eventually go to George Preston Marshall, who secured a league charter to place a team in Boston.

In an April 21, 1932, *Globe* story headlined "Pro Football Plans for Boston Outlined," Marshall noted that pro football attendance had risen 35 percent in the previous season. The story went on to say, "A canvass of this section where football is thoroughly understood has led the promoters to place a club in Boston." Though they may have understood the game, Boston sports fans were slow to embrace it.

Marshall named his team after the baseball Braves, with whom it shared Braves Field in its first season. The football Braves made their debut on October 2, 1932, losing at home to the Brooklyn Dodgers. A week later they secured their first win, 14-6, over the New York Giants. They completed their first season with a 4-4-2 record under head coach Lud Wray, but the games were so poorly attended that Marshall moved his team to Fenway Park in 1933.

Since his team was no longer playing in the same park as the Braves, Marshall changed the nickname to the Redskins—reportedly to honor their new head coach, William "Lone Star" Dietz, a Native American. The new nickname also allowed Marshall to continue to use the uniforms from the previous season.

In their first two years at Fenway, the Boston Redskins continued to play .500 football, finishing with records of 5-5-2 and 6-6. In 1935, the Redskins suffered from a punchless offense, scoring just 23 points during a seven-game losing streak en route to a 2-8-1 record.

The 1936 season—their final one in Boston—would also prove to be the Redskins' most successful on the field in Massachusetts. They won their final three games to capture the NFL's Eastern Division with a 7-5 record, outscoring their opponents, 74-6, in those three games. The Redskins featured a pair of future Hall of Fame players in running back Cliff Battles and offensive tackle Turk Edwards. But when they routed the Pittsburgh Pirates, 30-0, in their next-to-last game of the season, only 4,813 fans showed up at Fenway Park.

Marshall was so outraged by the meager turnout that he gave up the home field for the NFL championship game, choosing to face the Green Bay Packers at New York's Polo Grounds. The Redskins lost, 21-6, and citing the lack of fan support in Boston, Marshall moved the club to Washington, D.C.

On December 6, 1936, the *Globe*'s Paul V. Craigue was at the NFL title game in New York, and he wrote of the change of venue, "Nobody could offer a satisfactory excuse for the minor-league move by a 'major-league' club." Marshall claimed that he moved the game for the players' sake. "They get 60 percent of the playoff gate, with 20 percent going to the league and 10 percent to each club. We'll get a much bigger gate here than we would in Boston." Marshall went on to say, "We don't owe Boston much after the shabby treatment we've received. Imagine losing $20,000

Boston Redskins vs. New York Giants, 1933.

with a championship team."

Craigue defended the fans' indifference, noting that the Redskins "gave their worst exhibition of the season before their largest crowd and lost three of their five home games before starting their title surge against the lowly Brooklyn Dodgers. Maybe, after all, Boston would turn out for a real attraction."

He went on to ask, "Can you imagine the Red Sox winning the American League pennant and shifting their World Series games to Yankee Stadium in the interest of the gate?"

The franchise's move proved fortuitous for Marshall. The Redskins drafted a star college quarterback named Sammy Baugh before their first season in D.C., where they drew nearly 25,000 fans for their first home game. Baugh guided them to an 8-3 regular-season record in his rookie year and then threw three touchdowns to lead the Redskins over the Chicago Bears in the championship game. Baugh went on to a Hall of Fame career, and the Redskins had nine straight winning seasons in D.C. en route to becoming one of the NFL's most successful franchises.

Eight years after the Redskins' departure, another NFL club made an unsuccessful foray into Fenway Park. Ted Collins, a former recording executive who had become the manager and partner of popular singer Kate Smith, wanted to put a team in New York City and call it the Yanks. He was forced to settle for Boston, though he kept the Yanks nickname. Perhaps that name choice for a Boston team doomed it from the start.

The Yanks never had a winning season in Boston, going 2-8, 3-6-1, 2-8-1, 4-7-1, and 3-9. Collins was given permission to move the franchise to New York in 1949, though for some reason, he renamed his team the Bulldogs. They played three seasons in New York (the latter two, again, as the Yanks), before moving to Texas where they played as the Dallas Texans for one season. The franchise was sold and became the Baltimore (now Indianapolis) Colts in 1953.

The other early Boston NFL franchise was the Boston Bulldogs, who played just one season (1929) when the former Pottsville (Pa.) Maroons were sold to a New England-based partnership that included George Kenneally, a standout player for the Maroons. They played their home games at Braves Field, chalked up a 4-4 record and folded after one season in Boston.

A fire during renovations on January 5, 1934, destroyed much of the ballpark seen in this vintage postcard, though the original facade endures. The workforce was bolstered and repairs and improvements that included replacing wooden grandstands with steel and concrete were completed in time for the 1934 season.

were turned away. As attendance for the season ballooned past 600,000, the Sox ascended to the first division for the first time since Babe Ruth's departure and broke even with a 76-76 record. Had Lefty Grove not been sabotaged by abscessed teeth and a sore shoulder, they might have finished even higher than fourth place. "We were all set to shoot for third place," Harris said in April, "and I believe we could have made it until this terrible thing happened."

Grove, who'd won 172 games over the previous seven years, ended up going 8-8 and Mack, the Philadelphia owner, felt so badly that he offered to give Boston back its money. But Yawkey was in for the long term. Grove pitched another seven seasons in Boston, won nearly 100 more games and made the Hall of Fame.

The franchise clearly was on the rise and its new owner had no problem opening his overflowing wallet to fuel the ascent. But Yawkey's $250,000 bid for Senators shortstop Joe Cronin, twice what the Yankees had paid for Babe Ruth, was so extravagant that even Washington owner Clark Griffith couldn't believe he was serious. "Take it or leave it," Yawkey told him to his face. "I'll not be back."

Trading the man who'd just married Griffith's adopted daughter wasn't a bad way of shedding a son-in-law, one wag observed. And Cronin, who'd led the Senators to the pennant two years earlier as player-manager, was delighted to go to Boston in the same role. "A fellow with an Irish name like mine ought to get along there," he said.

The Sox were already in first place when they knocked off the Yankees in the Fenway home opener in 1935, giving rise to a rare case of spring fever in the Hub. "One hundred and forty seven more games before the World Series," Hy Hurwitz observed in the *Globe*. While the Fall Classic

would remain a pipe dream for another decade, the fans became entranced by a spirited and volatile club that could go from fifth to third to fourth place in three days and produce astonishing moments.

None was more bizarre than the triple play that Cronin hit into against the Indians on September 7 at Fenway, when his line drive skipped off the glove of third baseman Arvel Odell "Bad News" Hale, bounced off his forehead and into the glove of shortstop Bill Knickerbocker, who doubled up Bill Werber with a toss to second baseman Roy Hughes, whose relay to first nipped Mel Almada. "Nobody in all probability ever saw one like it," James O'Leary wrote in the *Globe*, "and nobody is likely to see another."

Even when the Sox were out of contention they were well worth the admission price. A record 49,000 turned up for a Sunday doubleheader with the Yankees in late September with another 10,000 refused entry. As it was, hundreds of fans stood behind a rope in the outfield where they were pelted with bottles by "bleacherites" whose view was blocked. "Boston was established beyond all doubt yesterday as the greatest baseball city in the universe," Gerry Moore declared in the *Globe*.

Yet for as many millions as the new regime had pumped into the park and the roster, it only had brought the Sox up to mediocrity. The club won just two additional games that year and still finished fourth. So Yawkey did what he would do for the next four decades—he brought in a right-handed wallbanger, sending $150,000 and two bodies to the Athletics for brawny Jimmie Foxx, whose 58 homers in 1932 were just two shy of Ruth's single-season mark. "Don't be surprised to see the Ruthian record fall," predicted the burly first baseman.

Though Double X whacked 41 homers and knocked in 143 runs, the Sox sagged badly in 1936. After sitting in first

The massive reconstruction, directed by new owner Tom Yawkey, dramatically upgraded Fenway Park before the start of the 1934 season.

Boston's boys of summer in the 1930s included (left to right) Jack Wilson, Jimmie Foxx, and Joe Cronin.

place in early May, the club went into a June swoon, going 4-13 on a 17-game road trip that was so horrific Yawkey was billed for the damage that his players did to clubhouses in Chicago and New York. In mid-July, only 2,500 witnesses turned up for an 11-3 home loss to Cleveland amid what the *Globe* termed "the unprecedented nose-dive of the most expensive collection of talent in the history of baseball."

They were the "Gold Sox" and the "Millionaires" who had a perverse attraction to Skid Row. A national poll declared Boston's sixth-place showing as the year's biggest sports "floperoo," far ahead of the knockout of Joe Louis by Max Schmeling and the U.S. tennis team's defeat by Australia in the Davis Cup. Yet Yawkey insisted that he still liked his club's chances for 1937. "People were beginning to think that nobody liked the Red Sox but their mothers," wrote John Lardner, who dubbed their owner a "dealer in second-hand ivory."

What Yawkey most liked was the future and, after spending seven figures on the expensive present, he now began looking to his embryonic farm system to deliver. While the Cardinals and Yankees had been growing their own talent, the Sox owner had been buying overpriced

and overripe produce from his competitors. So he looked at what seedlings were available on their minor-league affiliate in San Diego and came up with 19-year-old Bobby Doerr, who started immediately at second base in 1937 as the club's only field player under 23.

But Doerr wasn't quite ready for prime time—he played only 55 games—and though the Sox were clearly improving, they weren't anywhere near a match for the pinstriped champions. "You better warn the Yankees next time you see them," Foxx had advised a visitor in spring training. But when Boston had a chance to draw within grappling distance in August after climbing from fifth place to second, New York grabbed three of four games in a turbulent pair of midweek doubleheaders at Fenway that essentially ended the season for Boston.

The first of them, played before a crowd of more than 36,000 (with another 15,000 wanna-sees turned away), consumed just under six hours and after the opener went 14

FIRE AND ALL, IT WENT YAWKEY'S WAY

In its first 21 years—through a series of owners and the disastrous wholesaling of Red Sox talent—Fenway Park remained virtually unchanged, except for the effects of a fire on May 8, 1926, that destroyed the wooden grandstand past third base. Those seats were not replaced for years, leaving a wide gap in foul territory that remained until the sale of the team and the ballpark to Thomas A. Yawkey on February 25, 1933.

Yawkey immediately ordered a renovation of Fenway that reports of the day estimated would cost between $750,000 and $1.25 million. Yawkey promised a new team and a new image, and instantly began investing in his two assets—though those plans were jeopardized by yet another fire.

The Osborn Engineering Co., the Cleveland-based firm that designed Fenway Park in 1911, was hired for the reconstruction, which began in the fall of 1933. Fenway was largely unchanged in the area that horseshoed behind and around home plate. However, all the areas that had originally consisted of wooden grandstands, including left field, right field, and center field, were given a concrete base—and the outfield bleachers were expanded.

But on January 5, 1934, in the middle of renovations, a heater being used to dry the concrete overturned. A nearby canvas caught fire and the new left-field grandstand went up in flames. The fire quickly spread to the center- and right-field bleachers, and then jumped Lansdowne Street and engulfed five buildings across the street. The effort to fight the five-alarm fire was hampered by dense smoke and icy footing, but none of the roughly 700 workers on site or the more than 100 firefighters was seriously hurt. Damages from the fire were estimated at $250,000.

Red Sox general manager Eddie Collins admitted, "We may have to rebuild a large part of the bleachers we had just finished," but he was confident that the team would still open its season on time. Though the Braves offered the use of their field as a temporary home, the number of construction workers was boosted to nearly 1,000 and the work was completed on schedule. Yawkey, who was on a hunting trip in South Carolina when the fire broke out, did not cut his trip short.

The deepest region of Fenway Park, beyond the flagpole in center field, originally measured 468 feet and the right-field foul line extended 358 feet. In the renovation, center field was trimmed back to 425 feet and right field brought down to 326.

The look of the left-field wall and Duffy's Cliff also changed considerably in the makeover. The 10-foot cliff was all but eliminated, with only a very slight grade remaining (and that would disappear completely in the years to come). The now famous scoreboard that helps give the left-field wall its distinctive look was constructed at the base of the towering barrier, which was brought up to its current height of 37 feet.

The netting above the left-field wall wasn't installed until two years later, in 1936. The net, which rose at an angle over Lansdowne Street for another 23 feet 4 inches, not only saved on lost baseballs, it also prevented damage to cars and buildings along the street, before it was dismantled in favor of the Monster seats nearly 70 years later.

As part of the 1934 makeover, 15,708 new seats were installed at a cost of $45,556.10, or $2.90 each. The maximum attendance figure was increased to nearly 38,000. (By 1995, with more restrictive fire laws and allowances for fans to stand on the perimeter of the field a thing of the distant past, Fenway's capacity had been reduced to 33,583—the smallest in the major leagues.)

Like the original Fenway opener in 1912, the Red Sox went 11 innings on April 17, 1934, the day the renovated park was unveiled. With 30,336 watching, the Sox suffered a 6-5 setback to the Washington Senators.

Seated in the stands that day was George Wright, a Hall of Famer and one of the game's pioneers. Wright could remember playing baseball in 1871 at Boston's Walpole Street grounds, a ballpark that seated 5,000 spectators.

"As I looked around," Wright, then in his 80s, said that day in Fenway, "I thought how wonderful all this was, and how baseball had advanced in every respect. That is, every respect except ability. On that point, the players of my day were just as good."

Tom Yawkey and his first wife, Elise, at Fenway Park. They divorced in 1944.

Jimmie Foxx of the Red Sox slid safely back into first base ahead of the throw to Washington Senators first baseman Joe Kuhel.

ENTERING WILLIAMSBURG

On September 24, 1939, the Red Sox announced that the home and visiting bullpens would be moved from foul ground into right and right-center field at Fenway in time for the 1940 season. The common expectation was that Ted Williams would propel home run after home run over the shortened fence. As the *Globe* put it, Williams's "batting and home-run marks are expected to soar with the new layout."

"Everyone thought," Williams recalled years later, "that I was supposed to break Ruth's record."

After all, Williams was coming off a prodigious rookie season in which he had hit .327 with 31 home runs and a league-leading 145 RBI. There was little doubt that the reason for the ballpark reconfiguration ordered by Sox owner Tom Yawkey was to allow the Splendid Splinter, a pull hitter, to boost his number of round-trippers. The new warm-up pens were quickly dubbed "Williamsburg."

The bullpens were constructed at the base of the existing bleachers, taking more than 20 feet off the home-run distance for the start of the 1940 season. The modification also led to the construction of extra seating at the bottom of the right-field grandstand. The rounded portion of the right-field wall—often called the belly—was another offshoot of the changeover.

In announcing the change, Sox GM Eddie Collins estimated that 600 to 700 box and grandstand seats would be added and provide sorely needed revenue for the team. Fenway's home-run distance to the right-field foul pole shrunk from 325 feet to 302, while the right-field distance dropped from 402 to 380. As the *Globe's* Harold Kaese wrote in a story in 1952, "Some optimistic experts predicted [Williams] would hit 75 home runs, or at least break Babe Ruth's record of 60 with the park changed." However, Kaese contrasted Williamsburg's 380-foot distance in straightaway right field to the bullpens that had been constructed in the late 1940s in Pittsburgh, the so-called "Greenberg Gardens"—which required only a 335-foot poke from Pirates slugger Hank Greenberg. "Williamsburg," Kaese concluded, "is no joke, but Greenberg Gardens . . . is a big laugh for a slugger." Even with the new configuration, Fenway remained the longest right-center field fence to reach in the American League.

Kaese's analysis in 1952 led him to pronounce that Williams had gained a total of 48 home runs over nine seasons (1940-42; 1946-51), or just over five a year from the reduced distances. Indeed, in 1940, the first season of the change, Williams actually hit fewer homers overall (23, down from 31) and fewer to right field than he had in his rookie season of 1939 (seven in 1939; five in 1940—four of which landed in the pens, one of which reached the bleachers beyond). Perhaps, Kaese wondered, Williams had pressed because of the expectations.

If nothing else, Williams made shrewd adjustments over his career. Kaese noted that in his first five seasons, Williams had not hit a single home run over the left-field wall, but in his succeeding five seasons, he hit 15. Kaese noted that the uptick coincided with the introduction by Lou Boudreau, the Cleveland Indians' player-manager, of the Williams Shift, a realignment that left only one fielder to the left of the pitcher's mound.

Twelve years later, Williams recalled the inflated expectations for 1940. "I didn't hit the home runs that I had my first year," he said. "I got a lot of catcalls and criticism. That just irked me enough, so I got a little sour on everything and everybody."

That would not be the last time that Williams soured on the fans or the press in his brilliant, tempestuous 19-year career.

How Williamsburg Will Look Next Season

"BOY, WON'T I BE GLAD TO SEE THOSE SHORTER FENCES"—WILLIAMS
Above is a diagram of Fenway Park as it will look in 1940 and as announced by the Red Sox yesterday in confirming a Globe exclusive of seven weeks ago. The blackened spots are the present seats, with the shaded areas the positions where extra box seats and new bullpen will be constructed. The foul line now extends to the 332-foot mark and this will be shortened to 302 feet. The bleacher starts in right field, 402 feet from home plate and the building of the new bullpen there will reduce the home-run range at that point to 380 feet. In center is Teddy Williams, whose batting and home-run marks are expected to soar with the new layout.

HERE'S TO YOU, MISS ROBINSON

Ted Williams called her "Sunshine." Joe Cronin trusted her to babysit his sons. And Nomar Garciaparra never forgot to send her flowers.

For more than 60 years, Helen Robinson was the no-nonsense Red Sox switchboard operator who controlled access to the team's decision makers, guarded its most explosive secrets, and ultimately created a legacy of loyalty and longevity.

"Helen Robinson was a legend, really," said Red Sox GM Dan Duquette after Robinson, of Milton, Massachusetts, died of a heart attack in 2001 at age 85.

Robinson had witnessed it all with a telephone in her hand, all the sadness and glory that was Red Sox history for 60 years. She fielded condolence calls after the deaths of Thomas and Jean Yawkey, Tony Conigliaro, Joe Cronin, and one Sox great after another. And she endured the profanity-laced protests from fans after the most devastating losses on the field.

Robinson's greatest admiration was for Tom Yawkey. "He wasn't just a boss," she said, "he was also a friend." Although the switchboard went crazy whenever the Sox made a trade or were in a pennant race, Robinson remembered July 9, 1976, as her busiest day. That was the day the Red Sox announced Yawkey's death.

"She has lived through some of the greatest and most trying moments in Red Sox history," then-CEO John Harrington said at a ceremony marking Robinson's 60th year on the job—one month to the day before she died, "and she will forever be entwined with Red Sox lore."

A seamstress, Robinson knitted sweaters for Sox players who went off to World War II and Korea. Decades later, she helped sew tiny American flags on the backs of uniforms after the 9/11 terrorist attacks.

Robinson was working for New England Telephone in 1941 when she learned of an opening with the Red Sox. She was interviewed by Hall of Famer Eddie Collins, then the general manager, and landed the operator's job.

"I was the only non-uniformed personnel he ever hired," she proudly told people.

Those were the days of the telephone circuit board, when the operator needed to monitor the line to know when both parties were connected and disconnected on a call. Thus, she knew more about the inner workings of the Sox than almost anyone, but she never publicly whispered a word of it.

Nor did she betray the secrets she gathered by handling personal calls for players from Williams's early years to Garciaparra's heyday. And though the proliferation of cell phones curbed her contact with contemporary players, it was taken as much more than a minor observation when she first met Manny Ramirez and declared him "a fine young man."

Robinson never married ("The Red Sox were her life," Duquette said), and she counted Ted Williams among her closest friends. When they were young and single in the early 1940s, Robinson and Barbara Tyler, Collins's secretary, often socialized with Williams, Johnny Pesky, and Charlie Wagner.

"She loved Ted," Pesky said. "Ted always has called her 'Sunshine.'"

When Elizabeth Dooley, generally considered the greatest Sox fan, died in 2000, Robinson was on the phone trying to contact Williams. "I knew Ted would want to know," she said.

At her switchboard on the third floor at 4 Yawkey Way, Robinson worked from 9 a.m. until well after a home game ended, day or night. She left precisely at 5 p.m. when the team was on the road. And during weekend homestands, she arrived promptly on Saturdays and after church on Sundays.

In 60-plus years, Robinson was rarely absent. She kept working more than 20 years after she beat cancer in the 1970s. And she made no secret that she intended to work until she no longer was able.

"She went out doing what she wanted to do," Manager Joe Kerrigan said when she died. "She worked till the last day. . . . I hope she gets her due. I hope people realize what she meant to the Red Sox."

innings, the nightcap was called after seven because of darkness. "It looks like Tom Yawkey will still be among the scant few who isn't on W.P.A.," Hy Hurwitz observed in the *Globe* after more than 20,000 fans turned up the next day.

Although New York ran away with the pennant and the World Series, and the Sox ended up fifth, they still won more games (80) than they had since 1917 and their bankroller finally had a glimpse of a payoff. Boston would win a pennant "if it takes 1,000 years," Yawkey vowed before the 1938 season, but his checkbook had a limit. "I'm through playing Santa Claus," he declared when four players still were holding out on the eve of spring training.

As long as Yawkey had "The Beast," he had a potent holiday punch, particularly at Fenway, where Foxx's right-handed bat had the power of a cudgel. He had a monster campaign on the premises on the way to winning the league's most valuable player award, hitting .405 at home with 35 homers, 104 RBI, and an .887 slugging percentage. His loudest thunderclap came at the end of an August 23 doubleheader against Cleveland, when Foxx crashed a grand slam with two out in the bottom of the ninth to give his team a 14-12 triumph and a sweep after they'd trailed, 6-0.

"Who cares if the Yankees win the pennant after this?" crowed Cronin's wife, Millie, after Foxx had circled the bases with what the *Globe*'s Moore called "a grin as wide

as the Sahara Desert." By then New York had already run away with the league en route to a third straight world championship. But Boston's second-place showing was its best since Ruth had departed.

Another potential Ruth arrived in 1939 in the form of Ted Williams, a goofy and gangly 20-year-old out of San Diego who was so skinny that he eventually was dubbed the Splendid Splinter. He'd arrived at spring training a year earlier full of braggadocio that was deemed the prerogative of a veteran like Foxx, whose slugging credentials were beyond dispute. "Foxx ought to see me hit," he proclaimed.

Doc Cramer, Joe Vosmik, and Ben Chapman, who'd had the outfield jobs locked up, mocked Williams mercilessly. "Tell them I'll be back," Williams told clubhouse man Johnny Orlando as he was shipped up to Minneapolis for seasoning, "and I'm going to wind up making more money in this game than all three of them put together."

There was no keeping Williams down the following season, although Cronin, who'd originally dubbed him, "Meathead," was quick to sit the rookie when he threw a ball over the grandstand roof in Atlanta after misjudging an outfield fly in an exhibition game. "I'll continue to crack

Raising the backstop—an April ritual.

down on him until all the 'bush league' is out of him and he begins to act like a major leaguer," the skipper vowed.

There was nothing bush about his bat, though. "If he puts it there again, I'm riding it out," Williams promised after Red Ruffing had struck him out twice on Opening Day in New York, and then hammered a ball more than 400 feet that just missed going over the fence. In his third game at Fenway, Williams went 4 for 4 and hit his first homer. In Detroit, he launched the two longest homers ever hit at Briggs Stadium. "This kid can hit a baseball as far and as hard as any ballplayer that ever lived," a rival told sportswriter Grantland Rice. "And I'm not even barring the Babe."

"The Kid" was Ruthian in both his power and his personality, which was unapologetically adolescent, marked by what Moore described as "his constant boyish chatter, seldom possessing any meaning" and his "screwball acts." But his rookie numbers were irrefutably adult—.327 with 31 homers, 145 RBI, and 107 walks from pitchers reluctant to see their offerings sailing into the seats.

Even before Williams earned the nickname "Thumping Theodore," his colleagues had been optimistic about dethroning the Yankees, who'd been picked by their manager Joe McCarthy to win a fourth straight crown. "Perhaps the Fates will cross him up on the prediction," Cronin said. As always, though, it was a futile and frustrating chase that ended with a fiasco at the Fens on Labor Day weekend.

After winning the opener of the Sunday doubleheader by squeaking by the Yankees, 12-11, the Sox hoped to salvage the nightcap by stalling as the clock approached the 6:30 p.m. curfew with New York leading, 7-5, in the eighth. If the game couldn't be completed by then the score would revert to 5-5 (the score at the end of the seventh inning), so Cronin ordered an intentional walk to Babe Dahlgren to load the bases. But the Yankees countered by playing hurry-up, as George Selkirk and Joe Gordon trotted home and let themselves be put out.

After the fans littered the field with soda bottles, straw hats, and rubbish, umpire Cal Hubbard called Fenway's first forfeit and awarded a 9-0 victory to the visitors, a decision that later was rescinded by the league president, Will Harridge, who ordered a replay that was scrubbed by rainouts. Not that it mattered. Boston already was hopelessly in arrears and ended up 17 games behind. ⚾

Ted Williams at spring training in March 1938. The "Splendid Splinter" made his Red Sox debut in 1939, hitting .327 with 31 home runs and 145 RBIs.

HATS OFF TO ARTHUR D'ANGELO

BY STAN GROSSFELD

In blazing sunshine directly across the street from Fenway Park in 2006, Arthur D'Angelo, 79, was slowly and methodically pressure-washing the stale beer off the sidewalk in front of his souvenir store. By the time he finished, one side of Yawkey Way was clean enough to eat an *El Tiante* Cuban sandwich off it.

Inside the megastore, D'Angelo's 65-person staff was enjoying the air conditioning. But D'Angelo, a short man with a sweet smile, didn't want to delegate the cleaning chore.

Arthur and his twin brother, Henry, arrived in Boston's North End from Italy with their family in 1938, fleeing the dictatorship of Benito Mussolini. "I was 14 when we came to Boston," he said. "I couldn't speak a word of English."

The brothers started hawking newspapers, the *Daily Record* and the *Boston American*. The two eventually wandered from the North End to Dorchester to Fenway Park.

"We saw these crowds," D'Angelo said. "We didn't know what baseball was. We snuck into the ballpark. The game started at 2 p.m. and we thought, 'What are these idiots doing with a baseball bat?' But then it caught on and we loved the game. Why not capitalize on it?" They did, in a big way.

D'Angelo said that the Souvenir Store, run by Twins Enterprises, Inc., is the largest of its kind. Most locals refer to it as "Twins" even though Arthur D'Angelo's twin brother Henry died in 1987.

"We sell more caps than anybody in the world," said D'Angelo, who operates Twins Enterprises with his four sons. "We make them for all the major-league teams. We also have licensing for 200 colleges."

After a stint in the Army, D'Angelo was discharged in 1946 and returned to Fenway, hawking pennants. Interest in the team was high, as the 1946 Sox won their first American League pennant since 1918 and played to a record 1.4 million fans.

"Ted was back from the service," D'Angelo said. "They had Dave Ferriss, Bobby Doerr, Dom DiMaggio, and Johnny Pesky. Pennants were 25 cents. We had buttons with the players' pictures on them. We used to buy 'em for 12 cents and sell them for a quarter. You didn't need a license back then."

The D'Angelo brothers rented space outside Fenway until 1965, when they borrowed $100,000 and bought the building on Jersey Street (now Yawkey Way) that still houses the Souvenir Store. It almost folded.

In 1965, the Sox suffered through a 100-loss season, and the next season they drew just over 800,000 fans to Fenway to watch them finish ninth. "Nobody wants to remember a loser," said D'Angelo.

But then came the Impossible Dream team of 1967. "My favorite team was 1967," said D'Angelo. "The Sox won the pennant, then lost the World Series in the last game. Besides Yaz, there were no real standout players, but they all charged into it."

Arthur D'Angelo surveyed the scene on Yawkey Way from his office.

JANUARY 5
Fire ravages Fenway Park for about five hours, causing major damage.

APRIL 17
Crews manage to finish the reconstruction of Fenway in time for the season opener. Concrete bleachers replaced the wood bleachers in center field. Duffy's Cliff, a steep 10-foot embankment that ran in front of the left-field wall, is nearly leveled. The 37-foot wooden left-field wall is replaced by a more durable, 37-foot sheet-metal structure.

MAY 30
An estimated 8,000 fans watch the New York Yankees of the American Soccer League beat Scotland's Celtic F.C., 4-3. (The Yankees' goalie, Johnny Reder, would return to Fenway the following year to play for the Red Sox.)

DECEMBER 1
John Collins is hired as Red Sox manager, replacing Charles "Heinie" Wagner.

1930 1931 1932 1933 1934

JULY 3
The Red Sox play the first Sunday game at Fenway, a 13-2 loss to the Yankees.

JUNE 19
Collins quits as manager. Marty McManus is hired to replace him.

FEBRUARY 25
Thomas Austin Yawkey buys the Red Sox for $1.2 million, four days after his 30th birthday. He begins to plan a major overhaul of the park with General Manager Eddie Collins.

OCTOBER 2
Marty McManus is forced out as manager.

OCTOBER 8
The Boston Redskins football team plays the first game of its four seasons at Fenway.

OCTOBER 29
Stanley "Bucky" Harris is named as new manager.

JUNE 10
40,000 people gather in Fenway Park for Mass by William Henry Cardinal O'Connell, and speeches by Senator David Ignatius Walsh, Governor Joseph Buell Ely and Mayor Frederick W. Mansfield.

OCTOBER 26
Bucky Harris is forced out; Joe Cronin becomes the Red Sox player-manager.

APRIL 16
Shortstop Joe Cronin makes his debut as a Red Sox player-manager.

SEPTEMBER 22
A Yankees doubleheader draws a record baseball crowd of 47,627 to Fenway. After World War II, more stringent fire laws and league rules prohibited such overcrowding.

SEPTEMBER 29
The Sox finish in fourth place with a record of 78-75-1, the team's first winning record in 17 seasons.

JULY 4
A 23½-foot tall screen, held by 13 posts, is installed above the left-field wall to protect the windows of buildings on Lansdowne Street. The Globe headline reads, "13 Posts Do Not Jinx Homers."

NOVEMBER 29
The Boston Redskins play their last game at Fenway Park before moving to Washington, D.C.

DECEMBER 7
The Red Sox acquire a 19-year-old from San Diego named Ted Williams, who spends one more season in the minors before being called up to Boston.

OCTOBER 1
Jimmie Foxx sets a Boston club record by hitting his 49th and 50th home runs of the season in a 9-2 win over the Yankees.

APRIL 16
Ted Williams makes his Fenway debut in the annual city series between the Boston Braves and Red Sox.

APRIL 23
Williams hits his first career home run in the first inning of a 12-8 loss to the Athletics at Fenway Park off Philadelphia's Bud Thomas.

SEPTEMBER 24
Home and visiting bullpens are moved to right and right-center field to bring the fence 23 feet closer to home plate for Ted Williams. The new bullpens are dubbed "Williamsburg."

1935 1936 1937 1938 1939

Top of page (l-r): Red Sox outfielder Doc Cramer and pitcher Fritz Ostermueller in the dugout, 1936; groundskeepers covering the infield, 1937; fighting fire at Fenway, 1934. Timeline: Bobby Doer being adored by super fan Lillian Hopkins in the early 1930s; unidentified player executing a headstand on the edge of the dugout, 1935; Joe Cronin and Jimmie Foxx playing with umbrellas, 1938; Joe Vosmik getting behind the camera, 1938.

1940s

(left to right) Manager Joe Cronin, third baseman Jim Tabor, and left fielder Ted Williams at the Fenway Park batting cage.

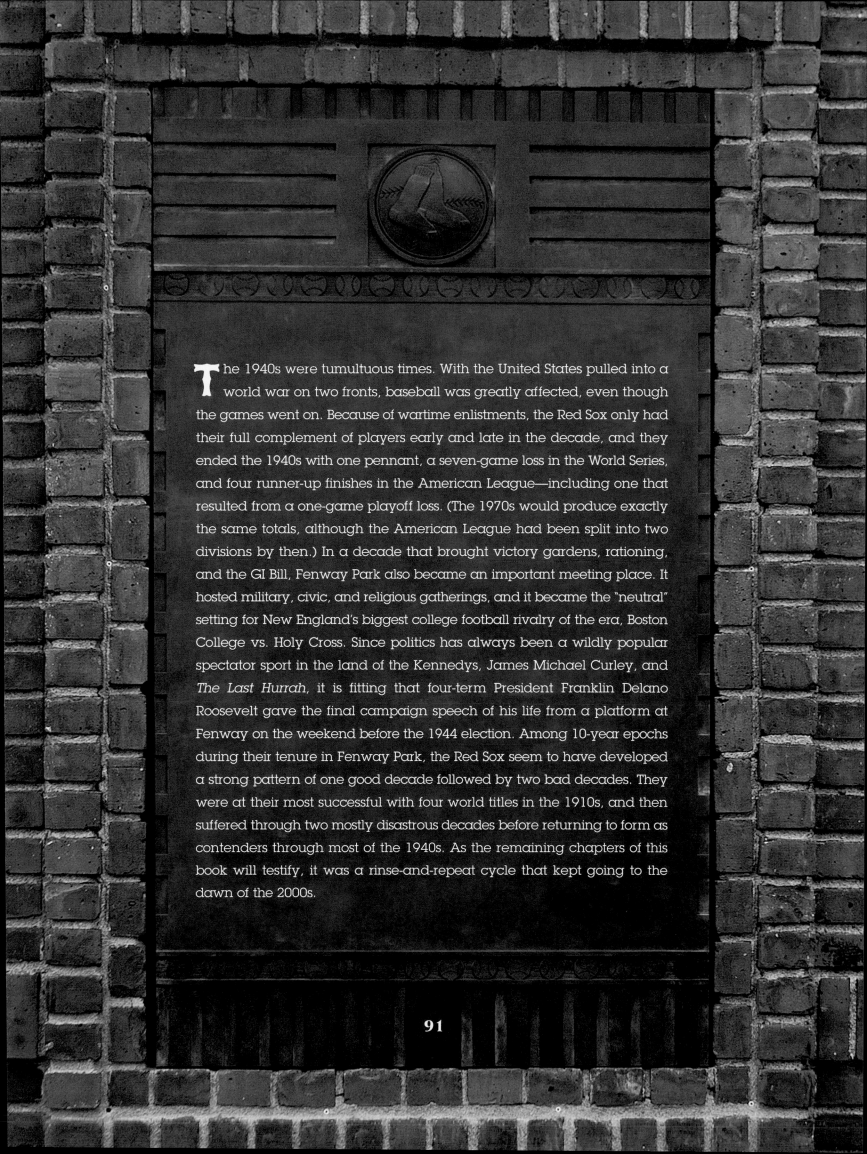

The 1940s were tumultuous times. With the United States pulled into a world war on two fronts, baseball was greatly affected, even though the games went on. Because of wartime enlistments, the Red Sox only had their full complement of players early and late in the decade, and they ended the 1940s with one pennant, a seven-game loss in the World Series, and four runner-up finishes in the American League—including one that resulted from a one-game playoff loss. (The 1970s would produce exactly the same totals, although the American League had been split into two divisions by then.) In a decade that brought victory gardens, rationing, and the GI Bill, Fenway Park also became an important meeting place. It hosted military, civic, and religious gatherings, and it became the "neutral" setting for New England's biggest college football rivalry of the era, Boston College vs. Holy Cross. Since politics has always been a wildly popular spectator sport in the land of the Kennedys, James Michael Curley, and *The Last Hurrah*, it is fitting that four-term President Franklin Delano Roosevelt gave the final campaign speech of his life from a platform at Fenway on the weekend before the 1944 election. Among 10-year epochs during their tenure in Fenway Park, the Red Sox seem to have developed a strong pattern of one good decade followed by two bad decades. They were at their most successful with four world titles in the 1910s, and then suffered through two mostly disastrous decades before returning to form as contenders through most of the 1940s. As the remaining chapters of this book will testify, it was a rinse-and-repeat cycle that kept going to the dawn of the 2000s.

(left to right) Star players Bobby Doerr, Ted Williams, and Dominic DiMaggio obliged the cameraman by posing for this 1940 image.

As the Thirties ended, the Red Sox franchise had made the transition from a losing proposition to a winning proposition, even though the Yankees still were a mile ahead of Boston in the standings. The lineup, too, was in flux with Jimmie Foxx, Joe Cronin, and Doc Cramer nearing the end of their careers, and Ted Williams, Dom DiMaggio, and Bobby Doerr at the beginning of theirs.

Whether Williams, his teammates, or the fans liked it, he clearly was the future of the franchise. After the front office redesigned the park to suit him, the Kid was feeling the pressure in 1940, particularly since the homers were slow in coming. Even though the Sox were in first place (thanks to a 17-6 start and a torpid spring in the Bronx) and Williams was hitting well over .300, he felt unappreciated and was vocal about it.

What especially irked Williams was his $12,500 salary, given what he felt was expected of him. "Here I am hitting .340 and everybody's all over me," he complained in early June. "I shoulda been a fireman." When Boston next played in Chicago, White Sox manager Jimmy Dykes, a notorious bench jockey, outfitted his players in papier-

mâché helmets, cranked up a siren, and had them howl, "Fireman, save my child!"

Once the Sox lost seven games in a row on the road in June—four of them to the fifth-place St. Louis Browns—and then dropped another eight straight in July, all of the engine-and-ladder companies in the Hub couldn't save them and they ended up in fourth place. Yet Williams, for all his angst, had an exceptional season, hitting .344, clouting 23 homers, and knocking in 113 runs. He even pitched the final two innings in a mop-up role against Detroit in late August. Williams held the Tigers to one run on three hits and struck out Rudy York on three pitches, though the Sox lost, 12-1.

That season was prelude to an achievement that has been unmatched since, as Williams hit .406 in 1941, even while opposing hurlers were pitching around him, walking him 147 times in 143 games. The biggest challenge for the club at first was to find him, as Williams absented himself from spring training, phoning in once to assure the front office that he hadn't been abducted. "Theodore says he has been so busy shooting wolves in a country so wild that no paths led from there to civilization," Mel Webb wrote in the *Globe*.

When Williams finally turned up, he was both relaxed and reflective, eager to put the tumult and torment of the previous season behind him. He even "shook hands all around" with newspaper reporters, the *Globe* reported on March 10. "They said I was a heel and I'll admit I had a lousy attitude," he later conceded in June. "But I don't think I deserved all they wrote about me, even though I have to admit the start of it all probably was my fault."

Nobody could find a flaw in his performance, as Williams went on a 23-game hitting streak during which his average soared to .436. "The Kid has grown up," the *Globe* declared.

When he hit the game-winning, three-run homer with two out in the ninth inning in Detroit to win the All-Star Game for the American League, there was no doubt about who was baseball's most electrifying player. By then the Sox had fallen out of contention after being swept at New York. The only two story lines keeping Boston fans intrigued were Ted Williams's quest to hit .400 (something no one had done for a full season since 1930) and Lefty Grove's push to reach 300 career wins.

It had been 16 years since his first victory and Grove

An American Legion memorial Mass on May 20, 1940.

FOOTBALL, FATE, AND THE COCOANUT GROVE

In 1896, Boston College and Holy Cross played the first game in what was to become one of the longest-running rivalries in college football. In 1916, the schools squared off at Fenway Park for the first time, and in 1920, BC capped an 8-0 season with a 14-0 victory over Holy Cross before 40,000 fans at Braves Field.

BC hired Frank Leahy as coach in 1939, and he turned the Eagles into a national power that won 20 of 22 games over the next two years, including an undefeated season in 1940 and two straight victories in the Sugar Bowl in 1940 and 1941.

The Eagles were routinely dominating their rivals from Worcester, and entering the 1942 matchup at Fenway Park, undefeated BC had routed its eight previous opponents that season by a combined 249-19 and was nearly assured of a berth in the Sugar Bowl. Holy Cross was 4-4-1, and the Crusaders were expected to provide little resistance. BC had already scheduled a victory party at the swanky Cocoanut Grove nightclub in Boston.

A crowd of 41,350 packed Fenway Park on November 28, and, led by halfback Johnny Bezemes, who scored three touchdowns and passed for another one, Holy Cross proceeded to rout the vaunted Eagles, 55-12. Seeing its expected spot in the Sugar Bowl vanish, BC canceled its victory party. That night, a deadly fire swept through the glitzy Cocoanut Grove nightclub, killing nearly 500 people in the worst nightclub fire in U.S. history. A BC victory surely would have resulted in the deaths of some of its football players, as a large table had been reserved for the team in the club's main dining room.

William Commane, a fullback on the 1942 BC squad, had planned to be at the Cocoanut Grove that night, but like his teammates, he switched plans after their loss and went to the Statler Hotel. "The next day, I was listening to the radio at home with my family," Commane recalled. "They read out the names all day; it was a terrible tragedy. The football game didn't mean much after that."

The teams' annual clash in 1956, a 7-0 Holy Cross victory, would be their final contest at Fenway Park, as the Red Sox banned football from the ballpark for several years. Shortly thereafter, the schools took different athletic paths, with Holy Cross deciding to de-emphasize the sport. In 1986, after losing 17 of the previous 20 games to BC, Holy Cross terminated the series.

LIB DOOLEY: ULTIMATE FAN

Elizabeth "Lib" Dooley got her first season ticket during World War II and didn't miss a Red Sox home game for the next half-century, attending more than 4,000 consecutive ballgames at Fenway. She had a direct link to the franchise's beginnings in 1901 through her father, and she sat in the first row behind the Red Sox on-deck circle in Box 36-A. Mickey Mantle would stick out his tongue at her when he homered for the Yankees, and she was Ted Williams's favorite fan.

"Forever, she's the greatest Red Sox fan there'll ever be," said Williams in 1996.

Dooley, who retired after 39 years as a physical education teacher in Boston, said that she attempted to guide her students in the right direction by telling them, "I don't drink, I don't smoke; I go to ballgames."

Dooley fell in love with the sport in an era when she was one of the comparatively few female baseball fans. She grew up hearing the men in her family share stories about the game and looked forward to days when she could accompany her father to the ballpark.

Dooley decided to buy her own season pass in 1944 and "make baseball my hobby." One of her sisters had taken up bridge, but Dooley didn't have the stomach for that: "I despise bridge and I hate gossip. I wanted something where I could go by myself without anyone ruining it by saying, 'I can't do it this week.' It gets you out in the fresh air and keeps you from talking about your neighbors."

Dooley's father, John Stephen Dooley, helped the upstart American League ballclub get a home at the Huntington Avenue Grounds in 1901. He was also the founder and president of a boosters group known as the Winter League, a forerunner to today's BoSox Club. According to family lore, Dooley attended every Boston baseball opener from 1894 until his death at the age of 97 in 1970.

Lib Dooley went on to become a member of the board of directors of the BoSox Club, the team's official booster club. In 1956, she moved to Kenmore Square so she could walk to Fenway. "It's seven minutes to the ballpark, a little more now as I get older and the crowds get bigger," she said in 1995.

Williams lived nearby, and during his playing days he would visit her apartment on his way to the park, stopping by for "her words of wisdom for the day."

"Theodore trusts me," Dooley explained, "because he knew I was a schoolteacher and I would talk to him straight." Dooley recalled telling Williams that he'd never know who his real friends were until he left the game.

For his part, Williams called her "Goddammit Red," as in: "Goddammit Red, how do you know that?"—even as her red hair became tinged with silver.

Along with Williams, her favorite players were Bobby Doerr, Dom DiMaggio, and Johnny Pesky. She called them "my four baseball brothers."

"She was just a perfect lady," said DiMaggio in June 2000, after Dooley died at 87. "I remember so well when she presented us with our American League championship rings after we won in 1946. She was so thrilled. The Red Sox were practically her whole life."

Dooley took at least one road trip with the team every year, and she claimed she'd seen five no-hitters. Despite her prime location, she fielded only one foul ball—a pop-up off the bat of Sox outfielder Carroll Hardy in the early 1960s. She broke two fingers in the effort and never attempted to catch another.

Jim Rice was a favorite in the 1970s and 1980s, and later on, she took to Nomar Garciaparra. "Nomar would give her a wink when he came into the on-deck circle," said David Leary, her grandnephew.

Her strongest negative feelings were reserved for the team in pinstripes.

"I despised the Yankees," she said, "because they gave us so much trouble. They always beat us, always." Joe DiMaggio, Phil Rizzuto, and Mantle "were the only three Yankees who I tolerated, because of their great talent."

"The fans are really baseball, not the players," Dooley said when a strike marred the 1994 and 1995 seasons. "You can always get someone to play ball—it doesn't have to be someone who gets $4 million to work two hours a day." A moment later, she added with a grin, "I wonder if I'm going to need a bodyguard to get back into that park."

Dooley once explained her position thusly: "I do not consider myself a fan. I am a friend of the Red Sox." An anecdote from her nephew, Owen Boyd, backed up that statement.

Boyd was at a game with Dooley when she directed him to dial a number for her on his cell phone. To his astonishment, "Happy birthday, Theodore" were the next words out of her mouth.

"You know Ted Williams?" Boyd asked in amazement.

"More importantly," she replied, "Ted Williams knows me."

Daily life for grounds crews in the '40s included pulling tarps and pushing lawn mowers.

HOMESTEAD GRAYS COME TO TOWN

The Homestead Grays, the two-time defending champions of the Negro League who featured Hall of Famers such as Josh Gibson and Buck Leonard, defeated the Fore River Shipyard team of the New England Industrial League, 1-0, in a game played at Fenway Park on May 26, 1944.

The Grays, who were based in Homestead, Pennsylvania, near Pittsburgh, played many of their games at Forbes Field in Pittsburgh while also using Washington's Griffith Stadium as a second "home" park. The team also barnstormed and often played two or three games a day against local amateur and professional teams.

The *Boston Globe* had published a one-paragraph story under the headline: "Negro Home Run King at Fenway Tonight." Second only to the legendary Satchel Paige among Negro League players in terms of fame and popularity, Gibson was generally considered to be the greatest hitter in the history of black baseball and was nicknamed the "Black Babe Ruth."

The story also reported, "A United States Marine band will furnish music. Jack Burns, Skinny Graham and Charlie Bird will be in the Fore River lineup." The game account the next day showed the Grays outhitting Fore River, 11-5, on their way to a 1-0 win. Some 3,000 fans attended the game.

Gibson reportedly won nine home-run titles and four batting championships during a 17-year career that ended in 1946. Paige called him "the greatest hitter who ever lived." Hall of Fame pitcher Carl Hubbell noted, "Any team in the big leagues could use him right now."

While Gibson certainly could have helped any major-league team that elected to sign him, the unwritten rules of baseball kept him out of the majors his entire career. Frustration over his lack of opportunity, various illnesses, and despondency over the death of his wife in childbirth caused Gibson to die of a stroke at the age of 35 on January 20, 1947, just three months before Jackie Robinson broke Major League Baseball's color barrier.

Two days after the Grays played at Fenway, the ballpark hosted a military memorial Mass that was attended by an estimated 6,000 people. In his sermon, the Reverend John S. Sexton, an American Legion chaplain, spoke out against racial and religious hatred, saying, "Jim Crow-ism and anti-Semitism are un-American, because in the first instance they are anti-God. Let's put America ahead of our own little cheap individual, and group interests."

On June 3, 1947, the *Globe*'s Hy Hurwitz wrote a story that said the Red Sox were considering signing Negro League star Sam Jethroe. The story noted that Jethroe, who was playing for the Cleveland Buckeyes of the Negro American Baseball League, was considered the best hitter in the Negro Leagues since Gibson. Jethroe had led the league in both batting average and stolen bases as the Buckeyes won the Negro League title in 1945, beating the Grays in the championship series.

Had they signed Jethroe, as they were reportedly considering, the Red Sox would have been the only Major League Baseball team other than the Brooklyn Dodgers, who had signed Jackie Robinson in 1945, with a black player on its roster. Jethroe ended up signing with the crosstown Boston Braves, and he would go on to be named the National League's Rookie of the Year in 1950. It would be more than a decade before the Red Sox promoted Pumpsie Green to their big-league club, making the Sox the final MLB team to integrate its roster.

was at the end of his career at age 41. When he took the mound against the Indians on Ladies Day in Fenway, he hadn't won a game in more than three weeks. The thermometer read 90 degrees and Grove fell four runs behind. "The toughest game I ever sweated through," he said. But Foxx's two-run triple and Jim Tabor's second homer gave the Sox a 10-6 triumph and Grove, who never won another game, his 300th career victory. Grove was elected to the Hall of Fame in 1947.

The Williams melodrama went until the last day of the season. His average was .406 after his final home game against the Yankees, which he punctuated with a home run. Going into the concluding doubleheader at Philadelphia, it had dipped to .3995. Though Cronin offered to let him sit out the final two games so that his average would be rounded up to .400, Williams was adamant about playing *both* games. "A batting record is no good unless it's made in all games of the season," he declared. Then he proceeded to go 6 for 8 with a homer against the last-place Athletics and finish the season at .406. "Ain't I the best goddamn hitter you ever saw?" Williams proclaimed in the clubhouse.

Joe DiMaggio, who strung together a record 56-game hitting streak as the Yankees breezed to the pennant, might have been the Most Valuable Player, but even he wouldn't challenge the Kid's primacy at the plate. Williams had a more than reasonable reprise in 1942, leading the league in batting average (.356), runs (141), RBI (137), and homers (36). But with the country at war after the bombing of Pearl Harbor, there was some dispute as to whether he should be playing at all.

Bob Feller, Hank Greenberg, and Sox teammate Mickey Harris already had been called to duty and Williams's draft board in Minneapolis had reclassified him 1A in January. But since he was supporting his mother, Williams was switched to 3A on appeal and turned up at training camp. "If Uncle Sam says fight, he'll fight," Cronin said in February. "Since he has said play ball, Ted has a right to play."

But only for one more year, Williams vowed at the end of March. "No matter what happens during the coming season, I'm going to enlist when it's over," he said. Williams began it auspiciously, lofting a three-run homer into the bleachers in his first at-bat in the Opening Day victory over the Athletics at Fenway. But despite the emergence of a brace of promising rookies (right-hander Tex Hughson and shortstop Johnny Pesky), the Sox couldn't catch the Yankees and finished nine games behind their rivals despite winning 93 games, their highest season total since 1915.

The season finale in the Fens, a symbolic 7-6 victory over New York, was telling. The story of the day was that the fans donated more than 46,000 pounds of scrap metal to the war effort. By 1943, the Sox would be donating a third of their lineup to the cause.

Williams and Pesky had enlisted with the Navy Air Corps and DiMaggio with the Coast Guard. So Cronin, who'd been easing out of his role as player-manager, pressed himself back into service at 36. The 1943 season figured to be a lost cause anyway after Boston dropped 10 of its first 14 games (seven of them to the Yankees) and sank into the cellar after the first week in May. So the skipper chose Bunker Hill Day, which commemorated a gallant but ultimately losing battle

The decade's renovations included a television and radio coop, perched atop the screen behind home plate.

by American rebels against the British in the Revolutionary War, to make a bit of history himself.

"I guess the old man showed them something today," Cronin crowed after he'd pinch-hit home runs in both ends of a doubleheader against the Athletics at Fenway, becoming the first major-league player to manage the feat. By the end of the season he'd hit .429 with five homers coming off the bench. But there was no way to salvage a lost campaign. The Sox ended up in seventh place—29 games behind New York—for their worst finish in a decade as attendance dwindled to its lowest level (358,275) since the Depression.

Nothing was close to normal during the war. Had it been, the Browns never would have won their only pennant in 1944, displacing the depleted Yankees with a "collection of misfits, 4Fs, brawlers and drunks," as they were described in *The Boys Who Were Left Behind*, by John Heidenry and Brett Topel. Still, Boston managed to stay in the pennant race until Labor Day, even after military enlistment took catcher Hal Wagner and Doerr, who'd

been leading the league in batting in late August, and Hughson, who'd won 18 games.

Their departures, plus a killer schedule that put the Sox on the road for their final 17 games, finished them off, as the front office didn't bother taking World Series requests. The club lost 10 in a row and finished in fourth place, a dozen games astern. "Maybe it's just as well," mused a *Globe* editorial, "because local fans are so badly out of practice they wouldn't know what to do with a championship."

By 1945, Uncle Sam had spirited away virtually all of the former regulars and the Sox were happy to consider anyone who might be capable of playing 154 games without tripping over himself. So the day before the season opener in New York, the club ran a Fenway tryout for three black players—Jackie Robinson, Sam Jethroe, and Marvin Williams—who were performing in the Negro League.

LEFT: His attitude wasn't always so sunny, but Ted Williams smiled for the camera when he left the Fenway Park locker room in July 1942.

BELOW: Several players who had enlisted as naval aviation cadets joined Lt. Cmdr. E.S. Brewer at Fenway Park on April 27, 1943, before the Red Sox-Yankees game. Front row, from left: Johnny Pesky of the Red Sox, Brewer, Buddy Gremp of the Boston Braves, and Joe Coleman of the Philadelphia Athletics. Back row, from left: Ted Williams, and Johnny Sain of the Boston Braves.

FDR'S ROAD SHOW

When U.S. President Franklin Delano Roosevelt's motorcade arrived at Fenway Park on the night of November 4, 1944, there wasn't a bare patch of ground between Kenmore Square and the ballpark, or for blocks around. It was three days before the presidential election, and FDR's race against Governor Thomas Dewey of New York had taken a nasty turn. Factor in that Roosevelt was preceded on stage by two enormous talents of music and film, and the ballpark and the surrounding neighborhood were rollicking in a boisterous but far different fashion than if the Red Sox were staging a ninth-inning rally.

Sound wagons blared campaign tunes and patriotic songs, and hawkers sold buttons promoting Roosevelt and Maurice J. Tobin, the Democratic candidate for governor of Massachusetts. Inside the park, red, white, and blue bunting and banners were draped along the infield wall, around uprights, and along the edge of the grandstand roof. More than 250 newspaper reporters were instructed by Secret Service men to meet in a garage on Ipswich Street, and they entered the park in columns of three at 8 p.m., an hour ahead of Roosevelt's entrance.

One of the key questions in voters' minds was the health of the three-term president, compelling Roosevelt to undertake a whirlwind tour of several cities, including a four-hour appearance in New York City a couple of weeks earlier in bitterly cold temperatures.

When he got to Boston on this Saturday night, the estimated 40,000 people inside the park and thousands more outside were treated to opening acts by Frank Sinatra, who sang the national anthem, and writer-director Orson Welles. Just three years removed from *Citizen Kane*, Welles boomed out an oratory as only he could. "The audience delightedly applauded each at frequent intervals," wrote *Globe* reporter Leslie G. Ainley.

When FDR's open car entered the park and he took the stage at the center of the field, the crowd was in a frenzied state. Announcers tried to still the tumult as he began to speak, but audience members continued their roaring welcome until the president himself reminded them in a shout over the loudspeakers that radio time costs money. He spoke for 36 minutes, firing back at charges leveled by Dewey, the Republican candidate, that Roosevelt had sold out to communists. FDR accused his opponent of "a shocking lack of faith in America."

The *Globe*'s Louis M. Lyons called the appearance "a thundering windup" to FDR's campaign for reelection and reported that the crowd was "almost delirious in their wild cheering" for him. Just over five months later, after winning an unprecedented fourth term handily, FDR died of a cerebral hemorrhage in Hot Springs, Georgia, on April 12, 1945, at the age of 63. The appearance at Fenway Park turned out to be the final campaign speech of his life.

WEATHER
SUNDAY—Generally colder
Monday—Fair, cold.

The Boston Sunday Globe

Reg. U.S. Pat. Off.

The United War Fund Drive Is On
The goal is $7,650,000. Increase your subscription this year.

VOL. CXLVI — No. 130 — The Globe Newspaper Co.   SUNDAY, NOVEMBER 5, 1944—68 PAGES   (S)   PRICE 10 CENTS

F.D.'s 'Confused Incompetence' Stiffened German Army, Dewey Charges

FDR LASHES AT DEWEY

Thrills Boston Crowd With Fighting Speech Answering Opponent's Boston Charges

Allies Gain in Holland, Yanks Lose Nazi Town

LONDON, Sunday, Nov. 5 (AP) —American troops, although driven back from the high water mark of their invasion of the Reich, the town of Schmidt, held their lines to the north firmly last night while Allied troops in southwestern Holland plunged ahead and the German radio said the battle of Walcheren Island was near its end.

The Doughboys scrambled out of Schmidt, 15 miles southeast of Aachen, under pressure by German infantry and tanks, but a few minutes after their withdrawal swarms of United States dive-bombers flattened the town, leaving, according to a frontline dis-

patch, the walls of only two houses standing.

A few thousand enemy troops still were fighting on Walcheren but with the Allies advancing on all sides of them and their main route of escape flooded, they could only swim, surrender or die.

Allied troops clearing the western flank in Southwestern Holland for the impending offensives hammered forward two miles in a general advance that swept to within three miles of the last German escape bridge at Moerdijk, now within easy artillery range.

The battle spread along the Maas nearly 20 miles east to a point west of S'Hertogenbosch, where the British under a violent artillery barrage broke across Afwatering canal and fought north more than a mile in a new drive to unhinge the enemy's east

ABOVE — ALL 40,000 SEATS in Fenway Park filled as F. D. speaks.
BELOW—PRESIDENT ROOSEVELT responds to cheers as he enters Fenway Park

Photos by William Tambeau, Globe Staff Photographers.

Dewey
G.O.P. Head Addresses N.Y. Crowd

(Dewey Text, Page 3)

NEW YORK, Nov. 4—Gov. Dewey climaxed his eight-week Presidential campaign tonight before 20,000 persons in Madison Square Garden with the charge that President Roosevelt's "own confused incompetence" is prolonging the war in Europe, and that "the blood of our fighting men is paying" for the delay.

Carrying the 1944 political battle aggressively to the President right up to the near-close of the campaign's home-stretch, the Republican Presidential candidate lashed out at the "improvised meddling which is so much a part and parcel of the Roosevelt Administration," and accused Mr. Roosevelt anew of claiming "for himself" the war achievement laurels rightfully due American

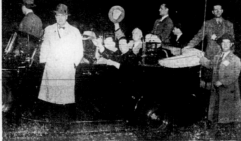

Blasts Campaign 'Filled With Distortion, Falsehoods'

(Roosevelt Text, Page 1)

By LOUIS M. LYONS

President Roosevelt brought his campaign for reelection to a thundering windup before a roaring crowd of 40,000 at Fenway Park last night.

Almost delirious in their wild cheering for "The Champ," the tightly packed stands yelled their responses to his hardest hitting speech of his campaign.

They heard the President accuse his opponent of such distortions and falsehoods as he had not known in a campaign in his lifetime.

He took up directly Dewey's charge made in Boston three nights earlier that he had sold out to the Communists. In terms of scorn, he turned aside the fear of communism to accuse his opponent of "a shocking lack of faith in America."

He had given America not less but more democracy he declared.

The kind of campaign his opponent has run has made him "anxious to win," the President told the yelling bleachers. He appealed for the biggest vote in history to answer the question if it is time for a change.

See ROOSEVELT   Page 6

Roxbury city councilor Isadore Muchnick had badgered the club to break baseball's color line and the players suspected that the workout was perfunctory. Though scout Hugh Duffy proclaimed them "pretty good ballplayers," the front office didn't sign them. "Not for one minute did we believe the Boston tryout was sincere," Robinson would remark. "We were going through the motions."

Robinson went on to play in six World Series with the Dodgers and was elected to the Hall of Fame; Jethroe was Rookie of the Year for the Boston Braves. But the Sox didn't suit up a black player for another 14 years and went on to finish seventh that year, 17½ games behind the Tigers. By then the war had ended and Williams and his fellow veterans would be coming home, ready for a renaissance.

Once their stars had exchanged one uniform for another, the Sox enjoyed a spring flowering in 1946. The return of Williams, DiMaggio, Doerr, and Pesky revitalized the lineup, which was further bolstered by the arrival from Detroit of slugging first baseman Rudy York, who knocked in 119 runs.

Williams, who'd missed three full seasons since enlisting, dramatically announced his return with a homer in his first

Jack Matheson of the Detroit Lions (right) stopped Johnny Grigas of the Boston Yanks for no gain in the second quarter of a November 4, 1945, game at Fenway Park. The Lions eked out a 10-9 victory in the game played during a heavy snowstorm.

at-bat against the Braves in spring training. From Opening Day until the season finale, Boston owned the league, spending all but one day in first place. The Sox won their first five games and 21 of 24, including a 15-game streak that began with a 12-5 belting of the Yankees at Fenway.

When their tally reached a major-league record 41-9, the pennant race essentially was over. But the Fenway turnstiles kept spinning as attendance more than doubled to over 1.4 million. One of the attendees, an Albany construction engineer named Joseph A. Boucher, found himself sitting in what became the most famous seat in the park on June 9 when Williams cracked a 450-foot homer that drilled a bulls-eye through his straw hat. "How far away must one sit to be safe in this park?" wondered Boucher, who was sitting in the 33rd row of the right-field bleachers, where the ball's landing place later was memorialized by a red seat.

Williams hit 38 homers that season, not counting his

IN RIGHT FIELD, A SEAT OF POWER

BY DAN SHAUGHNESSY

It sits in a sea of green, a single red chairback in the outer limits of Fenway Park's right-field bleachers. It is Seat 21 in Row 37 of Section 42. It is known simply as the red seat, and it marks the spot where Ted Williams hit the longest home run in Fenway history.

Like a fleck of red paint on a lush green canvas, the commemorative chair draws the eye. Someone is almost always sitting in it, even when just a few patrons are in the bleachers. New fans ask about the red seat, and citizens of Red Sox Nation are happy to relay the Fenway folklore.

Teddy Ballgame's mighty clout was struck in the summer of 1946, on a windy, sun-splashed Sunday afternoon in the first inning of the second game of a doubleheader against the Tigers.

"Hell, I can tell you everything about that one," Williams said from his Florida home in 1996—50 years later. "I hit it off Fred Hutchinson, who was a tough [righty] who changed speeds good. He threw me a changeup and I saw it coming. I picked it up fast and I just whaled into it."

Indeed. The ball sailed over the head of right fielder Pat Mullin, and then carried beyond the visitors' bullpen and kept on going. And then it crashed down onto the head of Joseph A. Boucher. More accurately, it landed on Boucher's straw hat, puncturing the middle of the fashionable skimmer.

Boucher was an Albany, New York construction engineer who kept an apartment on Commonwealth Avenue when he worked in Park Square during the week. He loved baseball and the Red Sox. But sitting more than 30 rows behind the bullpen, he wasn't expecting to catch any home-run balls.

Boucher spoke with the *Globe*'s Harold Kaese after the game and asked: "How far away must one sit to be safe in this park? I didn't even get the ball. They say it bounced a dozen rows higher, but after it hit my head, I was no longer interested. I couldn't see the ball. Nobody could. The sun was right in our eyes. All we could do was duck. I'm glad I didn't stand up."

Boucher went to the first aid room briefly, where he was treated by a doctor. He returned to watch the Sox complete their sweep of the Tigers.

The next day's *Globe* featured a Page One photo of Boucher holding his hat, his finger stuck through the hole. The caption read, "BULLSEYE!"

Newspaper accounts claimed Williams's homer traveled 450 feet, but the Red Sox measured the distance in the mid-1980s and arrived at an official distance of 502 feet.

"I got just the right trajectory," said Williams. "Jeez, it just kept going. In distance, it was probably as long as I ever hit one."

The bleachers were replaced with chairback seats in 1977 and '78. In 1984, Sox owner Haywood Sullivan decided to commemorate Williams's clout by putting a red chairback in the spot where Boucher sat on June 9, 1946.

If you find yourself sitting in Section 42, Row 37, Seat 21, don't bother to bring a glove. There was only one man who could hit a ball that far, and he's no longer with us.

Photo by William D. Tamberg, Globe Staff

BULLSEYE!—Joseph A. Boucher, Red Sox fan, happily sticks finger through hole knocked in his hat by Ted Williams' homer.

'How Far Away Must One Sit to Be Safe in This Park?'—Jos. A. Boucher, Sox Fan

Ted's Longest Homer Pierces Straw Hat on Head 450 Feet Away

By HAROLD KAESE

A singular honor fell to Joseph A. Boucher, a construction engineer from Albany, at yesterday's Red Sox-Tigers double-header. The longest home run ever hit by Ted Williams in Boston bounced squarely off his head in the first inning of the second game.

He had never sat in the Fenway Park bleachers before. There were 7897 fans besides himself perched on the sun-drenched wind-whipped concrete slope. Indeed was the elderly Mr. Boucher honored when crowned by a five-ounce baseball that the game's greatest hitter had socked some 450 feet.

"How far away must one sit to be safe in this park?" asked Ted's target for the day, feeling his pate tenderly.

WILLIAMS

He was sitting in the 33d row of the bleachers, next to the aisle dividing the first and second sections behind the home bullpen. This was a little more than half way up the slope, and surely out of range of anything less than light artillery, he though.

"I didn't even get the ball," said Mr. Boucher. "They say it bounced a dozen rows higher, but after it hit my head I was no longer interested."

See KAESE COLUMN   Page 6

TED'S CLOUT; ALL-STAR ROUT

If he threw it today—when it could be shown endlessly on TV replays and dissected on the Internet—Pittsburgh Pirate Rip Sewell's trick pitch would hardly rank as a novelty. But in 1946, Sewell's "eephus" pitch, an exaggerated lob that made it look like it was shot out of a mortar, was known only to a limited number of baseball fans.

That was before Ted Williams gave the eephus lasting fame when he hit one of them into the home bullpen in Fenway Park during the 1946 All-Star Game, won by the American League, 12-0. The July 9 victory, before 34,906 fans, still stands as the most lopsided in All-Star Game history.

"Yes, that was my first look at the eephus or oophus or whatever you call it," Williams said after putting on one of All-Star history's most memorable batting shows, a performance that included a second home run, two singles, a walk, and five RBI.

"That's the greatest exhibition of hitting I've ever seen," said National League manager Charlie Grimm, whose 1946 squad had fewer hits (three—all singles) than Williams did.

The Red Sox, who would go on to win the 1946 pennant, placed eight players on that All-Star team. One of them was Johnny Pesky, who said Williams was not even in the batter's box when he hit Sewell's eephus.

"The first one Sewell threw was high," Pesky recalled. "The crowd went 'Oooooh.' That pitch went up like 25, 30 feet in the air. Williams then moved up in the box, and the next one he hit it out of the park, but he was out of the batter's box."

Indeed, a front-page photo in the *Globe* shows that Williams's right foot had crossed the white line marking the front of the batter's box.

Sewell said he warned Williams in advance that he would throw the pitch to him.

"Before the game, Ted said to me, 'Hey, Rip, you wouldn't throw that damned crazy pitch in a game like this, would you?'" Sewell recalled afterward. "Sure, I said. I'm gonna throw it to you. So look out."

Sewell actually threw three of the bloopers to Williams. On the first, Williams swung mightily and fouled it off the tip of his bat. A second blooper pitch was outside, and then came the third.

"It was a good one, dropping right down the chute for a strike," Sewell said. "He took a couple of steps on it—which was the right way to attack that pitch, incidentally—and he hit it right out of there. And I mean he hit it."

The ball landed in the American League bullpen.

"Well, the fans stood up and they went crazy," Sewell recalled. "I told him, the only reason you hit it is because I told you it was coming. He was laughing all the way around the bases."

Truett Banks "Rip" Sewell broke into the big leagues in 1932 and won 143 games before retiring in 1949. He would later say that Williams was the only batter ever to hit a home run off his eephus pitch.

Elaborate religious and military demonstrations brought crowds to the park in the 1940s.

two in the All-Star Game at Fenway. But the most important and least expected was his unorthodox round-tripper at Cleveland on Friday the 13th of September, the day the Sox won the pennant. Williams had been frustrated yet challenged by Cleveland manager Lou Boudreau's "Williams Shift" that stationed everyone but the left fielder to the right of second base. "I've been planning for weeks to beat the crazy shift that Cleveland used against me," he said. So Williams knocked the ball deep to left and legged it out for the only inside-the-park homer of his career and the only run of the game.

When New York's Joe DiMaggio later hit a homer to beat the Tigers, Boston earned its first pennant since 1918. By then, though, the players had dressed and scattered and Yawkey, who'd been lugging champagne around the Midwest for days and spent millions for one pennant, sent Tom Dowd, the club's road secretary, around town for more than four hours to collect them.

Williams, who was visiting a dying veteran at an Army hospital, couldn't be located and Pesky was hanging out with former Navy buddies. But everyone else came to Yawkey's suite at the Hotel Statler to pop corks and toast what had appeared inevitable. "We ran away from 'em, didn't we?" said Del Baker, a Sox coach. "That's the best way to do it. Beat their brains out."

So Boston, which had won 104 games and left its pursuers a dozen games behind, was favored to win the World Series over a St. Louis Cardinals club that survived

MR. RED SOX, JOHNNY PESKY

BY BOB RYAN

Momma knew best. Johnny Pesky was ready to grab the cash—such as it was. He had been leaning toward Boston after Red Sox scout Ernie Johnson made his living-room sales pitch, but the St. Louis Cardinals moved in at the 11th hour and were offering a little more money than the $500 the Red Sox were discussing. It was 1939, Depression time. Any extra dollar would have meant a lot to the Paveskovich family of Portland, Oregon. But Maria Paveskovich did not want to hear it.

"She said, 'No, no, no, Johnny,'" Pesky recalled. "'I don't care about the money. You go with Mr. Johnson. He will look out for you.'"

And thus was born a 70-plus-year relationship in which Pesky would be so closely associated with the ball club that his name would become attached to Fenway Park itself.

About that right-field foul pole....

"[Sox pitcher] Mel Parnell started that," Pesky explained. "I won a game with a home run down the right-field line against the Athletics. But I didn't have any power, and I knew it."

The pole is a mere 302 feet from home plate and Pesky recalled wrapping eight of his 17 career homers down the line and around it. It was officially named "Pesky's Pole" in 2006. A lifetime .307 hitter, Pesky was a classic table-setter who led the American League in hits each of his first three seasons, a feat that has not been surpassed.

Pesky was an integral member of the Red Sox in those notable but frustrating post-World War II years between 1946 and 1950, when they won more games than any team in the league and only had one pennant to show for it.

"This is a game that can break your heart or build you to the heavens," Pesky mused. "The Red Sox have not been a lucky club."

Who better knows how cruel baseball fate can be than Johnny Pesky, who for so long was accused of "holding" the baseball on a relay throw from Leon Culberson while Enos Slaughter, running with the pitch, scored the winning run in Game 7 of the 1946 World Series?

He did, of course, no such thing. "Bobby Doerr defended me," Pesky said. "Ted Williams defended me. Even Slaughter defended me."

Johnny Pesky went away for a while. The Sox traded him in 1953 and he spent time managing in the Pittsburgh organization. But he always remained a Bostonian and now it's as if those years away from the Red Sox never happened.

Pesky remains a viable member of the Red Sox family into his 90s, having served the club as a player, coach, manager, broadcaster, and general all-around goodwill ambassador. He was one of the first inductees into the Red Sox Hall of Fame in 1995. In 2008, the team retired his No. 6.

HARRY AGGANIS: A TWO-SPORT STAR

In life, Harry Agganis was the perfect model for the great American sports novel. In death, he was the ironic portrait of a Greek tragedy.

The son of poor immigrant parents from nearby Lynn, Massachusetts, Agganis had vaulted from the wrong side of the tracks to stardom, first as an All-American quarterback at Boston University and then as a .300-hitting first baseman for the hometown Red Sox. When he died suddenly at age 26 in 1955, the American sports scene was stunned and eulogies echoed around the world.

As George Sullivan wrote in a *Globe* retrospective in 1980, you had to have seen Harry Agganis to believe him. He was born Aristotle George Agganis. His mother called him "Ari" but his friends Americanized it to "Harry." At the age of 14, Agganis played for a local semipro baseball team that often took on teams made up of servicemen, and he would routinely lace hits off major-league pitchers.

As a football player, Agganis led Lynn Classical High School to a 30-4-1 record in three seasons, including a national high school championship. He threw for 48 touchdowns and ran for 24 more, and more than 20,000 fans routinely filled the Lynn stadium to see Agganis play.

Frank Leahy, Notre Dame's famed football coach, declared, "That boy is the greatest prospect I've ever seen," and virtually every major college power in America recruited Agganis, to no avail.

He chose Boston University because he didn't want to attend college away from his widowed mother. He went on to become an All-American player on both offense and defense, and in 1951, Paul Brown, the famed head coach of the Cleveland Browns, shocked the football world by making Agganis Cleveland's No. 1 draft choice. Though Harry was only a junior and would not be able to play professionally for another year, Brown saw Agganis taking over for Otto Graham as his next star QB.

Crowds of 40,000 and more were common for games at Fenway Park when BU played college powers of the era. In Agganis's sophomore season, he led the Terriers to six straight victories before they lost a 14-13 heartbreaker at Fenway to Maryland.

While playing at BU, Agganis was the subject of feature stories in *Sport* magazine and the *Saturday Evening Post*, yet he was so unselfish a player that his coaches had to order him to call more plays for himself.

When the Greek community in Lynn held a dinner in his honor, Agganis refused the money raised by the dinner. Instead, he sent it to the Greek village in Sparta where his father had been born to buy soccer balls and uniforms for youngsters there. In 1955, the Varsity Club of Boston gave him a new car, but again, Agganis refused the gift, using the money to bestow a scholarship at BU for Greek-Americans.

He ended up spurning football for a $40,000 bonus from the Red Sox ("I've already proved myself in football," was his explanation) and, after a year with Boston's top farm team in Louisville, he was the Red Sox starting first baseman in 1954.

Still a few credits shy of his BU degree, Agganis took courses during his rookie season. One memorable Sunday after getting three hits against the Tigers—including the game-winning home run—he rushed up Commonwealth Avenue to BU Field to receive his diploma at commencement. The June 7 headline in the *Globe* read: "Agganis the Hunter Bags Two Trophies: Tiger Hide, Sheepskin."

Just a year later, in May 1955, Agganis was stricken by viral pneumonia and hospitalized for 10 days, but he rushed back into the lineup against doctor's orders. In his last game with the Red Sox, Agganis batted cleanup behind Ted Williams at Chicago's Comiskey Park and got two hits to boost his average to a team-leading .313.

He was stricken again on a train trip to Kansas City, and the severe infection was complicated by phlebitis. Just when he appeared to be recovering, he died suddenly of a massive pulmonary embolism at Sancta Maria Hospital in Cambridge on June 27. He was 26.

More than 25,000 paid their respects at St. George Greek Orthodox Church in Lynn. Every Greek Orthodox church in North and South America, more than 300 of them, held memorial services, an honor customarily reserved for Greek royalty and statesmen.

On a fall day in 1991, 36 years on, Agganis' nephew, George Raimo, visited his grave in Lynn's Pine Grove Cemetery and found a baseball placed there, with the simple inscription: "In everlasting respect."

A crowd gathered on the roof of the post office building overlooking Fenway Park during the 1946 World Series.

NIGHT BASEBALL DEBUTS AT FENWAY

The Red Sox played their first night home game on June 13, 1947, before 34,510 fans. And although some ominous signs were noted beforehand—it was played on Friday the 13th, as the opener of a 13-game home stand—it turned out well for Boston. The *Globe*'s Bob Holbrook reported the next day that the ball club "inaugurated night baseball at Fenway Park in a fashion pleasing to Bostonians as they tipped over the Chicago White Sox, 5-3, before a near-capacity crowd."

The Red Sox were the third-to-last of the 16 major-league teams of the time to install lights in their home park, and owner Tom Yawkey was clearly reluctant to do so. As a preview story in the *Globe* by Hy Hurwitz noted: "No special festivities will accompany the arc-light premiere at Fenway. If not for public demand, Tom Yawkey would never have installed the giant towers over his orchard. Like Walter O. Briggs of Detroit and Phil K. Wrigley of the Chicago Cubs, Yawkey believes that baseball should be played under sunlight." Indeed, the only ceremony accompanying the first night game was the lowering of the colors at sunset, five minutes before the 8:15 game.

The Red Sox teams of the era were the franchise's best in nearly three decades, and in 1947 they were coming off a league championship. Certainly, they didn't need gimmickry to fill the ballpark. As Hurwitz noted, "Yawkey is strictly in the baseball business. He doesn't believe in fashion shows, nylon hosiery door prizes and other nonsense. As for fireworks, he hopes they will be provided by Ted Williams, Bobby Doerr, Rudy York & Co."

The Red Sox provided little offensive firepower on opening night, as they scored all five of their runs in the fifth inning on a combination of walks, errors, and infield hits. The Sox and starting pitcher Dave Ferriss held on to win and the *Globe* story the following day noted, "You couldn't get breathing space in the park." It also said that the new lighting system—the brilliance of which "startled the capacity throng"—made it one of the two best-lighted stadiums in the world, equaled only by Yankee Stadium.

AT BAT STRIKE BALL HIT ERROR OUT INNING VISITORS 0
4   3   BOSTON   0

a best-of-three pennant playoff against the Dodgers. "Why they've made the Red Sox such heavy favorites is beyond me," Williams wrote in the *Globe*. "Those Cardinals have two arms and two legs like we have."

Yet the Sox filched Game 1 at Sportsman's Park as York deposited one of Howie Pollet's slow curves into the left-field seats with two out in the 10th inning. "I just shut my eyes and swung," said York after the 3-2 triumph. And after Harry "The Cat" Brecheen blinded them 3-0 in Game 2, Boston's Dave "Boo" Ferriss, who'd won 25 games, produced a dazzler of his own in the Fenway opener, which was all but decided in the first inning when York hit a three-run homer to left. "The ball which he hit struck the Cardinals right over the heart although it lodged in the fish nets many yards away," Nason wrote in the *Globe*.

Never had the citizenry been quite so febrile about Yawkey's paid performers. Nearly a half-million fans applied for Series tickets and hundreds of them jammed the Hotel Kenmore lobby. When standing room tickets went on sale, fans mobbed the ticket windows, nearly creating a riot.

The Cardinals, though, were unwilling to collaborate in the entertainment and they battered Boston in Game 4, matching the Series record of 20 hits set by the 1921 Giants in a 12-3 shelling. "I'd much rather lose a game 12 to 3 than 2 to 1 or 3 to 2," shrugged Williams, whose mates *Globe* columnist Nason said had played like married men at a church picnic. "We just had our ears pinned back."

Joe Dobson righted things in Game 5 with his "atom pitch," an explosive curve that all but vaporized the Cardinals and staked the Sox to a 6-3 victory, sending them back to Missouri with two chances to win the championship. But Brecheen confounded Boston again in Game 6 as St. Louis knocked out Sox starter Mickey Harris early. "Well, the Cat not only skinned us again, but this time he feasted on our flesh and scratched on our bones," Williams conceded in the *Globe*.

So for the first time since 1912, the Sox were pushed to the limit in the Series. After falling behind by two runs in the fifth inning of Game 7, Ferriss was sent to the showers. Boston drew even in the eighth when DiMaggio doubled

TEN MEN OUT

For once, someone else stole the spotlight with Ted Williams at the plate.

During a game at Fenway with the Cleveland Indians on August 26, 1946, Lou Boudreau, the Indians player-manager, employed his typical Williams Shift, moving the shortstop into short right field and the third baseman to second base. The Indians' Pat Seerey, who stood in short left field, was their only player on the left side of the diamond.

Suddenly, a midget jumped out of a box near the visitors' dugout and walked onto the field. The man, who was later identified as Marco Songini, a vaudeville performer, picked up the glove that had been left on the field by Red Sox third baseman Mike "Pinky" Higgins and took a fielder's stance, pounding the glove for effect. It was customary for fielders of that time to leave their gloves on the field between innings. It wasn't until 1954 that the practice was banned.

The players, umpires, and the 28,082 fans in the park that day stared in disbelief, and then began to laugh. The laughs continued when Songini was eventually ordered off the field. He got a boost over the infield fence by Buster Mills, an Indians coach, and then climbed atop the visiting dugout and struck a fighting pose before the game continued.

The headline in the next day's *Globe* read, "What Next at Fenway? Midget Plays Third, Indians Lose Anyway." The Red Sox won, 5-1, and as Gerry Moore's story noted: "Although a 10th man in the form of a dwarf-sized character tried to assist them by playing third base, Cleveland's Indians couldn't escape mathematical elimination from the American League pennant race."

Later in the game, Cleveland pitcher Bob Lemon and shortstop Boudreau combined to pick Williams off second base. Williams was so upset with himself that he kicked his glove all the way out to left field to start the next inning. Moore noted that, "The victory, the 10th man, and Ted's being picked off second seemed to satisfy the clients."

"I believe that these temples are our secular cathedrals and they tell us as much about what we care about as anything in our environment."

—Ken Burns, filmmaker

ABOVE: In August 1946, Red Sox fans' thirst was quenched by root beer, and by their team's pennant run.

BELOW: One happy Boston fan scored World Series tickets while another wrote the local newspaper to complain that many would not be as fortunate.

SAME OLD STORY

Letter to the editor [of the *Boston Globe*], August 27, 1946:

As a Red Sox fan of the last 25 years, I should like to make a suggestion now for sale of tickets to the forthcoming World Series.

Preliminary inquiries seem to indicate that only by luck, going to the ticket scalpers, or knowing someone who knows someone will the average fan be able to get a ticket to even one game.

So-called celebrities from Hollywood and New York will occupy seats that rightly belong to Boston fans.

Wouldn't it be fair to let Boston followers have first chance at available seats, even if it takes personal interviews with Eddie Collins and Mr. Yawkey?

—James Detrich, Brighton

FOWL PLAY

BY HAROLD KAESE

August 4, 1947—The Red Sox are really in a bad way. Not only did the Tigers claw them, 10-3, yesterday, but fans no longer bothered to ask, "What's the matter with the Red Sox?"

Instead they wanted to know, "What's the matter with the pigeon?"

Baseball indeed plunged to a new low at Fenway Park yesterday. The bird, identified as Parsley P. Pigeon, parked, perched, or roosted himself on the screen's western edge about 20 feet above the backstop. He remained there somewhat longer than three hours, turning this way and that, now and then fluttering his wings, but giving no great display of worry or anguish.

The major mystery was, how could he stand it? How could he sit there enduring such a tedious game when blue skies and green fields beckoned? Obviously, he was not a homer. He was stuck, a foot or toe caught in the wire mesh. Either that or he was a Detroit pigeon and was enjoying himself heartily.

Less than 15 minutes after game's end, a tall ladder was set up against the screen by Fenway Park's Ladder Company No. 4. No sooner had an MSPCA agent started climbing the ladder when Parsley flew away, briskly in the direction of South Williamsburg.

Fans calling up sports departments that evening asked first, "How did the pigeon make out?" and then, "What about the Red Sox?"

According to one press box worker, Parsley was not stuck at all. "He's just a lazy lout, that's all. I've seen him before sit all afternoon on that screen, even when there wasn't a game to watch."

A little boy with his mother was overheard to say, "Maybe he's going to build a nest, mama, and lay an egg."

That probably wasn't Parsley's intention at all. He knew that his wouldn't be the first egg laid at Fenway this season. Not the biggest. Nor the last.

Quoth the pigeon: "Bobby Doerr."

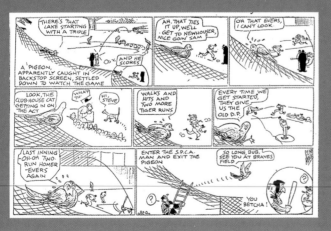

home two men. But when he twisted an ankle rounding the bag, it proved a most costly misstep. Leon Culberson replaced him in center field. With Enos Slaughter on first base and two out, Culberson didn't see DiMaggio motioning from the dugout for him to move more to the left.

When Culberson had to chase Harry Walker's looping liner, Slaughter took off on a mad dash around the bases. Culberson's throw to Pesky was weak enough ("He threw me a lollipop," the shortstop said decades later) that Slaughter decided to risk going all the way. "All I kept seeing was the World Series ring on my hand," he said. How long Pesky held the ball has been barstool debate fodder ever since. The *Globe*'s Nason said that Pesky "froze momentarily" and Pesky readily took responsibility. "I'm the goat," he said. "It's my fault. I'm to blame. I had the ball in my hand. I hesitated and gave Slaughter six steps. When I saw him, I couldn't have thrown him out with a .22."

After Brecheen shut down Boston in the ninth for his third victory of the Series, he was borne aloft by his triumphant birds of a feather. The Sox dressed quietly in their clubhouse. "We lost to a great team," concluded Cronin. But Williams, who wept in the shower and sat staring into his locker for a half hour, was inconsolable after hitting .200 for the Series. Boston Mayor James Michael Curley canceled his planned welcome-home reception for the club. "I guess the boys just simply aren't in the mood for a reception, anyway," he said. The railroad ride back to the Back Bay was somber. "This wasn't just an ordinary train," Harold Kaese observed in the *Globe*. "It was the Red Sox Special. It was a shield, bringing back to Boston a Red Sox corpse."

The renaissance in 1947 came from the Yankees, who hadn't won the pennant in four years and came out of the war disorganized and distracted, going through three managers in 1946 and finishing 17 games behind Boston in third place. Though the Sox were in second for most of the season, they dropped eight of nine games to fall eight games back on Independence Day and never were in contention again. With Ferriss, Hughson, and Harris all ruined by arm problems (they combined to win just 20 games), the rotation came apart and even Williams's Triple Crown season (.343, with 32 homers and 114 RBI) couldn't keep the Sox in contention.

As it was, early in the season Yawkey had come close to trading Williams to New York for Joe DiMaggio, which would have been the biggest one-for-one blockbuster in baseball history. But Boston also wanted catcher Yogi Berra, so Yankees owner Dan Topping nixed the swap. Yawkey did acquire a former Yankee icon, though, when he hired Joe McCarthy at the end of the season to succeed Cronin, who replaced Eddie Collins as general manager.

"I'm going up with the real Irish now," cracked McCarthy, who'd resigned from the Yankees for health reasons in May of 1946. McCarthy was 60 years old, but his résumé was top-drawer—nine pennants and seven Series championships with the Yankees and Cubs. "Now the Red Sox have as their manager a man who converses with gremlins," observed Kaese, "instead of one who converses merely with knives and forks."

So the front office soon made a deal with the St. Louis Browns, whose mascot resembled a gremlin, and brought in starting pitchers Jack Kramer and Ellis Kinder and shortstop Vern Stephens for cash and scrubs. Kramer and Kinder won 28 games between them in 1948, and Stephens led the club with 29 homers. Yet it wasn't until after Memorial Day, when they were in seventh place and nearly a dozen games out, that the Sox came alive, winning 15 of 16 at Fenway in late July to move into first. "It took the Red Sox 98 days of the season to chin themselves into first place," Kaese observed. "They have 70 left in which to elevate the rest of the body."

Boston wound up in an enthralling pennant chase that came down to the final weekend with three teams in contention. The Indians, who were two games up with four to play, had the edge and the Sox needed to beat the Yankees twice at Fenway to force a playoff. "Nevertheless, if you can manipulate an Oriental abacus, you can still juggle the little wooden pegs and come out with a Red Sox victory," Hy Hurwitz calculated in the *Globe*.

The Sox took care of one variable on Saturday when Williams, who'd been bothered by a head cold and had hit only one homer in six weeks, crushed a two-run shot in the first inning, spurring his mates to a 5-1 triumph and eliminating New York from the pennant chase. Then, as the Tigers were rocking ace Bob Feller en route to a 7-1 decision at Cleveland on Sunday, DiMaggio and Stephens each hit homers to rally the Sox to a 10-5 victory over the Yankees and set up the first pennant playoff in American

League history—a single elimination game against the Indians at Fenway the following day, October 4.

"We were counted out in the spring," remarked McCarthy, as thousands of fans were mobbing the ticket windows for reserved seats and thousands more were lining up overnight for bleacher spots. "We were counted out as late as last Wednesday. But those players never gave up."

The speculation was that Kinder, the most rested Sox starter, would face Cleveland's Bob Lemon for the pennant. But Boudreau opted for left-hander Gene Bearden, a 20-game winner. Bearden would be pitching after just one day of rest, but his knuckleball was unhittable when it was behaving for him. McCarthy not only skipped over Kinder, he also bypassed Mel Parnell, who'd won 15 games and had the staff's best ERA at home. Parnell was a southpaw and a rookie, which McCarthy concluded was a dangerous combination at Fenway with the pennant on the line and the wind blowing to left field. "Sorry, kid, it's not a day for left-handers," the manager told him. McCarthy instead went with a most unlikely starter in right-hander Denny Galehouse, a 36-year-old journeyman who had pitched only once since September 18.

Baffled, Boudreau had someone check to make sure McCarthy wasn't warming up his real starter beneath the stands. Galehouse served up two homers, a solo shot by Boudreau and a three-run blast by Ken Keltner, while the knuckleballer Bearden bollixed the Boston hitters, allowing only five hits as Cleveland won, 8-3. "It's pretty tough when you know what's coming and still can't hit it," said DiMaggio.

Instead of the Sox facing the Boston Braves in the first Streetcar Series in the city's history, the Indians went on to win their first championship since 1920, and Galehouse, who pitched only two more innings in his career, became a synonym for Sox failure for more than a half-century.

It didn't seem possible that the Sox could lose a pennant in a more wrenching fashion, but they did just that in 1949. Once again, they staged a second-half surge. Once again, they played with the pennant on the line in the season's final weekend against the Yankees.

That had seemed unlikely at the end of June when Joe DiMaggio, who'd been sidelined all season after heel surgery, swept Boston all by himself at Fenway in what he called the greatest series of his career. He hit a two-run homer and snagged Williams's long ball for the final out in

In April 1947, the pennant was hoisted at Fenway by (from left) MLB president Will Harridge, Red Sox manager Joe Cronin, and Ossie Bluege, manager of the Washington Senators.

a 5-4 victory in the Tuesday opener. He lifted up his pin-striped colleagues from a six-run hole with a three-run shot, and then hit another two-run homer in the eighth for a 9-7 revival on Wednesday. Then in the Thursday wrap-up game, DiMaggio hit a monster three-run blast off the left-field light tower in a 6-3 conclusion that brought a standing ovation from Sox fans who'd always claimed that Dom was the better DiMaggio. "You swing the bat and hit the ball," Joe explained after he'd scored five runs, knocked in nine more and batted .455 for the series.

After dropping a doubleheader in the Bronx on Independence Day, Boston seemed all but finished, sitting 12 games behind in fifth place. But the Sox went 42-13 in August and September to come storming back into contention. The season turned when the Sox won two pivotal games at Fenway to draw even with the Yankees. They took the first on Williams's 42nd homer, a 410-foot launch into the right-field stands, and a daring dash by Al Zarilla, who scored from second after catcher Yogi Berra bounced a throw to first trying for a double play.

"It was a chance and I took it," said Zarilla, who'd been picked up from the Browns in May. After Parnell had mystified the visitors for a 4-1 victory on Sunday, the Sox proceeded to New York, where they claimed first place after Doerr squeezed home the winning run in a 7-6 bleeder.

They were back at the Stadium for the endgame, with the Sox ahead by a game with two to play and hundreds of their fans already lining up on Jersey Street for Series tickets. But the Sox squandered a 4-0 lead in the opener of the double-header and lost on a homer to left by light-hitting Johnny Lindell that just went fair. Then, with his club trailing, 1-0, after seven innings in the finale, McCarthy pinch-hit for Kinder, came up with nothing, and then watched New York score four in the eighth on a solo homer and a three-run bloop double by Jerry Coleman. The Yankees went on to win, 5-3, and take the pennant. "Too bad we had to do it to you," his former Yankees players told McCarthy when he went over to his old clubhouse to congratulate them.

The train ride back to Boston was a funeral cortege and the players were greeted at the station by mourners who'd been at Fenway hoping to snap up World Series tickets. "If we can't win one out of two, we don't deserve it," Yawkey said. But it would be another 18 years before his players would come that close again. 🧦

The bullpen had plenty of company on October 4, 1948, when the Fenway faithful packed the bleachers to watch the Red Sox face the Indians in a one-game playoff. They were stunned when Cleveland won the game, 8-3.

FENWAY PARK

SEPTEMBER 27
At the end of a season in which he won the Triple Crown, Ted Williams plays his last game before joining the service in support of World War II efforts.

NOVEMBER 28
The favored Boston College football team goes down unexpectedly to Holy Cross, 55-12, in a game at Fenway, leading many BC fans and players to cancel celebration plans at the Cocoanut Grove nightclub. Fire engulfs the nightclub later that night, killing nearly 500 people in the most deadly nightclub fire in U.S. history.

JULY 12
Babe Ruth returns to Fenway Park as manager of a service all-star team, taking on the Boston Braves during the mayor's annual charity field day program, which also features a home run hitting contest that pits Ruth against Ted Williams. The event marks Ruth's final appearance in uniform before he's diagnosed with throat cancer.

NOVEMBER 4
President Franklin Delano Roosevelt delivers his final campaign speech at Fenway Park; Frank Sinatra sings and Orson Welles gives an oratory.

1940   1941   1942   1943   1944

Top of page (l-r): Hosting the 13th All Star game, 1946; the *Boston Globe*, 1948; a capacity crowd for the Red Sox vs. Braves series, April 1946.
Timeline: Ted Williams making his major league pitching debut at Fenway Park on Aug. 24, 1940; Robert Moses "Lefty" Grove Day, with Mayor Maurice Tobin presenting a plaque to the player on June 8, 1940; (l-r) Ted Williams, Mel Parnell, and Johnny Pesky, 1949; coffee urns shined and ready, 1949.

The Boston Daily Globe

2500 SERIES DUCATS ON SALE

McCarthy Reported Out as Sox Manager

APRIL 16
Negro League players Jackie Robinson, Sam Jethroe, and Marvin Williams have tryouts at Fenway; none gets a contract offer.

APRIL 19
Joe Cronin injures himself sliding into second base, ending his playing career. He continues as manager.

MAY 2
The Red Sox announce that lights will be added to the park for night games for the following season.

JUNE 9
Ted Williams hits the longest measurable home run ever inside Fenway Park off Fred Hutchinson of the Detroit Tigers. A seat in the right-field bleachers is later painted red to mark the spot where Williams's shot landed, 502 feet from home plate.

PRESEASON
Seven light towers are built at Fenway.

JUNE 13
The Red Sox defeat the White Sox, 5-3, in Fenway's first night game. The arrival of night baseball leads the team to replace the advertisements covering the left-field wall (which produced a lot of glare) with green paint. "The Green Monster" is born.

SEPTEMBER 29
Joe Cronin leaves Boston's managerial post to replace Eddie Collins as general manager. Joe McCarthy becomes the Sox new manager.

APRIL 3
Broadcasters announce that both Red Sox and Boston Braves games will be televised for the first time that summer.

OCTOBER 4
The first one-game playoff in American League history is played at Fenway. The Cleveland Indians beat the Red Sox, 8-3, preventing the only crosstown World Series in Boston history.

DECEMBER 5
In their last game, the last-place Boston Yanks football team beats the Philadelphia Eagles, 37-14. The team then moves to New York.

AUGUST 15
Boston signs African-American second baseman Piper Davis from the Negro Leagues.

NOVEMBER 25
Ted Williams wins his second American League Most Valuable Player Award.

1945   1946   1947   1948   1949

SEPTEMBER 19
A throw by Athletics outfielder Hal Peck hits a pigeon flying over Fenway Park.

JULY 9
In the first All-Star game at Fenway, the American League wins, 12-0. Ted Williams hits two homers and drives in five runs. Skyview seats are built for the press covering the game.

OCTOBER 1
Ted Williams is injured when he is hit on the elbow by a pitch in an exhibition game.

OCTOBER 9
The Red Sox host the Cardinals in the first World Series game at Fenway since 1918. They win, 4-0, but lose the World Series in seven games.

Ted WILLIAMS GOD'S GIFT TO BASEBALL

1950s

As the baby boom got into full swing, so did Boston's bats. The Red Sox put up one of the top offensive seasons of all time in 1950, scoring more than 1,000 runs for the only time in their history and batting over .300 as a team. But characteristically, the pitching staff had a bloated ERA (4.88), and the Sox finished four games behind the Yankees in third place. This combination of powerful offense and mediocre pitching kept the Red Sox in the top half of the league through most of the decade, but they never placed higher than third. So it went, with the Sox either staying in contention long enough or reviving late enough to keep interest alive among their saddle-shoed, flattop-wearing fandom. In 1955, for example, they crept up from sixth in May to fifth in June to fourth in July and were only three games back on Labor Day before losing 12 of 14. Boston's two major-league clubs, the Sox and the Braves, collaborated to host clinics for aspiring ballplayers in 1952, and when the Braves left town for Milwaukee at the end of that season, the Sox continued the practice, which lasted well into the 1970s. The 1950s at Fenway also featured the Harlem Globetrotters' hoop shtick on a basketball court set up in the infield, and some not-so-funny antics from Sox outfielder Jimmy Piersall, who overcame mental illness to eventually earn a spot in the team's Hall of Fame. Meanwhile, the team was overcoming its sad racial legacy by adding a pair of African–American players near the decade's end to become the last Major League Baseball club to integrate its roster.

he tease resumed at Fenway Park in the 1950 opener when Boston ran up a 9-0 lead, imploded, and lost, 15-10. Scoring runs wasn't a problem for a bunch of bashers who led the league in batting average (.302), runs (1,027), and homers (161). In one June week, the Sox pounded out 104 runs, 49 of them in a two-game pummeling of the St. Louis Browns at Fenway, during which the hosts broke five major-league records.

"Hot lava bubbled in the batter's box when the Red Sox had their innings," the *Globe*'s Harold Kaese reported after a 20-run explosion. There was an even bigger volcanic eruption the next day when Sox second baseman Bobby Doerr hit three homers and drove in eight runs in a 29-4 win in which Boston was up, 20-0, after four innings, having batted around three times.

Yet Browns Manager Zach Taylor was unimpressed. "Pitching wins pennants," he declared, "and pitching is what the Red Sox will need more of if they aren't going to have another battle on their hands this season." St. Louis bashed the Sox, 12-7, the next day, and then Detroit laid on an 18-8 whipping. After subsequently being banged around in Cleveland, Detroit, and Chicago, the club had dropped to fourth place.

It was enough to drive a manager to drink, and Red Sox Manager Joe McCarthy, a notorious tippler in the best of times, had become all but legless and soon was gone for what were described as health reasons. "When a man can't help a ball club any more, it's time to quit," said McCarthy, who was replaced by third-base coach Steve O'Neill and never managed again.

The Sox were world-beaters at Fenway, their angular playpen. When his club was out of town, Yawkey delighted in putting on a threadbare team jacket and wrinkled khakis and taking personal batting practice with new balls. "I hit the Wall eight times today," he'd brag. But Joe Cronin, who'd played shortstop for a decade and managed for another dozen years before becoming the Sox general manager in 1947, hated the cozy confines. "Trying to build a ball club here is almost impossible. You build it for here, you lose on the road; you build it for the road, you lose here," said Cronin, who called it a "pissy ballpark."

The Sox were 39-38 away from home that season but 55-22 in their yard, where they went 16-1 during an August home stand to draw within a game of the lead, even though Ted Williams was sidelined with a splintered elbow that he'd sustained by running into a wall at Comiskey

Park during the All-Star Game. But Boston struggled on the road, including an 8-0 blanking at New York on September 23, and was extinguished at Fenway by the Senators, who swept them in a Wednesday doubleheader as Boston was shut out at home for the first time in two years. "The ignominy of the Red Sox demise yesterday will not soon be forgotten in these precincts," Kaese wrote as the club went on to finish third behind New York.

Yet the fandom happily succumbed to temporary amnesia in 1951 when the Sox surged past New York and into first place just after the All-Star break. "Hey, looks like we'll be in the World Series THIS year, baby," clubhouse attendant Johnny Orlando taunted Joe DiMaggio as the Yankees quietly filed through the home clubhouse on their way to the bus after having been swept in early July. "Long ways to go, John," DiMaggio reminded him. "Don't count your money. Long ways to go."

Boston remained aloft, thanks to Clyde Vollmer, who'd apparently struck a Faustian bargain on Independence Day. "Dutch the Clutch" crammed an entire career into one month, hitting 13 homers and driving in 40 runs and hitting

Mel Parnell made his pitching delivery wearing skis after the Red Sox home opener against the Washington Senators was postponed by a snowstorm on April 14, 1953. Parnell went on to win 21 games for the Red Sox that season. He pitched 10 seasons, all with Boston, and threw a no-hitter in 1956.

Clyde Vollmer crossed home plate after delivering a big hit for the Red Sox in July 1951.

HE WAS "DUTCH THE CLUTCH"

One July, a journeyman ballplayer had a month that rivaled nearly any that the game has ever seen. It wasn't just that Clyde Vollmer had a lot of hits for the Red Sox in July 1951, but that nearly every one seemed to win a game for Boston.

"I've never seen anybody come through like Vollmer—and I mean nobody," said then-Red Sox first-base coach Earle Combs, who had once teamed with Babe Ruth and Lou Gehrig in the Yankees' legendary Murderer's Row lineup.

Vollmer would never again come close to duplicating the heroic performances of those four weeks, during which he would become known as "Dutch the Clutch." Vollmer clubbed as many home runs as singles—13 of each—along with a triple and four doubles, while compiling a 16-game hitting streak. Though his batting average during the spree was a less-than-stunning .298, almost every hit was a key one—including a pair of grand slams off two of baseball's top pitchers.

"That month belonged to Vollmer as no single month has ever belonged to a major leaguer before or since," Red Sox broadcaster Curt Gowdy later recalled in a *Globe* story by George Sullivan.

Vollmer, 29, was obtained from Washington a year earlier as a backup outfielder and pinch hitter. During his memorable month, he drove in 40 runs and scored 25 more to almost single-handedly lift the Sox into first place.

Fittingly, his explosion began on July 4, when he homered in the first game and singled in the nightcap as the Sox swept a doubleheader from the Philadelphia A's.

On July 7, Vollmer ripped a first-inning slam off Yankee ace Allie Reynolds to ignite a 10-4 rout of New York at Boston. From July 12-14, the Red Sox took over first place from the White Sox by winning three out of four at Chicago in a series that featured Vollmer's clutch hitting in all four games.

The binge continued for two more weeks and included a three-homer, six-RBI game at Fenway on July 26. On July 28, he had a single in the 15th inning to tie the score against Cleveland at Fenway, and then rocked a grand slam off Bob Feller, baseball's top pitcher of the time, to win it an inning later. But at month's end, Vollmer dramatically struck out in the last of the ninth inning as the Sox lost to the Indians, 5-4.

As Vollmer faded, so did the Red Sox. They finished third, 11 games behind the Yankees and five behind the Indians. By season's end Vollmer had reverted to his lifetime average of .251. And by early 1953 he was sold back to Washington, where he finished his major league career a year later.

"Those were my happiest years in baseball," Vollmer said later. "Coming to the Red Sox was the greatest break I ever got."

safely in 16 straight games in July. But when he returned to earth in August, so did his teammates, and the season ended with a brutal five-game sweep in New York, where fireballer Allie Reynolds no-hit the Sox in the series opener to clinch the pennant. Boston ended up third, 11 games out.

Yawkey, who'd never seen his club held hitless, didn't stick around to watch Yogi Berra catch Williams's foul pop-up for the final out just after the catcher had dropped one. "Even he couldn't stand the sight of the once proud team stumbling all over the stadium," Bob Holbrook wrote in the *Globe*.

Terminal summer siestas had become the norm for the Sox and after Williams was recalled to duty by the Marines at the end of April 1952 to fly a fighter jet in the Korean War, it seemed possible that they might go dormant before the solstice. Yet one combustible personality took up for the other as rookie Jimmy Piersall put the club in first place in early June with a bit of clownish agitation that was as worrisome as it was entertaining.

His target was Satchel Paige, the St. Louis pitcher whose age (allegedly 46) was little more than a random number. "Satchmo, I'm going to bunt on you. And then watch out!" Piersall shouted as he came to the plate in the ninth inning with Boston trailing, 9-5. After he'd reached safely and advanced to second, Piersall began flapping his arms and making porcine grunts. "Oink, oink, oink," he snorted. After a walk moved him to third, Piersall resumed his taunting: "You look awful funny to me. Oink, oink, oink. Gosh, but you look funny out there on the mound."

Paige, who hadn't allowed a run in more than 26 innings and was renowned for his imperturbability, clearly was rattled. He walked Billy Goodman to force in Piersall,

ABOVE: Birdie Tebbetts, Mel Parnell, and Vern Stephens posed in the Fenway clubhouse after a game in 1950.

BELOW: A clubhouse attendant tidied up the home team locker room in '53.

YOUTH BASEBALL CLINICS

Over more than two decades, between 1952 and 1974, tens of thousands of youngsters attended baseball clinics with Red Sox coaches and players at Fenway Park. The clinics—billed as a one-day "spring training" for players from Little League to high school age—were sponsored by the Red Sox and the *Boston Globe*. Said Red Sox General Manager Joe Cronin on the announcement of the inaugural clinic in 1952, "Who knows but someday one of the pupils may be wearing a major-league uniform."

Indeed, at least two players who attended clinics as high school students went on to become instructors: Bill Monbouquette of Medford and Wilbur Wood of Belmont. In May 1960, Monbouquette threw a one-hit shutout for the Red Sox over the Tigers in front of thousands of youths who had attended a clinic earlier in the day.

The first clinic, in April 1952, featured players from the Red Sox and the Boston Braves, who would leave town a year later for Milwaukee. The event brought an estimated 5,000 young ballplayers and coaches into the park, and they stayed for the fourth game of the exhibition city series between the Red Sox and Braves. The youngsters were treated to a display of new Red Sox skipper Lou Boudreau's famous pickoff play, and instruction from the Braves' Tommy Holmes on hitting to the opposite field.

In a *Globe* article promoting the first clinic, Boudreau directed clinic attendees: "If you get your heart set on becoming a Major League Baseball player, nothing will stop you. . . . Don't shirk your work. No manager likes a loafer. Play hard and for keeps, even if it's only a practice game."

Among the players who participated in the youth clinics over the years were Warren Spahn, Dom DiMaggio, Johnny Pesky, Jackie Jensen, Jimmy Piersall, Frank Malzone, Carl Yastrzemski, Tony Conigliaro, George Scott, and Carlton Fisk. In later years, some of the youngsters were brought out to work with the players on the field, and the clinic always concluded with a crowd-pleasing home-run contest.

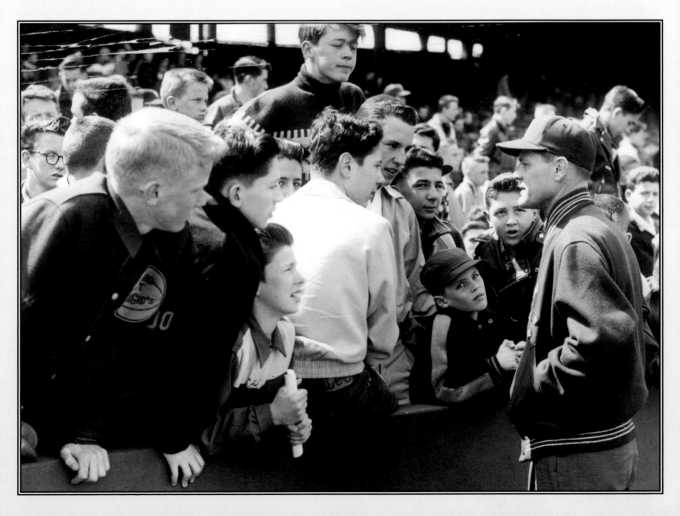

THE KID BIDS ADIEU FOR THE FIRST TIME

In 1960, Ted Williams closed out his career at the age of 42 with a home run in his last at-bat, a moment celebrated by John Updike in his essay, "Hub Fans Bid Kid Adieu." But more than eight years earlier, Williams had batted for what many then thought would be his final time, on April 30, 1952—the day before he left for active duty as a fighter pilot in the Korean War. Ted was nearly 34 years old, and no one knew how long his military duty would last, or whether he would return.

Williams was brash and outspoken, and he had a tempestuous relationship with the Boston press. But he knew better than to complain when he was called to active military duty in early 1952. In 1941 Williams had been classified 3-A by his draft board, due to the fact that his mother was totally dependent on him. When his classification was changed to 1-A following U.S. entry into World War II, Williams appealed to his draft board, and the board agreed with him. He announced that he intended to enlist once he had built up his mother's trust fund, but the press and some fans were merciless in their complaints that Williams was ducking his duty. He enlisted in the Navy in 1942, and unlike many wartime ballplayers who played for service teams while in uniform, Williams was awaiting orders as a Marine pilot when the war ended.

Fast-forward to early 1952: Williams was now 33 years old, married with a child, and had not flown in eight years. But the Korean War was raging and he was called to active duty. After completing refresher training, he returned to the military service that would cost him almost five seasons of his career and very nearly take his life. He flew 39 combat missions over Korea, including one that ended in a crash landing and escape from the flaming wreckage of his crippled aircraft after it was hit by enemy fire. Soon after that, he contracted pneumonia and developed an inner-ear infection. He was discharged in July 1953.

The pregame stories on that April day in 1952 called it Williams's Fenway farewell, and the *Globe*'s Jack Barry wrote the following day,

"Fittingly climaxing a 14-year career, in what may have been his last appearance at bat . . ."

The Red Sox had declared it "Ted Williams Day" and the 24,764 fans, the Tigers players, and Ted's teammates joined hands and sang "Auld Lang Syne" during a pregame ceremony in which Williams received a new Cadillac. A day later, he would report to Willow Grove, Pennsylvania, for training, but not before putting an exclamation point on his career to that point.

The Red Sox and Tigers were tied, 3-3, in the bottom of the seventh inning when Teddy Ballgame came to the plate. Barry wrote, "In this most dramatic and tense moment, with every fan in the ballpark cognizant of what Williams has done under pressure in the past, the amazing Kid delivered."

Williams ripped a curveball from the Tigers' Dizzy Trout eight rows deep into the right-field grandstand. It was his 324th career homer.

After the game, former teammate Rick Ferrell, then a coach with the opposing Detroit Tigers, speculated that Williams could come back, even if he missed two seasons, because "he keeps in great shape."

Although Williams would miss nearly all of the next two seasons, he would return to hit nearly 200 more home runs. And before his third and final "curtain call" at-bat in 1960, he had a second one. In April 1954, Williams told the *Saturday Evening Post* that the coming season would be his last, as most of his contemporaries had retired and the team was emphasizing its younger players. On September 26, in the season's final game, Williams came up in the seventh inning and homered into the right-field stands. However, the Sox batted around and he came up again in the eighth, this time popping out. Sure enough, after the game he confirmed his plan to retire, saying, "That's it."

But by May of 1955, he was back again, returning for six more seasons and a final adieu.

and then served up a grand slam to Sammy White to give his hosts a most improbable 10-9 triumph as White crawled across the plate on all fours. "I don't care what anybody thinks about what I was doing," Piersall proclaimed. "We won the ball game, right?"

But the Browns were convinced that the zany provocateur was unbalanced. "Want to know something? I believe that man's plumb crazy," said catcher Clint Courtney. "Yuh, he's nuts altogether." A few weeks earlier, Piersall had brawled in the dugout at Fenway with Billy Martin, the Yankees' own time bomb. Sox Manager Lou Boudreau worried that Piersall was becoming unhinged and forbade photographers to take posed photos of him without the skipper's consent.

By the end of the month, the club had sent Piersall to its minor-league team in Birmingham, where his erratic behavior continued. "He just got worse every day," Cronin observed. A month later, Piersall was being treated in a Massachusetts hospital for what was described as nervous exhaustion, but, in fact, was mental illness. He recovered, returned the next season and played six more in Boston and 15 more years in the majors. But his teammates faded without him during the 1952 stretch run, losing 20 of 27 games in September and finishing sixth, 19 games behind the Yankees.

That was enough for the front office, which decided to go with bonus babies in 1953. Except for Williams, who was on sabbatical above the 38th parallel, the 1946 pennant winners were gone. Doerr had retired after the 1951 season and Johnny Pesky had been dealt to Detroit. When Boudreau elected to go with rookie Tom Umphlett in cen-

ter, Dom DiMaggio called it a career in early May after playing only three games that season. "After all the good years I've had," said the 36-year-old, "I'm not going to be sitting on the bench."

Boston had finished in the second division for the first time since the war, attendance had dropped by nearly a half-million in three years and the Yankees had won four more rings. Investing in the past was a losing proposition, Yawkey concluded. "We take the long view," said Boudreau. "We can't expect to be a pennant contender for at least two years."

Yet the "Green Sox"—the league's youngest bunch in 1953—still managed to be entertaining, winning 35 one-run games and clubbing the Tigers by 16 and 20 in a two-day June outburst at Fenway. In the second bashing, Boston rolled up a record 17 runs in the seventh inning alone, batting around twice. "Who made the three outs?" cracked pitcher Skinny Brown in the wake of the 23-3 victory.

Not that the sound-and-light show counted for much. The Sox already were in fourth place, 14 games behind New York, and were still there when Williams returned from Korea at the end of July and promptly whacked a pinch-hit homer against the Indians. "There's no doubt about it—flying jet planes improves the eyesight," Yankees Manager Casey Stengel cracked after Williams knocked in four runs during a Labor Day weekend doubleheader at Fenway. "Baseballs now look as big as grapefruits to Williams."

Red Sox catcher Lou Berberet took time out to mingle with the Topsfield girls' softball team during its Fenway visit in 1958.

Ted Williams launched yet another Fenway home run on September 26, 1954, against the Washington Senators.

"I can't wait to see the new park when it's done. I want Boston to have the best. If any city needed a new park, it's Boston. I won't shed a tear."

—Ted Williams, Hall of Fame Red Sox slugger

ECHOES OF "SWEET GEORGIA BROWN"

The Harlem Globetrotters made a pair of stops at Fenway Park in the mid-1950s, and the antics of the famed troupe included star dribbler Reece "Goose" Tatum punching a basketball into the crowd behind the third-base dugout, part of a faux-baseball skit performed in deference to the ballpark surroundings.

The exhibition on July 29, 1954, was part of a 12-city "Summer in America" tour organized by Globetrotters founder and promoter Abe Saperstein. The famed basketball road show was in its 27th season of play and fresh off a tour of South America. The hoop doubleheader drew a crowd of 13,344. Preview stories alluded to the possibility of attracting the largest basketball crowd ever in New England, but the attendance turned out to be smaller than a typical sellout crowd at Boston Garden.

Still, Francis Rosa of the Globe reported that fans "thrilled to the gyrations of Tatum, Leon Hillard, and Sweetwater Clifton" of the Trotters, who incidentally won the game, 61-41, over a collection of NBA players and draft picks that included future Hall of Famers Paul Arizin and Frank Ramsey and local stars Togo Palazzi and Ronnie

Perry of Holy Cross. A preliminary game between the Boston Whirlwinds and the traveling House of David squad ended in a 47-46 win for the Whirlwinds, although Rosa noted that none of the winning team's players were actually from Boston.

The doubleheader was played on the Globetrotters' own portable court, which measured 80 feet by 50 feet and covered much of the infield, stretching from just in front of home plate almost to second base. The six-ton court was cutting-edge for the time and included a skid-proof surface developed by the U.S. Navy that would allow the Trotters to play in driving rain and other daunting conditions.

A small crowd of 3,332 watched the Globetrotters defeat the Honolulu Surfriders, 45-38, the following August at Fenway. The Trotters "clowned and capered their way through another victory," though the team was in transition and did not feature their longtime stars Tatum or the retired Marques Haynes. Among the opponents, the best-known player was Clyde Lovellette of the Minneapolis Lakers. The evening also featured a variety of vaudeville performers before the game and at halftime.

HOSTING THE BRAVES

The Boston Braves built the 40,000-seat stadium known as Braves Field in 1915, and they were its primary tenants until the end of the 1952 season when the team left for Milwaukee. The Braves played second fiddle to the Red Sox for nearly all of their Boston years, even though their National League franchise began in 1876, a quarter-century before Boston's American League entry was founded in 1901.

Ironically, when the "Miracle Braves" rallied to win their only World Series in 1914, they played their World Series home games at nearby Fenway Park because Braves Field, just off Commonwealth Avenue about a mile away, was under construction. It would not be ready until the following season, and in 1915 and 1916, the Braves returned the favor and allowed the Red Sox to host their own World Series games at new Braves Field, now the much larger stadium. The ballpark would host its only Braves' postseason games in 1948, when the Braves lost the World Series in six games to the Cleveland Indians. The Indians had beaten the Sox in a one-game playoff the previous week to spoil the prospect of Boston's only two-team "trolley" World Series.

Though the Boston Braves were marginal at best on the field (with only 11 winning seasons in 38 years at Braves Field), they had their share of historic feats. The longest major-league game in history was played at Braves Field on May 1, 1920, when they battled the Brooklyn Dodgers to a 26-inning, 1-1 tie

before the game was called because of darkness. It was also the site of several Boston baseball firsts, including the Hub's first night game and the first televised game, and the Braves also had the first black player to wear a Boston uniform: Sam Jethroe in 1950, who was named NL Rookie of the Year that season. The National League's longest hitting streak, 37 games, was compiled by the Braves' popular Tommy Holmes in 1945, though Pete Rose broke the record years later.

The Braves' most successful seasons came too late—from 1945-48. Beyond that, they were a tough draw, attracting only 245,000 in 1943. It wasn't until 1947 that the team drew a million fans in a season.

Meanwhile, local football fans had an equally fickle relationship with another Braves team. The NFL's Boston Braves played their inaugural season (1932) at Braves Field, and then moved to Fenway Park, changing their name to the Boston Redskins. The team headed to Washington four years later because of a lack of support in Boston.

A sold-out Braves Field on Gaffney Street in Allston. Though crowds of 43,000-plus at one time packed Braves Field to watch the likes of Warren Spahn pitch—including 1.4 million in 1948—owner Lou Perini moved the team to Milwaukee in 1953 because of dwindling attendance.

WHEN FEAR STRUCK OUT: JIMMY PIERSALL

No one who lived in Boston in the 1950s can forget Jimmy Piersall, the center fielder for the Red Sox. A swift, graceful, handsome athlete, he would be off at the crack of a bat, racing toward the wall at Fenway Park, running, straining, and then timing his leap to spear the ball at the last moment.

One day in the summer of 1953, Roger Birtwell, a *Globe* sportswriter not given to excesses, was so moved by Piersall's fielding that he wrote: "35,000 persons sat spellbound in Cleveland Municipal Stadium yesterday and watched the greatest exhibition of outfielding in major-league history as the Red Sox beat Cleveland, 2-0, 7-5, and went into third place."

But Piersall suffered from mental illness, reportedly bipolar disorder. In his rookie season of 1952, he was involved in fights with the Yankees' Billy Martin, and teammates Mickey McDermott and Vern Stephens. Finally, a series of bizarre demonstrations on and off the field led to several ejections from games and culminated in a breakdown. Piersall was confined to Westborough State Hospital for electroshock therapy and psychotherapy. To everyone's surprise, he recovered and the next year he returned to the Red Sox and became a star. Piersall was selected to the American League All-Star team in 1954 and 1956, thanks in great part to his outfield play. In 1956, he posted a league-leading 40 doubles, scored 91 runs, drove in 87, and had a .293 batting average. The following year, he hit 19 home runs and scored 103 runs. He won a Gold Glove Award in 1958, but that winter he was traded to the Cleveland Indians for first baseman Vic Wertz and outfielder Gary Geiger. Piersall earned a second Gold Glove with the Indians in 1961, also finishing third in the batting race that season with a .322 average.

In June 1963, while playing with the New York Mets, Piersall famously ran the bases while facing backward after hitting the 100th home run of his career.

He described his breakdown in a 1955 book, *Fear Strikes Out: The Jim Piersall Story*, which became a movie in 1957 starring Anthony Perkins and Karl Malden. (After seeing Perkins play Piersall in the film, director Alfred Hitchcock signed the actor to portray Norman Bates in *Psycho*.) Though in his autobiography Piersall blamed much of his condition on pressure from his father, he later disavowed the film, saying it distorted the facts.

One afternoon in the early 1980s, *Globe* writer Jack Thomas, who idolized Piersall as a youngster, visited him in South Carolina and accompanied him to a psychiatric ward at a Charleston hospital. When Piersall stepped off the elevator, there was a bustle among the patients, who loved Piersall, not as a ballplayer, but as a symbol of hope that perhaps they too could overcome mental illness. Piersall shook hands with the doctors, admonished two

nurses for smoking, and then settled into an easy chair to chat with the children hospitalized for psychiatric care.

"Have you read my book or seen the movie about me?" he asked. "It will let you know that we all have problems. . . . I don't have a college degree, but I've got a PhD in some other things. Don't ever let anyone tell you there's no stigma to mental illness. You're going to have to prove yourself all over again. I know how tough it is to be alone. I'm a graduate of a mental institution."

Suddenly, when Piersall said he was opposed to women as umpires, there was a sharp exchange between the Sox legend and a 13-year-old patient named Cynthia. It was brief, but acrimonious, and both seemed hurt. As Piersall and Thomas were leaving, Cynthia's voice called out, "Jimmy?" He turned and walked to her quickly, knelt, and the two embraced. He kissed her cheek, and she squeezed him hard, turning her face so he wouldn't see her tears.

"You're a doll," he said, "and you're going to be OK. You're going to make it."

On September 17, 2010, Jimmy Piersall was inducted into the Boston Red Sox Hall of Fame.

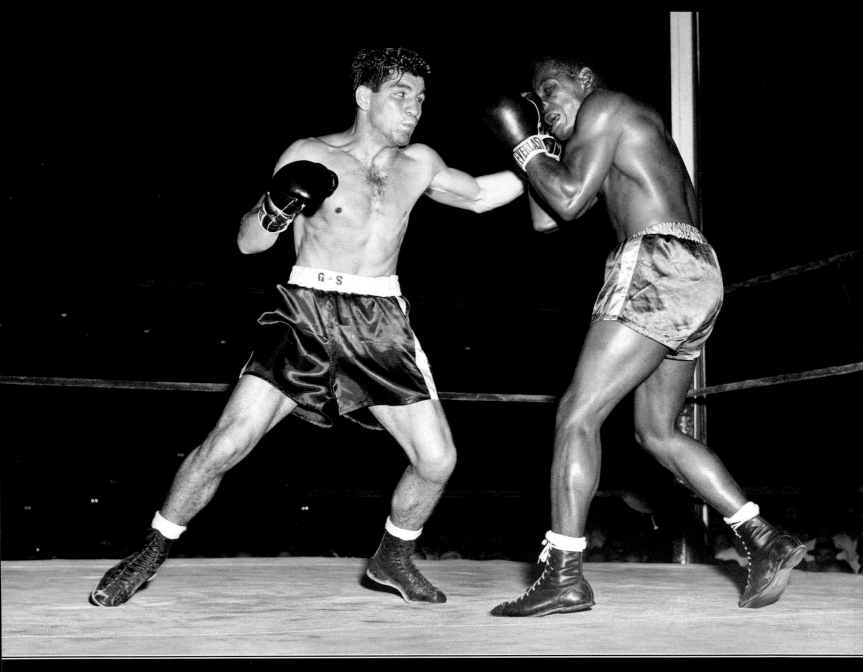

ABOVE: Fenway Park played host to numerous boxing matches over the years. In July 1954, Tony DeMarco, left, a welterweight from Boston's North End, fought lightweight George Araujo of Providence. DeMarco won by a TKO in the fifth round.

BELOW: In June 1958, park personnel prepped for the arrival of television personality Ed Sullivan, who came to host the annual Mayor's Charity Field Day.

JOHN KILEY: A THREE-SPORT STAR

Radio station WMEX was on Brookline Avenue, adjacent to Fenway Park, and John Kiley was the station's musical director and studio organist from 1934 to 1956. When Kiley played in the studio in the early 1950s, he had a regular visitor. Unbeknownst to Kiley, that listener was Red Sox owner Tom Yawkey, and Yawkey wanted to hire him.

"He was a very delightful, pleasant man," Kiley once recalled, "and he complimented me a lot when he was around the studios, but I'd just tell him to be quiet [because Kiley was on the air]. I didn't know who he was until he offered me the job."

Yawkey brought Kiley on board in 1953 when he decided to add music to the Fenway experience. Kiley was also the house organist at Boston Garden from 1942 to 1984 and was proud to be the answer to the trivia question: "Who played for the Bruins, the Celtics and the Red Sox?" Kiley was quick to point out that he also played for the Boston Braves before they left town—in fact, the Braves became his first sports gig in 1941.

Kiley began taking piano lessons when he was 6 and he later quit Dorchester High School to enroll in the Boston Conservatory. He landed jobs playing for the silent movies at the old Criterion Theater in Roxbury and several other theaters, starting at age 15, before taking over at the opulent Keith Memorial Theater downtown. When *The Jazz Singer* ushered in talking pictures in 1927, Kiley found himself out of work before taking over at WMEX and the sports venues.

Kiley started at Fenway in an era when the goal was to please the owner's wife with songs like Rodgers and Hart's "Where or When?" (Tom and Jean Yawkey's favorite song). He was known to pump out "White Christmas" on a scorching day, and his 20-minute pregame medley of songs might include "Embraceable You," "Clarinet Polka," "Misty," and "The Way We Were."

Kiley was not a flamboyant organist, but he did add the occasional flourish, including his spirited playing of the "Hallelujah Chorus" when Carlton Fisk hit his historic Game 6 home run in the 1975 World Series. Kiley retired in 1989 and died at age 80 in 1993.

These days show tunes on the ballpark organ are fading out in favor of loud rock on expensive sound systems. Fenway is one of a handful of ballparks that still feature organ music. "We try to do either of two things at every game: make a child fall in love with baseball, or remind an adult where, when, and why they fell in love with baseball," Red Sox Vice President Charles Steinberg explained in 2005. "That's why it's essential to use the organ and pop music at Fenway."

remained just competitive enough to justify the price of a ticket, either staying in contention long enough or reviving late enough to keep their adherents interested. In 1955, they crept up from sixth in May to fifth in June to fourth in July and were only three games back on Labor Day before losing 12 of 14. "Our tank went dry when we needed gas," Piersall concluded, "and we just couldn't get a refill."

There was always enough wall-banging to keep the customers reasonably satisfied, always a new prospect—a Harry Agganis, a Jackie Jensen, a Gene Stephens—for them to check out. And, always, there was Williams—prodigious and profane, invigorating and infuriating. He vowed that the 1954 season would be his last, saying, "You think I'm kidding, but I'm not." But he came back by mid-May of 1955 (too late to qualify for the batting title) and hit .356 to lead the league.

His chilly relationship with "the knights of the keyboard" had turned acerbic by 1956 when he twice spat in the direction of the press box. Soon after came "The Great Expectoration," when Williams, after being booed for muffing a two-out fly ball in the 11th inning against the Yankees, reeled in a blast by Yogi Berra and, on his way in to the dugout, directed several saliva shots at a record crowd of 36,350. "I'm not a bit sorry for what I did," later declared Williams, who'd walked to produce the winning run in a 1-0 decision. "I was right and I'd spit again at the same fans who booed me today. Some of them are the worst in the world."

Yet they were cheering him a day later after Williams, who was fined a record $5,000 by Yawkey (who never bothered collecting), smashed the game-winning homer, and then theatrically covered his mouth as he rounded the bases. "Atta boy, Ted," one grandstand denizen applauded. "We're all with you." Homers always had been an instant remedy at Fenway. But there were other ways to please a crowd. Spectators were startled three weeks earlier when former ace Mel Parnell, spurned after two injury-ruined seasons, became the first Sox hurler in 33 years to pitch a no-hitter.

Parnell, who'd been knocked around by the Yankees 10 days earlier on Independence Day and hadn't appeared since, baffled the White Sox with sinkers, facing only one

Said Yogi Berra: "He don't look like he used to; he looks better."

The Splinter, who ended up hitting .407 with 13 homers and 34 RBI in his abbreviated season, immediately jacked up Fenway attendance by more than 3,000 a game. Not that Boston fans had a better alternative. Once the Braves decamped for Milwaukee just before the season, the Sox literally were the only game in town.

Even though the club was in seventh place by mid-May (losing Williams with a broken collarbone on the first day of spring training didn't help), and ended up 42 games behind the Indians in 1954, nearly a million spectators came through the Fenway turnstiles, with more than 85,000 turning up for a weekend series with the Yankees in late August that the Sox swept.

So it went for the next several years with the Sox, who

"There are two places that I've played in my entire career that you can actually feel momentum change: Fenway Park and Yankee Stadium. You can actually feel it change."

—Tim Wakefield, Red Sox pitcher

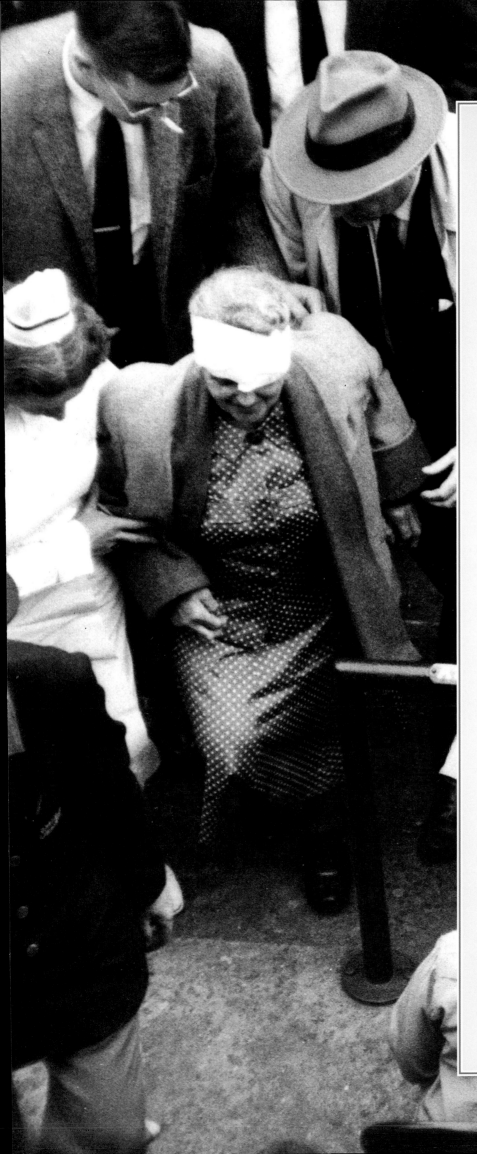

TED AND GLADYS

As the *Globe's* Bud Collins recalled it, "Gladys Heffernan was one hardheaded woman. You can bet your Louisville Slugger on it. Sweet, congenial, grandmotherly, but—lucky for her and for Ted Williams that September Sunday afternoon in 1958—she was topped by a skull that could have gone 10 rounds with Gibraltar."

Collins was in the Fenway press box when Williams struck out against the Washington Senators' Bill Fischer (who would go on to become the Red Sox pitching coach in the 1980s). Williams's temper was legendary, even at age 40, and he was so furious at striking out that, as he strode away from home plate, he took a vicious cut at the air—but the bat slipped from his hands.

There was no time for the 69-year-old Heffernan, sitting a few feet away in the first row near the Sox dugout, to react. Like a guided missile, the speeding bat beaned her. A communal gasp of horror and concern swept the park, followed by choruses of boos, as attendants rushed to the felled woman. A distraught Williams was quickly over the low wall and beside her.

As Collins told it, by the time he had run down the staircase from the press box and along an aisle to where she had been sitting, he was told by an usher that she was in the first aid room. Was she dead? The usher didn't know.

Outside the room, Red Sox General Manager Joe Cronin greeted Collins with, "She's fine. Nothing to worry about."

"Fine?"

"Of course," Cronin said with a smile. "Ted has talked to her. Apologized. She told him she knows he didn't mean it, that it was an accident. Just a little bump."

"But maybe a big lawsuit, Joe?"

"No, no, no. There'll be no lawsuit," he said firmly.

Collins frowned. "This happened five minutes ago. How can you be so certain there'll be no suit?"

"Because," Cronin smiled again, "Gladys happens to be my housekeeper."

Williams reportedly cried in the dugout after the accidental beaning. In his next at-bat, he doubled to drive in the second run in a 2-0 Boston win. Williams would go on to finish with a .328 average that season to win his final AL batting title.

Cronin's daughter, Maureen, who was 13 years old at the time, recalled the incident years later. She said Heffernan spent a week in the hospital, and Williams felt awful about it. "He went to see her every day in the hospital and bought her a diamond wrist watch," Cronin said. "She loved Ted and forgave him, but she never went to another game."

Joe Cronin decided the family's seats were a little too close to the action and moved them back a few rows, much to his four children's displeasure.

"That moment, when you first lay eyes on that field—the Monster, the triangle, the scoreboard . . . the left-field grass where Ted [Williams] once roamed—it all defines to me why baseball is such a magical game."

—Jayson Stark, ESPN analyst

man over the minimum. "That makes up for a lot of those days the past few years when things didn't go so good," said the 34-year-old left-hander after he'd done on July 14 what no Boston pitcher had done since Howard Ehmke in 1923—and no Sox pitcher had done at home since Ernie Shore in 1917. "Boy, it felt good to hear those people cheering me."

It was the last great moment for Parnell, who tore an elbow muscle and retired after the season. For nearly a decade, he'd been the mainstay of a staff that never had enough pitching, which is why Boston perennially ended up double-digits behind New York. In 1958, when Williams and teammate Pete Runnels finished 1-2 in the batting race and Jackie Jensen was Most Valuable Player, the Sox still finished 13 games out.

Had Jensen been able to play all of his games in the Fens, he might well have been a Hall of Famer. But his acute fear of flying exhausted him. When his teammates were heading for Logan Airport, Jensen often was jumping into a car and driving all night to the next city. He could handle Bob Lemon but not Rand McNally, so he quit the game a year later.

For Williams the most difficult opponent had become Father Time. He turned 41 in 1959, when a pinched nerve in his neck wrecked him for the season. The Sox sank with him and when they were in the cellar in July, Yawkey decided to ax Manager Mike "Pinky" Higgins, the former infielder who'd taken over for Lou Boudreau at the end of the 1954 season.

Yawkey dispatched General Manager Bucky Harris to Baltimore to give Pinky the pink slip. "The little one (Harris) keeps saying, 'You gotta quit, you gotta quit,'" a barmaid told two Boston sportswriters who'd paid her to provide a report. "And the big one (Higgins) keeps telling the little one to go bleep himself."

Higgins was given a scouting job and Billy Jurges, a Washington coach, was brought in to supervise the remainder of the season, which was most notable for the arrival of infielder Elijah Jerry "Pumpsie" Green and pitcher Earl Wilson, the franchise's first two black players. Green made his Fenway debut on August 4, 1959, two weeks after he first played for the Red Sox on the road in Chicago. Ever since the club had turned up its nose at Jackie Robinson at a 1945 tryout, the Sox had shown little interest in signing African-Americans. Perhaps it was a coincidence that the owner was from South Carolina and the manager from Texas, but Boston was the last team to integrate and its all-white roster all but assured continued mediocrity. ♣

BELOW: Elijah "Pumpsie" Green made his first major league start for the Red Sox in 1959. Green, the first black player for the Sox, was honored during the team's annual Jackie Robinson Day ceremony at Fenway Park on April 18, 2009.

FENWAY PARK

APRIL 18
The Sox run up a 9-0 lead, but lose, 15-10, to the Yankees in season opener.

JUNE 8
The Sox set a scoring record with a 29-4 win over St. Louis at Fenway.

JUNE 23
Manager Joe McCarthy resigns and is replaced by third-base coach Steve O'Neill.

MAY 15
With Cy Young in attendance, the Red Sox mark the franchise's 50th anniversary.

JUNE 8
Dom DiMaggio hits an inside-the-park home run in the fifth inning, boosting the Red Sox over Chicago, 1-0. The ball gets lost under the Boston bullpen bench and DiMaggio circles the bases while White Sox outfielder Wally Moses tries to retrieve it.

OCTOBER 22
Lou Boudreau becomes manager, replacing Steve O'Neill.

APRIL 12
The first baseball clinic organized by the Red Sox and the *Boston Globe* is held.

APRIL 30
In his last at-bat before leaving for Korean War duty, Ted Williams hits a home run.

MARCH 17
The Boston Braves move to Milwaukee, leaving the Red Sox as the only Major League Baseball franchise in Boston.

JUNE 18
In one inning, the Red Sox score 17 runs against the Detroit Tigers, setting a record. The Sox go on to win, 23-2.

JULY 28
Ted Williams participates in his first batting practice since returning from war duty.

APRIL 13
Hometown hero and All-American football quarterback Aristotle George "Harry" Agganis debuts with the Red Sox after Tom Yawkey outbids the Cleveland Browns for him; Agganis nearly has an inside-the-park home run, but is delayed by a slow runner in front of him.

JUNE 6
Harry Agganis hits a home run at Fenway, and then races up Commonwealth Avenue to receive his Boston University diploma.

1950 • 1951 • 1952 • 1953 • 1954

JULY 29
The Harlem Globetrotters put on their first show at Fenway.

OCTOBER 13
Mike "Pinky" Higgins takes over as Red Sox manager, replacing Lou Boudreau.

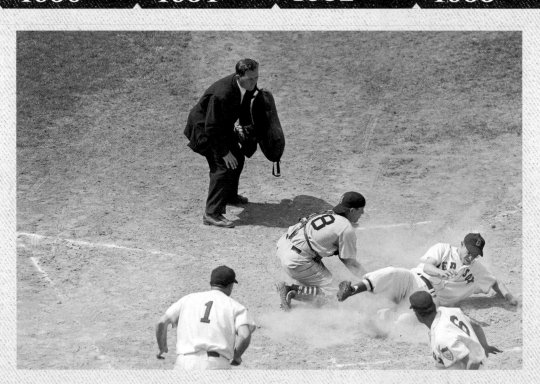

GREEN GIANT

The Wall, now known affectionately as the "Green Monster," is unquestionably the defining feature of America's most beloved ballpark. It stands 37 feet tall and 240 feet long, and its legend has been building since 1934.

Fenway Park was created in 1912, when then-owner John I. Taylor moved the home of the Red Sox from the Huntington Avenue Grounds to an undeveloped piece of land he owned in the Fenway area. With Lansdowne Street already established, architect James McLaughlin was left with no option but to truncate the field boundaries.

The short distance to the left-field boundary from home plate was compensated by the dead-ball era of the time and the height of the wall, and though much has happened to it since then, the large, storied structure remains formidable to hitters, pitchers, and fielders today.

BELLY OF THE MONSTER

Inside the Wall, it's scorching in the summertime and cold in the spring and fall, but scorekeepers get spectacular front-row seats and a chance to chat with outfielders, who can enter through a door that opens onto the field, during breaks in play. Manny Ramirez was particularly fond of ducking inside, sometimes barely making it back out before the game resumed. There is no permanent bathroom, although portables have been used.

GRAFFITI AND AUTOGRAPHS:

The interior walls are covered with graffiti. Some of it is illegible, but you will find signatures from many American League players of the last half-century, not to mention non-baseball celebrities such as James Taylor and Neil Diamond. Lyrics by Tom Petty, "The waiting is the hardest part," grace one beam. And somebody inside the Wall logged the home runs hit by Ted Williams in 1951 (there were 30, including the 300th of his career).

THE HAND-OPERATED SCOREBOARD:

The scoreboard today is very similar to the one that was constructed in 1934 and is still manually updated by a pair of attendants who work inside the Wall during games. The linescore of the game – as well as the day's other American League scores – is displayed on 16-inch-by-12-inch steel plates weighing two pounds that are changed by hand from within the Wall. In 2003, a panel for National League scores was added; those numbers must be changed from the outside between innings.

THE MORSE CODE:

The initials of former owner Thomas A. Yawkey and his wife, Jean R. Yawkey, are written in Morse code vertically – in two columns on the scoreboard.

LIGHTS:

When the scoreboard was added in 1934, the colored lights indicating balls, strikes, and outs were considered cutting-edge technology.

TV CAMERA:

The late NBC-TV director Harry Coyle put a camera inside the left-field wall. It captured what many consider the best baseball video clip of all time: Carlton Fisk's 12th-inning home run in Game 6 of the 1975 World Series, when Fisk waves his arms, willing his fly ball to stay fair.

HISTORY OF THE WALL

When Fenway Park was built in 1912, there was a 10-foot-tall, sloping embankment in front of a wooden wall in left field. The incline, which served as lawn seating and a picnic area for overflow crowds during the dead-ball era, as well as support for the wall itself, was tough on outfielders. However, Boston's Duffy Lewis mastered it and the hill became known as "Duffy's Cliff."

When Thomas A. Yawkey bought the Red Sox in 1933, Duffy's Cliff was scaled down, elevating the importance of the 37-foot metal fence behind it.

1930 **1940** **1950**

1934: Yawkey spent about $1.25 million in Depression-era dollars to renovate and modernize his ballpark. The fence became more wall-like with the addition of a scoreboard that featured colored lights and American and National League scores. Today's Fenway looks much the same as when Yawkey reopened the park to record-breaking crowds.

1936: A 23-foot-tall wire screen, set at a 45-degree angle, was installed above the 37-foot left-field wall to protect windows of buildings across Lansdowne Street. The screen stretched 240 feet from the left-field foul pole to the flagpole in center field.

The Wall was originally plastered with advertisements for companies such as Calvert Whiskey, Gem Blades, Lifebuoy Soap, and Vimms Vitamins.

In 1947, the ads were covered with green paint to accommodate TV broadcasts and the Green Monster was born. The Red Sox also became the 14th of 16 major league teams to install lights so that the team could play games at night.

FISK POLE:

The pole on the left-field foul line atop the Green Monster is known as the Fisk Foul Pole, in honor of Carlton Fisk's game-winning homer that struck the pole in the 12th inning of Game 6 of the 1975 World Series.

310:

At the foul pole, the Wall is only 309 feet, 3 inches from home plate, but for most of the century the Red Sox posted a sign that read "315." Club officials refused to allow an independent measurement of the distance, but when a *Boston Globe* reporter snuck into Fenway and came up with the new figure, the Sox grudgingly changed the sign to read 310 feet in 1995. Major League rules today stipulate that no fence in any new park be closer than 325 feet to home plate.

96:

Metric distances were added to the outfield walls in 1976, when it was thought that the U.S. would adopt the metric system; thus the 315-foot marker had a smaller accompanying 96-meter marking in yellow. The metric figures were painted over during the 2002 season.

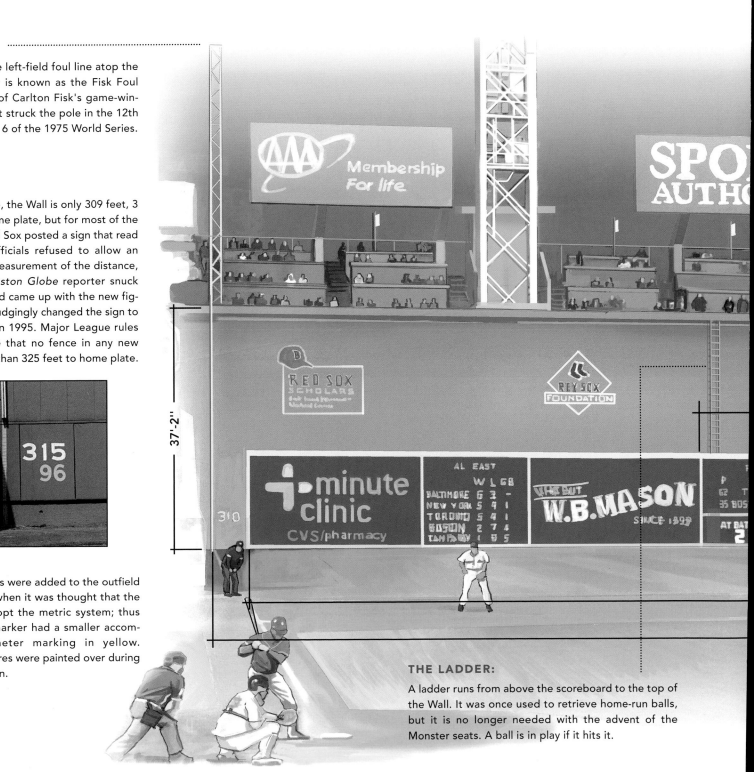

THE LADDER:

A ladder runs from above the scoreboard to the top of the Wall. It was once used to retrieve home-run balls, but it is no longer needed with the advent of the Monster seats. A ball is in play if it hits it.

JUNE 27
Harry Agganis dies
of a pulmonary
embolism at age 26.

JULY 14
Mel Parnell pitches a
no-hitter, the first at
Fenway in 33 years,
as Boston beats
Chicago.

JULY 23
Joe Cronin is
inducted into the
Baseball Hall of
Fame.

FEBRUARY 6
Ted Williams re-
signs with the Red
Sox for $135,000,
making him the
highest-paid player
in MLB history up to
that point.

JANUARY 15
Bucky Harris
becomes the general
manager of the
Red Sox after Joe
Cronin is voted in
as American League
president.

JULY 3
Billy Jurges is named
manager of the Red
Sox, replacing Mike
"Pinky" Higgins.

AUGUST 4
The first black player
to play for the Red
Sox, Elijah Jerry
"Pumpsie" Green,
makes his Fenway
debut.

1955   1956   1957   1958   1959

NOVEMBER 28
The Red Sox
sign Notre Dame
sophomore Carl
Yastrzemski to
a minor league
contract for
$108,000.

Top of page (l-r): Snowed in, 1955; Frank Malzone, Don Buddin, and Pumpsie Green, 1950s; Cub Scouts enjoying a May game, 1959. Timeline: Red Sox Dom DiMaggio completing an inside-the-park home run in June 1951; Ted Williams after playing his last game in April 1952; Harry Agganis taking a swing; *Globe* story on Mel Parnell's no-hitter, 1956; Joe Cronin endorsing Ted Williams's new contract, 1958.

2000   2010

2003: About 270 seats, over three rows and 10 sections, plus a standing-room area, were constructed atop the Green Monster.

Side view of the Wall

37'-2"

Bank of A

"FENCE GREEN"

The green paint used on the wall is a 100 percent acrylic made by California Paints, which was founded in Cambridge, Mass. in 1926 and is now based in Andover, Mass. The color, called "Fence Green," is considered proprietary by the Red Sox; it is not sold publicly, and the formula of colorants is a secret. The hue of Fence Green has apparently been the same since the wall was first painted in 1947, although California Paints didn't start producing the color until the 1970s. It takes about 35 gallons of paint to cover the wall. Other green hues are used around Fenway Park, including Scoreboard Green, Box Green, and Special Green.

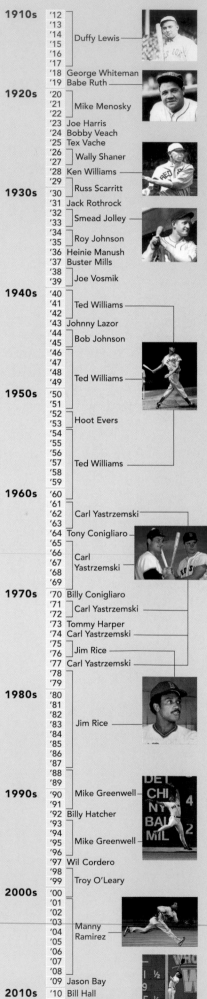

FENWAY'S LEFT FIELDERS

Red Sox players who played most games in left field for each of the last 100 years.

1910s	'12	
	'13	
	'14	Duffy Lewis
	'15	
	'16	
	'17	
	'18	George Whiteman
	'19	Babe Ruth
1920s	'20	
	'21	Mike Menosky
	'22	
	'23	Joe Harris
	'24	Bobby Veach
	'25	Tex Vache
	'26	Wally Shaner
	'27	
	'28	Ken Williams
	'29	
1930s	'30	Russ Scarritt
	'31	Jack Rothrock
	'32	Smead Jolley
	'33	
	'34	Roy Johnson
	'35	
	'36	Heinie Manush
	'37	Buster Mills
	'38	Joe Vosmik
	'39	
1940s	'40	
	'41	Ted Williams
	'42	
	'43	Johnny Lazor
	'44	Bob Johnson
	'45	
	'46	
	'47	
	'48	Ted Williams
	'49	
1950s	'50	
	'51	
	'52	
	'53	Hoot Evers
	'54	
	'55	
	'56	
	'57	Ted Williams
	'58	
	'59	
1960s	'60	
	'61	
	'62	Carl Yastrzemski
	'63	
	'64	Tony Conigliaro
	'65	
	'66	Carl Yastrzemski
	'67	
	'68	
	'69	
1970s	'70	Billy Conigliaro
	'71	Carl Yastrzemski
	'72	
	'73	Tommy Harper
	'74	Carl Yastrzemski
	'75	Jim Rice
	'76	
	'77	Carl Yastrzemski
	'78	
	'79	
1980s	'80	
	'81	
	'82	
	'83	Jim Rice
	'84	
	'85	
	'86	
	'87	
	'88	
	'89	
1990s	'90	Mike Greenwell
	'91	
	'92	Billy Hatcher
	'93	
	'94	Mike Greenwell
	'95	
	'96	
	'97	Wil Cordero
	'98	
	'99	Troy O'Leary
2000s	'00	
	'01	
	'02	
	'03	Manny Ramirez
	'04	
	'05	
	'06	
	'07	
	'08	
	'09	Jason Bay
2010s	'10	Bill Hall
	'11	Carl Crawford

1976: The park underwent major improvements following a play during Game 6 of the 1975 World Series, when Red Sox center fielder Fred Lynn was injured after crashing into the cement base of the Wall. Protective padding was installed, and the Wall was also stripped of its metal skin and fitted with a smoother, fiberglass covering. The new surface allowed balls to bounce evenly off any part of its surface, but a unique home-field advantage was lost for the Sox: The various materials of the old wall created odd caroms that were mastered by Sox outfielders while opposing players were often fooled by the bounces.

The old green facade was cut into snapshot-size rectangles and mounted on wood, then sold to Red Sox fans, with proceeds going to the Jimmy Fund.

CITGO SIGN:

Every time a player hits a home run over the Green Monster, the CITGO sign is seen by fans at the ballpark and on television. The computer-operated sign is double-faced and measures 60 feet by 60 feet. In early 2005, the sign received a major restoration and technology upgrade from neon light to LEDs.

1960s

Carl Yastrzemski follows the flight of his second home run of Game 2 of the 1967 World Series, a 5-0 Red Sox victory. Yaz supplanted Ted Williams in left field for the Red Sox and created his own legacy, including an MVP season in '67 and his stature as the first American League player to have at least 400 home runs and 3,000 hits.

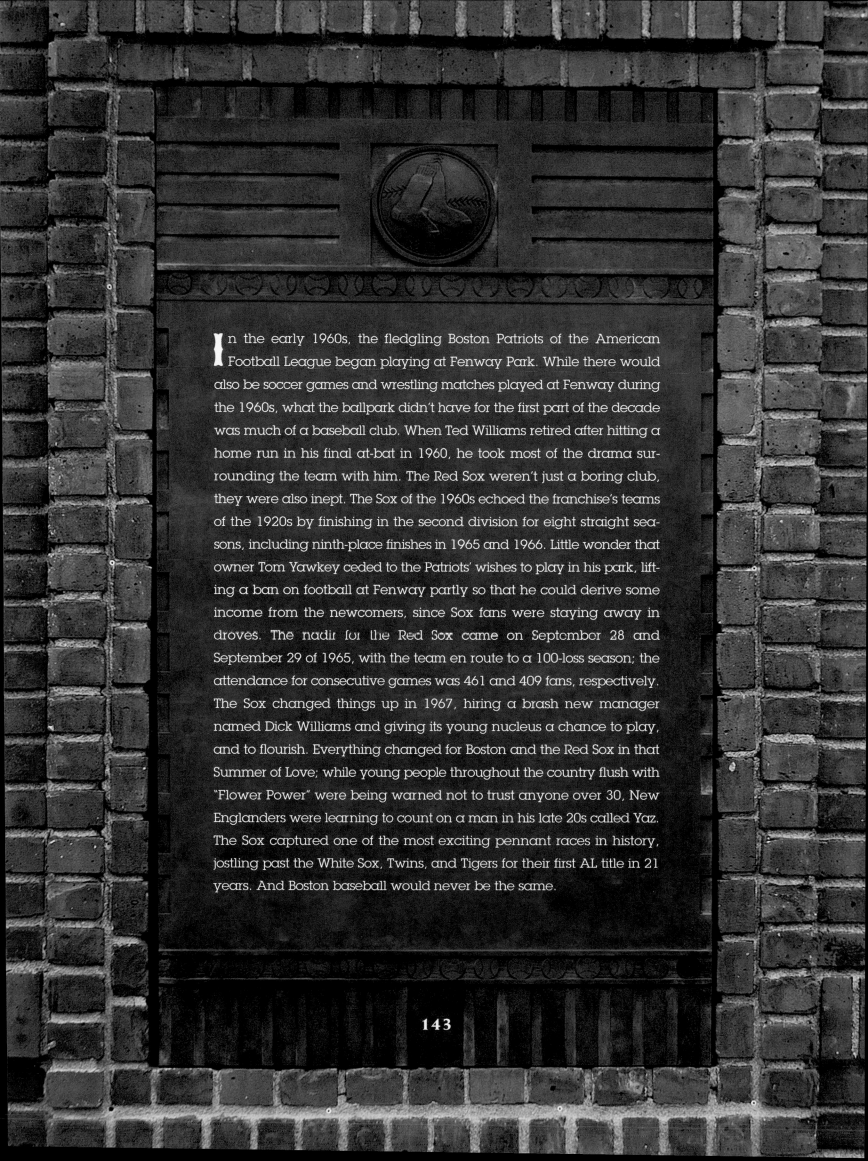

In the early 1960s, the fledgling Boston Patriots of the American Football League began playing at Fenway Park. While there would also be soccer games and wrestling matches played at Fenway during the 1960s, what the ballpark didn't have for the first part of the decade was much of a baseball club. When Ted Williams retired after hitting a home run in his final at-bat in 1960, he took most of the drama surrounding the team with him. The Red Sox weren't just a boring club, they were also inept. The Sox of the 1960s echoed the franchise's teams of the 1920s by finishing in the second division for eight straight seasons, including ninth-place finishes in 1965 and 1966. Little wonder that owner Tom Yawkey ceded to the Patriots' wishes to play in his park, lifting a ban on football at Fenway partly so that he could derive some income from the newcomers, since Sox fans were staying away in droves. The nadir for the Red Sox came on September 28 and September 29 of 1965, with the team en route to a 100-loss season; the attendance for consecutive games was 461 and 409 fans, respectively. The Sox changed things up in 1967, hiring a brash new manager named Dick Williams and giving its young nucleus a chance to play, and to flourish. Everything changed for Boston and the Red Sox in that Summer of Love; while young people throughout the country flush with "Flower Power" were being warned not to trust anyone over 30, New Englanders were learning to count on a man in his late 20s called Yaz. The Sox captured one of the most exciting pennant races in history, jostling past the White Sox, Twins, and Tigers for their first AL title in 21 years. And Boston baseball would never be the same.

UPDIKE HIT IT OUT OF THE PARK, TOO

BY BOB RYAN

On September 28, 1960, John Updike, 28 years old and, though raised in Pennsylvania, a Ted Williams fan since childhood, decided it was a good idea to attend the afternoon game between the Red Sox and Baltimore Orioles. He, like all members of the public, knew only that it would be the final home game of Ted's career. Not until the game was concluded did people learn that it would be Ted's last game, period, that he had decided before the game he would not be making a season-ending trip to Yankee Stadium.

The times were different. The word "hype" had barely entered the language. Today, there would be special editions, minted coins, and live shots galore.

"The world was a simpler place," Updike noted.

But Wednesday, September 28, 1960, was a dank, dreary day. And the Red Sox, Ted Williams aside, were a dank, dreary team on their way to a 65-89 record and a seventh-place finish. Accordingly, a mere 10,454 fans showed up. And it could very easily have been 10,453. Updike's first choice that day was to visit a lady on Beacon Hill. Fortunately, the lady was not home.

Updike explained in a 1977 epilogue: "I took a taxi to Beacon Hill and knocked on a door and there was nothing, just a basket for mail hung on the door. So I went, as promised, to the game and my virtue was rewarded."

The resulting "Hub Fans Bid Kid Adieu," published in the October 22, 1960 edition of the *New Yorker*, is the most spellbinding essay ever written about baseball. Some, like critic Roger Dean, go even further. "It is simply the greatest essay I have ever read," he said.

"It influenced me in a big way," said Roger Angell, who would become the foremost baseball writer of the late 20th century, but in 1960 had yet to publish a word about it. "And it has influenced just about every sportswriter who followed. The great thing is that he went expecting something amazing and incredible—and it happened. Only baseball provides in any number those totally unexpected turns."

"My one effort as a sportswriter," explained Updike. "It's had a longer life than I would have expected."

We all know how the story ends. In the eighth inning, battling horribly adverse weather conditions that had already cost him one shot at a homer, Williams hit a 1-1 pitch from Jack Fisher onto the canopy covering a bench in the Red Sox bullpen. He ran the bases hurriedly amid relentless applause and did not tip his cap. He took

his place in left field at the start of the ninth and was replaced by Manager Mike Higgins with Carroll Hardy, in the hopes that Williams would acknowledge the crowd, and again he did not tip his cap. He had not tipped his cap since 1940 and he had no remote intention of deviating from his policy.

Wrote Updike, "No other player visible to my generation concentrated within himself so much of the sport's poignance, so assiduously refined his natural skills, so constantly brought to the plate that intensity of competence that crowds the throat with joy."

Williams liked the piece. At least, that's what was conveyed to Updike by a third party. And Ted even suggested Updike be a collaborator on a biography, an offer that Updike, a longtime resident of Boston's North Shore who died in 2009, politely declined.

"I'd said all I had to say on the subject," he said in the epilogue.

Of Ted's stubborn refusal to tip his cap that day, despite being given three separate opportunities to do so (coming to the plate, rounding the bases, and trotting in after being removed from the field), Updike sagely noted, "Gods do not answer letters."

But they sometimes leave behind epic accounts of epic events.

"Everything is painted green and seems in curiously sharp focus,
like the inside of an old-fashioned peeping-type Easter egg."
—John Updike, from "Hub Fans Bid Kid Adieu"

Teammate Jim Pagliaroni offered congratulations after "Teddy
Ballgame" hit his 521st home run in the final at-bat of his career.

"We knew almost all the fans in the stands by name."

—Dick Radatz, the top closer in baseball when he pitched
for the woeful Red Sox teams of the early 1960s

There were only 2,466 fans in the stands on April 11, 1962, when the Red Sox played the
Cleveland Indians, winning the contest 4-0 on a Carroll Hardy grand slam in the 12th inning.

As mediocre as most of the fifties had been for the Red Sox, the club at least had been finishing in the money at a time when that meant that most of its players wouldn't have to spend the off-season selling tires. But by 1960, the Sox were bouncing around the bottom of the league and their owner was growing exasperated. "Want to buy a ball club?" Tom Yawkey asked broadcaster Curt Gowdy after a 12-3 home loss to the Indians. "I'll sell it for seven million. Seven million will take it."

It was early June and Boston already was stuck in eighth place, nearly a dozen games out of first. To shake things up one game, manager Billy Jurges switched Bobby Thomson, who'd hit the "Shot Heard 'Round The World" to win the 1951 pennant for the Giants, from the outfield to first base, where Thomson made two of his team's four errors in the fourth inning.

"I can't believe what I saw here tonight," declared Yawkey, sipping bourbon in his office after the game to blot out the memory. "A guy playing first base in the major leagues with a finger glove on. A finger glove at first base. I'll sell this club. Take it off my hands. This is the major leagues? THIS is the major leagues?"

And yet more than a million spectators came through the Fenway turnstiles that year, most of them to watch Teddy Ballgame play his final season. After his miserable 1959 campaign, by far the worst of his career, Ted Williams actually demanded that the club chop $35,000 from his $125,000 salary. Though Yawkey had suggested during the off-season that the slugger retire, Williams wanted one more .300 season and to reach 500 career home runs before he put away his bat. He easily accomplished both, batting .316 and hitting 29 homers to finish with a lifetime average of .344 and 521 career homers.

While everyone in the park knew that the midweek game against the Orioles at the end of September would be Williams's last at Fenway, nobody but he, Yawkey, Gowdy and the clubhouse denizens knew that it would be the last

of his career. Williams had a nasty cold and had asked the owner if he could skip the final series in New York. So when he deposited Jack Fisher's fastball atop the Sox bullpen in the eighth inning, it made for a grand finale and a farewell that was completely in character.

"I thought about tipping my hat, you're damn right I did, and for a moment I was torn," Williams later confessed. "But by the time I got to second base I knew I couldn't do it. It just wouldn't have been me." Yet Manager Mike Higgins, who'd supplanted Jurges on June 12, wasn't going to let him get away without one last ovation. "Williams, left field," he declared at the top of the ninth— then sent Carroll Hardy out after him once Williams had been saluted for a final time.

The club already had Williams's successor—there was no replacement—in mind. Carl Yastrzemski, who'd grown up on a Long Island potato farm and whose father had spurned the Yankees' lowball offer for his son, had signed a $100,000 deal while he was at Notre Dame. "We're paying this kind of money for THIS guy?" said skeptical general manager Joe Cronin when he met his skinny bonus baby.

The Sox gave Yastrzemski the jersey No. 8 because it was nearest to his predecessor's legendary No. 9, and assigned him the locker adjacent to Williams's at spring training, where Williams, now a batting instructor, gave Yaz a thorough tutorial. But by midsummer, when he was stuck in a prolonged slump and haunted by Yaz-vs.-Ted comparisons, the overwhelmed rookie went to see the owner. "I feel guilty about not giving you your money's worth," Yastrzemski recalled telling Yawkey in his autobiography. "Could Ted come in for a day or two and take a look at me?"

'PATRIOTS DAY' AT FENWAY

Almost from the time it opened, Fenway Park served as a professional and collegiate gridiron for several teams. But Red Sox owner Tom Yawkey banished football from his ballpark in the late 1950s and early '60s because he wanted to protect the grass for baseball. When Sox attendance plummeted, however, Yawkey welcomed the Boston Patriots of the American Football League to Fenway in 1963.

It's hard to fathom today, but the Patriots operated on pretty much a shoestring budget for their first decade. The team offices were in a basement in Kenmore Square, and when it came time to draft players, reporters sat alongside as team officials flipped through the *Street & Smith* football guide to make their choices. Former Patriot star Gino Cappelletti would typically rush from training camp to anchor WBZ television sportscasts five nights a week to supplement his $7,500 salary. The Patriots played their first three seasons at Boston University's football field (the former Braves Field) before the Red Sox offered their ballpark.

"We had played at BU and that was appreciated," said Cappelletti. "But once we got to Fenway Park, it immediately gave us a feeling of having arrived."

Fenway's football configuration put one end zone on the third-base line and the other in front of the bullpens in right field. Gil Santos called the games from a makeshift booth atop the first-base grandstand, and temporary stands were erected in front of the Green Monster. Both benches were initially situated in front of the temporary stands to avoid blocking the sightlines of fans sitting behind the first-base dugout.

"Funny thing about those side-by-side benches," said Cappelletti. "During the games, we would get closer and closer to the other team and start eavesdropping. I remember one game when we heard [Chiefs' head coach] Hank Stram calling for a screen pass. The next year, they put us over on the first-base side."

A receiver/placekicker, Cappelletti booted a lot of footballs into the stands. "The bullpens in right were pretty close to the end zone so most of my extra points went over the bullpens and into the bleachers," he recalled.

One summer, because of the uncertainty over where they would be playing, the Patriots printed tickets for three potential locations. Patrick Sullivan, the son of Patriots' founder Billy Sullivan and the team's former general manager, said his favorite venue was Fenway, where the Pats played for much of six seasons, until 1968.

"It was a great place to watch a football game, for precisely the same reason it is for baseball," he said. "If you were in the temporary seats that we set up against the Green Monster—it was a big grandstand with about 5,600 seats—you were right on the action. The conversations that occurred between some of the coaches and our fans were hysterical. I was a ball boy, so I would listen in on them."

Sullivan also remembered how players and fans would mingle on the field after games, which created a connection that doesn't exist today.

"Romances were started, business relationships were formed, and guys got jobs during those times," he said. "The visiting players would hang out, too, and one time I bumped into [Bills quarterback] Jack Kemp. One of the things he later told me was that it was a Patriots' season ticket holder who convinced him to later go into politics: Tip O'Neill." Kemp went on to a successful political career after his playing days, which included a run for the presidency in 1988.

Cappelletti and quarterback Babe Parilli were two of the team's big stars of the time, and running back Jim Nance's appearance on the cover of *Sports Illustrated* gave the Patriots national recognition in the mid-1960s. The AFL gradually gained acceptance, and later, a merger with the NFL.

"When we first got there, I don't think many of us realized that pioneering was what we were doing," said Cappelletti. "The original dream was survival. First, you had to survive to make the team. Then, you hoped for franchise survival. And then you hoped that the league would survive."

"Get behind by four runs, no problem. Ahead by four in the eighth, delay the champagne. Nothing was—or is—certain, not even a pitcher sailing along. One little hit, an error maybe, can open a door to a pop-fly homer in the net. . . . That's the magic of Fenway Park. That's why people love it so."

—Ned Martin, longtime Red Sox announcer

So Williams abandoned a fishing trip to give Yastrzemski a refresher course that made for a respectable debut season highlighted by 80 RBI and 11 homers. His teammates, few of whom would deign to speak to a rookie, didn't do nearly as well, and the Sox finished in sixth place, far enough behind that they would have needed a spyglass to locate the Yankees. The highlight of the season came against the last-place Senators on a Sunday in mid-June when the Sox staged the greatest comeback in franchise history, coming from seven runs down with two out in the ninth to win the opener of their doubleheader, 13-12. They then claimed the nightcap in 13 innings, 6-5.

"You had a real bad day at the plate today," an observer jokingly told Jim Pagliaroni, who hit the killer grand slam in the first game and the walk-off homer in the second. "You were only 2 for 11." "Gee, that's right," the catcher realized. "My batting average is going to blazes."

In a season when the Sox finished 33 games out of first place, novelties of any kind were welcome. The most notable came in the season's finale in the Bronx when Tracy Stallard proffered the ball that Roger Maris launched for his record-breaking 61st homer of the season. "I have nothing to be ashamed of," concluded the rookie, who pitched only one more inning for the club, but ended up as a Cooperstown footnote, albeit with an asterisk. "Maris hit 60 other homers, didn't he?"

It was otherwise a forgettable summer that engendered several more of the same. "There may be more broken beer bottles than broken hearts in the trail they leave behind them," concluded *Globe* columnist Harold Kaese on the morning of the club's Fenway finale.

Boston fans (they were not yet a Nation) derived their satisfaction from rare and wondrous moments that season. For instance, who would have predicted that the club's first no-hitter in a half-dozen years would be pitched by an African American?

Earl Wilson, who'd grown up in Louisiana, had been signed in 1959 as Boston's second black player after

Pumpsie Green, as much for his demeanor as his ability. "Well-mannered colored boy," said the club's first scouting report on him. "Not too black, pleasant to talk to, well-educated, very good appearance." Wilson had come up from the minors before the 1962 season, but he was flawless when he faced the Angels on June 26, feeding them a steady diet of fastballs. "It's hummin', man," catcher Bob Tillman assured him as Wilson strung together a row of zeros and won the game, 2-0, with a homer off Bo Belinsky, who'd thrown a no-no of his own in May.

"All I can say is the Good Man was with me tonight," proclaimed Wilson, the first black pitcher to toss a no-hitter in the American League, and the first Red Sox pitcher to hurl one since Mel Parnell in 1956—and the first right-hander to pitch a no-hitter at Fenway since Ernie Shore in 1917. Fenway's man upstairs was suitably appreciative, as Yawkey made a rare visit to the clubhouse, gave Wilson a $500 bonus, and bumped up his salary by $1,000.

Little more than a month later, Bill Monbouquette threw another no-hitter in Chicago. It was the first time a pair of Boston pitchers had managed the feat since Dutch Leonard and George Foster both pitched no-hitters in 1916. By then, though, the season had been long lost. The Sox were entombed in eighth place, 17 games out, and Higgins, who'd morphed from caretaker to undertaker, was dismissed.

Succeeding him was Johnny Pesky, the former Sox shortstop and manager of their Triple A affiliate in Seattle. He was determined to put a stop to the "country club" culture that had become embedded over the previous decade. So during spring training in Scottsdale, Arizona he established a midnight curfew, banned swimming (because "It dulls the reflexes") and discouraged golf. "I'm not a slave driver," the new skipper insisted. "I'm just trying to be helpful."

What the 1963 club needed was something close to unearthly intervention. It arrived in the form of Dick "The Monster" Radatz, a hulking closer who was coming off a percussive rookie season during which he'd led the league in relief appearances, victories, and saves and was voted

Helicopters were employed to help dry out the field in March 1967 as preparations for the season got underway. Later in the year, veteran groundskeeper Jim McCarthy used a riding mower to keep the grass in check.

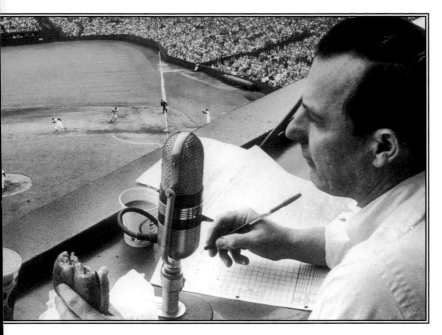

Ned Martin broadcast—on radio and TV—for 31 Red Sox seasons, partnering first with Curt Gowdy and last with Jerry Remy.

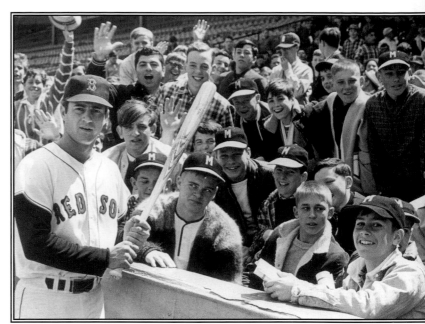

Carl Yastrzemski supplanted Ted Williams in left field in 1961 and went on to create his own Hall of Fame legacy.

"Fireman of the Year." His repertoire consisted of one pitch—a fastball—but it was delivered from a 78-inch frame that weighed 245 pounds.

During a season when victories were again hard won, Radatz's was the only number on Pesky's bullpen speed dial when the game hung in the balance. In June and July alone, Radatz made 30 appearances, once working six times in six days and closing out both ends of consecutive doubleheaders. In one 15-inning victory over Detroit on June 11, he pitched the final nine innings. "God bless Dick Radatz," proclaimed Pesky. "He's our franchise." The *Globe*'s Kaese avowed that Radatz was to the Red Sox "what (Pablo) Casals is to music, the Prudential Tower is to Boston's skyline."

In the All-Star Game at Cleveland, Radatz pitched two innings and struck out five men, including future Hall of Famers Willie Mays, Willie McCovey, and Duke Snider. But his 15 victories and 25 saves couldn't rescue a club that went into a summer swoon, falling from second place to seventh and finishing 28 games behind the Yankees. The Sox poster boy for the season was first baseman Dick Stuart, nicknamed "Dr. Strangeglove" for his mystifying fielding. While Stuart led the club with 42 homers and 118 RBI, he also struck out a franchise-record 144 times and made 29 errors.

Wood always had been a higher priority than leather around Fenway, so when a 19-year-old rookie from Swampscott cracked a 450-foot homer against the Indians in spring training, he immediately was plugged into the 1964 starting lineup, despite having only played a year of "A" ball. The only challenge was getting Tony Conigliaro into, and then out of, bed.

When the Sox scheduled a workout for Yankee Stadium after their season opener with New York was rained out, the rookie still was dozing at the hotel. "What a way to start a career," he moaned. "I can hear my kids asking me some day, 'What did you do on your first day in the big leagues, Dad?' And I'll say, 'I slept.'"

Tony C., as he immediately was dubbed, was wide awake on Opening Day in the Fens though, launching the first pitch he saw from Chicago's Joel Horlen over the left-field wall. He hit 22 more homers before the season was done, even though he missed about six weeks with various injuries, including a broken wrist and forearm. Broken curfews also were an issue, as Conigliaro was casual about bedtimes. "I am not a playboy," he insisted after Pesky fined him for being AWOL in Cleveland.

Not that it would have set Conigliaro apart on a club that usually played as if it had been up all night. The Sox snoozed through the rest of 1964 and Pesky was dismissed two games before the end with third-base coach Billy Herman, who hadn't managed since 1947, inheriting a club that finished eighth. They were the Dead Sox now, flatlining by May. In 1965 Boston was buried in seventh place after 14 games, en route to 100 losses with foul balls clanging off empty seats.

"When I was with Kansas City we played in Fenway one day and I was in right field, counting people in the stands," recalled Ken Harrelson, who ended up in Boston in 1967. "There couldn't have been more than a couple hundred." Only 1,274 turned up on September 16 when Dave Morehead, a 23-year-old right-hander who'd lost 16 games that

THE PATRIOTS FLOP IN FIRST MEANINGFUL GAME

Gino Cappelletti peeked through his bedroom curtains and couldn't believe his eyes. Snow? Can't be, he said to himself.

The date was December 20, 1964, and the Patriots would be taking on the Buffalo Bills at Fenway Park in the biggest game in team history.

The game was for the AFL's Eastern Division championship. Buffalo, led by Jack Kemp, Cookie Gilchrist, and Elbert Dubenion, came to Boston with an 11-2 record. The Patriots were 10-2-1 and had halted the Bills' 10-0 start by beating them at Buffalo. With a win, the Patriots would capture the division and face the San Diego Chargers for the AFL title at Fenway. The Patriots sought revenge for the 51-10 whipping the Chargers had administered in San Diego a year earlier in the Patriots' only championship game appearance.

For the first time in history, a Patriots' game not only was going to sell out Fenway Park, but it would also be the national TV game of the day. The surprise snowstorm that had hit Boston the night before meant that the game had to be delayed for 45 minutes while the grounds crew finished clearing the field. And with 38,021 fans converging on the snow-covered streets around Fenway, the entire area was in chaos.

Said Cappelletti, "I got stuck on Route 9 on the way in [from his home in Wellesley]. Thank goodness the game was delayed. The rumor in the locker room was that I got kidnapped by gamblers. No kidding. That was the story going around, and some of the guys believed it."

Much of the crowd stood throughout the game because the seats were never cleaned. The *Globe*'s Bud Collins described Fenway as a glacier: "There were snowball fights and fist fights and drawing from the hip flasks." When the game finally started, it was all Buffalo. On the first play from scrimmage, Gilchrist, a powerful fullback, leveled Patriot cornerback Chuck Shonta, who was shaken up but stayed in the game. Two plays later, Dubenion beat Shonta for a 57-yard touchdown pass.

"You could see the Bills get a lift after that," said Cappelletti. "They also had an excellent defensive game plan."

The Bills won, 24-14, and went on to beat the Chargers for the AFL championship. For the Patriots, it would be 21 more years before they would play in a league championship game, and it took them 37 years to win their first league title in Super Bowl XXXVI.

The Fenway Park gridiron was bathed in white after an unexpected storm dumped four inches of snow on December 20, 1964. The Patriots (led by Gino Cappelletti, above) played the Buffalo Bills later that day for the AFL's Eastern Division title, falling to the eventual AFL champions, 24-14.

season, pitched a no-hitter against the Indians, missing a perfect game on a full-count walk in the second inning.

Even that feat wasn't enough to keep Yawkey from dumping Higgins as his general manager in the middle of the game—Higgins's second sacking by the Sox in six years. The former skipper, who'd been the primary target of fans' displeasure, had advised the owner to fire him. "You'd be better off with somebody else," Higgins said. "I'm not popular in this town."

Yawkey first said the change would be made during World Series time. But he lowered the boom in the fifth inning ("I'd like to make that change now"), giving Morehead 45 minutes to savor his no-hitter before announcing the decision to the public. Replacing Higgins was Dick O'Connell, who quickly shook things up by moving spring training from Arizona to Florida and promoting farmhands like George Scott, Joe Foy, Reggie Smith, and Mike Andrews.

But the club still finished ninth in 1966, dropping its first five games and 20 of 27. By mid-May, the Sox were in last place. "You're always optimistic in spring training," Yastrzemski wrote in his memoir, *Yaz*, "but that optimism's gone after the first two months of the season when you're 25 games out of first place and looking at 2,000 people in the stands in springtime."

It was no consolation that Boston finished the season ahead of New York. The franchise was going sideways and attendance still was well under a million. So O'Connell brought in Dick Williams, who'd been the Triple A manager in Toronto and who insisted on two things—a one-year con-

Tony Conigliaro worked on his batting stance in the Fenway Park dressing room under the watchful eye of then-Red Sox vice president Ted Williams on July 21, 1966.

tract and absolute autonomy in the dugout. "I decided if I'm going to go down, I'm going down my way," said Williams, who'd been a reserve infielder on the Sox soporific 1963 and 1964 teams where "nobody really cared about winning."

Given the dismal denouement of the previous campaign, expectations for the coming season were modest by the players and less-than-modest by oddsmakers, who listed the Red Sox as 100-1 long shots. "If our pitching holds up, we'll finish fifth," reckoned Yastrzemski, the club's perennial cockeyed optimist. "No kidding. I think we can make it to the first division."

That's precisely where the Sox found themselves in mid-July after a 10-0 home loss to the Orioles. Though none of them predicted what was about to occur—a 10-game winning streak that lifted Boston to second place, a half-game behind Chicago, and bestirred a fandom that long ago had been lulled into somnolence.

"Our mouths were open," shortstop Rico Petrocelli said after 15,000 Sox fans turned up at Logan Airport to salute the players upon their return from a four-game sweep of the Indians in Cleveland. "We were shocked. That's when we started believing."

The summer of 1967 was a revival, a daily salvation show for both the Sox and their supporters, whose souls had been deadened by decades of disappointment. It was

In the annual Father-Son Game, on July 24, 1966, Mike Yastrzemski, 4, threw a pitch as dad Carl offered support. Vin Martelli, 5, godson of Sox outfielder Tony Conigliaro, was the batter, while George Thomas of the Red Sox caught and umpire Hank Soar called the balls and strikes.

BALLPARK BACKDROP ENDURES

For nearly five decades, Red Sox fans have watched home-run blasts over the Green Monster soar against the backdrop of a Boston landmark. When the Citgo sign in Kenmore Square was first illuminated in 1965, it replaced a 1940 neon sign that displayed the shamrock logo of Cities Services, the predecessor to Citgo.

The pulsating, computer-controlled design of the 60-by-60-foot sign was an immediate hit in the psychedelic age, and an avant-garde filmmaker made a critically acclaimed three-and-a-half-minute film in 1967 called *Go, Go Citgo*, in which he set the sign's display to music by the Monkees and Indian sitarist Ravi Shankar.

The sign became so renowned that even opposing managers knew it well. In 1978, with Sox slugger Jim Rice on a particularly torrid stretch, Royals manager Whitey Herzog deployed a four-out-fielder shift. "What I'd really like to do is put two guys on top of the Citgo sign and two in the net," Herzog quipped. Rice beat the shift by hitting one over the left-field wall and the netting for a home run.

Bostonians have taken their skyline pretty seriously ever since Robert Newman placed two lights in the tower of the Old North Church in 1775 as a beacon to Paul Revere. This may explain why plans to tear down the Citgo sign caused an uproar in 1982.

In September 1979, at the urging of state officials, Citgo had turned off the sign to set an energy-conservation example, even though it cost only $60 a week to light. By November 1982, Citgo was preparing to tear it down.

The public was outraged. The sign's supporters even urged the Boston Landmarks Commission to make it an official landmark. A man who testified before the commission said, in complete seriousness, "Paris has the Eiffel Tower, London has Big Ben, and Boston has its Citgo sign." On November 16, the Landmarks Commission issued a cease and desist order.

"We had no idea it would receive such a response. Now we know how much people in Boston love that sign," Citgo spokesman Kent Young later said. By August 1983, the sign was again aglow.

In 2005, more than 1.7 miles of LED lights replaced the existing 5,878 glass tubes of neon, which saved thousands of dollars in energy costs. But when those LED lights went out of production in 2010, crews replaced the sign's 218,000 lights with brighter, more weather-resistant versions.

Citgo is a division of Venezuela's government-owned oil company, and in a 2005 relighting ceremony, Mayor Thomas M. Menino of Boston flipped the ceremonial switch with Juan Barreto, then mayor of Caracas, and former Red Sox shortstop Luis Aparicio, the only Venezuelan in the Baseball Hall of Fame.

The sign continues to glow, part symbol of roadside culture, part Boston icon, and some fans still call out "See it go!" (C-IT-GO) when a Red Sox player blasts a home run in its general direction.

Jim Lonborg laid down the bunt for a base hit that triggered the winning Red Sox rally in the final game of the 1967 "Impossible Dream" season. The Red Sox trailed the Minnesota Twins, 2-0, in the sixth when Lonborg set the table for a five-run inning and an eventual Boston victory. The Red Sox edged the Twins and Tigers by one game for their first pennant in 21 years.

WHEN RED SOX NATION WAS BORN

They listened on transistor radios in the clubhouse for the crackling report from Detroit's Tiger Stadium. It was October 1, 1967, and the Red Sox had held up their share of the deal by defeating the Twins earlier in the day, clinching no worse than a tie for the AL pennant. Fans had stormed the field to hoist pitcher Jim Lonborg onto their shoulders, and players bathed in adulation from success-starved Bostonians who couldn't quite believe that their longtime American League doormats could be going to the World Series.

The Red Sox had started that 1967 season with a victory on Opening Day—before a mere 8,234 fans. It turned out to be the Summer of Love nationally, but in New England, it was the summer when the lovable losers of Fenway became a team that mattered, a team that played meaningful games in late summer and fall. *Globe* columnist Dan Shaughnessy, who was 13 years old that year and had never seen a decent Sox team, years later wrote: "The Red Sox of the new century are still beholden to the Impossible Dream crew."

Red Sox teams of that era didn't fall out of the pennant race in the final weeks—no, they were usually out of any consideration by the Fourth of July. The Boston clubhouse was known as a "country club" where star players had only to run to the owner, the benevolent Tom Yawkey, if they thought a manager wasn't treating them fairly. They had coasted to eight consecutive losing seasons, finishing eighth, seventh, eighth, ninth, and ninth in a 10-team league the previous five seasons.

Now, as the "Age of Aquarius" dawned, a rookie manager named Dick Williams was in charge, and it seemed he had some backing from above. The Sox, a collection of retread players and youngsters led by two stars who were having the seasons of their lives, had reawakened a generation of Red Sox fans. By July, they were in first place, a totally unexpected perch. They hung on with improbable determination and entered the season's final weekend with two home games against the Minnesota Twins, who led them by one game in the standings. Win two, and the Sox could do no worse than tie for the pennant with the Detroit Tigers.

Boston fans were wild for "Gentleman Jim" Lonborg's pitching, and yet he triggered a game-changing rally with—of all things—a bunt single, as Boston defeated the Twins on the season's final day. It was Lonborg's 22nd victory of the season, and it would help earn him the Cy Young Award, the first such honor for a Red Sox pitcher.

The tale of Don Quixote was all the rage on Broadway that season, and, thus, the Red Sox rebirth was tagged—forever and always—as the Impossible Dream season. They won their first pennant in 21 years in the culmination of baseball's best-ever pennant race, which was finally settled when the radio told the tale and the champagne was uncorked: the Tigers had lost, and no playoff game was necessary. They would finish the season one game behind the Sox with Minnesota. With 44 homers, 121 RBI, and a .326 batting average, Carl Yastrzemski won the Triple Crown (no one has done it since, or even come close). He capped the year with a 7 for 8 hitting performance in the last two games. That season was the launching pad for all of the team's success since then. After eight straight losing campaigns, the Red Sox would go on to have 16 straight winning seasons and establish the base of Red Sox Nation.

LEFT: The annual Bat Day promotion at Fenway Park was just one more reason to love 1967.

RIGHT: October '67, as seen through a fish-eye lens.

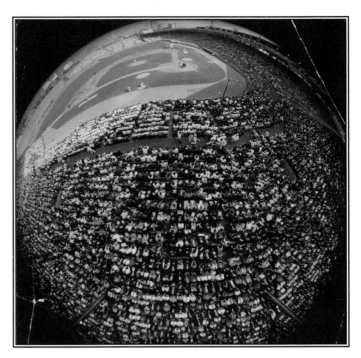

the wildest ride in memory as the club went from first place to ninth to first to eighth, all before Memorial Day. Attendance was on its way to doubling to more than 1.7 million—the franchise's highest ever.

For one terrifying moment on August 18 at Fenway, when Angels pitcher Jack Hamilton hit Tony Conigliaro in the face with a fastball that left him motionless in the dirt, the magic vanished. "I thought I was going to die," said Conigliaro, who suffered a fractured cheekbone, a dislocated jaw, and a damaged retina that prevented him from playing again until 1969. "Death was constantly on my mind."

Yet his shaken teammates won, 12-11, that night and swept the Sunday doubleheader, coming from eight runs down to claim the nightcap, 9-8. From then until the end of the season, Boston was never more than a game out of the lead. "We were doing the impossible," said Petrocelli, "and we were doing it together."

It was the Impossible Dream, a quixotic adventure that swept up all of New England in its giddy unlikelihood. No ball club ever had come from ninth place to finish first in one season. But as Boston remained in contention into September, the possibility created both anticipation and anxiety. "I can remember people saying, 'How can you stand the pressure?'" said Yastrzemski, who found himself on the cover of *Life* magazine. "I'd say, 'Pressure? This is fun. This is what the game is about.'"

"The Yaz Song," radio humorist Jess Cain's ditty, became the summer's refrain as the slugger defied the game's laws of probability. "I was in the zone," Yaz recalled decades later. "You usually stay in it for 10 days, but I was in it for a month."

As the season came down to its final week, the Sox still were very much in the chase with Minnesota, Detroit, and Chicago. The standings shuffled by the hour. "You were in first place or fourth, depending on the time of day," said Williams.

Scoreboard-watching became an obsession, particularly in the home dugout. "At Fenway we had the best way of keeping score—the guy in the Wall," ace pitcher Jim Lonborg noted. "You would see that number disappear and wait for the next one to come up. It wasn't like it was being blurted out on a Jumbotron."

Even the improbable numbers worked for Boston in the last few days. After the club was beaten, 6-3 and 6-0, by Cleveland at home, the players figured they were out of the race. "We thought it was over," conceded Yastrzemski. "Everyone was saying, 'Well, we had a great year.'"

But when the Twins lost at home to the Angels that same day and the Athletics swept the White Sox in a doubleheader, the Red Sox realized they were still alive, tied with the Tigers and only a game behind Minnesota, with the Twins coming to town for the final two games. "We got up the next morning and said, 'You know, we still have a chance,'" Yastrzemski said.

What the hosts needed was for Detroit to lose two of its four at home to the Angels while Boston took both games from a Minnesota club that had beaten them in 11 of 16 meetings and that had aces Jim Kaat and Dean Chance scheduled to pitch. The Sox won the first meeting, 6-4, on a three-run homer by Yastrzemski, and then pinned their hopes on the gentlemanly and scholarly Stanford grad who'd won 21 games for them.

"This is the first big game of my life," Lonborg mused Saturday evening. "I haven't seen a big one until tomorrow. Never." To prepare for it, he borrowed teammate Harrelson's room at the Sheraton-Boston and fell asleep reading *The Fall of Japan*.

After such an enchanted campaign, it was inconceivable that the finale would be without drama or quirkiness. With his team trailing, 2-0, in the sixth, Lonborg began the comeback with a leadoff bunt that ignited a five-run rally marked by a two-run single by Yastrzemski, two wild pitches, and an error. With victory imminent, Fenway organist John Kiley played "The Night They Invented Champagne" and after Rich Rollins popped up to Petrocelli to end things, Fenway erupted in joyous disbelief. As youngsters tried to scale the backstop screen, the crowd rushed the diamond and hoisted Lonborg atop its shaky shoulders on a hero's ride, ripping off parts of his uniform for souvenirs.

Since Detroit had won the opener of its doubleheader,

Carl Yastrzemski launched a three-run homer off Minnesota Twins pitcher Jim Merritt in the seventh inning of the penultimate game of the 1967 season. The Sox won their first pennant in 21 years the next day.

YAZ MANAGED TO OUTLAST HIS DREAM SEASON

BY BOB RYAN

"Tris Speaker may have done it, or Duffy Lewis, or some other Red Sox giant of long ago, but Ted Williams didn't, nor Jimmie Foxx. If any player in baseball history ever had a two-week clutch production to equal Carl Yastrzemski's, let the historians bring him forth."

—Harold Kaese

Most baseball careers are measured in years. Carl Yastrzemski's was measured in epochs. He was in left field the day Roger Maris hit his 61st homer in 1961. He was still playing the day *M*A*S*H* aired its final episode in 1983 (not that there was much chance he had ever heard of Hawkeye Pierce).

No one has ever played as long for one team, and one team only, as Carl Yastrzemski. He is one of the select few with 3,000 hits and 400 home runs. He was handed the thankless task of replacing Ted Williams in left field in 1961, and by the time he retired 22 years later, he had found a way to create his own distinct legend.

But perhaps Yastrzemski's most significant achievement was that he managed to overcome the bizarre handicap of having that one transcendent season. He could have been Orson Welles, never able to top *Citizen Kane*. He could have been Don McLean, still waiting for the appropriate follow-up to "American Pie." He could have let 1967 engulf him, but in due time, he allowed it to define him.

1967. If you weren't there, you'll just never know. You won't understand what Boston was like, when every night in June, July, August, and September you could follow every pitch with Ken Coleman and Ned Martin from stoplight to stoplight and front porch to front porch and business to business, because the entire city was recaptured by baseball and the Red Sox, thanks to Yaz and his teammates. Before Yaz won the Triple Crown in 1967, before the Impossible Dream season, you could pretty much have any Fenway seat you wanted at any time.

In 1967, Carl Yastrzemski showed us what grace and determination under athletic pressure could produce, and while he never again had an all-around season like that, neither has anyone else. With his bat, glove, arm, and will, he personified the idea of the Most Valuable Player.

Hyperbole? OK, you judge. In the final 12 games of a sizzling four-team pennant race, Yaz was 23 for 44 (.523), with five homers, 16 RBI, and 14 runs scored. Throw in the Gold Glove Award and underline the 7 for 8 hitting in the final two games of the season, and then put the exclamation point on the performance by throwing out Bob Allison trying to stretch a single to squelch an eighth-inning Minnesota rally on the season's final day. In the ensuing years, we have not seen a more valuable Most Valuable Player.

Manager Billy Herman told him after the 1966 season, "You can't be a leader the way you played this year. You can be a great ballplayer if you'll work at it."

Yaz hired a Hungarian immigrant fitness trainer named Gene Berde and said, "I'm yours." No baseball player had ever done such a thing. He reported to training camp with a new body and a new sense of purpose in 1967 to play for Dick Williams, a new, energetic, no-nonsense manager. But as heroic as Yaz was in leading the Sox to the pennant, he could not win the World Series all by himself. He certainly did his part, batting .400 with three home runs, but the Sox lost in seven games to Bob Gibson and the St. Louis Cardinals.

Yaz would go on to have good years, but never anything like 1967. What he did was last long enough at a high enough level to construct a new image, that of the ultimate grinder. His toughness, his consistency, and his unmatched work capacity—along with that unforgettable 1967 campaign—remain his legacy.

the celebration in the clubhouse was exuberant yet restrained as the Sox drank beer and smeared each other with shaving cream. If the Tigers won the nightcap, there would be a one-game playoff at Detroit for the pennant.

So the players waited several more hours, listening to the play-by-play from Michigan. "For us to be sitting around a radio instead of a TV, it reminded me of an old-time movie where you were listening for news of some important event," Lonborg said. When the Tigers grounded into a double play with the tying run at the plate to complete an 8-5 loss, Williams leaped up. "It's over, it's over," the skipper proclaimed. "It's unbelievable!"

Now it was time for champagne and tears. "This is the happiest moment of my life," declared Yawkey as he sipped Great Western from a paper cup, relishing the end of two desiccated decades. "THE SMELL OF THE PENNANT . . . THE ROAR OF THE CROWD" declared the headline on the front page of Monday's *Globe*.

Just getting to the World Series was such a miracle that few fans had time to ponder the upcoming challenge—the formidable St. Louis Cardinals club of Lou Brock, and Bob Gibson, Curt Flood, and Orlando Cepeda that had won the National League flag by a mile over the San Francisco Giants. Gibson, its glaring ace, had missed nearly two months after his right leg was broken by a line drive in July, but he was overpowering in the opener at Fenway, yielding only a solo homer to counterpart Jose Santiago in the third inning while holding hitless Yastrzemski, Petro-

celli, and Harrelson, all of whom took batting practice after the 2-1 loss.

Yastrzemski responded with two homers and four RBI the next day, but his team needed just the bare minimum as Lonborg befuddled the Cardinals, taking a perfect game into the seventh inning and coming within four outs of a no-hitter before Julian Javier smacked a double, in a 5-0 whitewash. "I hope we can end the Series on Monday," Williams said with brash optimism.

On Monday, though, his club was teetering on the edge of extinction after St. Louis had administered 5-2 and 6-0 tutorials at Busch Stadium. It was left to Lonborg to bring the Sox back home alive and he delivered with a 3-1 decision. "Same lineup, same result," Williams decreed for the sixth game in Boston. But his pitching choice was startling. Gary Waslewski had started only four games all season and had been sent down twice to the minors.

Nobody with that little experience had ever been tapped for a decisive World Series game, but Waslewski performed superbly until the sixth inning and Boston hitters worked over eight St. Louis hurlers. The Sox set a post-season record with three homers in the fourth as Yastrzemski, Reggie Smith, and Petrocelli chased starter Dick Hughes. Boston then broke things up with four more runs in the seventh for an 8-4 triumph.

The outfield wall got a thorough scraping in March 1968.

REMEMBERING TONY C

Mike Higgins, the general manager, thought he was too young. But Johnny Pesky, the manager, had already seen enough of Tony Conigliaro in spring training in Arizona in 1964 to know he had a natural power hitter in camp, and he brought him up to stay at age 19.

On Opening Day at Fenway Park that season, Conigliaro, a year out of St. Mary's High School of Lynn, Massachusetts, stepped to the plate and in his first at-bat unloaded a home run off White Sox pitcher Joel Horlen.

Conigliaro went on to become the youngest American League player to reach the 100-homer mark, and the youngest ever to lead the majors in homers (with 32 in 1965, at age 20). At the height of his popularity, the handsome, dark-haired Tony C also did a little singing, and he performed on *The Merv Griffin Show*, among other places.

Conigliaro was hitting .287 with 20 homers and 67 RBI in 1967 as the Red Sox chased their first pennant in 21 years. But on Friday, August 18, at Fenway, his life changed forever. Conigliaro "was never one to back off from an inside pitch," said Pesky, and Tony C was struck in the face by a fastball from Angels pitcher Jack Hamilton.

The ball shattered Conigliaro's cheekbone and cracked the orbital bone encasing his left eye. The impact also severely damaged the retina of his left eye. The beaning was so severe that Conigliaro dropped to the ground face first, bleeding from the nose and eye.

Later, Conigliaro described the impact: "His first pitch came in tight. I jumped back and my helmet flew off. There was this tremendous ringing noise. I couldn't stand it. . . . I kept saying to myself, 'Oh, God, let me breathe.' I didn't think about my future in baseball. I just wanted to stay alive."

Conigliaro sat out the entire 1968 season, and after two comeback attempts, he retired in 1975 at age 30. Teammate Rico Petrocelli remembered the comebacks, the first of which produced a remarkable 36-homer, 116-RBI season in 1970, before Conigliaro was traded to the Angels.

"He wouldn't quit. He made the greatest comeback, I think, in the history of baseball. He was the most courageous player I ever saw," said Petrocelli.

Tony C remained a popular figure in Greater Boston, running a nightclub with his brother Billy, who had also played for the Red Sox. While he was being driven to the airport by his brother on January 3, 1982, Conigliaro suffered a massive heart attack; his heart stopped for several minutes, and he suffered a stroke and lapsed into a coma.

Conigliaro remained in a vegetative state until his death on February 24, 1990. He was 45 years old.

The Tony Conigliaro Memorial Award is presented annually by the Boston Baseball Writers Association to the major-league player who has overcome adversity with the spirit and courage demonstrated by Conigliaro.

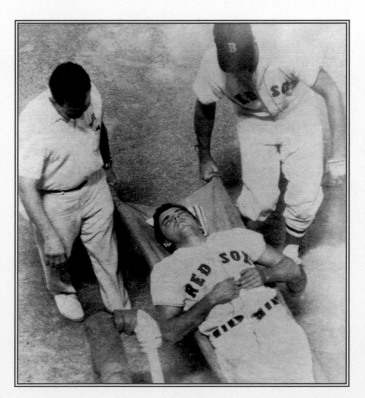
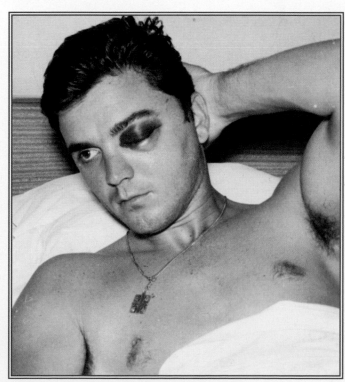

On August 18, 1967, Tony Conigliaro's life changed forever when he was struck in the face by a pitch from the Angels' Jack Hamilton. "Tony C" had led the league in home runs in 1965 with 32, at age 20 the youngest to do so at the time. His injuries from the beaning kept him out of baseball for almost two years, and after two comeback bids, he retired from the game in 1975.

ABOVE: Fenway has played host to lots of soccer matches. In this 1968 contest, Ruben Sosa (17) of the North American Soccer League's Boston Beacons fired on Chicago Mustangs goalkeeper Gerd Langer.

LEFT: Nuns' Day, which was a park tradition in the '60s, brought an added dimension to the term "Fenway faithful." Boston Archbishop Richard Cardinal Cushing (seated) was often in attendance.

"Lonborg and champagne," Williams predicted for the finale even though his ace would be dueling Gibson on two days' rest. "CINDERELLA TRIES ON THE SLIPPER," read the *Globe* headline on the morning of Game 7 as all of New England anticipated a fairy-tale finish. "This is a story that has to have a happy ending," Kaese declared. If the Sox lose "it will be the wolf gobbling up Little Red Riding Hood."

The wolf licked its chops.

The Sox couldn't solve Gibson, who struck out 10 and hit a homer off the depleted Lonborg, who departed after six innings with St. Louis leading by six runs. "Lonborg and champagne, hey!" the Cardinals chanted in the clubhouse after they'd claimed their second world championship in four years by a 7-2 count. "Now it's our turn to pop off," shouted outfielder Flood as he pried open a bottle of Mumm's. "Pop this."

As the club packed for the winter, hundreds of Red Sox fans lingered in their seats, unwilling to let go of the most enthralling season of their lives. "The laurels all are cut, the year draws in the day, and we'll to the Fens no more," Roger Angell wrote in his *New Yorker* account.

While the Dead Sox days were over, it would be another eight years before the Sox suited up for a playoff game.

Even before the club convened for spring training in 1968, the chances for a reprise had lessened markedly when Lonborg tore up his knee skiing at Lake Tahoe before Christmas. That was the prelude to a procession of problems that sabotaged the season. Lonborg returned, but posted a losing record. Santiago hurt his arm and never won another game. Scott saw his average plummet from .303 to .171 and failed to hit a homer at Fenway. And Conigliaro's comeback bid ended before it began, undone by blurred vision.

The Sox, who never were in first place after Opening Day, were out of contention by Flag Day. "We'll win it next year," declared Yastrzemski, after Boston had finished fourth, 17 games behind the Tigers. "There's no doubt in my mind about that."

When Conigliaro smashed a two-run homer and scored the winning run in the 12th inning of the opener at Baltimore in 1969, Boston fans saw it as a harbinger of a restoration. But nobody that year was going to catch the Orioles, who won 109 games and claimed the East Division in the first season of baseball's four-division format. When Boston slipped from second to third in August, player discontent grew with Williams and his whip-hand ways. The friction peaked in Oakland when the skipper yanked Yastrzemski after the first inning for not hustling, bawled him out, and fined him $500.

With nine games to go in the season, Yawkey dumped Williams, who went on to win two championships with Oakland and be enshrined in the Hall of Fame. Memories of the Impossible Dream had been soured by an irremediable dyspepsia. "The days of wine and roses didn't last long, which should have been predictable," *Globe* columnist Ray Fitzgerald mused. ⚾

JUNE 26
Earl Wilson pitches a no-hitter against the Angels, becoming the first black pitcher to accomplish the feat in the American League. He also hits a home run to win the game, 2-0.

AUGUST 1
Bill Monbouquette throws a no-hitter against the White Sox, making it the first time that two Boston pitchers had managed that feat in the same season since 1916.

OCTOBER 6
Pinky Higgins steps down as Red Sox manager but remains as general manager. Johnny Pesky becomes manager.

APRIL 11
Carl Yastrzemski makes his major-league debut at Fenway Park, going 1 for 5 with a single as the Sox lose the season opener, 5-2, to the Athletics.

JULY 31
The All-Star Game at Fenway ends in a 1-1 tie.

OCTOBER 11
The Boston Patriots play their first game at Fenway Park, beating the Oakland Raiders 20-14. Among the game highlights: Babe Parilli throws two touchdown passes, Gino Cappelletti kicks two field goals, and the Patriots' defense forces five turnovers.

APRIL 17
In his first at-bat at Fenway Park, 19-year-old Tony Conigliaro hits a home run over the left-field wall on Opening Day to help Boston beat Chicago, 4-1.

OCTOBER 1
Just 306 people, the smallest crowd in Fenway Park history, watch the Red Sox beat the Indians, 4-2.

OCTOBER 2
Johnny Pesky is fired with two games remaining in the season; Billy Herman becomes manager.

1960   1961   1962   1963   1964

JUNE 8
Manager Billy Jurges leaves the team; Del Baker takes over briefly until Pinky Higgins returns as manager on June 12.

SEPTEMBER 28
Ted Williams ends his MLB career by slugging a home run—his 521st—into the Red Sox bullpen in his last at-bat. The classic John Updike essay "Hub Fans Bid Kid Adieu," chronicles the event.

DECEMBER 20
The Patriots play the Buffalo Bills after a surprise snowstorm at Fenway for the AFL's Eastern Division championship. Bills win, 24-14.

Top of page (l-r): Manager Dick Williams getting a shower after the Red Sox win the 1967 pennant; Boston Globe coverage of the pennant win; Senator Eugene McCarthy campaigning for president at Fenway Park, 1968. Timeline: Ted Williams bowing out as a player, 1960; Carl Yastrzemski warming up, 1961; catcher Bob Tillman congratulating pitcher Earl Wilson on his 1962 no-hitter; Yaz hitting a home run in Game 6 of the 1967 World Series; pitchers Jim Lonborg, Dick Ellsworth, and Ray Culp, 1969.

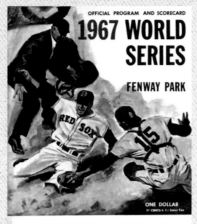

OFFICIAL PROGRAM AND SCORECARD

1967 WORLD SERIES

FENWAY PARK

ONE DOLLAR

BOSTON **RED SOX** ST. LOUIS **CARDINALS**

AUGUST 18
Tony Conigliaro is knocked unconscious by a pitch at Fenway.

AUGUST 20
Reggie Smith becomes the first Red Sox player to hit home runs from both sides of the plate in a single game as Boston wins, 12-2, against the Angels.

OCTOBER 1
In what comes to be called the Impossible Dream, the Red Sox secure a tie for the American League title with a 5-3 victory over the Twins at Fenway Park, then celebrate winning the AL pennant when the Detroit Tigers lose.

JUNE 28
Professional wrestling good guy Bruno Sammartino wallops villainous Killer Kowalski before a reported 17,000 "screaming, chanting, hollering" fans in Fenway's first wrestling carnival since the 1930s.

SEPTEMBER 23
Manager Dick Williams is fired, with nine games to go in the season, and Eddie Popowski is named interim manager.

OCTOBER 2
Eddie Kasko is named manager.

SEPTEMBER 16
Dave Morehead no-hits Cleveland. During the game, Pinky Higgins is fired as general manager and later replaced by Dick O'Connell.

SEPTEMBER 8
Manager Billy Herman is fired; Pete Runnels is named interim manager.

SEPTEMBER 28
Dick Williams is hired as manager.

FULL SEASON
Fenway Park serves as home field for the North American Soccer League's Boston Beacons during their 1968 season.

1965 1966 1967 1968 1969

OCTOBER 5
In Game 2 of the World Series, Jim Lonborg pitches a one-hitter—just the fourth in Series history—leading the Sox to a 5-0 win over the St. Louis Cardinals.

OCTOBER 12 The Impossible Dream season ends as Boston loses the seventh game of the World Series, 7-2, at Fenway Park.

NOVEMBER 15
Triple Crown winner Carl Yastrzemski gets the American League Most Valuable Player award. Jim Lonborg wins the AL Cy Young Award with a 22-9 record.

1970s

It is one of the most famous images in all of sports: Carlton Fisk willing (and waving) his fly ball to stay fair for a walk-off home run in Game 6 of the 1975 World Series.

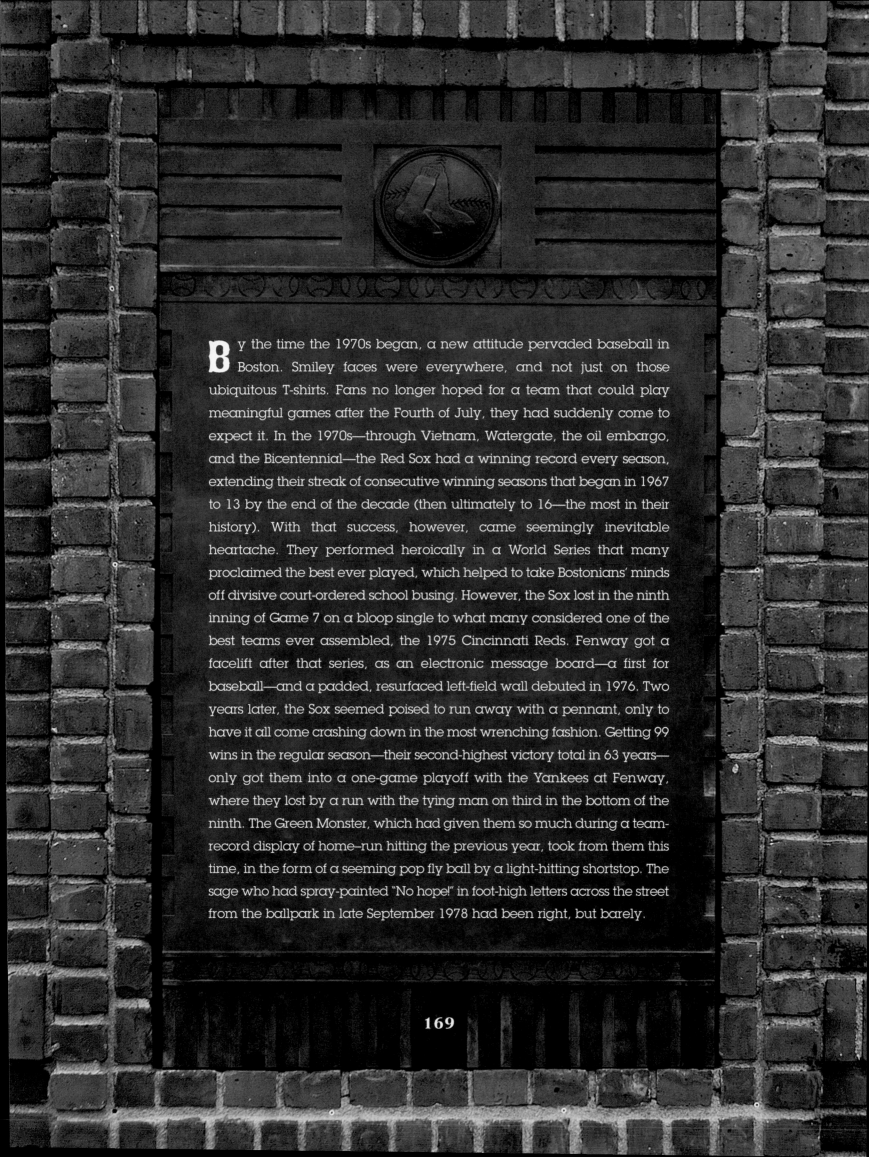

By the time the 1970s began, a new attitude pervaded baseball in Boston. Smiley faces were everywhere, and not just on those ubiquitous T-shirts. Fans no longer hoped for a team that could play meaningful games after the Fourth of July, they had suddenly come to expect it. In the 1970s—through Vietnam, Watergate, the oil embargo, and the Bicentennial—the Red Sox had a winning record every season, extending their streak of consecutive winning seasons that began in 1967 to 13 by the end of the decade (then ultimately to 16—the most in their history). With that success, however, came seemingly inevitable heartache. They performed heroically in a World Series that many proclaimed the best ever played, which helped to take Bostonians' minds off divisive court-ordered school busing. However, the Sox lost in the ninth inning of Game 7 on a bloop single to what many considered one of the best teams ever assembled, the 1975 Cincinnati Reds. Fenway got a facelift after that series, as an electronic message board—a first for baseball—and a padded, resurfaced left-field wall debuted in 1976. Two years later, the Sox seemed poised to run away with a pennant, only to have it all come crashing down in the most wrenching fashion. Getting 99 wins in the regular season—their second-highest victory total in 63 years— only got them into a one-game playoff with the Yankees at Fenway, where they lost by a run with the tying man on third in the bottom of the ninth. The Green Monster, which had given them so much during a team-record display of home-run hitting the previous year, took from them this time, in the form of a seeming pop fly ball by a light-hitting shortstop. The sage who had spray-painted "No hope!" in foot-high letters across the street from the ballpark in late September 1978 had been right, but barely.

ABOVE: Manager Eddie Kasko had a few words for his team in the clubhouse on April 5, 1973.

RIGHT: A vendor sold popcorn and ice cream on Van Ness Street outside Fenway Park in August 1974.

After his vocal and volatile predecessor, the bespectacled Eddie Kasko seemed decidedly buttoned-down and dialed-back. But the new Red Sox manager was not averse to the occasional outburst if provoked. "I've been known to throw furniture around," he said. Since most of the key members of the 1967 squad still were in place, the clubhouse mood was optimistic going into the 1970 season. "We'll win the pennant," Carl Yastrzemski declared during spring training.

They did win the opener at New York. But the Sox never spent another day in first place. After they went 9-17 in May, they were stuck in fifth. The low point came on June 25 when the club lost, 13-8, to Baltimore in 14 innings at home, despite having led, 7-0. They gave up six runs with none out in the final inning. Before long even Yastrzemski, the team's only All-Star starter, was being booed at Fenway.

Kasko's Mr. Chips mien was fraying, too. One day in Anaheim, he stormed into the press box after the organist had played "Tiptoe Through the Tulips" during one of his mound visits.

"We need players," general manager Dick O'Connell told Tom Yawkey in the press room one August evening when the Sox were stuck in fourth. "We've only got eight players."

"We do?" the owner replied. "Who are they?"

After Boston finished almost exactly as it had in 1969—21 games behind in third place, with an 87-75 record—changes were inevitable. The most startling was a trade that sent Tony Conigliaro, who had led the team in RBI the previous season, to the Angels for three players. "Honest, I never thought I'd be traded. [I thought] that being a hometown boy meant something," said Conigliaro, who'd spent all of his previous seven major-league seasons in Boston.

Mike Andrews was shipped out, too, dealt to the White Sox for Luis Aparicio. "The fans want a winner and I think we've got one now," Kasko declared before the 1971 season. The club was in first place by the end of April, and won 13 of 15 in late April and early May, putting them up by four games. But the Memorial Day weekend was fol-

THE SPACEMAN COMETH

William Francis Lee once told Bowie Kuhn, the commissioner of baseball, that he sprinkled marijuana on his pancakes. Lee was an outspoken nonconformist who famously called his Red Sox manager, Don Zimmer, a gerbil. He jogged five miles to the park on the days he was scheduled to pitch, and he once staged a 24-hour walkout when the Red Sox released friend and teammate Bernie Carbo. He said, "Baseball's a very simple game. All you have to do is sit on your butt, spit tobacco, and nod at the stupid things your manager says."

Lee also won 119 games over his 13-year career, appearing in the most games ever by a Sox left-hander (321), and recording the third-most victories (94) by a Sox lefty.

Lee won 17 games in three consecutive seasons for the Red Sox and started two games in the 1975 World Series. Lee's loathing for the Yankees endeared him to Sox fans. In 1976, a collision at home plate resulted in a bench-clearing brawl and Yankee third baseman Graig Nettles threw Lee to the ground in the melee. After the game, Lee called Yankee manager Billy Martin "a Nazi" and the team "Steinbrenner's Brown Shirts." Lee missed two months with torn ligaments in his shoulder.

For much of his time in Boston, Lee also feuded with Zimmer, as Lee's attitude and lack of respect for authority clashed with Zimmer's old-school personality. Zimmer relegated Lee to the bullpen, and at the end of 1978, the Sox traded Lee to the Montreal Expos for Stan Papi, a utility infielder. The furious Lee bade farewell to the Red Sox by saying, "Who wants to be with a team that will go down in history alongside the '64 Phillies and the '67 Arabs?" Lee went on to win 16 games for the Expos in 1979, but the team tired of his antics as well, releasing him in 1982 after he staged a one-game walkout over the release of infielder Rodney Scott.

As *Globe* columnist Ray Fitzgerald once said, "He marches to a drummer no one else would let into the ballpark."

As for himself, Lee said he was either long before or long after his time. He tried to keep the game in perspective. "I think about the cosmic snowball theory," Lee explained. "A few million years from now, the sun will burn out and lose its gravitational pull. The earth will turn into a giant snowball and be hurled through space. When that happens it won't matter if I get this guy out."

Bill Lee and young fan Tammy Patterson surveyed a pumpkin carved in the likeness of Luis Tiant.

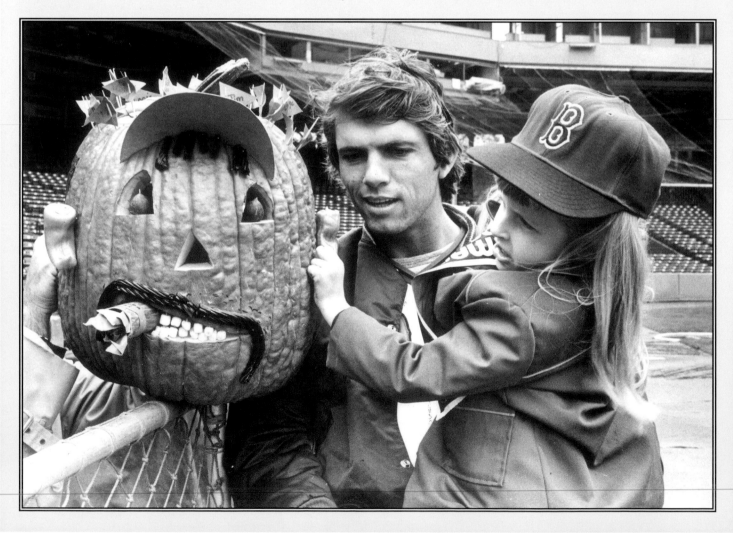

lowed by a slump in which they dropped 11 of their next 14 outings to fall five games off the pace. A lifeless 6-1 loss at New York in early June prompted Kasko to close the clubhouse door and upbraid his underperforming crew. "I'm sick of watching guys hang their heads around here just because we're in a rut," he barked.

Still, the Sox lost to the Royals for the fifth straight time in mid-June, and slipped into third place. They never regained the lead, finishing 18 games behind Baltimore. That gave management the green light to clean house and by the time the team convened for spring training in 1972, only four players remained from the Impossible Dream team.

The biggest part of the exodus came with a 10-player deal that sent six Boston players, most notably Jim Lonborg and George Scott and Billy Conigliaro (younger brother to Tony), to Milwaukee. "I'm sick of listening to some of those people," said general manager Dick O'Connell, who'd been annoyed by clubhouse grumbling.

When the season started, Tommy Harper was in center, Danny Cater at first and imposing rookie Carlton Fisk behind the plate. It took until late summer for the new group to coalesce and after losing 10 of their first 14 games, the Sox were buried in fourth place and had slipped to fifth as June was coming to an end. But as the pitching improved with Luis Tiant and Marty Pattin, Boston won 19 of its next 25, including a dozen in a row at Fenway.

The midsummer run peaked with two extra-inning home victories over the Athletics, both wins coming from Oakland miscues. After A's skipper Dick Williams intentionally (and inexplicably) had Doug Griffin walked to load the bases in the 11th inning so that Darold Knowles could face Yastrzemski, his pitcher walked in the winning run to give Boston a doubleheader sweep. The next night, with 1967 notable Gary Waslewski on the mound for Oakland in the 14th inning, Yastrzemski bounced a grounder off the glove of A's third baseman Sal Bando to score Griffin from first base.

By Labor Day, the Sox had taken over first place, beating the Yankees, 10-4, on three-run homers by Harper and Rico Petrocelli as the fans chanted "We're Number One!" The season came down to a three-game series on the final weekend in Detroit after the Tigers had swept the Brewers (bashing ex-Sox Lonborg in the opener). "I wish the Red Sox a lot of luck and hope they win," said former Sox teammate Joe Lahoud after Detroit had run up a 30-10 aggregate

Fans scaled a billboard to peer into Fenway Park in 1971.

on Milwaukee over three games. "But God help them."

Boston needed divine intervention after losing, 4-1, in the series opener against the Tigers. Beating Tigers ace Mickey Lolich, who posted 15 strikeouts, would have been challenging enough. But the Sox literally tripped over themselves as Aparicio, who would have scored the lead run, stumbled rounding third on Yastrzemski's third-inning double in a painful reprise of his Opening Day pratfall at Tiger Stadium that cost the club a victory. "I stepped on top of the bag instead of the corner and then I hit a soft spot on the grass," said Aparicio, who gashed his right knee with his left foot when he went down. "How dumb can I be, spiking myself?" he groaned.

Yet it was Yastrzemski who made the killer mistake, steaming toward third without noticing that his teammate had gone down and that Eddie Popowski had called Aparicio back to the bag. "There was no way then to hold Yaz to second," the third-base coach said after Yastrzemski had been tagged out. When the Tigers finished them off the next day, some Sox players wept in the clubhouse. "You came a long way and have nothing to be ashamed of," Kasko told them.

Had Boston not given up so much ground in the early going, the season might not have come down to an untimely slip. "I told Haywood Sullivan I didn't want to come to Boston next June and find the team eight or nine games back," Yawkey said. "We've tried that too often."

The 1973 season started sublimely, as the Sox swept the Yankees at Fenway for the first time in an opening series since 1933. "Ah, Tiant et Fisk et Yaz, quisque cum clangore epico ballatorum ex Iliade," *Globe* columnist George Frazier exulted in Latin after the Tibialibus Rubris had clobbered Eboracum Novum by a count of XV-V.

The introduction of the designated hitter provided added oomph to a Sox lineup that needed more production, with Orlando Cepeda clouting the winning homer in the ninth inning of the third game. "I see about 15 guys at home plate," marveled Cepeda, who'd been signed as a free agent. "It looks like the World Series kind of homer."

But the early euphoria vanished when Boston dropped four to Detroit at home. By the beginning of May, the club was stuck in sixth place and didn't get above .500 until late June. Though four victories in New York in early July moved the Sox from fifth place to third, even an eight-game winning streak in mid-August made up no ground on the runaway Orioles, and Boston ended up eight games in arrears.

That was enough to get rid of Kasko, who was dismissed before the final day of the season and never managed again. "We are the ones who let him down," said pitcher

RAY, LITTLE STEVIE AND ALL THAT JAZZ

On July 27 and 28 of 1973, the famed Newport Jazz Festival came to Boston. Not only that, it came to Fenway Park for two shows, with a stage set up near second base and a portion of the ballpark's seats cordoned off. Attendance was reported as 14,000 for the first night, and 21,500 for the second night of the festival, which is traditionally held in Newport's Fort Adams State Park. Concertgoers were both fascinated and disoriented. The *Globe*'s Ernie Santosuosso admitted that "even I kept casting instinctive glances toward the board for out-of-town scores."

Globe reporter William Buchanan covered the first night's five-hour-plus performances, and he was obviously unaccustomed to the ballpark comforts. "All due respect to you, Mr. Yawkey," he wrote, "those Fenway seats could test the mightiest of Spartans after an hour or two."

The featured artists on Friday were Freddie Hubbard, Billy Paul, War, Herbie Mann, the Staples Singers, and Ray Charles. Not a bad lineup for a ballpark concert, although some fans were irate when it turned out that they had bought counterfeit tickets from scalpers, while, Buchanan noted, "There is still an obvious problem with pickpockets [outside the ballpark]. Youthful teams of two or three would jostle an unsuspecting fan and woosh, the wallet is gone." Inside the park, he noted, "Boston police were polite but firm, and that made for a generally relaxed feeling."

Among the highlights were: Paul's "Me and Mrs. Jones," which had won him a Grammy Award earlier in the year; War's 50-minute set, and the "musical and spiritual togetherness" it inspired; and Charles's "What'd I Say," though Buchanan noted that the lineup of backup singers to Charles, known as the Raelettes, was "a bit weak."

The second night's lineup included B. B. King (in a silver-gray suit and accompanied by a nine-piece band), Stevie Wonder and Donnie Hathaway, plus Charles Mingus and Roland Kirk. During Hathaway's set, according to the *Globe*'s Ray Murphy, "hundreds streamed onto the Fenway infield, but they finally returned to their seats after the earnest pleading of Hathaway himself."

John Curtis. "I can't look at this season and say we gave it our best shot."

With the new manager (and former Pawtucket skipper), Darrell Johnson, preaching defense and equality ("All of us have the same rules, nothing special for anyone"), the Sox remained near the top of the standings in 1974, moving into first place on May 22 after bashing the Yankees, 14-6 and 6-3, at Fenway and staying there for most of the summer even without Fisk, who tore knee ligaments in a home-plate crash in Cleveland at the end of June. "We're no longer a team that waits for something to happen," declared Yastrzemski. "Over 162 games, this is going to be a better team."

But as the bats lost their pop, Boston began losing ground and fell out of first place with a home loss to New York in September. When the club was starved, 1-0, in both ends of the Labor Day doubleheader in Baltimore with aces Luis Tiant and Bill Lee on the mound, the slippage began in earnest. The Sox soon fell out of first after losing to the

Luis Aparicio, a Hall of Fame shortstop who played three seasons with the Red Sox, turned this double play on September 27, 1972.

Yankees and ended up dropping 16 of 21 games. When the soaring Orioles took two of three in their next series at Fenway, bashing Sox hurler Reggie Cleveland, 7-2, in the finale, a young man rose behind the home dugout in the ninth inning, put a bugle to his lips, and played "Taps." "We're going to have to win almost every game now," acknowledged Johnson.

When the end came, with barely 5,000 witnesses rattling around the Fenway stands for a date with the Indians, the Sox were seven games out, finishing third behind Baltimore and New York. "Well, to say that I'm not disappointed would make me a damn liar," said Yawkey as he prepared to head to his South Carolina plantation for the winter.

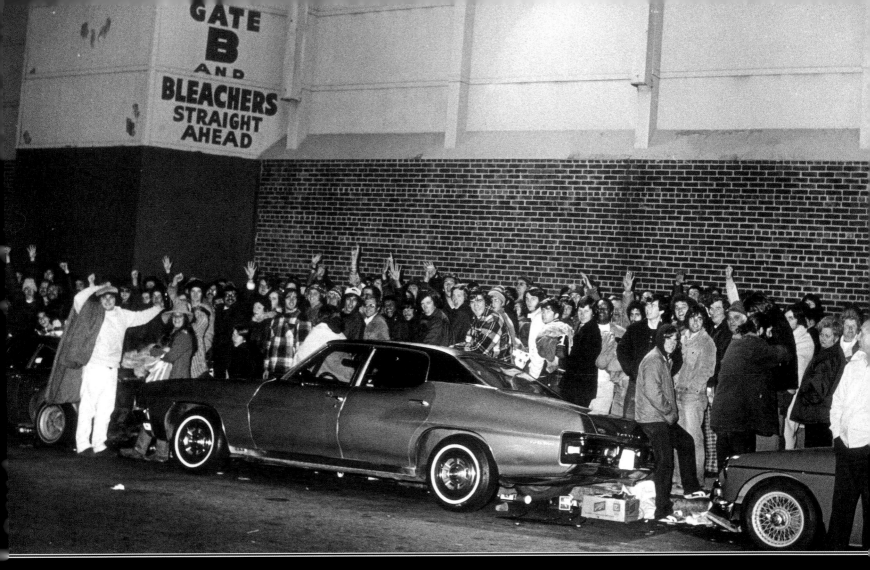

LEFT: A hot dog vendor on Lansdowne Street awaiting the game-day bleacher crowd in August 1975.

ABOVE: The prospect of World Series tickets prompted crowds to camp out all night in October 1975.

BELOW: Fans awaited the sale of bleacher seats for Red Sox-Yankees games in June of 1978.

JOE MOONEY: SPLENDOR IN THE GRASS

From 1971 to 2000, Joe Mooney was the keeper of the greensward, the man behind the meticulously manicured Kentucky bluegrass at Fenway Park that always leaves first-time visitors—not to mention some frequent attendees—agape. As the head groundskeeper for the Red Sox for some 30 years, he liked to point out that his career in baseball stretched from Schilling to Schilling—Chuck to Curt.

"I worked for the minor-league team in Minneapolis in the late 1950s and used to pitch batting practice to [former Red Sox] Chuck Schilling and Carl Yastrzemski," said Mooney.

A native of Dunmore, Pennsylvania, Mooney worked at Red Sox minor-league parks in Louisville, San Francisco, and Minnesota before he broke ranks and went to work in Washington, D.C. There he kept up D.C. Stadium (later renamed RFK Stadium) for professional teams that featured a pair of legendary coaches. Former Red Sox legend Ted Williams managed the Washington Senators at the time, and Vince Lombardi then coached the Washington Redskins.

"Imagine working for those two guys," said Mooney. "It didn't come any better than that."

Mooney also credits Williams for helping him land his job with the Red Sox. He had spent much of his 10-year stint in D.C. improving a poorly designed field, and Fenway was in need of an overhaul as well.

"They had tried out a different grass—rye, I think—that couldn't take the gaff, and they had a lot of fungus," he recalled. Mooney solved the Fenway woes and transformed the park into a dazzling beauty. Ask Yaz, who patrolled left field and first base while Mooney groomed the grounds: "Fenway is the best there is, at least since Joe Mooney started working on it."

Mooney was known to throw interlopers off his field, regardless of their title or temperament. His customary explanation was this: "You walk on grass too much, it gets beat up."

In 2001, Mooney ceded control of the field to Dave Mellor while he continued to supervise maintenance of much of the rest of the park. In the winter of 2004, the Fenway drainage system was renovated, leaving Mooney shaking his head.

"When I came here, we had three drainage pipes; now there will be 50," he said. Even for groundskeepers, "it's a different game."

"Why? Why should the bond between a people and their baseball team be so intense? Fenway Park is a part of it, offering a physical continuum to the bond, not only because Papi can stand in the same batter's box as Teddy Ballgame, but also because a son might sit in the same wooden-slat seat as his father."

—Tom Verducci, sportswriter

But Yawkey, who'd been the club's spiritual 26th player for four decades, was exuberant a year later as his club won the pennant for the first time since 1967 and went on to face the Reds in a World Series that featured the most dramatic game in postseason history.

Nobody would have predicted it after Boston had lollygagged its way through a listless spring training that prompted Yastrzemski to rip into his teammates in a closed-door meeting before the April 8 opener with the Brewers. "The worst attitude I ever saw," the captain railed. "If it keeps up, we'll finish in last place."

That opener featured Hank Aaron making his American League debut after 21 years with the Braves, and Tony Conigliaro coming back as a designated hitter for the Sox after three-and-a-half years away from the game while his injured eye healed, Fenway was awash in emotion, especially when the once-favorite son singled in his first at-bat. "The ball looked like a basketball," he said following his team's 5-2 victory. "That's what counts."

While Conigliaro's renaissance lasted only until June, the town soon was captivated by the Gold Dust twins, rookies Jim Rice and Fred Lynn, who had extraordinary debut seasons, with Lynn hitting .331 with 105 RBI and 21 home runs and Rice hitting .309 with 102 RBI and 22 homers.

With Tiant and Lee anchoring a pitching staff that received career seasons from Rick Wise (19-12) and Roger Moret (14-3), the club took over first place on May 24 after Lee, who'd mocked California's flaccid lineup ("The Angels could take batting practice in the lobby of the Grand Hotel and not bother a chandelier."), blanked them, 6-0, at Fenway. "He popped off and backed it up," conceded Angels manager Dick Williams, whose players had taken batting practice in the Sheraton-Boston lobby that day using Wiffle bats and Nerf balls, until a hotel security guard halted the antics.

Boston soon proved that it was a genuine contender,

winning nine straight at home to take a five-game lead following the All-Star break. For punctuation, Rice smashed a homer off the Royals' Steve Busby that went over the center-field bleachers next to the Fenway flagpole. "I think the ball is on the New Hampshire toll road somewhere," reckoned Busby. After taking beatings of 8-3 and 9-3, the visitors had seen enough. "Get me the hell out of here," growled Royals Manager Jack McKeon.

But Boston's biggest challenge was the Orioles, who'd won 10 of 12. When they came to Fenway for two pivotal games in mid-September, Tiant and Jim Palmer hooked up in a showdown for the ages. "Lou-eee, Lou-eee, Lou-eee," the fans chanted as El Tiante befuddled Baltimore, 2-0, while Petrocelli and Fisk each rocked Palmer for homers. "We hurt them bad," concluded Johnson, whose employers immediately invited fans to mail in applications for playoff tickets. "Sure, they can beat Oakland," Palmer said. "Why not?"

While it was conceivable that Boston could win a postseason series against the Oakland A's, who had won the three previous World Series ("Four In a Row?" *Sports Illustrated* mused in its pre-playoff cover story), nobody was predicting a sweep. But the Sox made the Athletics look like bushers in the Fenway opener as Tiant mesmerized them, conceding three hits across nine innings. "This is Lou-eee's palace," proclaimed Yastrzemski after Boston had punished the visitors with five runs in the seventh inning of a 7-1 rout. "In here, he can do no wrong." And Oakland, which had won its division by seven games over Kansas City, could do no right, committing four errors, three of them on five batted balls in the first inning. "We embarrassed ourselves," admitted A's center fielder Billy North.

Even with Vida Blue, their 22-game winner on the mound, the A's went down again the next day as Boston, sparked by Yastrzemski's two-run homer in the fourth and Petrocelli's leadoff shot off Rollie Fingers in the seventh, came from three runs down to win, 6-3, while the jubilant

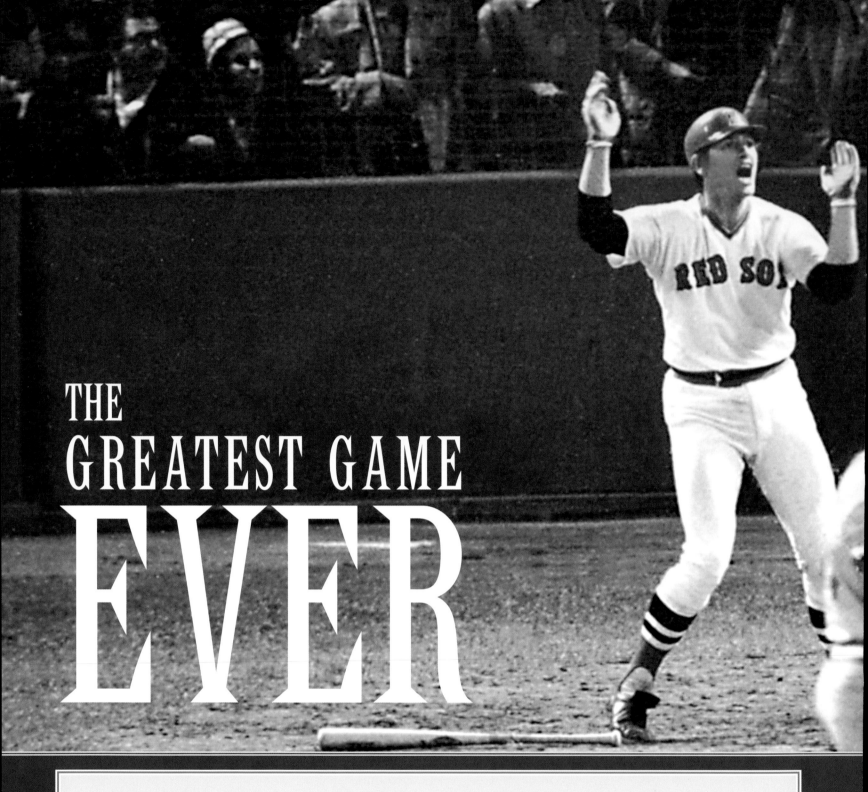

THE GREATEST GAME EVER

It was 1975, Clark Booth recalled in a *Globe* story many years later, and the nightmare of Vietnam had just ended. The country was still shaking off Watergate. In Boston, court-ordered busing had turned neighborhoods into battlegrounds. These were not the best of times. Then along came the Reds, the Red Sox, and Game 6, and we discovered that baseball could still inspire us.

In 1975, the Red Sox came into their first World Series in eight years in a familiar position: although they were not the out-of-nowhere pennant winners of 1967, they were again facing a team that had dominated the National League. In 1967, it had been the 101-win Cardinals; this time, it was the 108-win Reds, and few people gave the Red Sox much of a chance against the "Big Red Machine." They went down to defeat, but the Series went down as possibly the greatest ever played.

By the time Carlton Fisk was urging his dramatic 12th-inning home run fair in Game 6 on October 21, the Red Sox had made believers of much of the nation. And although Game 7 was decided

on a ninth-inning looping single to center field, the Red Sox and Reds had compiled enough highlights to squarely put baseball back into the forefront of American sports fans' collective consciousness, after it had languished behind football for several years.

"If this ain't the national pastime, tell me what is," Reds third baseman Pete Rose asked after Game 6. Rose would go on to be named the Series MVP.

Boston's 7-6 victory in Game 6 was the first home night game in Red Sox postseason history, and it took four hours and almost 12 innings to complete. Each team seemed to have the game won at least once: the Reds were leading, 6-3, with two outs in the eighth before Bernie Carbo hit a dramatic three-run, pinch-hit homer; the Sox had the bases loaded and none out in the ninth inning of a 6-6 game, only to fail to score. The Reds seemed poised to take the lead in the 11th when, with a man on base, Joe Morgan laced a drive over Dwight Evans's head in right field. Evans managed a leaping, lunging catch at the fence, and Boston finally prevailed an inning

later on Fisk's blast off the left-field foul pole, which was officially christened the "Fisk Pole" 30 years later when the Reds visited Fenway Park in June 2005.

Roger Angell of the *The New Yorker* wrote: "What can we say of Game 6 without seeming to diminish it by recapitulation or dull it with detail?"

Fisk remembered telling Fred Lynn going into the 12th inning that he would hit one off the wall and that Lynn, whose earlier home run had given Boston a quick 3-0 lead, should drive him home. Instead, at 34 minutes past midnight, Fisk gave us one of the most oft-replayed clips in sports history, as he leaped, waved, and coaxed his drive off Reds pitcher Pat Darcy fair.

Fisk started down the line, carrying his bat the first few steps. He dropped the bat and started to yell at the ball, "Stay fair! Stay fair!" He never actually ran. He skipped sideways, watching the ball, and then began waving his arms from left to right. The dance was immortalized by a camera inside the left-field wall. (Legend holds that NBC

got the shot because a rat scared the cameraman from his chair and the camera never moved, but the camera trails Fisk's first few steps up the line.) The ball clanged off the foul pole high above the Green Monster, and Reds left fielder George Foster caught the winning home run on the fly as it ricocheted back toward the field. Ballpark organist John Kiley broke into the "Hallelujah Chorus" as Fisk tore around the bases, and in Fisk's hometown of Charlestown, New Hampshire, David Conant—who had known Fisk since the catcher was a baby—rang the bells of the Episcopal church.

Foster kept the Fisk home-run ball at his mother's house in California for the better part of the next 24 years. It sold at an auction in July 1999 for $113,273.

Despite being just 12 outs away from victory in Game 7 on October 22 (the Red Sox held a 3-0 lead as late as the sixth inning), Cincinnati's Big Red Machine won the game and the World Series, both 4-3. The world championship drought in Boston would continue another 29 years.

CLEAN PLATE CLUB?

BY RAY FITZGERALD

May 25, 1975—Carl Yastrzemski, long known as a man of the soil, tried to show Lou DiMuro yesterday at Fenway Park how they plant potatoes on Long Island, but the umpire misread Carl's intentions entirely.

DiMuro had just called Yaz out on a 3-2 pitch that the Red Sox captain judged to be somewhere in Jamaica Plain. Yaz, perhaps thinking that DiMuro should get into another line of business, proceeded to give the umpire a tip on truck farming.

Carl lovingly gathered some Fenway dirt in his hands and spread it over home plate to a depth of, oh, three inches.

He covered the middle and he covered the corners. He was nothing if not thorough.

Then Yaz flipped his batting helmet on the dirt, the way potato farmers always do back in East Hampton to protect their precious crop from grubs, cutworms and the common blight.

As a gracious afterthought, Yaz grabbed Rick Burleson's dark glasses and tossed them in DiMuro's general direction in case there should be a sudden eclipse of the sun.

DiMuro looked upon the heap of dirt not as a back-to-the-earth movement, but as a back-to-the-locker-room invitation.

And that's where he consigned Capt. Yaz. He calmly uncovered home plate with his whisk broom and said, in effect: "To the clubhouse, Euell, and don't forget your pail and shovel."

So Yaz went, to join the already banished Bernie Carbo and Manager Darrell Johnson.

fans gave Oakland owner Charlie Finley a mocking farewell serenade: "So long, Charlie, we hate to see you go!"

Two days later at the Coliseum, the Sox were spraying each other with champagne for the first time in eight years. "I don't know if this stuff feels better when you drink it or have it poured over your head," said Fisk after Boston had closed out the series with a 5-3 decision. Next up were the Reds, who would be playing in their third World Series in six years, but were looking for their first ring since 1940.

Boston's drought was longer by 22 years. But in the wake of an effortless 6-0 victory in the Fenway opener on October 11, a bejeweled ring finally seemed possible. "In the National League we don't face anyone who throws a spinning curve that takes two minutes to come down," observed third baseman Pete Rose after the gyrating Tiant had twisted them into knots, and then touched off a killer six-run seventh with a single off a misplaced Don Gullett changeup.

The Sox came tantalizingly close to winning Game 2, carrying a 2-1 lead into the ninth before the visitors scored a pair of two-out runs off Dick Drago to escape with a 3-2 win. "Nobody said it was going to be easy," Lynn remarked as the club packed for Cincinnati. "No way."

Nobody said it would be fair, either. In Game 3, umpire Larry Barnett, misinterpreting the rules, called Fisk for interfering on pinch hitter Ed Armbrister's 10th-inning bunt. The Reds, who'd led 5-1 before a Sox comeback, won it, 6-5, on Joe Morgan's single. "This is brutal," declared Fisk. "I never saw anything like it in my life."

Fortunes were reversed the next night. It took a five-run inning and 163 pitches by Tiant, but Boston hung on for a 5-4 victory. Then came another shift in momentum: Gullett mastered his opponents, 6-2, in Game 5 and the Sox returned home on the brink.

A three-day nor'easter gave them time to regroup and allowed Johnson to start Tiant instead of Lee. "Tiant is our best," he said. "We're down 3-2. We have to win the sixth game first."

It took the Sox until after midnight to do it and Tiant was long gone when they did. But after pinch hitter Bernie Carbo's two-out, three-run homer in the eighth brought Boston back even, Fisk won it in the 12th with a homer that bounced off the left-field foul pole and set church bells ringing in triumph in his hometown of Charlestown, New Hampshire. "I straight-armed somebody and kicked him out of the way and touched every little white thing I saw," said Fisk after his celebratory gallop around the bases through fans and teammates on his way to touch the plate.

For five innings the next night, the faithful could envision a championship flag flapping as the Sox took a 3-0

ATTACK OF THE GREEN MONSTER

Game 6 of the 1975 World Series was noteworthy for, among other things, one catch that was made (by Dwight Evans, to steal a possible home run from Joe Morgan in the 11th inning) and one that was not (by Fred Lynn when he slammed into the left-field wall in pursuit of Ken Griffey's two-run triple).

As part of the modifications for the 1976 season, the wall was stripped of its metal skin and fitted with a smoother, Formica-like covering. Protective padding was added to the wall's base to prevent serious injury, a move swayed at least in part by Lynn's scary World Series collision.

The new surface made caroms off the wall more predictable, and the Jimmy Fund, the Red Sox-supported charity, was made a little richer. The green sheet metal of the old façade was turned into paperweights and sold to fans to benefit cancer research.

The biggest change, however, was the addition of a huge electronic message board and scoreboard in center field—a first in Major League Baseball. The manually operated left-field scoreboard was reduced in width, with the elimination of the section of the board devoted to National League scores (which would instead be shown intermittently on the message board).

The new scoreboard cost $1.5 million, which was more than the cost of the complete stadium overhaul that took place in 1934. The board was 40 feet wide and 24 feet high, flashed 8,640 lights and was equipped to show both film and videotape, including instant replay.

Did the new scoreboard affect the game? A flagpole stood in center field for much of Fenway history. Jim Rice was the last man to hit a ball completely out of the park in that direction when he homered to the right of the flagpole off the Royals' Steve Busby in 1975. It's nearly impossible to do now because of the center-field scoreboard, the 2011 version of which is even larger.

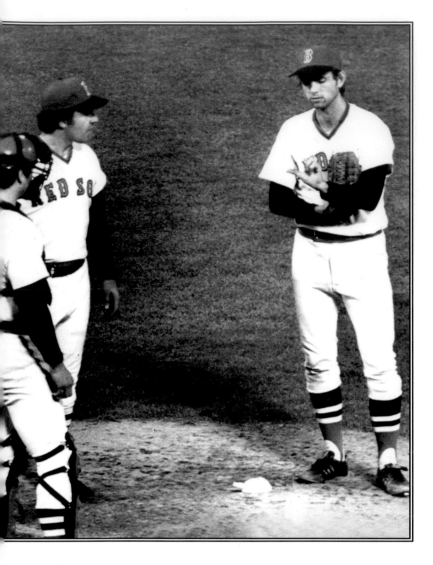

Bill Lee showed teammates Carlton Fisk and Rico Petrocelli the blister on his thumb that would force him to leave Game 7 of the 1975 World Series in the seventh inning. The Red Sox lost the game, 4-3, after holding a 3-0 lead.

lead. But Lee served up a looping, ill-timed "Leephus" pitch with two out in the sixth to slugger Tony Perez, who launched it over the Wall for a two-run homer. "Lee threw it to the wrong guy," Morgan mused years later. "He could have thrown it to me, Pete Rose, Johnny Bench, anybody. But Perez was the best off-speed hitter on our team."

Lee left with a blister in the seventh. Then Rose tied it up. After Johnson yanked reliever Jim Willoughby for pinch hitter Cecil Cooper and brought in rookie Jim Burton for the ninth, Morgan won the game and World Series with a two-out blooper to center. "It was a slider low and away, and I couldn't have asked for a better location," Burton said as his teammates glumly put on their street clothes. "He didn't even hit it well."

The Sox were honored the next day at City Hall Plaza by thousands of fans for their gallant run, but second place in October brings no reward. "We're going to win that Series yet," vowed Yastrzemski.

Any chance that Boston had of a reprise vanished early in 1976 when the owners locked out the players in March after the Basic Agreement had expired and Lynn, Fisk, and Rick Burleson held out. "The togetherness, it wasn't there," Johnson would say at the conclusion of the club's most tur-

"There's nothing in the world like the fatalism of the Red Sox fans, which has been bred into them for generations by that little green ballpark, and the wall, and by a team that keeps trying to win by hitting everything out of sight and just out-bombarding everyone else in the league. All this makes Boston fans a little crazy and I'm sorry for them."

—**Bill Lee**

ABOVE: Senator Ted Kennedy and nephew Joe were faces in the crowd during 1975 World Series play.

BELOW: Resilient Red Sox Nation returned to its "wait till next year" philosophy in the wake of the '75 loss.

SIZING UP THE WALL

The sign at the base of Fenway Park's famous left-field wall long indicated that the fence was 315 feet from home plate. Yet, from the day that sign was posted, batters insisted that the wall was less than 315 feet from home plate.

No doubt some of this skepticism was due to the height and breadth of the wall. Its imposing dimensions make it appear closer than it really is. But it turns out there was more to it than perception—there was proof.

In 1975, *Globe* sports editor Dave Smith was presented with aerial photos of the park, accompanied by the report of an expert who flew reconnaissance in World War II. The military man concluded that the distance from home plate to the left-field wall was 304.779 feet. Smith made a formal request to the Sox to have someone from the *Globe* measure the foul line. The team refused to comply, and the next day it was Page One news in a story by Monty Montgomery. Original blueprints from the Osborn Engineering Co.—which built Fenway in 1912—indicate that the wall is 308 feet from home plate.

Citing various reasons, the Red Sox for years had been reluctant to let anyone measure the debated distance. It was part of the Fenway mystique. Author George Sullivan once used a yardstick and came up with a distance of 309 feet 5 inches. It turns out that Sullivan was darned close.

One day in March 1995, in broad daylight, armed with a 100-foot Stanley Steelmaster measuring tape, the *Globe*'s Dan Shaughnessy vaulted the railing and measured the line. He found it to be 309 feet 3 inches, give or take an inch, and he said so in a story on April 25. In May, the Red Sox surreptitiously admitted to their longstanding fib. Groundskeeper Joe Mooney re-measured the distance, and after huddling with Sox management, quietly changed the numbers on the wall to "310" feet. For a while, it went unnoticed.

"I was sitting in the stands before the game wondering when someone would come up and ask about it," said Mooney later. "Nobody did."

When Shaughnessy's estimate of 309 feet 3 inches was mentioned, Mooney said, "That's about what it is. We rounded it off. It came out in that story, so why hide it?"

After all those years, why indeed?

Even at 310 feet, Fenway's dimensions would be against the rules if the ballpark were being built today. The league now stipulates that fences must be no less than 325 feet from home plate.

bulent season in memory. "With those men playing out their options, I could see something was different, right from the start."

By autumn, Johnson had been fired, Yawkey had died, a blockbuster deal with Oakland had been voided and the Sox, who never spent a day in first place, had to make a magnificent closing surge just to finish third as they posted their fewest number of victories (83) in a decade. Ten straight losses, half of them at Fenway, buried the club in sixth place and it never recovered.

The troubles in the '76 season began early. Eight days after a brawl-filled May meeting in the Bronx that put Lee on the sidelines for two months with a torn shoulder ligament, the Sox met the Yankees at the Fens, where extra security was added in case the fans sought retribution. Though Boston dropped two of three and sank to fourth, prospects seemed markedly brighter when O'Connell made a bold deal with the cash-strapped Finley, buying A's pitcher Rollie Fingers and first baseman/outfielder Joe Rudi for $1 million apiece.

"We had to make up our minds that we're trying to win the pennant this year," said the general manager. The deal, though, seemed too good to be true, and it was. Commissioner Bowie Kuhn soon nixed the sale "in the best interests of baseball."

"Bowie Kuhn is acting like the village idiot," fumed Finley, whose sale of Vida Blue for $1.5 million to the Yankees also was voided.

Three weeks later Yawkey, who'd had no problem open-

The Fenway grounds crew caught a few Zs in July 1978.

"I love Fenway. I love it in spite of the things about it that I hate."

—Stephen King, author

ing his pocketbook if it would have meant another pennant, died at 73 after battling leukemia for several years, ending an era both in Boston and in baseball. "He gave so much to this city," said Mayor Kevin White. "Over the years so much pleasure. Last year so much excitement. And always so much class."

The Sox soon went into free fall, losing 11 of 13 games on the road to drop to fifth. That meant the end for Johnson, who'd been Manager of the Year in 1975, but couldn't find a way to keep his club in contention in 1976. "What happened? I just ran out of answers," he said. It was easier, O'Connell conceded, to change the manager than the team, "which would be practically impossible."

So Don Zimmer, the Sox third-base coach who'd previously managed the Padres for two years, took over as skipper and the club caught fire as summer turned into fall, winning 15 of their final 18. "Third place is no big thing," Zimmer acknowledged, "but it was an outstanding finish."

Except for signing Twins reliever Bill Campbell to a seven-figure deal, the front office opted not to shop in what it deemed an overpriced bazaar during the first year of MLB free agency, instead bringing back George Scott and Bernie Carbo from the Brewers for Cecil Cooper. That created a cadre of wallbangers that rivaled the 1927 Yankees for percussive power.

The 1977 club set franchise records for homers, hitting 124 at home and 213 in all, with Rice contributing 39, Scott 33, Hobson 30, Yastrzemski 28, and Fisk 26. Its most jaw-dropping—and delightful—display came on a mid-June weekend in Fenway when Boston cranked 16 round-trippers off the Yankees amid a three-game sweep in which the hosts outscored their archrivals by a combined 30-9 on national television.

The shelling began immediately as the Sox battered Catfish Hunter for four homers in the first inning of the opener, and then added two more in a 9-4 bashing. "They beat the hell out of us tonight," acknowledged New York's Reggie Jackson. "They were sending bombs everywhere." Unfortunately, the triumph was marred by bleacher oafs who pelted New York center fielder Mickey Rivers with metal bolts. "If it happens again, I'm going to pull my team off the field," vowed Yankees Manager Billy Martin. "We won't stand for that kind of stuff. Somebody could get killed."

The Sox were doing enough damage to the visitors with horsehide, thumping another five homers (with two apiece from Carbo and Yastrzemski) in a 10-4 drubbing on Saturday that was equally notable for a dugout confrontation between Martin and one of his star players, Jackson, who chafed at being pulled from the game because the skipper thought he'd loafed on a fly ball.

The Yankees left the Fens both squabbling and reeling after dropping the finale, 11-1, on Sunday in a game highlighted by another five Boston homers. "We just had our men playing in the wrong spots," observed Martin, whose own club didn't manage a single shot. "We should have stationed them in the screen."

It was the most rewarding home stand in memory for the Red Sox, who went 9-1 and vaulted from third to first place. Nobody who'd witnessed the humbling of New York would have bet that the Yankees would come back to win the division or that the Sox soon would turn into a white-knuckle carnival ride. They lost nine in a row, and then won seven of eight. During a West Coast road trip in late July and early August, they won nine straight as part of a 16-1 surge, and then lost seven straight to fall into second place.

Despite winning 11 of 13 to start September, Boston never again was atop the pile and the season ended with an ironic twist as the Sox gave up six homers to the Orioles in an 8-7 loss that eliminated them and let the Yankees spray champagne. "Just like the horses I bet on, I came up a little short," Zimmer joked in a telegram to Martin. "Congratulations."

While the Yankees went on to beat the Dodgers to win the World Series for the first time since 1962, the Sox were left to ponder yet another near miss. "You start out in April and you hope to be in a pennant race when it ends," mused Yastrzemski, after Boston had finished in a second-place tie with Baltimore. "We were in this one until the end and I have no regrets. The better team won."

In 1978, the Sox were in the race to the end and beyond, and the payoff was the most painful October moment in three decades. There had been significant changes before

GAME NO. 163

After 162 games, there was only one way to settle one of the most tumultuous playoff races in baseball history: with Game No. 163. One of the two teams—the Yankees or the Red Sox—would reach the 100-victory mark and move on to the 1978 American League Championship Series vs. the Kansas City Royals. The other would have a litany of questions to answer about a final duel that would define this six-month roller-coaster ride of a season.

That 1978 AL East battle is remembered mostly for a Red Sox collapse. What many forget is that the Red Sox actually rallied to post a 12-2 record in their last 14 games, winning their final eight, to catch New York on the season's final day and set up the one-game playoff at Fenway.

Boston was sailing along with a 2-0 lead in the seventh inning when light-hitting Yankee shortstop Bucky Dent (who had a batting average of .140 over the previous 20 games) sent a fly ball into the screen off Mike Torrez with two men on, deflating Sox fans and surprising Dent himself, who didn't think his hit would clear the wall. ("I couldn't believe it," he later admitted.) New York extended its lead to 5-2, and just as they had played it out over the long season, the Sox would be forced to rally from behind in the late going.

The collective will of more than 35,000 Sox fans, along with a couple of timely hits, brought Boston back to within 5-4, and Carl Yastrzemski, who had homered earlier in the game when the day held such promise, stepped in with two outs in the last of the ninth and Rick Burleson on third base representing the tying run. Yaz managed only a towering pop fly off the Yankees' flamethrower Rich Gossage, and the most agonizing season in Red Sox annals was complete.

After 163 games over more than six months, the Sox had come up shy by one base, the distance between third and home plate. They had won 99 games, fourth-most in their history, but finished second to the Yankees' 100 victories. New York would go on to win its second straight world title. "We have everything in the world to be proud of," said Yaz afterward, "what we don't have is the ring."

Teammates welcomed Bucky Dent after his three-run homer in the seventh inning gave the Yankees the lead in the 1978 one-game playoff. Afterward, Yankees' owner George Steinbrenner (right) consoled Red Sox catcher Carlton Fisk.

the club reconvened in Florida with the Yawkey Trust shifting control of the franchise to widow Jean, former vice president and catcher Haywood Sullivan, and former trainer Buddy LeRoux. After dismissing O'Connell, management reshaped the roster, shipping out Jim Willoughby, Ferguson Jenkins and, eventually, Wise and Carbo—the bulk of the bohemian "Buffalo Heads" clique that Zimmer abhorred—and bringing in Mike Torrez and fellow pitchers Dennis Eckersley (who won 20 games), Dick Drago, and Tom Burgmeier.

The result was an explosive start (45-19, 28-4 at home) that astounded even the most pessimistic Sox fans and had Boston in first place by seven games on June 17. At the All-Star break, the Sox led Milwaukee by nine games, with New York a distant 11½ astern. But in the wake of a spate of injuries, the pitching, hitting, and defense all collapsed, and the Sox began drooping by late summer.

By the time Boston met its traditional tormentors, the Yankees, at Fenway in September, New York had replaced Billy Martin with the less acerbic Bob Lemon, healed their internal divisions and closed to within four games. By the

It was just another rainy June evening at Fenway Park in 1977.

time New York left town, the Yankees had drawn even with a four-game sweep so devastating that it was labeled "The Boston Massacre." The visitors, who'd won 12 of their previous 14 outings, teed off on Torrez, who'd won two Series games for them the previous year, and administered a 15-3 flogging that was so unsightly that thousands of fans fled early. "Maybe we tired (the Yankees) out," Zimmer said, wryly. "They had scheduled extra hitting Friday afternoon. They called in the fifth inning and canceled it."

There was no joking the following night when the Yankees breezed to a 13-2 decision (aided by seven Boston errors) with a scoreline—2600210—that prompted one press-box imp to dial that number in New York. "No one was home," Peter Gammons reported in the *Boston Globe*. "Perhaps he was out looking for playoff tickets."

After a 7-0 loss, and then a 7-4 defeat in the finale, the Sox saw a season's work vanish in a weekend. "I'm not happy and I'm not worried," proclaimed second baseman

Jerry Remy. "We're tied and we shouldn't be. But we're not going to roll over and cry."

Indeed, despite dropping 13 of 16 games during their September swoon, Boston rallied heroically, winning its final eight dates with Detroit and Toronto. (Tiant shut out the Blue Jays, 5-0, on two hits at Fenway on the final day.)

When the Indians hammered Hunter and the Yankees, 9-2, Boston found itself in a one-game playoff for the first time since 1948, when it met Cleveland at Fenway. "There is no way any of us right now can appreciate or even understand how it came to this," said Burleson. "But what we do know is that this is the biggest day of our lives."

For six innings, the division title appeared within grasp after Boston had nicked Ron Guidry for two runs. But with one swing, the least likely Yankee, light-hitting Bucky Dent, lofted what seemed to be a harmless two-out fly ball to left. Torrez, assuming that the inning was over, walked off the mound. "Then I looked over my shoulder on the way to the dugout and couldn't believe it," he said. "Yaz is back to the wall, popping his glove, looking up. I said, 'What's this? What the . . .'"

It was a three-run homer that put the visitors ahead, 3-2. The Yankees would take a 5-4 lead into the final frame. With two out in the bottom of the ninth, Burleson stood on third representing the tying run. But Yastrzemski, whose homer originally put his team ahead, popped up to third and the season was gone. The Yankees went on to win the World Series again and the Sox simply went home. "We won, but you didn't lose," New York owner George Steinbrenner told the disconsolate Sox, but none of them believed him. "We just blew it, that's all," said Burleson.

It was a particularly bitter ending for Yastrzemski, who craved not only his third pennant, but also his first championship ring. "Someday we're going to get that cigar," declared the 39-year-old captain, who'd wept in the clubhouse after watching the last ball off his bat drop into Graig Nettles's glove. "Before old Yaz retires, he's going to play on a world champion."

Except for Eckersley, who went on to claim a ring with Oakland in 1989, none of the players on that Red Sox team ever did. By the time the 1979 season began, Tiant had taken his rhumba delivery to the Yankees as a free agent and Lee and his extraterrestrial aura had been dealt to the Expos. Still, optimism reigned as author John Updike (who 19 years before had penned "Hub Fans Bid Kid Adieu," the famous farewell essay to Ted Williams) wrote an Opening

Day story for the *Globe* describing the "first kiss of another prolonged entanglement."

But while the Sox started briskly, winning 12 of their first 16 games to lead the division by two-and-a-half games, they were demolished, 10-0, at home by the Yankees in their first meeting with Torrez on the mound and Dent, who was heartily hooted on sight, knocking him out of the game. "I turned on the radio this morning and heard that the season was over," said Drago, whose teammates were booed the next day when they came out for infield practice.

Despite magnificent seasons from Lynn (a league-leading .333 batting average with 39 homers and 122 RBI) and Rice (.325, 39, 130), Boston never saw first place again and finished third, 11½ games behind Baltimore. 🔴

Opening day always drew a crowd in the 1970s.

FENWAY PARK

PRESEASON
Fenway Park's flagpole in center field, which dated to the park's opening and was part of the field of play, is removed from the field of play.

MAY 16
A three-run homer by Carl Yastrzemski clears the back wall in center field in what may be the longest home run ever hit at Fenway. The hit propels the Sox to a 6-2 victory over Cleveland. "When I hit it, I knew it was something special," Yaz says.

SEPTEMBER 2
Sonny Siebert pitches a complete-game shutout and hits two home runs (he remains the last American League pitcher to hit two home runs in a single game), as Boston defeats Baltimore, 3-0, at Fenway Park.

NOVEMBER 21
Red Sox catcher Carlton Fisk is named the American League Rookie of the Year, becoming the first unanimous selection in the award's history.

JANUARY 18
Veteran slugger Orlando Cepeda signs with the Red Sox, becoming the first player to be signed by a team to exclusively fill the role of designated hitter.

APRIL 8
Orlando Cepeda gets his first hit as a designated hitter—a walk-off home run that gives Boston a 4-3 win over New York at Fenway Park.

JULY 27-28
The Newport Jazz Festival is held in Fenway, which would not host another major concert for 30 years.

MAY 25
The last Red Sox-*Boston Globe* Baseball Clinic is held at Fenway Park.

APRIL 14
A foul ball hit by Detroit Tigers outfielder Willie Horton strikes a low-flying pigeon, which falls dead in front of home plate.

1970   1971   1972   1973   1974

JULY 5
Infielder John Kennedy, making his debut with Boston, hits a pinch-hit, inside-the-park home run at Fenway Park.

AUGUST 1
Yankee Thurman Munson crashes into Carlton Fisk in a failed suicide-squeeze attempt. The two fight, launching a bench-clearing brawl. They get tossed out; the Red Sox win, 3-2.

SEPTEMBER 30
Manager Eddie Kasko is fired and replaced by Darrell Johnson.

Top of page (l-r): Dwight Evans dropping back for a spectacular 11th-inning catch in Game 6 of the 1975 World Series; Fenway's new electronic scoreboard, 1976; new bleacher windows, 1979. Timeline: Red Sox catcher Carlton Fisk, 1972; Fisk erupting after Yankees' Thurman Munson crashed into him during a suicide squeeze in August 1973; a boy hawking souvenirs outside the park in 1979.

OCTOBER 4-5
The Red Sox win two games at Fenway on their way to sweeping the Oakland A's in the ALCS.

OCTOBER 21
In the eighth inning of Game 6 of the World Series, the Red Sox tie the score, 6-6, on Bernie Carbo's three-run, pinch-hit home run with two outs. In the 12th inning, Carlton Fisk's iconic home run off the left-field foul pole wins the game, 7-6, ending what many consider the best game in World Series history

MARCH 1
Padding at the bottom of both the left-field and center-field walls at Fenway Park is installed. The wall's metal surface is also replaced to eliminate dead spots and make caroms off it more consistent.

APRIL 3
Fenway's first electronic scoreboard, 40 feet wide and 24 feet high, is installed in center field. (The new technology is viewed warily at first by the Fenway faithful.) New construction at the park also includes an enclosed press box.

JANUARY 24
Jersey Street adjacent to Fenway Park is renamed Yawkey Way in honor of the late Red Sox owner.

OCTOBER 24
Dick O'Connell is fired as general manager and replaced by Haywood Sullivan.

MARCH 30
In a trade with the Indians, the Red Sox acquire pitcher Dennis Eckersley (who will go 20-8 for the season).

SEPTEMBER 10
In what is known as "The Boston Massacre," the Yankees complete a four-game sweep at Fenway, wiping out what had been a 14-game lead for the Sox.

OCTOBER 2
In a one-game playoff for the AL East title and a berth in the ALCS, the Yankees win, 5–4, taking the lead for good on a three-run homer by Bucky Dent.

JULY 24
Carl Yastrzemski hits his 400th career home run.

SEPTEMBER 12
Carl Yastrzemski becomes the 15th player in baseball history to reach 3,000 hits—and the first in American League history to accumulate both 400 home runs and 3,000 hits in a career—with a single during a 9-2 win over the Yankees at Fenway.

1975 1976 1977 1978 1979

OCTOBER 22
The Sox lose Game 7 to the Reds, 4-3, dashing their World Series hopes, again.

NOVEMBER 26
Fred Lynn becomes the first MLB player to win Most Valuable Player and Rookie of the Year in the same season.

JULY 9
Tom Yawkey, owner of the Red Sox for 44 years, dies. His wife, Jean, becomes president of the club.

JULY 19
Darrell Johnson is fired and is replaced by Don Zimmer, the Sox third-base coach.

1980s

Red Sox manager Joe Morgan fumed after Rich Gedman was called out for crashing into Oakland's Mike Gallego at second base during Game 3 of the AL Championship Series in 1988.

The signature moments of the decade—on the diamond at least—occurred a couple of weeks and thousands of miles apart—in Anaheim, California, and in Queens, New York. But swirling around the historic Dave Henderson homer and the haunting Bill Buckner gaffe of 1986 were plenty of Fenway Park vignettes, both celebratory and shocking. Seemingly for the want of a stamp on an unmailed contract offer, native son and stalwart catcher Carlton Fisk walked away from the team in 1981. Soon after, the luxury-box era debuted at Fenway, and ultimately 40 of the revenue-producing suites were built on the ballpark roof. In 1983, an ugly ownership rift was exposed on a June night that had been reserved for celebrating the wondrous 1967 pennant and one of its stricken heroes. In the fall of that same season, Captain Carl, who had kept his feelings in check for pretty much his entire 23-year career, said farewell with an emotional lap around the ballpark. On a cold April 1986 night, Boston's "Rocket Man," Roger Clemens, was propelled into the spotlight by a record 20-strikeout game, the opening salvo in his first Cy Young Award season. Sparked by the "Hendu" home run, the Sox made the World Series for their only time of the decade; it had been 11 years since they had been there, and it would be 18 more before they returned. When the team foundered in 1988, Joe Morgan, the bullpen coach, assumed the duties as manager on an "interim" basis. But the Sox took off on a remarkable run, winning a league-record 24-straight home games. All the while, Morgan, who hailed from nearby Walpole, kept things on a "six, two and even" keel as he guided the team to the playoffs twice in three years. Once in the postseason, though, his Sox struggled mightily—their losing streak, which began with Game 6 of the 1986 World Series, would last 13 games and 12 seasons.

The club never got rolling in 1980. Stalwarts like Jim Rice, Fred Lynn, Carl Yastrzemski, and Butch Hobson were among the lame and the team was stuck in fifth place at the All-Star break. At the end of September, when attendance had dropped by 400,000, management dumped Manager Don Zimmer with a year left on his contract. "A change was needed and we made it," said General Manager Haywood Sullivan, who promoted Johnny Pesky from coach to manager for the rest of the season. "Economics has something to do with it, fan reaction, public relations, on-the-field things. Let's be fair about it, sometimes change creates attitude. I'm looking for a little different tone, that's all."

Zimmer, whose 411 victories in four-plus seasons still put him in the top seven in club annals, was sanguine about his dismissal. "I've heard a lot of boos," acknowledged the man who'd never been fired nor held a job outside of the game. "I've made a lot more friends than I have enemies in my stay here. That certainly holds true in the clubhouse. This has been a good club to manage. A damn good club."

What the front office wanted, Sullivan stated, was "a strict disciplinarian, a solid baseball man and a motivator." The choice was Ralph Houk, a decorated Army major who'd directed the Yankees to consecutive World Series championships in the early 1960s, and then returned to oversee their reconstruction before moving on to Detroit, where he took on another renovation job before retiring to Florida. "My golf game didn't get very good," Houk said

upon returning to baseball. "The fish weren't biting. How often can you cut the grass?"

Houk was a transition specialist, which made him a natural fit for a 1981 Boston club that had lost three prominent regulars—Fred Lynn, catcher Carlton Fisk, and shortstop Rick Burleson—during the off-season. Burleson was traded with Butch Hobson to the Angels for Carney Lansford, Rick Miller, and Mark Clear. Fisk and Lynn took advantage of a baffling oversight by the Boston front office to switch uniforms; because management hadn't offered them new contracts by the December deadline before their option year, Fisk and Lynn were able to declare themselves free agents.

While the dispute was being heard in January, the club traded Lynn and pitcher Steve Renko to the Angels for outfielder Joe Rudi and pitchers Frank Tanana and Jim Dorsey. When arbitrator Raymond Goetz ruled for Fisk, "Pudge" exchanged red socks for white and decamped for Chicago. Through a scheduling coincidence, Fisk played in his 10th Opening Day at Fenway (but his first as a visitor), where he cracked a three-run homer in the eighth that gave his new confrères a 3-2 decision.

"I honestly wasn't concerned about how the fans were going to react to me," said Fisk, whose line-drive home run quieted a crowd that hadn't been sure all afternoon whether it should applaud or boo him. "I thought it would be mostly positive, which I feel it was. I knew there would be some hooters, but I thought the majority would be favorable because I don't think I ever gave them any reason in all of the years I played here to feel any differently."

Rich Gedman, up from the minors, was the part-time new man behind the plate with Glenn Hoffman at short and Miller in center, and the syncopated Sox were essentially out of contention by the end of April after dropping seven straight, including four games by a 28-8 aggregate during a sobering sweep by the Twins at Fenway. So a two-month players' strike actually was a blessing, since Major League Baseball went to a split-season format when play resumed in mid-August, giving everyone a clean slate.

"Well, we're only a game out," Houk reckoned after Boston had been mugged, 7-1, by Chicago in Opening Day II at Fenway. Since the Sox had been four behind when the strike began, that constituted progress. By season's end, though, the deficit was two-and-a-half games, which turned out to be the club's closest finish to the top for five years.

While there was some satisfaction in playing a full slate in 1982, the Sox experienced a peculiar season that was as disappointing as it was encouraging. Despite winning 89 games (only five times in 30 years had they won more), they

Red Sox manager Don Zimmer kicked at the dirt after being ejected by umpire Marty Springstead on April 14, 1980.

ABOVE: An electrician tinkered with some of the 95 lights on one of Fenway Park's light towers in March 1983.

BELOW: In April of '83, for the 10th straight year, Jane Alden put up bunting on the Red Sox dugout and along the right-field line.

JIM RICE'S ONLY CAREER SAVE

One of the more emotional moments in Fenway history started as just another perfect summer Saturday at the ballpark.

On August 7, 1982, Tom Keane drove down to Fenway from his home in Greenland, New Hampshire, on the Granite State's sliver of a seacoast, with his sons Jonathan, 4, and Matthew, 2. Keane had scored tickets for an afternoon game against the White Sox, and these weren't just any seats. Through a friend, Keane had gotten tickets from Red Sox Executive Vice President Haywood Sullivan, and they were two rows from the field, just to the left of the Red Sox dugout.

"You were actually right there," Keane told an ESPN reporter years later. "It was a seat that everybody would dream of when they had little kids and you wanted to get them close to the action. It was just ideal."

The boys had cheered wildly when Sox second baseman Dave Stapleton—Jonathan's favorite player—came to the plate in the fourth inning. But Stapleton swung late at a pitch and slashed a foul ball into the stands. The elder Keane didn't see the ball, but he did hear a cracking sound. He thought the ball had hit the side of the dugout—until he turned and saw the blood coming down his son's face. Jonathan had been hit by the foul ball and suffered a fractured skull.

Red Sox left fielder Jim Rice, who had been perched on the top step of the dugout, waiting his turn to hit, reacted instinctively. "Jim Rice was right there with his arms immediately," Keane said, "I mean immediately."

Rice was described by the media of the day as standoffish, or even sullen. His reserved manner was fortified for a time by an impression that, as an African-American ballplayer, he wasn't as warmly received by Boston fans as a white superstar would have been. And as an eight-time All-Star and the American League's MVP in 1978, Rice certainly qualified as a superstar. But none of those perceptions mattered one bit on that day, when Rice's quick reaction may have saved Jonathan Keane's life.

Rice, a father of two young children, later said he was thinking of one thing, and one thing only. "My child," he said. "Just someone, myself, just taking care of my child, picking my child up and taking him to the clubhouse."

"I was kind of chasing Jim Rice; he was carrying Jonathan," said Keane. "There was an ambulance waiting. When we got to the hospital, they were set up for neurosurgery."

Doctors at Children's Hospital, just a mile away, relieved the pressure on Jonathan's brain and gave him medicine to guard against seizures. He was hospitalized for five days.

Eight months later, Jonathan was reunited with Rice. On April 5, he threw out the first pitch at Fenway to open the 1983 season.

"Obviously, as we sit here today, what he did saved [Jonathan's] life," Keane said. "I mean you had a young child, his left skull is fractured open, it is bleeding profusely. The worst could have happened."

Said Rice, years later, "Playing baseball was more of a talent than a gift. The reaction to save somebody's life, that's entirely different."

finished third, six games behind the Brewers. And though they were in first place at the end of June, the Sox subsequently dropped 10 of 13 games and never recovered. "We just weren't quite good enough," observed Clear.

Boston was nowhere near good enough in 1983, when the club finished 20 games out in sixth place with its worst record (78-84) since 1966. Everything went sour in early June, when minority owner Buddy LeRoux announced a takeover (the so-called "Coup LeRoux") that provoked an immediate riposte from Sullivan. The dueling press conferences, observed *Globe* beat man Peter Gammons, resembled "the staging of a Mel Brooks parody of post-Mao China."

The front-office turmoil sent an aftershock through the clubhouse as the Sox promptly were swept at home by the Tigers and went on to lose seven in a row, tumbling from first place to fifth in less than a week. "I can't believe what I saw," said a nonplussed Houk after a comedy of errors resulted in a 10-6 loss to the Orioles. "I've never seen so many things happen like that in my life."

The rest of the season was forgettable, except for the finale, when Yastrzemski made a farewell tour of the park where he'd performed with both dignity and distinction for 23 years. "They just kept saying, 'We love you, Yaz,' over and over," he said after the fans had saluted him. "I'll never forget it."

That was the end of an era that began with the departure of Ted Williams and ended with the blossoming of Wade Boggs, who won the batting title in only his second year with the club by hitting .361 in 1983. Yastrzemski wasn't the only familiar face missing from the starting lineup when the club convened for 1984. Gedman had taken over for Gary Allenson behind the plate; Bill Buckner (obtained from the Cubs for Dennis Eckersley) was at first; Marty Barrett stood in for the hobbled Jerry Remy at second; Jackie Gutierrez replaced Hoffman at short; and Mike Easler (obtained from Pittsburgh for John Tudor) was the designated hitter.

It was a dramatic changeover and after losing 10 of their first 14 outings, the Sox were 10 games off the pace by the end of April. Yet with a young rotation—that included Bruce Hurst, Dennis Boyd, Bob Ojeda, and Al Nipper—gradually finding its way, the club's stock clearly was on the rise, most notably with the arrival of right-hander Roger Clemens, the top draft pick from the previous year who debuted on May 15 and quickly established himself as an overpowering force.

His dominance of Kansas City in an August date at Fenway was a high-octane preview of future performances, with Clemens striking out 15 batters with no walks and only 31 balls to 33 batters. "The sound you heard was me: Owww!" testified catcher Jeff Newman. "He done hurt

IN THE LAP OF LUXURY

The 1980s gave us the concept of corporations slapping their names on stadiums for a price, and the debut of the luxury box, including at Fenway Park.

In 1980, the Red Sox began to realize they could no longer survive with the park as it stood. With only about 34,000 seats and an escalating payroll that could not be met by ticket sales alone, Fenway Park was in danger of crumbling under the financial stresses of the day.

Before 1970, players made an average of $20,000 per year; by the early 1980s, they were making more than $100,000 on average. There once was a time when owner Tom Yawkey didn't worry about finding new ways to generate revenue, but Yawkey was gone. He had died of leukemia in 1976.

The Red Sox constructed 21 luxury boxes on the roof of the ballpark along the first-base side that debuted during the 1982 season. They later added boxes on the third-base side and behind home plate that brought their total to more than 40 luxury boxes (or suites), with an average of 14 seats per box, at a rental price of $50,000 to $70,000 per season.

From the day he took over the Sox business operations, Red Sox co-owner Buddy LeRoux set out to raise revenues. Along with constructing the luxury boxes, he increased ticket prices dramatically and eliminated Yawkey's policy of saving 6,500 bleacher tickets for sale on the day of a game. The interest on money deposited for advance ticket sales was believed to have brought the Red Sox as much as $2 million a year at that time. LeRoux's plan to add a second tier of seats, some 6,000 of them, atop the luxury boxes was never implemented.

LeRoux's approach ran counter to the Yawkey philosophy that no one should invest in sports to get rich.

Eventually, the ownership battles between LeRoux and his limited partners on one side and Sullivan and Jean Yawkey, Tom's widow, on the other, culminated in LeRoux being bought out of his ownership stake by Mrs. Yawkey in 1987.

Ted Williams stood, typically forgoing a tie, during the ceremony in which his No. 9 was retired, along with Joe Cronin's No. 4, on May 28, 1984. Team owner Jean Yawkey and former teammate Johnny Pesky joined the festivities.

YAZ SHOWS HE'S HUMAN

Carl Yastrzemski always wanted the other team to think that he was a machine. He wanted the pitcher to stare in and see a hitting robot staring back from the plate.

But on October 1, 1983, in his final game after 23 years of faithful service, Yaz broke down in full public view, before a sellout crowd at Fenway Park.

"I thought I had it under control," Yastrzemski said. "But then, when I started to hear the fans . . . that's why I put my head down when I got to first base."

For most of his final season, Yaz hadn't wanted any fuss. He just wanted to be what he always had been—the ballplayer, the worker. On this day, he endured the speakers and their kind words and the bows, until Yastrzemski himself was speaking, asking for a moment of silence for his mother and for former owner Tom Yawkey.

"New England, I love you," Yaz finally said, and then he was running around the perimeter of the field, touching as many hands as he could.

"I wanted to show my emotions," he said. "For 23 years, I always blocked everything out. I wanted to show these people that deep down, I was emotional for all that time."

When Yaz retired, he had played in more games (3,308) than anyone in baseball history, all of them for the Red Sox.

"I've always had tremendous happiness coming to this ballpark," said Yaz in a 1989 interview. "Never in my life did I think I'd make the Hall of Fame and have my number retired. I worked, and just working so hard overshadowed everything. I never enjoyed it after a game in which I did well. I was always thinking about tomorrow. I just never dwelled upon the success."

"I came to love Fenway. It was a place that rejuvenated me after a road trip; the fans right on top of you, the nutty angles. And the Wall. That was my baby, the left-field wall, the Green Monster."

—Carl Yastrzemski

my hand." The Royals, who managed one run across nine innings, were duly impressed. "That was the best stuff we've seen all season and we're not going to see better," declared Mike Ferraro, a Royals coach. "He has the best stuff in the American League, hands down."

Clemens went on to submit a 9-4 record, and with the outfield of Rice, Tony Armas, and Dwight Evans combining for 103 homers and 349 RBI, Boston managed to post 86 victories and climb to fourth place.

The club's transition complete, Houk retired at the end of the season and was succeeded by John McNamara, who'd been managing the Angels. "Am I too late to apply for the job?" Don Zimmer jokingly asked Sullivan over the phone after the announcement was made. Even before he'd checked into his hotel room upon arrival, McNamara discovered what Zimmer had learned—that everyone in New England was a would-be manager. "Is Rice going to hit fourth?" the Sheraton-Boston bellman inquired.

Rice batted third until August, but his 1985 season was cut short by a knee injury. Armas missed nearly two months with a torn calf muscle, and Clemens, dogged by a shoulder injury that required late-summer surgery, had only 15 starts as Boston finished fifth, more than 18 games behind the Blue Jays. "It's certainly not the kind of record I had in mind when I came here," McNamara conceded after his club was swept at home by the Brewers on the final weekend to end with a .500 record. "To me, this has been a very disappointing season."

In 1986, the disappointment was limited to two October nights in Queens, but it was painfully profound. The regular season, highlighted by Clemens's record 20-strikeout performance against the Mariners in April, proved surprisingly easy as the Sox held first place from May 16 until the end, won 95 games and claimed the division by five-and-a-half games despite losing the final four to the Yankees at home. "The usual rallying cry around here is, 'Wait until next year,'" remarked McNamara as his men prepared to take on the Angels in the league championship series. "Well, next year starts Tuesday night. We're prepared."

Boston hadn't played a postseason game since the one-game divisional playoff in 1978 with the Yankees, and the ALCS opener at Fenway was over almost as soon as it began. The visitors rocked Clemens for four runs in the second inning. "We'll be all right," Clemens insisted after California counterpart Mike Witt took a no-hitter into the sixth inning and wrung out the Sox by an 8-1 count.

Boston indeed bounced back the next afternoon. The sun-blinded Angels ran into outs, watched balls skip over and away from them, and made three errors in the seventh inning—when the hosts scored three runs on one hit. But

THE LEROUX COUP

In the annals of bizarre incidents at Fenway Park, probably none can top the night of June 6, 1983. The Red Sox had announced plans to honor former player Tony Conigliaro, who had been in a coma for months following a stroke. Many of his teammates from the revered Impossible Dream team of 1967 were gathered, along with a large media contingent.

Co-owner Buddy LeRoux interrupted the proceedings to announce that enough of the team's partners had voted in his favor to give him control of the Red Sox over co-owners Haywood Sullivan and Jean Yawkey, with whom he had been feuding for years. A half hour later, Sullivan and John Harrington, representing the Yawkey Foundation, held a rebuttal news conference to announce that the team's chain of command was intact, and that LeRoux's announcement was "illegal, invalid and, above all, not effective."

"Le Coup LeRoux," as it was dubbed, reduced the celebration of the 1967 team and the stricken Conigliaro to an afterthought.

In the next day's paper, *Globe* columnist Michael Madden wrote, "Buddy LeRoux and his bottom-line men did not have the patience, the class, the sensitivity, the good taste or even the most basic respect to wait another day." Madden called it "a sideshow, a shoddy, slippery coup by banana-republic generals. . . . What was to have been the Night of the Impossible Dream was transformed meanly into the Day of the Shameful Scene."

Former player George Thomas watched the competing news conferences, both held directly under a color portrait of the late, longtime owner of the Sox, Tom Yawkey.

"If he could see this now," said Thomas, "he'd be spinning in his grave."

Ironically, LeRoux had developed a strong bond with the Yawkeys as the team's trainer in the 1960s. He went on to build a real estate empire, and in 1977, with Sullivan as his partner, LeRoux led a group that sought control of the Red Sox after Tom Yawkey's death. When some questions arose about financing, Jean Yawkey joined the consortium and the sale was approved by Major League Baseball.

LeRoux took over the business end of the Sox operations, guiding the construction of luxury boxes at Fenway and signing lucrative TV and radio contracts. Before long, however, the ownership group became divided, leading to the stunning events of "Tony C Night."

The outcry over LeRoux's takeover bid was immediate and harsh. He was taken to court by Yawkey and Sullivan and eventually lost the battle for control of the team. Once he realized that he would never be able to buy the others out, LeRoux sold his shares to Yawkey in 1987.

THE ROCKET'S AWESOME COMING-OUT PARTY

As the 1986 Red Sox season opened, Roger Clemens was a 23-year-old question mark coming off shoulder surgery that curtailed his 1985 season. But he turned the question mark into an exclamation point on a weeknight in late April when the Red Sox game was playing a distant second fiddle to a Celtics-Atlanta Hawks playoff game that featured Larry Bird across town at the old Boston Garden.

Only 13,414 fans were on hand at Fenway Park on April 29 to see "Rocket Roger" do something that no pitcher in 111 years of major-league history had managed to do before: strike out 20 batters in a nine-inning game.

The Mariner lineup included a couple of guys who would later factor into Boston's amazing run to the 1986 World Series: Spike Owen and Dave Henderson. Owen had also been Clemens's teammate at the University of Texas. Clemens came into the game with a 3-0 record, which would eventually grow to 14-0 en route to a 24-4/MVP/Cy Young Award season. Clemens struck out the side (all swinging) in the first inning. He fanned two more in the second and one in the third. Although he went to three balls on five of the first nine batters, he ended up with zero walks to go along with his 20 strikeouts.

After giving up a single to Owen to start the fourth, Clemens struck out eight in a row, tying an American League record. But in the seventh inning, Seattle's Gorman Thomas drove a 1-2 fastball into the center-field bleachers to give Seattle a 1-0 lead. Amazingly, Clemens was on his way to history, but was in danger of losing the game. Fortunately, Dwight Evans crushed a three-run homer in the bottom of the inning to put the Sox ahead, 3-1, the eventual final score.

Clemens had 18 strikeouts after eight. Owen struck out on a 1-2 fastball to open the ninth, and when umpire Vic Voltaggio rang up Phil Bradley on an 0-2 fastball for No. 20, Wade Boggs jogged to the mound from third base and shook Clemens's hand. Ken Phelps grounded to shortstop for the final out on Clemens's 138th pitch.

Clemens would go on to throw another 20-strikeout game (no walks again) in Detroit 10 years later, but this was the night that signaled Clemens's ascendancy.

"In the clubhouse afterward," General Manager Lou Gorman said, "even the veterans were awed."

'OIL CAN' KEPT US GUESSING

In the 1980s, few people called him by his given name, Dennis. Years later, "Oil Can" Boyd told Dan Shaughnessy, "I'm blessed with this mystique. I got a nickname and I know how to pitch."

The Can started 207 games in his 10-year MLB career. He started the third game of the 1986 World Series and was lined up to pitch Game 7 before rain and Red Sox Manager John McNamara changed history. The Can went 78-77 in the big leagues with a 4.04 ERA and pitched the division-clinching game for the Sox in 1986. But his favorite baseball memories come from his younger days in Meridian, Mississippi.

"That was the most fun, around when I was 12-15 years old," he recalled. "Baseball was the epitome back then. I played a lot of baseball when I was little, so I have big reminiscences of baseball and that's how I came to be the player I came to be."

Boyd could throw a ton of innings and he always wanted the ball. Baseball was in his blood. His dad, Willie James Boyd, once faced Henry Aaron and Willie Mays at the ballpark in Meridian.

Dennis Ray Boyd was nicknamed "Oil Can" because of his fondness for beer (the nickname gets a special citation from Susan Sarandon in *Bull Durham*), and he became one of the more delightful characters on the Boston sports scene after splashing down in 1982. Manager Ralph Houk—and later McNamara—didn't know quite what to make of the Can, but they knew he wanted the ball every fifth day and that he could pitch.

There was plenty of controversy. The Can was hospitalized with a mysterious liver ailment in 1986, and then went into a rage and temporarily quit the Sox when he didn't make the All-Star team. There were rumors of drugs, and he got into a jam with the police. The Sox subjected him to a psychological evaluation and went public with their concerns. When teammate Wade Boggs announced he was a sex addict a few years later, Can said, "Now who needs the psychiatrist?"

In the end, blood clotting in his throwing shoulder took Boyd away from the game he loved. He pitched for the Expos and Rangers before retiring after the 1991 season.

the Sox dropped the next two in Anaheim, including a killer 11th-inning loss in Game 4 after they'd blown a 3-0 lead in the ninth with Clemens on the mound. It seemed that the season would end on the Left Coast, especially when the Angels took a three-run lead into the ninth inning of Game 5. Don Baylor cranked a two-run homer to draw the Sox to within 5-4, but pretty soon the visitors were down to their final strike, and the home team was preparing to rush the diamond in triumph. "I looked across the field and I could see everyone in the Angels dugout getting ready to celebrate," said Boston's Dave Stapleton. "Gene Mauch. Everyone. They had those little smiles that you get before you start hugging everyone."

Then Dave Henderson, picked up from Seattle in August, whacked another homer off Donnie Moore to tie the score in the ninth. And it was Henderson again in the 11th inning, knocking in Baylor with a sacrifice fly to put the Sox ahead, 7-6. "If we lost this game today, it wouldn't have been fair," concluded Baylor after Calvin Schiraldi, a mid-season call-up turned closer who had blown the save in Game 4, had set down the Angels in the bottom half of the 11th to preserve the Game 5 victory.

Once back in their own yard, the Sox closed out the Angels with a pair of emphatic blowouts. In Game 6, Boston easily evened the series with a 10-4 decision, knocking out starter Kirk McCaskill by way of five runs in the second inning. "Both teams have shown they know how to play and win," Mauch observed. "Now we'll find out which one knows how to win when they have to win."

Not since the 1912 World Series had the Sox won an October postseason series that had gone the distance. But

the finale was nearly a walkover. Clemens stifled the Angels while his mates laid a battering on John Candelaria, who gave up seven runs in the first four innings. The Sox outburst was punctuated by Rice's three-run shot over the left-field wall. "Yogi's quote gets better and better," exulted McNamara after his club had banished the Angels by an 8-1 margin to advance to the World Series for the first time in 11 years. "It's still never over until it's over. For me, it is a dream come true to get there."

The Sox hadn't won the Fall Classic since 1918. But after they had mastered the Mets, 1-0 and 9-3, in the first two meetings at Shea Stadium, the Fenway faithful began believing that they could see it happen in person, even though Boston had been a decided underdog when the Series started. "You look at some of the guys on our ball club," mused Buckner. "You go down the names, and then you wonder what the bookies were thinking. I think those guys are sorry now. I wish I could have made a bet."

Boston never had lost consecutive postseason games at home, but New York dealt them two sobering defeats in two days. The Mets knocked around Boyd for a 7-1 triumph in Game 3. Then Bob Ojeda, who had been traded in 1985, mastered his former teammates, as the Mets ran up a 5-0 lead in Game 4 en route to a 6-2 decision that evened the Series. But Hurst, who'd blanked the Mets in the opener, held them off again, 6-2, in Game 5 and the Sox returned to Queens with two chances to win their rings. "Our backs are not at the door," declared Rice. "Their backs are."

The Mets seemed all but finished in Game 6 after Henderson's leadoff homer and Barrett's RBI single gave Boston a 5-3 lead in the 10th inning and Schiraldi had the hosts down to their last strike with two on. But Ray Knight laced a single to score one run and Bob Stanley, who came in to close, uncorked a wild pitch with two strikes on Mookie Wilson that enabled New York to draw even. When Wilson's bouncing grounder went through Buckner's legs to score Knight from second, millions of Sox fans, many of whom had awakened children and propped them in front of the TV so that they could bear witness to history, went to bed in shock.

"I had dreamed of this moment," said Stanley after the Mets had escaped, 6-5, in the only Series game ever decided by an error. "How I would be on the mound for the clincher and how it would wipe out all the bad things. I was there tonight . . . but the dream turned into a nightmare."

Yet Boston had another chance to end 68 years of autumnal futility. A Sunday rainout enabled McNamara to start Hurst for a third time and the Sox staked him a 3-0

ABOVE: Young Red Sox fans bought up every souvenir in sight to cheer on the 1986 team during postseason play at Fenway.

RIGHT: Fenway fans saluted Jim Rice after his three-run homer sealed the Game 7 victory over the Angels in the 1986 AL Championship Series.

BUCKNER'S REDEMPTION

It was October 6, 1986, and Bill Buckner was talking to a Boston TV reporter at Fenway Park about the upcoming postseason for the Red Sox, their first since 1975. "The dreams are that you are going to have a great series and win, and the nightmares are that you are going to let the winning run score on a ground ball through your legs," said Buckner. "Those things happen, and I think a lot of it is just fate."

Fate brought Buckner to the plate in the top of the ninth inning of Game 5 of the ALCS in Anaheim against the Angels, who led the game, 5-2, and the series, 3-1. The Angels were three outs away from advancing to their first World Series. Buckner's single started a rally that concluded with Dave Henderson's dramatic, final-strike, game-tying homer that helped to propel the Red Sox into the Series.

Fast-forward a couple of weeks to Shea Stadium, to the play in Game 6 of the World Series that propelled the Mets to the world title and unfairly defined Buckner's career. We can close our eyes and see the videotape of Mookie Wilson's ground ball, we can hear announcer Vin Scully exclaim, "A little roller up along first . . . behind the bag! It gets through Buckner! Here comes Knight . . . and the Mets win it!"

Buckner played in four decades. He collected more hits (2,715) than either Ted Williams or Joe DiMaggio did. He won a National League batting title in 1980 and was an All-Star in 1981. But that one play, which has been called the Zapruder film of baseball, took on a life of its own and made him the poster boy for the Curse of the Bambino.

Years later, Buckner said, "This is the honest-to-God's truth. My first thought was, 'We lost the game.' The second thought was, 'Oh man, we get to play the seventh game of the World Series.' There was no doubt in my mind we were going to win the last game."

The Sox lost the last game to the Mets, of course, and Buckner was vilified, made the butt of hundreds of bad jokes. He played half of the 1987 season for the Red Sox, and played the final 22 games of his career in Boston in 1990, but then he moved far away, to Boise, Idaho, and for a long time he stayed away, including when the 1986 Sox team was honored in 2006.

In a 2003 interview with the *Globe*'s Stan Grossfeld, Buckner acknowledged that all was not forgotten. "I still hear stuff," he said. "I laugh at it. Sports are for teaching young people to deal with success and failure. The saddest thing is, what are you teaching kids today? That you can't make a mistake? You make an error and you don't win, so you say, 'I don't want to play.' That's not what sports is all about."

On Opening Day 2008, after enduring years of hecklers and worse, Buckner came back to Fenway to throw out the first pitch to former teammate Dwight Evans and received an emotional, four-minute ovation.

"I didn't think I was going to do it," said Buckner later. "I told them I'd think about it, but I made up my mind I wasn't going to come. Then I prayed about it a little, and here I am. Glad I came."

RIGHT: Bill Buckner wiped his eyes during the extended ovation he received when he threw out the first pitch to open the 2008 Red Sox home season.

lead in the second inning. Redemption seemed at hand. But New York squared things in the sixth off a tiring Hurst, and went ahead 6–3 the next inning. After Boston had drawn to within a run on Evans's double, the Mets stung Al Nipper for two more in the bottom of the eighth, and soon were spraying themselves with bubbly. "It's a wrong ending to a storybook year," said Henderson as his teammates quietly packed their gear.

The hangover continued through the following season as Boston finished 20 games out in fifth place in 1987, posting a losing record (78-84) for only the second time in 21 years. Things had begun trending downward during spring training when both Hurst and Boyd were injured and Clemens held out; the club already was 0-3 when the pennant was hoisted at the home opener. "It made me mad," said Evans, after the players received rings for winning the American League the previous season. "There should have been 'World Championship' on that ring."

By early May, the Sox already were sagging badly after dropping eight of 10 on a trip to Texas and the West Coast. Just after mid-month, they were buried in sixth place and never rose above fifth for the rest of the season. "I'm just waiting now for October 4th to get here," McNamara remarked on September 23. The dismal season wasn't the manager's fault, Lou Gorman declared. "There's no way you can blame him for this year," the general manager concluded. "I'm sure some people will do it, but I don't think he's responsible at all for the kind of season we've had."

McNamara did get the blame in 1988 when a $6 million palimony suit filed against Wade Boggs by companion Margo Adams made national news and created clubhouse dissension. With the team barely above .500 at the All-Star break, owner Jean Yawkey concluded that McNamara had to go and fired him against the wishes of both Sullivan and Gorman. "We want to try and turn this thing around," said Gorman. "We're not saying that John McNamara didn't do a good job, but the manager is always the scapegoat—

fairly or unfairly."

Stepping in with just a few hours of notice was Third-Base Coach Joe Morgan, a Walpole, Massachusetts, native who'd managed the PawSox for nine years and was the first local resident to manage the Boston Red Sox since Charlestown-born Shano Collins in 1932. "Communication is important," he acknowledged during his first day on the job. "You have to talk to players. But if they get out of line, you have to step on 'em."

The first to feel Morgan's tread was the captain. When Rice objected loudly after being pulled for pinch hitter Spike Owen, he and Morgan shouted and scuffled in the dugout and Rice was suspended for three games. "I'm the manager of this nine," Morgan declared.

By then the Sox already were up and away on their best run since 1948, a 12-game winning streak that included a six-run comeback over the Royals. "It's unbelievable, really," marveled Stanley. "I'm shocked. We're winning games we were losing before."

It was "Morgan Magic," the press declared, a spell conjured by a plainspoken citizen who channeled the catchphrase, "Six, two and even," drove a snowplow along the Massachusetts Turnpike during the off-season, and seemed unfazed by a position that had driven some of his predecessors to drink. "There is no pressure, gentlemen," Morgan declared as his nine ascended the standings, winning 19 of 20. "I had more pressure trying to hit in the big leagues than I do managing."

By Labor Day, the Sox were in first place for good and despite dropping six of their final seven games—including 11-1, 15-9, and 1-0 home losses to Toronto—Boston still won the division by a game over Detroit and earned a playoff date with Oakland. Boston had dismissed the Athletics en route to the 1975 World Series, but this edition of the A's proved to be decidedly more stubborn.

In the opener at Fenway, Hurst pitched well enough to have won most playoff outings. But Oakland pitcher Rick

THE MANIACAL ONE

"Sometimes the truth hurts," said Chuck Waseleski with a chuckle when asked about his nickname. "It's true. I can't refute it."

Waseleski, known as "The Maniacal One" for his devotion to baseball record-keeping, came along before computers and fantasy baseball exploded onto the sports scene, before situational statistics, before obscure but telling numbers became necessary fodder for sports talk shows and play-by-play announcers looking to fill airtime. He provided these statistical insights to Peter Gammons, who began to include them in his nationally recognized Sunday baseball column for the *Globe*.

"You hear that so-and-so is a good two-strike hitter," he said to the *Globe*'s Dan Shaughnessy in 1987. "I hate that. I want to know how good. Be specific."

Maniacal Chuck was born and raised in the village of Millers Falls, Massachusetts, and he went to Turners Falls Regional High, where he was class valedictorian in 1972. Like a lot of New Englanders, he was a casual Red Sox fan until the 1967 Impossible Dream season. "That hooked me for good," he said.

In 1982, he began corresponding with Bill James, author of the annual *Baseball Abstract*. "It was then that I realized there was some demand for this material," Waseleski recalled. "People would ask, 'Is Jim Rice a clutch hitter?'"

Waseleski had the information. He could tell you that "Wade Boggs is hitting .488 (21 for 43) on 1-0 counts this year." Or, "Ed Romero hit the ball off the left-field wall twice in 1986." Waseleski has watched and charted every Boston game—every single pitch—since 1983, which happens to be the year Boggs won his first batting title.

"Oh, yeah," Boggs told *Tampa Tribune* columnist Martin Fennelly just before he was inducted into the Baseball Hall of Fame in 2005. "He was the guy that would tell everyone how many times I popped up to the infield and kept crazy stats on me, like how many times I swung and missed."

Before long, players and their agents were using such numbers to their advantage in salary arbitration cases. Waseleski compiled negotiation files for 30 players after the 1985 season, and for 70 players after the 1986 season.

In October 2004, when the Red Sox won their first World Series since 1918, many people wept. Waseleski typed into his Dell.

"I can tell you exactly what I wrote when we won it. I have it right here. I wrote that it was a 1-0 count, a fastball, and a ground ball back to the pitcher. It was Keith Foulke's 14th pitch," he told Fennelly.

Maniacal as always.

Honeycutt starved the hosts until old friend Dennis Eckersley entered in the eighth to finish off his former mates, whiffing Boggs on three pitches with two on and two out in the ninth. "We've got to come back tomorrow with the hammers of hell," declared Morgan. That meant Clemens firing ingots from the mound. But the visitors rallied from two runs down on Jose Canseco's two-run blast in the seventh, nicked Lee Smith for the winner with two out and two strikes in the ninth, and brought in Eckersley again to tie the Sox in knots.

Morgan shook up his lineup as the series moved to the Bay Area and Boston grabbed a 5-0 lead in the second inning of Game 3. But Oakland's bashers quickly pounded Mike Boddicker for six runs and went on to a 10-6 decision that left the visitors on the brink. "We got a game left," said Boddicker, who'd arrived from Baltimore at the end of July. "We got a bullet left. It hasn't been done in baseball, but records are broken all the time."

Not this time. In the finale, Oakland's Dave Stewart scattered four runs across six innings and Eckersley came in to complete the sweep by closing out his fourth game. "All we have is some [hats and T-shirts] that say 'AL East champs,'" Boston's Todd Benzinger commented once the drubbing was done. "We never really got to enjoy it."

Joy remained scarce in 1989 as Boston finished third, a half-dozen games off the pace and with no playoff hopes. The dissolution began in late May, when the club lost six of eight games at Fenway and drifted downward from first place. By far the worst of the defeats—in fact, the biggest collapse in franchise history—was a 13-11 loss to Toronto in which the Sox blew the 10-0 lead they had mounted in six innings. "What a loss," moaned Morgan, after Ernie Whitt had crushed a grand slam off closer Lee Smith in the ninth and Junior Felix had clouted a two-run shot off Dennis Lamp in the 12th inning of the four-hour-and-36-minute fiasco. "This is the worst defeat of my managerial career in any league or city, hands down."

When Boston had climbed back to within one-and-a-half games of the lead in mid-August, the Blue Jays returned to put them out of the race with a sweep. "Is it the president?" someone asked Morgan when the phone rang after the season finale with Milwaukee. "I doubt it," the skipper said. 🐦

FENWAY PARK

OCTOBER 1
With just a few games remaining in a dismal season, manager Don Zimmer is fired with just a few games remaining and is replaced by Johnny Pesky.

OCTOBER 27
Ralph Houk is named manager; Pesky returns to his roles as batting and bench coach.

DECEMBER 20
The Red Sox miss the deadline to tender Carlton Fisk and Fred Lynn contracts for the 1981 season, making them both free agents.

MAY 25
Carl Yastrzemski plays in his 3,000th career game, and scores the winning run in an 8-7 win over Cleveland at Fenway Park.

JUNE 10-AUGUST 10
A baseball strike truncates the season.

APRIL 12
The Red Sox construct 21 luxury boxes on the roof of the ballpark on the first-base side as part of a long-term ballpark expansion project.

MAY 1
The first Old Timers game is played at Fenway; 64-year-old Ted Williams participates.

JUNE 22
Rookie Wade Boggs hits his first major-league home run in the bottom of the 11th inning to give Boston a 5-4 win over Detroit at Fenway Park.

JUNE 6
In what is called the LeRoux Coup, co-owner Buddy LeRoux interjects himself into an event honoring Tony Conigliaro to announce that he and his partners are taking over the Red Sox. He was later removed from the team's administration.

JUNE 6
Boston selects pitcher Roger Clemens in the first round of the amateur draft.

1980 | 1981 | 1982 | 1983 | 1984

SEPTEMBER 3-4
The Red Sox lose, 8-7, to the Mariners in 20 innings, the longest game in Fenway Park history.

AUGUST 7
Jim Rice climbs into the stands to rescue a 4-year-old boy who had been struck on the head by a Dave Stapleton line drive. It turned out that the boy had a fractured skull and might have died if not for Rice's quick actions.

OCTOBER 1-2
Carl Yastrzemski wraps up his days as a professional baseball player. Yaz is presented with a car, a boat, an SUV, a silver bat, silver bowl, and a rocking chair. He retires with a lifetime .285 average, 452 home runs, and 3,419 hits.

FEBRUARY 1
Lou Gorman is hired as general manager, replacing Haywood Sullivan, who becomes CEO.

MAY 25
Dennis Eckersley gets traded to the Cubs for Bill Buckner.

MAY 28
The Red Sox retire Ted Williams's No. 9 and Joe Cronin's No. 4, the first uniform numbers retired by the organization.

OCTOBER 14
Just after his 65th birthday, Ralph Houk announces his retirement, and John McNamara is named manager.

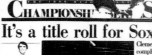

CHAMPIONSHIP SERIES

It's a title roll for Sox

Weak ace still a winner

Finally, Rice has spotlight

JULY 25
Wade Boggs extends a 28-game hitting streak in a 5-3 Red Sox win over the Mariners at Fenway Park.

SEPTEMBER 21
Wade Boggs sets a new American League mark with his 185th single of the season in the fifth inning of Boston's 7-6 win over Detroit.

APRIL 29
Roger Clemens strikes out 20 Seattle Mariners in nine innings at Fenway, setting a major-league record.

MAY 17
The Red Sox Old Timers game at Fenway features all three DiMaggio brothers (Dominic, Joe, and Vince), as well as Bobby Doerr, Johnny Pesky, and Ted Williams.

OCTOBER 23
The Sox win Game 5 of the World Series at Fenway, putting the team up, 3-2.

PRESEASON
The Fenway playing area is completely re-sodded. In addition, a new function facility (Diamond at Fenway) and souvenir store (The Lansdowne Shop) are constructed.

MARCH 31
Jean Yawkey buys out Buddy LeRoux's partnership stake in the Red Sox.

OCTOBER 4
On the last day of the season, Roger Clemens earns his 20th victory with a two-hit shutout against the Brewers at Fenway Park.

MAY 21
Boston retires former second baseman Bobby Doerr's No. 1.

JULY 14
John McNamara is fired and replaced by Joe Morgan, ushering in a period called "Morgan Magic."

AUGUST 13
The Red Sox win their 24th straight game at Fenway Park, establishing the longest home winning streak in American League history.

OCTOBER 5-9
The Oakland Athletics sweep the Red Sox in the ALCS.

FEBRUARY 24
The Red Sox add 610 stadium club seats. "The 600 Club" (later to be renamed the .406 Club in honor of Ted Williams) sits above the grandstand behind home plate, the site of the former press box. New broadcast booths and a press box are installed atop the club.

JUNE 4
The Red Sox blow a 10-run lead and lose, 13-11, in extra innings to the Blue Jays at Fenway Park. It is the biggest blown lead in franchise history.

AUGUST 6
Carl Yastrzemski's No. 8 is retired.

1985   1986   1987   1988   1989

Top of page (l-r): Washing down seats before a game, 1988; Globe coverage of Red Sox pennant win, 1986; young fans seeking autographs, 1989.
Timeline: Carl Yastrzemski tipping his hat at "Yaz Day," 1986; Jim Rice getting props for a game-winning homer in August 1984; Catcher Rich Gedman embracing "Oil Can" Boyd after clinching the AL East Championship, 1986; "Oil Can" Boyd with son Dennis in August 1989.

1990s

Catcher Mike Macfarlane (15) and outfielder Matt Stairs celebrated a win over Milwaukee that clinched the division title in 1995.

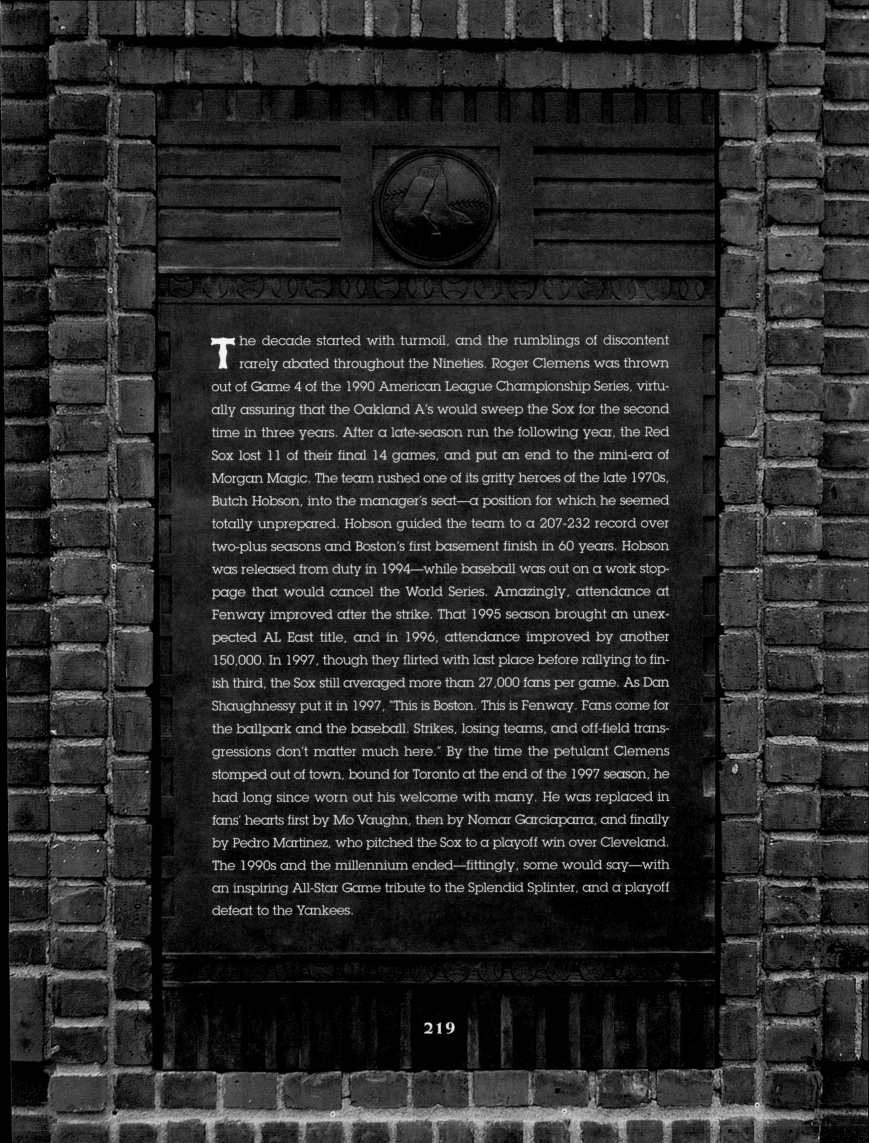

The decade started with turmoil, and the rumblings of discontent rarely abated throughout the Nineties. Roger Clemens was thrown out of Game 4 of the 1990 American League Championship Series, virtually assuring that the Oakland A's would sweep the Sox for the second time in three years. After a late-season run the following year, the Red Sox lost 11 of their final 14 games, and put an end to the mini-era of Morgan Magic. The team rushed one of its gritty heroes of the late 1970s, Butch Hobson, into the manager's seat—a position for which he seemed totally unprepared. Hobson guided the team to a 207-232 record over two-plus seasons and Boston's first basement finish in 60 years. Hobson was released from duty in 1994—while baseball was out on a work stoppage that would cancel the World Series. Amazingly, attendance at Fenway improved after the strike. That 1995 season brought an unexpected AL East title, and in 1996, attendance improved by another 150,000. In 1997, though they flirted with last place before rallying to finish third, the Sox still averaged more than 27,000 fans per game. As Dan Shaughnessy put it in 1997, "This is Boston. This is Fenway. Fans come for the ballpark and the baseball. Strikes, losing teams, and off-field transgressions don't matter much here." By the time the petulant Clemens stomped out of town, bound for Toronto at the end of the 1997 season, he had long since worn out his welcome with many. He was replaced in fans' hearts first by Mo Vaughn, then by Nomar Garciaparra, and finally by Pedro Martinez, who pitched the Sox to a playoff win over Cleveland. The 1990s and the millennium ended—fittingly, some would say—with an inspiring All-Star Game tribute to the Splendid Splinter, and a playoff defeat to the Yankees.

ollowing the 1989 shortfall, there was little reason to believe that Boston would be playing in October of 1990. But when Bill Buckner came back as a spring-training long shot, it seemed a cosmic sign of faith renewed. Buckner received a warm and redemptive Opening Day ovation from the forgiving, if not quite forgetting, Boston fans. Then he legged out an inside-the-park homer against the Angels on his first day in the lineup.

So it went for the Sox, who beat the Twins, 1-0, in a July game where they hit into two triple plays in five innings after conceding only two in the previous 25 years. Buoyed by magnificent pitching from Roger Clemens and Mike Boddicker, Boston built a lead of more than a half-dozen games by Labor Day. But after Clemens went down with a sore shoulder, the club dropped 10 of 12 and slipped behind the Blue Jays. The season came down to the final day at Fenway, with Boddicker on the mound; Boston needed a victory over the White Sox to avoid a playoff at Toronto, where Clemens already had been dispatched, just in case.

With the hosts ahead, 3-1, in the ninth and Chicago down to its last strike, champagne was at the ready. But Sammy Sosa singled and Red Sox closer Jeff Reardon plunked Scott Fletcher. Then up stepped future manager Ozzie Guillén to rip a line drive toward the right-field corner. Had it bounced past a diving Tom Brunansky, the game

at least would have been tied. "No time to think about what I should do," said Brunansky, who raced toward the no-man's-land by Pesky's Pole. "I just had to do it."

What resulted was one of the greatest catches in Fenway history, with Brunansky snaring the ball just before sliding into the wall. "Timmy, I've got the ball, I've got the ball," he shouted to Tim McClelland, the first-base umpire, one of the few people in the park who had a clear view. "I saw the play," McClelland said. "He never dropped the ball."

Thus did Boston claim the divisional title and earn a rematch with Oakland. "They called us misfits from the North Pole, castoffs," said Wade Boggs. "We were etched in stone for seventh place. But this team has got heart and desire I've never seen before. A heart as big as the Pru."

But up against A's aces Dave Stewart and Bob Welch, the Boston bats were as useless as toothpicks, managing only two runs in the first two games at Fenway. "A beautiful game turned into a horrible evening, didn't it?" mused manager Joe Morgan after the 9-1 opening loss, when Oakland bashed his bullpen for nine runs—seven in the ninth inning—after Clemens had blanked the visitors for

Wade Boggs rejoiced after the Red Sox clinched the 1990 East Division title with a victory over the Chicago White Sox.

the first six innings.

The next evening was less horrid, but the 4-1 defeat sent the Sox to the Bay Area in a formidable pickle. "You don't have to tell 'em too much now," Morgan said. "They can read that easy enough." Another 4-1 stumble in Game 3 put Boston on the verge of an early winter and after Clemens was ejected in the second inning of Game 4 for yapping at plate umpire Terry Cooney, his teammates went down by a 3-1 count, swept again and bitterly criticizing their manager.

"Those things don't bother me," Morgan said. "They don't amount to a row of beans. I'll tell you this—if a guy is going to manage in Boston, that guy better have some thick skin on his body. We've won two out of three years, so we must be doing something right."

Boston would not play another playoff game for five seasons. The front office signed Clemens to a five-year contract worth more than $20 million. But before the 1991 season, there were multiple departures (Boddicker, Dwight Evans, Oil Can Boyd, Marty Barrett) and a few notable arrivals (Jack Clark, Danny Darwin, Matt Young). While Clark, acquired from the Padres, made a concussive entrance on Opening Day, clouting a grand slam in a 6-2 decision over Toronto, his new comrades were all but buried by midsummer, falling nine games behind after the Twins swept them by a 33-6 aggregate.

The Sox made a heroic late run, winning 12 of 14 in August and 17 of 21 in September, and found themselves only a half-game out of the lead on September 21 in the wake of hammering the Yankees, 12-1, at Fenway. "It's not over yet," cautioned Clark. "We're still in second place." That proved to be the summit for the Sox, who dropped 11 of their final 14 games to tumble out of contention. They came home to Yawkey Way for a somber farewell weekend. "Have a good autumn, a good winter and we'll have a better year next year," Morgan promised the fans before the Sunday finale against the Brewers.

Two days later, Morgan was gone, replaced by Butch Hobson, the Pawtucket skipper and former Sox third baseman the front office feared it would lose without a promotion. Morgan shrugged off his dismissal. "I think they just wanted a change, that's all," said the man who'd been the only manager other than Bill Carrigan to direct the Sox to the postseason twice in three years. "If they thought I wasn't doing the job, they had every right to fire me."

Hobson, who'd been in Winter Haven with the instructional team, was startled to learn he'd been upgraded. "I can't believe this is happening to me," he said following his Fenway introduction. "This is the greatest feeling in the world."

LIGHTS OUT

Red Sox outfielder Ellis Burks was standing in the batter's box, awaiting a 2-2 pitch from Chicago's Jack McDowell, when Fenway Park did its best imitation of Boston Garden.

The Garden was where Bruins fans had seen games interrupted by blackouts, fog, and an occasional stray rodent on the ice, and where Celtics fans had seen games suspended by condensation on the court and interrupted by a pigeon on the parquet. But no such incidents interrupted the national pastime at 4 Yawkey Way. At least, not until the blackout of May 13, 1991.

As the Red Sox were waging a futile battle to erase a 2-0 deficit with two outs in the third, a power outage plunged Fenway Park and its crowd of 31,032 spectators into darkness for 59 minutes.

When the park went dark at 8:45 p.m., it was as though someone had begun a New Year's Eve-style countdown. The blackout touched off a raucous ovation and created a rock concert atmosphere, complete with flickering lighters and a battery of flashbulbs.

The likely cause was a blown manhole cover that cut through a power line and knocked out electricity to several buildings in the area, including Fenway Park.

Radio station WRKO and cable TV channel NESN lost their broadcasts. Auxiliary power illuminated the seating areas, but the rest of the park remained shrouded in darkness.

Public address announcer Sherm Feller, in a partially lit press box, played to the fans as though he were doing a vaudeville routine in a dimly lit nightclub. Announcing to the crowd that the power outage was the result of a problem outside the park, Feller cracked, "Boston Edison's working on it right now. If they send us a bill, we'll pay it."

The Fenway power outage was not unprecedented, though the previous one had gone relatively unnoticed by fans. "It was a weekday day game back in April 1981," said Josh Spofford, Red Sox director of publicity. "We didn't have any power the whole game. It was back when we were in the press box that was closer to the field, and Sherm led the crowd in the anthem a cappella and did the lineups with a bullhorn."

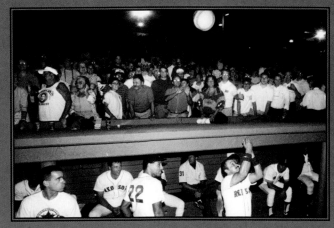

Players and spectators killed time batting beach balls during the Fenway blackout of May 13, 1991.

SOX CARETAKER

When Jean Yawkey died in 1992, John Harrington was entrusted to run the Red Sox. Harrington said that his goal was quite simple. "I just want to honor Jean's generous legacy—and prove myself worthy of that trust."

Harrington grew up in Boston and graduated from Boston College. While working as an accounting professor at BC, he was hired by Joe Cronin, president of the American League, to be the league's controller in 1970. From there, he was hired by Red Sox owner Tom Yawkey to be the team's treasurer. He eventually returned to the Red Sox in the mid-1980s and became an important adviser to Mrs. Yawkey.

After Mrs. Yawkey died, most observers expected that minority owner Haywood Sullivan, a former Red Sox player and executive, would buy out the Yawkey trust's majority share of the team. Instead, Harrington, acting on behalf of the trust, bought out Sullivan's general partnership stake in late 1993.

Sullivan talked about the relationship between Harrington and Mrs. Yawkey. "As the years passed, he became a kind of surrogate son. Certainly she depended on him more and more . . . and when he talked, you knew he was speaking for Jean."

Harrington reveled in his role as Red Sox CEO, jesting that "every kid under 12 wants to be Nomar or Pedro, and every kid over 40 wants my job." He acted as the chief negotiator for MLB owners during the 1994-95 strike, and he helped guide baseball's divisional realignment to accommodate the wild-card playoff format in 1995. But in 2000—with the team in good financial and competitive shape, and state lawmakers apparently poised to approve funding for Harrington's new ballpark project—he decided to sell the team on behalf of the trust. It was time to say good-bye.

"It was the right time for the team and the trust, and I knew I had to sell," Harrington said.

But what had seemed a dream to the new manager, who brought back his old skipper Don Zimmer as third-base coach, turned into a summer nightmare in 1992 as the Sox went into a June swoon on the road, falling 9½ games out on the way to their first cellar finish since 1932, the year before Tom Yawkey bought the franchise. "This team isn't as good as people think," Morgan had declared on his way out the door.

With no .300 hitters and Clemens as their only dominant starter, the 1992 Red Sox lost 89 games—the most the franchise had dropped in a single season since 1966—and finished 23 games behind Toronto. It was a rude awakening for Hobson, who had never experienced a losing season as a player. "Maybe I was a little in awe of managing Wade Boggs or having Roger Clemens on my pitching staff," he said. "That hasn't sunk in with me." It was an unsettling year for the franchise, which was thrown into transition when Tom Yawkey's widow, Jean, died in February of complications from a stroke. John Harrington, Yawkey's longtime confidant, stayed on as president of JRY Corp., which owned the Sox.

After another underwhelming campaign in 1993, when the Sox finished 15 games out in fifth place, Harrington shook up both the clubhouse and the front office. Gone after 11 years and more than 2,000 hits was Boggs, who departed for the Bronx. So was Ellis Burks, who changed red stockings for white.

During the autumn, Harrington bought out Haywood Sullivan's interest in the franchise. He moved General Manager Lou Gorman to executive director for baseball operations and brought in Dan Duquette from the Expos as GM. The 35-year-old Duquette, a lifelong Boston fan from Dalton, Massachusetts who'd made the most of a shoe-string budget in Montreal, arrived with a five-year mandate to make the club better by going both cheaper and younger, and to revamp a clubhouse that had 15 men who were 30 or older. "We're going to renew the roster with new life," Duquette vowed during spring training. By August, the Sox had suited up 46 players, half of them pitchers.

But the 1994 season was a lost cause by then. A 12-game home losing streak in June had mired Boston in third place, 10½ games behind. The breaking point came in a 10-4 home loss to New York during which Hobson had a meltdown and was ejected. He was later suspended five games for arguing with plate umpire Greg Kosc and bumping crew chief Larry Barnett after pitcher Sergio Valdez had been warned for throwing behind a Yankee batter. "There is a rage inside the guy [Hobson] that a lot of people don't know about," commented slugger Mo Vaughn. "If it goes, it goes. Behind this big job of being a

Red Sox manager is a man."

On July 22, when his club returned to Boston 13 games behind after having been swept in Anaheim, Hobson passed out towels to his battered ballplayers. "I ain't throwing mine in," he told them. "Don't throw yours in."

Three weeks later, the towel was tossed in for baseball itself as the players went on strike for the first time since 1985. "See you at the Patriots games," Vaughn told sportswriters after the finale at Baltimore had been washed out. The 54-61 record represented Boston's third straight losing season, its worst stretch since 1966, and it marked the end for Hobson, who was summoned from his Alabama home to be dismissed in September.

"I believed in my heart that this day would never happen," said Hobson, who later resurfaced as a scout and minor-league manager in Sarasota. "I'm not going to burn any bridges. When new faces come in, they want to bring in new faces. I know that." The new face belonged to mustachioed Kevin Kennedy, who'd been Montreal's minor league field coordinator and bench coach during Duquette's time there and had just been fired by the Rangers. "This is the first and only place I wanted to be," said Kennedy, who'd called Duquette as soon as Texas let him go.

An unprecedented winter of discontent followed the first canceled World Series, with the labor dispute remaining unsettled until March of 1995. It was unclear how the players would be received by fans when they took the diamond on April 26 for Opening Day.

Knowing the importance of public relations, new Sox

ABOVE: Dan Duquette, a native of Dalton, Massachusetts, achieved his childhood dream of running the Red Sox in 1994. And though the Sox made back-to-back playoff appearances for the first time in more than 80 years on his watch, Duquette's eight seasons as general manager were ultimately more tumultuous than triumphant. Duquette was considered one of baseball's brightest young executives when then-CEO John Harrington hired him away from Montreal as the Sox GM. Though he showed some flashes of brilliance, he was fired in March 2002 when the team's new ownership group led by John Henry decided they wanted their own man. "I've never had a bad day at Fenway Park," Duquette said after his ouster.

BELOW: A youngster had nowhere to go but down after making a lunge for a foul ball in a game at Fenway Park against the Chicago White Sox on April 29, 1995.

slugger Jose Canseco, who'd been acquired from the Rangers in December, was outside Fenway by 8 a.m., meeting and greeting ticket holders. "We can't forget what really counts," said his Sox teammate Mike Greenwell, who signed autographs for an hour after batting practice. "It's the fans."

And Sox fans seemed forgiving once their team had crushed Minnesota, 9-0.

The rebuilt and rededicated club took over first place on May 13 and stayed there for the rest of the season. Duquette, who'd reworked the roster (only three of the original 1994 starters were still in the lineup), kept tinkering, with 53 players (26 of them pitchers) suiting up by season's end.

Boston ran away with the AL East, winning the divisional title for the first time since 1990 and clinching at home on September 20 with a 3-2 victory over Milwaukee. For their triumphal procession around the premises, the players mounted police horses—even Vaughn, their resident Clydesdale. "Everyone got on the horse and so I had to get on the horse," Vaughn said, after John Harrington admitted that he was more worried about the horse than about his top slugger. "That's the way this team is."

The Sox were quickly unhorsed, however, in the playoffs by the Indians, who'd posted the league's best regular-season record with 100 victories. The 5-4 loss in the 13-inning opener at Jacobs Field was doubly hard to take since the Sox led, 2-0, and then 4-3, in the 11th—and since Tony Pena, their former catcher, clouted the winning homer off Zane Smith with two out. After Orel Hershiser blanked the Sox, 4-0, in Game 2, the season came down to what knuckleballer Tim Wakefield, who'd won 16 games after being picked up from Pittsburgh, could do with his notoriously unpredictable pitch.

The visitors were so confident they would finish off the Sox that they checked out of their hotel before the game. They then tagged Wakefield for seven runs in six innings, completing the sweep with an 8-2 triumph while extending Boston's postseason losing streak to an unlucky 13. "Sometimes I wish I could throw a hundred miles an hour like Randy Johnson," said Wakefield. Still, there was no disgrace in losing to a Cleveland club that went on to play in the World Series for the first time since 1954. "There are no excuses to be made for this series," reasoned Kennedy. "We lost, they won, and we'll be back."

But it was the Yankees who were back in 1996, winning their first World Series since 1978. The Sox finished in the middle of the pack after pretty much dooming themselves

TED AND JIMMY TOUCH BASE

He had been a symbol and a secret for a half-century, a New England icon frozen in time, representing all children with cancer. Then, in 1998, the Jimmy Fund logo came to life when Carl Einar Gustafson of New Sweden, Maine, revealed that he was the true "Jimmy." On July 9, 1999, in a thrill for both of them, he met Ted Williams, the Jimmy Fund's all-time biggest booster.

Anyone born in New England in the past 50 years knows of this charity dedicated to eradicating cancer in children. In 1948, Gustafson was chosen by Dr. Sidney Farber, the godfather of modern chemotherapy, to represent stricken kids everywhere on a national radio broadcast. They called him "Jimmy" to protect his privacy. The show was a hit, and the Jimmy Fund was launched.

As decades passed and treatments progressed, there was less curiosity about what happened to the original Jimmy. It made sense to assume that the child had died—as did almost all cancer patients of that era. A Maine man to the core, Gustafson never bothered to call attention to his role. "In my day, we were taught to keep things quiet," he explained. "There really was nothing to say about it. That was bragging."

In 1997, a year before the 50th anniversary of the fund's launch, Gustafson's sister sent a letter to Mike Andrews, the fund's executive director, explaining that her brother was alive and well. "We'd had a lot of leads like this before," said Andrews, who temporarily set aside the letter. "They were like Elvis sightings." An investigation based on hospital records and Gustafson's correspondence with Farber finally convinced Andrews that Gustafson was the real "Jimmy."

Williams finally met Gustafson when he visited Boston for the All-Star Weekend in 1999. They met at the Dana-Farber Cancer Institute and visited with dozens of patients—people who had a better chance of survival, in part, because of Williams's tireless efforts, in concert with an army of doctors, nurses, technicians, administrators, and fund-raisers.

"How are you, Jimmy baby?" Williams asked as Gustafson greeted him. "This is the biggest thrill of my trip, right here! Jeez, you look great! You're an inspiration to everybody!"

Gustafson appeared at numerous functions and recorded public service announcements for the Jimmy Fund. His story was featured in *People* magazine and *Sports Illustrated*. As for meeting Williams, he said, "I can't tell you how proud I feel to have met him."

Gustafson died in 2001 at age 65 after suffering a stroke.

"After 50 years, to find out he was alive was a miracle," said Andrews. "Then he turned out to be the most wonderful man. If we had tried to create a Jimmy, we couldn't have done better. And he was just thrilled to be part of it."

"Guys like George Will and Bob Costas come in and want to romanticize Fenway Park. But how many times have they had to sit in Section 1, 2, 3, 4, or 5? You sit in sections 6, 7, 8, or 9, you could get a crick in your neck from having to turn to the left all the time; you're looking straight at center field."

—Ted Sarandis, Boston radio talk-show host

On Opening Day in 1995, the woman at the center paid a scalper $50 for this obstructed-view seat behind home plate. Today, that would be called a steal.

by losing 19 of their first 25 games, and then falling 17 games behind in early July. Despite posting the best record in baseball over the final two months, Boston ended up in third place. Taking three of four from New York on the final weekend in Fenway provided a small bit of consolation. "It was emotional," said Kennedy after the Sox had won the finale by a 6-5 count, and then packed their bags for the winter. "Maybe it wasn't the intensity of winning a World Series game, but it was one we wanted."

A day later, Kennedy was gone for good, dismissed by Duquette after taking the fall for his club's wayward start and its perceived lack of cohesiveness. "It hurts," said Kennedy, whose players were startled by his firing. "I love what I do and I poured everything I had into it. You can ask the players how much I cared and how much they wanted to do well for me." By the time successor Jimy Williams arrived, Clemens had filed for free agency and then was gone in December, off to Toronto for what was then the richest contract ($31 million over four years) in baseball history.

When Clemens returned as a Blue Jay on July 12, 1997, after having once vowed that he'd never appear at Fenway in another team's uniform, he received a decidedly mixed reaction as he strolled out to warm up. Then he blinded his former mates, striking out 16 of them in an overpowering performance that had his former supporters chanting "Ro-ger, Ro-ger." "He came to make a point and he did,"

The Fenway outfield, where the bullpens are located, has always offered a spectacular view of the park.

conceded Vaughn, who whiffed three times.

Clemens—who had been characterized by Duquette upon his departure from the Sox as being in the "twilight of his career"—was jubilant.

"It was a special day, a beautiful day," said the Rocket, who went on to win the Cy Young Award as the league's best pitcher. The Sox, who were 17 games out and buried in last place that day, ended up fourth despite having a quintet of .300 hitters, including rookie shortstop Nomar Garciaparra.

The club clearly needed a pitching infusion and Duquette made a trade with his old club for ace Pedro Martinez, who signed a new contract with Boston for six years and $75 million. Martinez won 19 games in his first season in Boston, but it was Vaughn's bat that set the tone for 1998 with a mighty grand slam that brought his team back from the dead after thousands of discouraged fans had left the premises on Opening Day. "It felt like the World Series," noted winning pitcher Rich Garcés after the Sox had come from five runs down in the ninth to win, 9-7.

Vaughn, who'd squabbled with management over his salary during the off-season, became a fan favorite with his

MO'S PUZZLING DEPARTURE

For six seasons, Maurice Samuel "Mo" Vaughn, a native of Norwalk, Connecticut, was the heart and soul of the Red Sox. He twice led the team into the postseason, won an MVP Award and made three All-Star teams. He hit 230 home runs and drove in 752 runs in his tenure with the Sox, and in 1998, the "Hit Dog"—as he came to be known—had a career-best .337 batting average.

But following that 1998 season, Mo was gone, signed away by the Anaheim Angels as the Red Sox made a late, low-ball counteroffer that they had to know would virtually guarantee his departure.

Vaughn's souring relationship with Sox management had caused it to look past his good work on and off the field.

Mo's supporters included the *Globe*'s Bob Ryan, who wrote in July 1998 as the "Should they re-sign Mo?" debate was raging: "Here was a star player—a star player of color, on top of that—who was reflecting glory on the organization because he really was a man in, and of, the community. Central casting couldn't have shipped over a better player to the Red Sox. And now Mo is the bad guy? Don't believe it."

For a long time, Ryan noted, the Sox were eager to tout Vaughn's standing in Boston and his tireless work with youngsters.

But Vaughn also had gotten into a fight outside a Boston nightclub, and in 1998 he crashed his truck on the way home from a Rhode Island strip club and was arrested for failing field sobriety tests. (He was later tried and found not guilty of drunken driving.) These incidents, along with concerns about Vaughn's weight, created a growing chorus of Mo detractors.

As the 1998 season went on, his relationship with Sox management deteriorated, and his decision was made for him by the Angels when they made him baseball's highest-paid player at the time with an $80-million deal.

And though Mo appeared to be on the fast track to Cooperstown when he left the Sox, in the five succeeding seasons, he played just 466 games for the Angels and Mets before injuries forced him to retire.

Still, Vaughn later insisted he had no regrets. "It was just time to move on," he said. "If I had stayed in Boston, I would have retired as an angry player, and that's wrong, because I love this game."

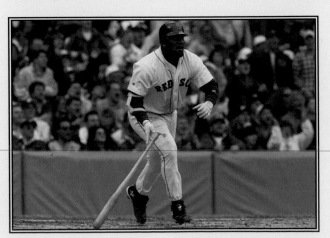

game-ending shot off Paul Spoljaric. "Sign Mo Now!" fans chanted as he circled the bases. By early May, the club already had come from behind seven times to win in the final inning.

While the Sox didn't come close to catching the Yankees (who won 114 games en route to another World Series ring), Boston did return to the playoffs for the first time in three years. "We made it, we made it," exulted Martinez, hugging Duquette and dousing Vaughn and Garciaparra with champagne after Boston had beaten Baltimore to clinch a wild-card berth.

Again, the opponent was Cleveland, and this time the Sox sensed that they were in for a reversal of fortune. Martinez stifled the Indians and Vaughn whacked two homers and knocked in seven runs in an 11-3 slamdown at Jacobs Field. "This is just the start," declared Dennis Eckersley after Boston had won its first postseason game since 1986. Everything was going the visitors' way when Indians Manager Mike Hargrove and starting pitcher Dwight Gooden were ejected and the Sox took a 2-0 lead in the first inning of Game 2.

But the Indians battered Tim Wakefield to salvage a split, and when they cranked three homers off Bret Saberhagen and another off Eckersley in the ninth inning of the first Fenway game, the Sox suddenly found themselves on the brink of elimination. "Please, Jimy, please pitch Pedro," Boston fans implored Sox Manager Jimy Williams as he walked toward the clubhouse.

Rather than use Martinez on three days' rest, Williams opted for a fresh Pete Schourek, who'd been scooped up from Houston in August. "The bottom line is we've got to win two games," said Saberhagen, "and Pedro can't win them both."

For seven innings of Game 4, Boston thought that it would even the series. Schourek was pitching a shutout and Garciaparra, who had a divisional series record 11 RBI, had put his team ahead with a leadoff homer in the fourth. When Tom "Flash" Gordon came in to wrap up things in the eighth, it seemed that the Sox would force a decisive fifth game with Martinez on the mound.

But Gordon, who'd strung together 43 saves in a row and hadn't blown one since April, conceded a two-run double to David Justice that gave the visitors a 2-1 decision. If Red Sox third-base coach Wendell Kim hadn't rashly waved home John Valentin for a damaging out in the sixth or if the autumnal wind hadn't reduced Vaughn's would-be tying homer to a Wall double in the eighth, Boston might have survived. "I'm pretty surprised it ended this way," Valentin remarked as the Sox cleaned out their lockers. "I anticipated that we'd go far." Instead the Indians

THE LONG GOOD-BYE

In May 1999, the Red Sox were gearing up for their first hosting of baseball's All-Star Game in 38 years. As far as the team was concerned, that summer's All-Star festivities would also provide an opportunity to say a gracious good-bye to Fenway Park, then 87 years old.

"Fenway is a wonderful ballpark," said John Harrington, chief executive officer of the Red Sox at the time. "But the sad truth is it's economically and operationally obsolete. It just doesn't allow us to compete like teams with modern ballparks do."

What the Sox hoped to sell to fans, political leaders, and the public was a new Fenway Park built right next door to the old one, "with the intimate scale and feel of the old" but up to 30 percent larger with modern conveniences and revenue streams.

As head of the JRY Trust that controlled the team, Harrington wanted to replace the existing 33,871-seat park with a new facility for 45,000 fans. Plans called for it to be built on roughly 14 acres bordered by Boylston Street, Brookline Avenue, and Yawkey Way.

Residents of the Fenway neighborhood and ballpark preservationists demanded that the park not be razed, but renovated. Harrington said he had studied several renovation options and rejected all of them.

Said Dan Wilson, a leading member of a group called "Save Fenway Park" and a Boston lawyer: "The Red Sox will be throwing out their most important asset if they build a new ballpark."

The Sox attempted to assuage that argument by offering plans to forever preserve parts of Fenway—a portion of the left-field wall, the 1912 brick entrance, and the entire infield—as a tourist attraction and open space.

After years of wrangling with city planners and park preservationists, the JRY Trust abandoned its new ballpark bid and put the team up for sale. Among the final five bidding groups in 2002, only the New England Sports Ventures group led by John Henry was committed to retaining the original ballpark. Interestingly, several of the options proposed by the Save Fenway Park contingent were ultimately implemented by Henry and his winning group, including the expansion of walkways and concession space inside the park, and the closing off of Yawkey Way to provide a game-day fan concourse.

Red Sox CEO John Harrington pointed out details of the proposed new Fenway Park to MLB commissioner Bud Selig (center) and Red Sox General Manager Dan Duquette (right) before the 1999 All-Star Game.

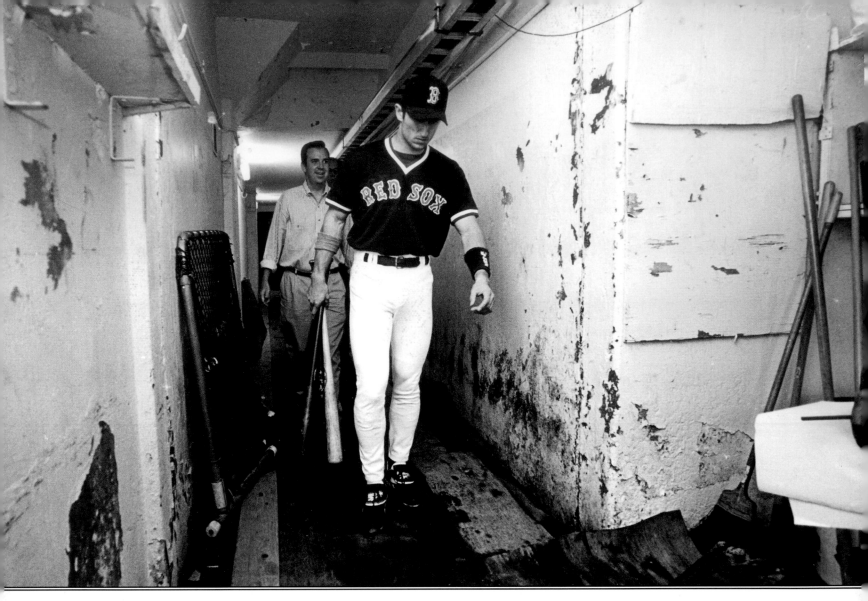

earned a quixotic date with the Yankees. "There's nothing to watch," declared Garciaparra. "We won't be there."

Boston was there in 1999, even after Vaughn decamped for Anaheim for $80 million over six years. Despite spending time on the disabled list with an uncooperative shoulder and squabbling with Duquette, Martinez won 23 games, including a one-hitter at New York in September. Though the Yankees, as usual, proved uncatchable, Boston did snare another wild-card spot for the playoffs and another meeting with the Indians.

After the Sox dropped the first two games of the divisional series in Cleveland—the second by an ugly 11-1 margin—they returned to Fenway facing extinction yet again. But they managed to stay alive with a pyrotechnic display in the seventh inning of Game 3, scoring six runs with two out on Valentin's two-run, bases-loaded ground-rule double, rookie Brian Daubach's three-run homer, and Lou Merloni's two-on single, to secure a 9-3 triumph.

Few would have predicted the next day's result, when the Sox literally put up telephone numbers in a 23-7 T-ball contest that drew them even. "Everything we threw up, they hit and where it came down, we weren't standing," observed Hargrove. No Boston team ever had punished as much horsehide in one October day. Three homers, two of

Nomar Garciaparra walked down the runway toward the Red Sox dugout with Red Sox Director of Communications Kevin Shea in 1998.

them by Valentin, who knocked in seven runs. Twenty-four hits, including a dozen for extra bases. A 10-2 lead after three innings, 15-2 after four, 18-6 after five. "It's a one-gamer now," concluded Williams.

So the Sox headed back to The Jake for the finale with a most appropriate, yet least likely figure providing their deliverance. Martinez had lasted only four innings in the opener before straining his back trying to blow a fastball past strongman Jim Thome. "I didn't know when Pedro could pitch again," admitted Joe Kerrigan, the Sox pitching coach. But after the Indians had pummeled Saberhagen and Derek Lowe for eight runs in three innings, Martinez came out of the bullpen to hurl six scoreless innings and stake his compañeros to a 12-8 triumph that put them into the league championship series for the first time since 1990.

The club's first postseason series victory since 1986 earned the Sox their first October date with the Yankees since the one-game 1978 playoff. "They better sweep us," warned Valentin. "They better sweep us, baby." By the time

ABOVE: A vendor offered soda (real New Englanders call it tonic) in July 1995.

BELOW: Programs were hawked on Yawkey Way before the 1997 home opener.

The view from atop the Green Monster at sunset, with both the ballpark and Lansdowne Street packed.

A STAR AMONG STARS

Baseball's All-Star Game frequently fails to live up to its hype. When Fenway Park hosted its third All-Star Game in 1999, the result was a 4-1 American League victory that featured zero home runs. But there will never be another sight like that of Ted Williams, who threw out the ceremonial first pitch, being engulfed by other baseball greats, including Stan Musial, Willie Mays, Bob Feller, Hank Aaron, Bob Gibson, and Cal Ripken Jr., just to name a few.

The ovation was loud and long. "I thought the stadium was going down," said Pedro Martinez afterward.

·The moment made a lasting impression on Mark McGwire of the St. Louis Cardinals. "When you have a chance to meet one of the best hitters in the game," said McGwire, "and you see tears running down his eyes because of the appreciation that the fans and all of us gave him, it becomes a very special time."

Introduced as "the greatest hitter who ever lived," Teddy Ballgame, 80, rode into Fenway on a golf cart. After a lap around the field, Williams was brought to the mound, where he was surrounded by both All-Star squads and 31 of the top 100 ballplayers in baseball history. It was without question the greatest assemblage of hardball talent ever gathered on any diamond. With a giant No. 9 stenciled into the outfield grass, and the ancient theater shaking on its foundation, Williams stood in front of the mound and delivered a strike to Carlton Fisk, the longtime Red Sox catcher and his soon-to-be fellow Hall of Famer.

The hero of the 1999 AL victory was Red Sox ace Pedro Martinez, who struck out five of the six batters to face him—Barry Larkin, Larry Walker, Sammy Sosa, McGwire, and Jeff Bagwell—and was voted the game's MVP. But even Pedro took a backseat to Williams.

"I don't think that there will be any other man that's going to replace that one," said Martinez.

"It was like something out of *Field of Dreams*," said Cleveland's Jim Thome.

Said a young woman in the stands, "Oh, my God. Ted Williams threw a pitch to Carlton Fisk. I'm going home happy."

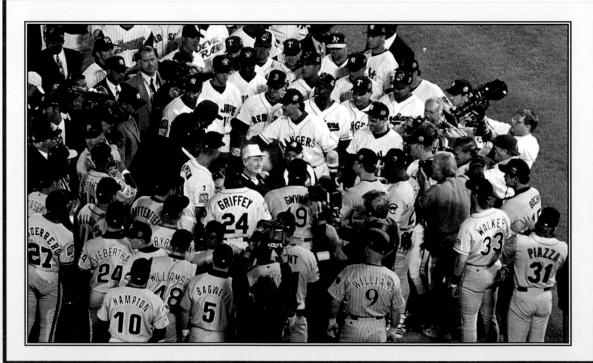

the Sox returned to Fenway, they were down two games after being edged, 4-3 and 3-2, in the Bronx, despite leading each night. They still had one defiant and glorious game left in them, though, and their 13-1 destruction of New York on Saturday afternoon delighted the full house, especially since it came at the expense of Clemens, who'd exchanged plumage for pinstripes in February.

Valentin's two-run homer in the first was the opening shot in a barrage that put Boston up, 6-0, after three innings and put New York starter Clemens out of the game. "Where is Roger?" the fans chanted gleefully in the seventh inning, when the lead had soared to 13-0 and Martinez still was throttling the visitors. "In the shower." It was the worst beating that the Yankees ever had taken in October and it made owner George Steinbrenner dyspeptic. "This can happen once," he told his players in the clubhouse, "but it can't happen again."

New York turned the tables emphatically on Sunday night with a 9-2 victory that put Boston on the brink. Everything turned on a bad call by umpire Tim Tschida, who allowed an inning-ending double play in the eighth with Boston trailing, even though Yankees second baseman Chuck Knoblauch missed tagging José Offerman after fielding Valentin's weak grounder. "No, I didn't make the right call," admitted Tschida. The furious crowd had agreed, littering the diamond with bottles in the ninth after Williams was ejected from the game for tossing his cap in the air.

As both teams were sent to their dugouts during an eight-minute delay, public address announcer Ed Brickley informed the spectators that the game would be forfeited unless order was restored. When play resumed, the Yankees ended things emphatically as pinch hitter Ricky Ledee hit a grand slam off Rod Beck. "It's the first one to win four and it's not over yet," Williams declared in a statement while remaining secluded in his office.

But New York made sure of it a day later, clinching the series in five games with a 6-1 victory that produced its 36th pennant and set the stage for another Series ring. "We wanted to finish it here," said Derek Jeter, who hit a two-run homer off Kent Mercker in the first inning. "We didn't want to give them any life or confidence."

While the Yankees sprayed each other with nonalcoholic champagne, the Sox, who'd had their best season in 13 years, were philosophical in defeat. "There's nothing for us to hang our heads about," Garciaparra proclaimed. "Disappointed? Of course. Any year we don't win the World Series, I'm disappointed. But I'm not going to hang my head."

Pedro Martinez argued his case to manager Jimy Williams in the Red Sox dugout on August 14, 1999. Williams had refused to let the late-arriving Martinez start the game; instead, he went with Bryce Florie. Martinez pitched the last four innings and Boston came away with a 13-2 victory over Seattle.

FENWAY PARK

MARCH 18
In the largest art heist in history, two thieves make off with 13 works of art, now valued at more than $300 million, from the Isabella Stewart Gardner Museum in the Fenway.

APRIL 18
The first baseball Beanpot tournament is held at Fenway Park. Boston College beats Northeastern, 4-1, for the championship.

JUNE 27
Mo Vaughn makes his major-league debut, going on to bat .260 with four homers and 32 RBI for the season.

SEPTEMBER 23
Joe Morgan is fired as manager and replaced by Butch Hobson.

FEBRUARY 26
Jean Yawkey, the widow of Tom Yawkey and the owner of the Red Sox, dies at age 83. Ownership of the team passes to the JRY Corporation, later renamed the JRY Trust, headed by John Harrington, team CEO.

SEPTEMBER 24
Father Guido Sarducci (comedian Don Novello) conducts an exorcism outside Fenway Park designed to banish the Curse of the Bambino.

DECEMBER 15
Wade Boggs signs a free-agent deal with the Yankees.

NOVEMBER 23
John Harrington buys out minority owner Haywood Sullivan, a former Red Sox player and executive, and the JRY Trust becomes the sole owner of the Red Sox.

JANUARY 27
Native son Dan Duquette is named Red Sox general manager, replacing Lou Gorman.

JUNE 2
Shortstop Nomar Garciaparra is selected by the Red Sox in the first round of the amateur draft.

AUGUST 12
A Major League Baseball strike begins. The Red Sox are already out of the playoff picture and near last place with a 54-61 record.

SEPTEMBER 20
Butch Hobson is fired as manager, to be replaced by Kevin Kennedy.

1990   1991   1992   1993   1994

OCTOBER 3
Boston clinches the AL East with a 3-1 win over Chicago at Fenway Park when Tom Brunansky makes a spectacular catch in the right-field corner for the final out.

OCTOBER 6-10
The Red Sox are swept by the Oakland Athletics in the ALCS. Roger Clemens is ejected from Game 4 for arguing balls and strikes.

APRIL 2
The Major League Baseball strike ends, but not before forcing the cancellation of the previous season's World Series.

APRIL 26
Knuckleballer Tim Wakefield is signed.

NOVEMBER 16
Mo Vaughn is named the American League's Most Valuable Player for the 1995 season.

DECEMBER 13
Roger Clemens, now a free agent, leaves the Red Sox and signs with the Toronto Blue Jays. GM Dan Duquette, in an often-misquoted statement, says, "The Red Sox and our fans were fortunate to see Roger Clemens play in his prime, and we had hoped to keep him in Boston during the twilight of his career."

SEPTEMBER 30
Manager Kevin Kennedy is fired and replaced by Jimy Williams.

MARCH 19
A 25-foot Coca-Cola three-bottle sign is built atop the left-field wall light tower. (The bottles were later removed in 2007, but Coca-Cola still has a prominent sign at Fenway.)

JULY 31
The Sox acquire Jason Varitek and Derek Lowe in a trade with the Mariners.

NOVEMBER 25
Mo Vaughn leaves the Red Sox and is signed as a free agent by the Anaheim Angels, who make him baseball's highest-paid player with a six-year, $80-million deal.

MAY 15
The Red Sox announce plans to replace Fenway with a new, modern facility nearby, and the rallying cry of "Save Fenway Park" is sounded. (The plans were abandoned in 2005.)

JULY 13
The 70th All-Star Game is held at Fenway Park. Retired Sox greats Ted Williams and Carlton Fisk make guest appearances. The AL defeats the National League, 4-1. Pedro Martínez is named the game's MVP.

1995   1996   1997   1998   1999

NOVEMBER 18
The Red Sox acquire Pedro Martínez in a trade with the Montreal Expos.

SEPTEMBER 27
Pedro Martinez strikes out 12 and gives up one earned run in eight innings against the Orioles to notch his final win of a season when he claims pitching's Triple Crown with a 23-4 record, 2.07 ERA, and 313 strikeouts. Martinez would go on to win the AL Cy Young Award in a unanimous vote and finish second in the American League MVP balloting.

OCTOBER 13-18
The Red Sox lose the ALCS to the Yankees in five games.

Top of page (l-r): Installing new seats, 1999; a nervous new mascot, Wally, debuting at Fenway, 1997; celebrating Mo Vaughn's game-winning grand slam on Opening Day, 1998. Timeline: "Ted Williams Day," May 1991; players saluting the silver anniversary of the Impossible Dream season, 1992; conductors Seiji Ozawa and John Williams rally the crowd before Game 3 of the ALCS, 1999; Globe coverage of the 1999 All Star game at Fenway Park.

2000s

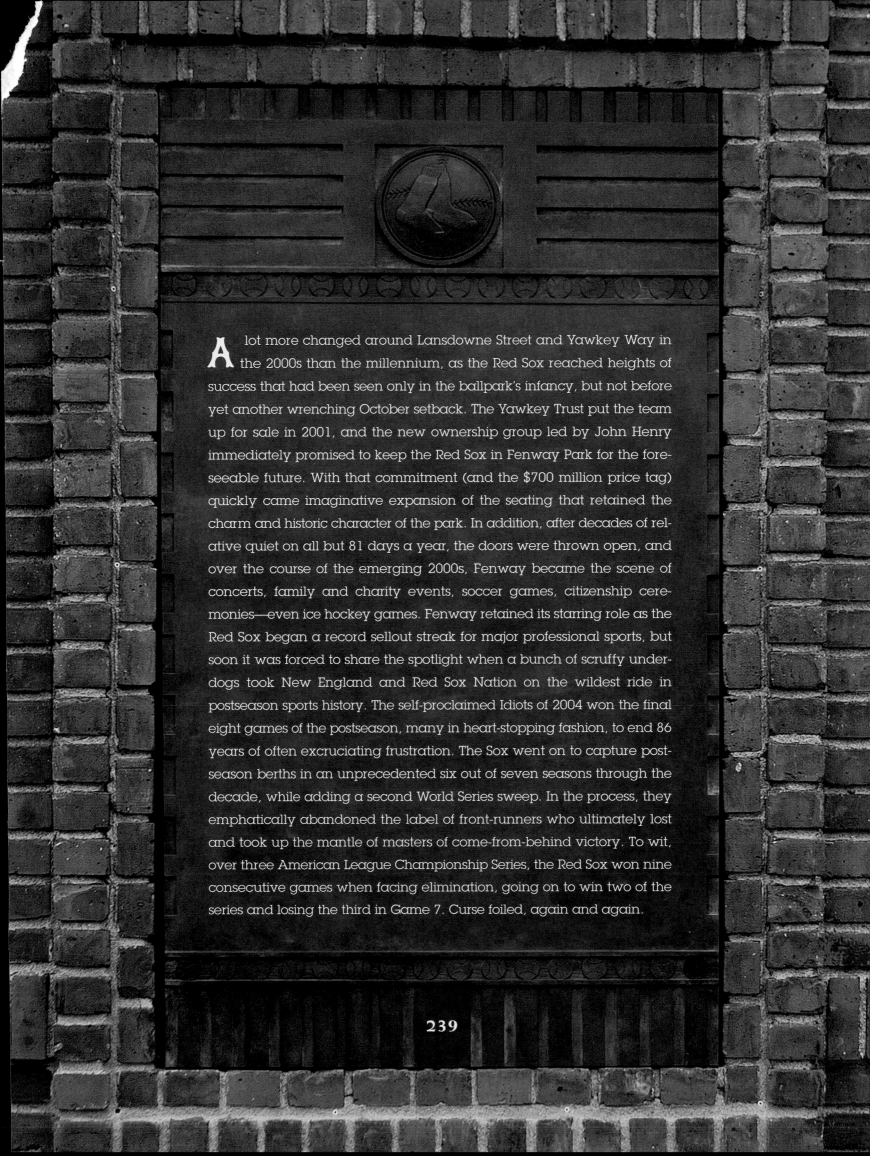

A lot more changed around Lansdowne Street and Yawkey Way in the 2000s than the millennium, as the Red Sox reached heights of success that had been seen only in the ballpark's infancy, but not before yet another wrenching October setback. The Yawkey Trust put the team up for sale in 2001, and the new ownership group led by John Henry immediately promised to keep the Red Sox in Fenway Park for the foreseeable future. With that commitment (and the $700 million price tag) quickly came imaginative expansion of the seating that retained the charm and historic character of the park. In addition, after decades of relative quiet on all but 81 days a year, the doors were thrown open, and over the course of the emerging 2000s, Fenway became the scene of concerts, family and charity events, soccer games, citizenship ceremonies—even ice hockey games. Fenway retained its starring role as the Red Sox began a record sellout streak for major professional sports, but soon it was forced to share the spotlight when a bunch of scruffy underdogs took New England and Red Sox Nation on the wildest ride in postseason sports history. The self-proclaimed Idiots of 2004 won the final eight games of the postseason, many in heart-stopping fashion, to end 86 years of often excruciating frustration. The Sox went on to capture postseason berths in an unprecedented six out of seven seasons through the decade, while adding a second World Series sweep. In the process, they emphatically abandoned the label of front-runners who ultimately lost and took up the mantle of masters of come-from-behind victory. To wit, over three American League Championship Series, the Red Sox won nine consecutive games when facing elimination, going on to win two of the series and losing the third in Game 7. Curse foiled, again and again.

With the new millennium and the club's 100th season at hand, the Red Sox made two blockbuster announcements in 2000: there would be both a new ballpark and new ownership. Despite Fenway's quirky charm and rich history, it was the oldest and smallest facility in the major leagues. "If we do nothing," chief executive John Harrington declared in a *Globe* op-ed column on May 25, "we will be left behind."

By the end of July, the front office, state, and city had agreed on a $665 million project, with nearly half of it to be publicly funded. The site, though, was undetermined, with management preferring the South Boston waterfront and Mayor Thomas Menino preferring the Fenway neighborhood. Meanwhile, the team was engaged in its annual battle—trying not to be left behind by the Yankees.

With Pedro Martinez and Nomar Garciaparra on track to retain their Cy Young and batting crowns, the Sox were in first place as late as June 22. But they faded during the summer and essentially were finished off on September 10 after the Yankees swept them at Fenway for the first time since 1991.

So the Sox finished second in the division for the third straight time and the Yankees went on to win their third consecutive World Series. And five days after the season ended, the For Sale sign went up on a franchise that had borne the Yawkey name since the Depression.

While Harrington wanted the next owner to be "a diehard Red Sox fan from New England," management estimated that it would take at least a year to have a buyer step forward and be approved.

In the interim, the Sox were under pressure to close the gap between them and their pinstriped overlords in 2001. So the front office lured away Manny Ramirez from the Indians with an eight-year deal worth $160 million, the fattest contract in franchise annals and second only in all Major League Baseball to the $252 million deal that Alex Rodriguez signed with the Rangers that same day.

"I'm just tired of seeing New York always win," said Ramirez, who grew up in Washington Heights, not far from Yankee Stadium, but who enthusiastically chugged a symbolic cup of chowder during his Fenway introduction. Ramirez, acquired for his prodigious ability to drive in runs, knocked in three against Tampa Bay in his new team's home opener. That came just two days after right-hander Hideo Nomo had celebrated his Sox debut in Baltimore with a no-hitter, the first by a Boston hurler since 1965. So the fans began dreaming about October in April.

But as Martinez, Garciaparra, and Jason Varitek all struggled with injuries, things went sour in midsummer. Jimy Williams was replaced by Joe Kerrigan, the pitching coach, and the season came apart in late August with an 18-inning loss at Texas. The club lost 12 of its next 13

A "Save Fenway Park" mural outside the State House in Boston drew signatures from fans of all ages.

games, the death knell coming at Fenway with a weekend sweep by the Yankees. "We don't have a monkey on our back," Red Sox outfielder Trot Nixon muttered. "We've got a goddamned gorilla on our back."

At season's end, Boston was 13½ games behind New York and the collapse set the stage for a massive transformation before the 2002 season that featured new ownership, a new GM, and a new manager. The biggest change came in December when a group headed by Marlins owner John Henry bought the franchise from the Yawkey Trust for $700 million, more than twice the previous record paid for a Major League Baseball team.

It was the first time since 1933 that the club had been sold.

Henry, who gave up his Florida Marlins stake, took over as the club's principal owner, while former San Diego owner Tom Werner became chairman, and former San Diego and Baltimore chief executive Larry Lucchino assumed the role of president.

When the new group took over in March, they immediately made changes, replacing General Manager Dan Duquette with assistant Mike Port on an interim basis and hiring Grady Little, a former bench coach, to succeed Kerrigan, whose tenure lasted only 43 games.

There were changes to Fenway, too, as the owners endeavored to show the faithful that they were committed to restoration instead of relocation. "When I think of Paris I think of the Eiffel Tower," Henry mused. "When I think of

A Red Sox groundskeeper scaled the ladder to the top of the Green Monster to retrieve baseballs hit into the netting during batting practice.

Boston, I think of Fenway."

Before Opening Day, the ballpark was painted, the club-houses freshened, and 10 new concession stands and 400 new seats were added. "Fans want to be at the game," said Henry, who ensconced himself in a front-row box for the unveiling. "So we'll put them on the field, we'll put them on the rooftops, we'll even put them on the bench."

The fans soon got a close-up of the first Fenway no-hitter since Dave Morehead's in 1965 and it came from an unlikely source—Derek Lowe, who'd been booed mercilessly during his 5-10 campaign the previous year. "It's surreal," marveled Lowe, whose teammates presented him the ball on a silver platter after he'd allowed Tampa Bay only one base runner during his 10-0 masterpiece on April 27.

While Lowe went on to start the All-Star Game and have a career year (21-8), his teammates faded after a 40-17 start that helped them stay in first place until late June; they finished more than 10 games astern.

Sport's most storied rivalry heated up during the off-season when Lucchino referred to the Yankees as the "Evil Empire" and New York owner George Steinbrenner called the Sox president the game's "foremost chameleon of all time." The clubs fought each other to a near-standstill in

SWEET SEATS

They have been voted the best seats in baseball by ESPN SportsTravel and *USA Today*. And even Fenway purists would have to admit that when the Red Sox added seats atop the left-field wall, they did it right.

When his ownership group took over the team in 2002, John Henry broached the idea of putting seats atop the 37-foot-tall Green Monster, which has been called the most famous wall this side of China. It wasn't the first renovation project Henry & Co. undertook, but, initially, it was the most controversial.

"Certainly there were raised eyebrows," recalled Charles Steinberg, former Red Sox executive vice president for public affairs. But by the time the project was finished, it became the most popular of the many ballpark upgrades. Henry credits Janet Marie Smith, the Red Sox senior vice president of planning and development, with the design of 269 stools with bar rails. The section has three rows, plus a fourth of standing-room-only and concession stands. The Red Sox resisted the urge to cram in as many seats as possible.

The challenge, said Smith, was "how to put seats up there without overpowering the Green Monster. We wanted to make the seats special even after the novelty wore off."

"They should've done it years ago," Marty Feeney, of Quincy, Massachusetts, told the *Denver Post* when he attended the 2007 World Series. "Now you get the real feel of a home-run shot. The camera's on you. You get your one minute of fame."

During a game in 2008, one fan atop the Monster was swamped with text messages from friends within seconds after he narrowly missed catching a home-run ball.

Smith was with the Red Sox for nearly eight years (she left in 2009 to help renovate the Rose Bowl), during which time the team spent roughly $150 million on improvements to the park, increasing Fenway's capacity by 5,000, while waterproofing its leaky stands and reinforcing its foundations to last another 40 years.

Another of the most popular changes is just outside the walls of the park: the Yawkey Way concourse, which debuted in 2002. The street named for longtime owner Tom Yawkey is closed to traffic and non-ticket holders on game days, creating a sort of street carnival with entertainment, food carts, vendors, and often a chance to visit with and get an autograph from a former Sox player.

RECENT CHANGES MADE TO FENWAY:

2002: Dugout seats and Yawkey Way concourse.

2003: Green Monster seats and right-field concourse.

2004: Right-field roof seats.

2005: Third-base concourse and Game On! Sports Bar.

2006: EMC Club and State Street Pavilion.

2007: Jordan's Third-Base Deck.

2008: State Street Pavilion expansion, Coca-Cola Corner, Bleacher Bar under center-field bleachers.

2009: Right-field roof renovations, repair of original 1912 seating bowl.

"When I was there, I always realized there was something bigger than us as players: these people that had bled, cried tears, and cheered over the years. Winning a World Series in Boston is more than an individual player winning a World Series—it was winning a World Series for these people."

—Nomar Garciaparra, March 2010

2003, with New York winning the season series, 10-9. "They know we are here," Little proclaimed in late July. "And they know that we are not going away."

The Sox had become relentless buckaroos who rode into the late summer with a sense of urgency, sporting red T-shirts that declared "THE TIME IS NOW . . . SO COWBOY UP." Yet Boston needed a near-miracle to earn a postseason date with the Yankees after losing the first two games of their best-of-five divisional series at Oakland. "I know it can be done," said Varitek, who had played on the 1999 club that had come back to beat the Indians after spotting them a 2-0 advantage in the playoffs. "Just let us get home and see what happens."

The odds, though, were daunting, especially given that the Sox had lost 10 straight playoff games to the Athletics.

"[Our fans] may be jumping off bridges," conceded Garciaparra, "but I guarantee they'll get out of the water and they'll be out there supporting us on Saturday."

It was almost Sunday morning by the time the club began its great escape with Trot Nixon's long, looping pinch-hit homer into the center-field seats for a walk-off victory in the 11th inning. "There was a little gust of wind from the good Lord," said Nixon, after his homer sealed the 3-1 triumph, "and it ended up going out of the ballpark."

There was an earthly intervention on Sunday afternoon

A street-fair atmosphere took root on Yawkey Way outside Fenway Park beginning in 2002, but it's for ticket-holders only. No ticket? The Cask 'n Flagon still accepts all comers.

SO LONG, TEDDY BALLGAME

When Ted Williams died at 83 on July 5, 2002, there was no wake and no funeral. Only the makings of a circus, with his three children battling over what exactly his last intentions were, and son John Henry Williams insisting that his father had signed an agreement to be cryonically frozen in Arizona.

Though the legal battle over Williams's remains would play out for months, the Red Sox held a ceremony in his honor on July 22 at Fenway Park, where lifelong friends and former teammates found kinship and a measure of closure for the passing of "Teddy Ballgame."

"The tribute was to him and his life, what he did on and off the field," said former Sox shortstop Rico Petrocelli. "And that's the way it should have been. I think we needed this, we being Boston and the former players, needed this closure."

Jerry Coleman, a former Yankee rival and fellow fighter pilot, met Williams at the 1950 All-Star Game. He said he immediately admired Williams. "He went to the wall to make a catch and crashed into it. He broke his arm," said Coleman. A few innings later,

Williams came to the plate and singled. "I was thinking, 'Geez, this guy hits better with a broken arm than most guys do with two arms.'"

Said Dan Shaughnessy: "Teddy Ballgame was our own Babe Ruth, an oversized figure who forged his way into every New England household. . . . Forget cryonics. The Kid stays alive through folklore, the telling of tall tales. He's a baseball Bunyan."

In a sad footnote to the Williams ceremony, longtime Sox announcer Ned Martin died of an apparent heart attack at the Raleigh airport after participating in the tribute at Fenway. Martin, who delighted New England with his erudition and gentle wit, described the Sox action on radio and television between 1961 and 1992.

Martin served in the Marines in World War II and saw action in Iwo Jima. He worked with Ken Coleman on Sox TV broadcasts from 1966-72. He famously cried, "There's pandemonium on the field" when Petrocelli caught the pop-up to end the final game of the 1967 regular season, as the Sox won their first pennant in 21 years.

from David Ortiz, who cranked the winning double off the Oakland bullpen in the eighth. "I've never cried at a baseball game before but I couldn't help it," said Henry after Ortiz, who'd been 0 for 16 in the series, knocked in Garciaparra and Ramirez for a most unlikely 5-4 decision. "It was an unforgettable moment."

As a closer, Lowe held off the A's to save Martinez's win in the finale on the Coast, and then he and his mates headed for the Bronx, and grabbed the ALCS opener from the Yankees with three homers and Wakefield's devilish knuckler. That was the beginning of what would be the most spirited, memorable and, ultimately, painful October meeting between the two rivals.

The first game in the Fens produced a bench-clearing brawl that included Don Zimmer, the former Sox skipper turned pinstriped Buddha. Zimmer charged Martinez, who'd thrown at Karim Garcia's head, and the 72-year-old was tossed to the ground in the scuffle. "When this series began everyone knew it was going to be quite a battle, very emotional, with a lot of intensity," said Little after the visitors had prevailed, 4-3. "But I think we've upgraded it from a battle to a war."

Though Wakefield evened things in Game 4, the Yankees countered with a 4-2 victory that sent them home with two

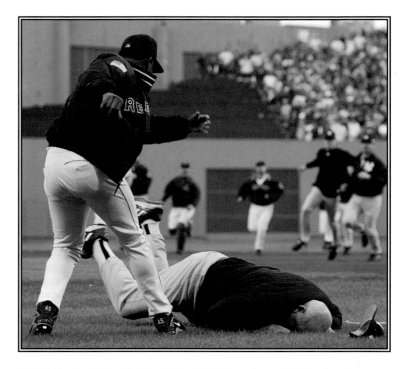

ABOVE: Red Sox pitcher Pedro Martinez threw Yankee bench coach Don Zimmer to the ground after Zimmer accosted him during a brawl in the fourth inning of Game 3 of the AL Championship Series on October 11, 2003 in Fenway Park.

BELOW: Despite his controversial antics, Manny Ramirez never lacked a following in Boston, on or off the field.

Jason Varitek grappled with the Yankees' Alex Rodriguez after Rodriguez was hit by a pitch from Bronson Arroyo on July 24, 2004 at Fenway Park. They were among four players ejected after a bench-clearing brawl. The Red Sox rallied from a 9-4 deficit to win the game, 11-10.

ROCKIN' THE PARK

This time, when Fenway Park echoed with the chords of "Take Me Out to the Ball Game," it was different.

The organist was Danny Federici of the E Street Band, and Bruce Springsteen was taking the field for the first rock concert in the park's 91 years.

It was September 6, 2003, and it had been 30 years since Stevie Wonder, War, and Ray Charles had played at Fenway as part of the Newport Jazz Festival. But this was different.

"What this park needs is a rock 'n' roll baptism, a rock 'n' roll bar mitzvah . . . a rock 'n' roll exorcism," Springsteen told the capacity crowd of more than 35,000 as he and his bandmates played a typical "Boss" show that encompassed 28 songs and three hours, ending appropriately with a cover of the ubiquitous Beantown anthem, "Dirty Water," helped along by Peter Wolf, former lead singer of the Boston-based J. Geils Band.

Bruce was starting the final month of a 14-month world tour in support of his *The Rising* album, a paean to America in the aftermath of the 9/11 attacks. His Boston audience was receptive to all of it, except his teasing about the Yankees rivalry. When he brought up the "evil citizens" to the South, the crowd booed lustily.

Still, Springsteen obviously got it. Toward the end of the show, he said, "There's not many places where you can walk into an empty place and feel the soul of the city, but this is one."

Since Springsteen headlined Fenway's coming-out party as a rock music venue, it has hosted at least one major rock or pop act per year, and it often plays host to the Dropkick Murphys, the backbeat of Red Sox Nation.

21ST CENTURY PLAYERS

2003: Bruce Springsteen and the E Street Band

2004: Jimmy Buffett and the Coral Reefer Band

2005: The Rolling Stones

2006: Dave Matthews Band with Sheryl Crow

2007: The Police

2008: Neil Diamond

2009: Dave Matthews Band with Willie Nelson

2009: Phish

2009: Paul McCartney

2010: Aerosmith and the J. Geils Band

2011: New Kids on the Block and Backstreet Boys

Standing atop the Red Sox dugout, the Dropkick Murphys played "Dirty Water" in October 2004.

"Other places have spectators;
Fenway has 35,000 participants."

—Bill Veeck, longtime owner and baseball executive

ABOVE: Teammates swarmed David Ortiz after his 10th-inning home run clinched a three-game sweep of the AL Division Series against the Anaheim Angels on October 8, 2004.

BELOW: A fan was rewarded for keeping the faith in the 2004 AL Championship Series against the Yankees: David Ortiz rounded third after hitting a home run in the eighth inning of Game 5, which Boston went on to win, 5-4, in 14 innings.

chances to win the pennant. "The clock is ticking on us right now," acknowledged Little. "This isn't something we've never been through before. We were through this about a week ago."

Resurrections had become routine. So when Boston came from two runs down to force a seventh game with a 9-6 victory, anything seemed possible. Before the Sox took the field, the Fenway grounds crew painted a 2003 World Series logo on the grass behind home plate. "They're crazy!" remarked Yankee closer Mariano Rivera. "It's silly. . . . Maybe they want to believe they won."

The finale, with Martinez and Clemens dueling again, was more painful than the 1986 World Series nightmare in Queens. With his club ahead, 5-2, in the bottom of the eighth and a fresh bullpen in reserve, Little left Martinez on the mound as the Yankees rallied and erased the Sox lead. The season slipped away in the 11th inning when pinch hitter Aaron "Boone-bino" Boone, a light-hitting infielder, lofted a Wakefield knuckler into the left-field seats. "Go back to Boston, boys, good-bye!" New York owner George Steinbrenner crowed as the buses pulled out of the stadium lot.

That was the end for Little, who was let go before the end of the month. "Yes, we came up short of our goal," Little acknowledged in a statement, "and to the Red Sox Nation I say: I hurt with each of you. It was painful for all of us."

For his successor, the front office selected Terry Francona, who knew about working in a demanding town after managing for four years in Philadelphia. "Think about it for a second," said Francona, who'd been a big-league player like his father, Tito. "I've been released from six teams. I've been fired as a manager. I've got no hair. I've got a nose that's three sizes too big for my face and I grew up in a major-league clubhouse. My skin's pretty thick. I'll be okay."

Prospects for an autumn rematch seemed remote in 2004 after the Sox had fallen well behind the Yankees by late July. But one startling turnabout at Fenway foreshadowed what ranks as the greatest resurrection in baseball history. Aroused by a brawl touched off by Varitek shoving his mitt in Alex Rodriguez's face after he'd been plunked by Bronson Arroyo, the Sox rallied from two runs down in the ninth and won on Bill Mueller's two-run homer off Rivera.

"I hope we look back a while from now and we're saying that this brought us together," Francona said. "I hope a long time from now we look back and say this did it."

That set the stage for another October showdown with New York. But Boston first had to finish off the Angels, who arrived at Fenway on the verge of extinction in their divisional series after being hammered twice at home. What the Sox needed, on the heels of setting a dubious record by blowing a 6-1 lead in the seventh, was a coup de

grace. Ortiz provided it with a two-run shot over the Green Monster off Jarrod Washburn with two outs in the 10th for an 8-6 triumph and the second Sox sweep of a postseason series since 1903.

"Now we have two more celebrations to go," observed Theo Epstein, who had become the youngest general manager in MLB history two years earlier when the Red Sox named him their GM at the age of 28.

That seemed impossible when Boston dropped the first two games of the championship series at New York, and then absorbed an ugly 19-8 smackdown at home that was the worst postseason loss in franchise history. No major-league ball club in history had won a seven-game series after losing the first three matchups. The only way to do it, Francona pointed out, was to win one each day.

His club came within one inning of a devastating sweep, trailing by a score of 4-3 in Game 4 with Rivera on the mound in the ninth. Then Kevin Millar drew a leadoff walk and the greatest comeback in MLB history was underway.

Dave Roberts, who'd been picked up from the Dodgers at the trading deadline as a speedy spare part, was sent in as a pinch runner and stole second on the next pitch. Then Mueller knocked him in with a single to center to tie the game and send it into extra innings. David Ortiz won it in the 12th with a two-run homer into the visiting bullpen off Paul Quantrill at 1:22 a.m. "This is a team that never gives up," Ortiz declared after Boston had won the five-hour duel by a 6-4 count. "Great heart."

Fenway was more than ready for World Series action as Game 1 got underway in 2004. A historic sweep was ahead.

The Sox again defied probability later that same day with another far-fetched escape. This time, it was a 5-4 triumph that required 14 innings and five hours and 49 minutes to complete, and ended with another killing blow from Ortiz, whose two-out single to center scored Johnny Damon. "To continually do it night in and night out, it's ridiculous," marveled Red Sox first baseman Doug Mientkiewicz. "It's a freak of nature."

Had Ortiz not clouted a homer in the eighth to help his teammates climb out of a two-run hole, the season likely would have ended an inning later. "Being down 3-0 and being down the last two nights shows the depth, the character, the heart, the guts of our ball club," proclaimed Wakefield, who collected the victory as Boston's seventh pitcher. "And it took every ounce of whatever we had left to win tonight's game and to win last night's game."

Still, the Sox trailed, 3-2, in the series going back to the Bronx, where the previous season had ended painfully. "We're in the same position as last year and we came awfully close," Henry observed. "But the odds are still against us."

Yet the club continued its historic resurrection in Babe Ruth's old playpen as Curt Schilling, pitching on a sutured right ankle that bled through his sock, dazzled the Yankees,

PEOPLE OF THE PARK

STANDELLS GET A SECOND ACT

BY BRIAN MACQUARRIE

Any time the Red Sox prevail at Fenway Park, you hear it: the slinky raunch of the guitar, the snide snarl of the vocals, the backhanded celebration of Boston in the lyrics. Hundreds of thousands of Sox fans recognize the Standells' "Dirty Water" as the unlikely anthem for their beloved team and city.

But for one Red Sox fan in California, "Dirty Water" means much more. For Dick Dodd of Buena Park, the song's surprising staying power has provided a link to his rock 'n' roll past, which included opening for the Rolling Stones, and a connection to a place he had never seen before "Dirty Water" came out.

Dodd sang the 1960s proto punk ode to a grungy Boston. Dodd was the drummer for the Los Angeles-based Standells when "Dirty Water" hit the airwaves, and he is the one who added the raspy opening that set the mood for the attitude-laced song.

"I'm gonna tell you a story," Dodd said one day in 2005, repeating his lyrics as he looked upward into a sunny California sky. "I'm gonna tell you about my town. I'm gonna tell you a big bad story, baby . . ."

After the Standells broke up in the early 1970s, Dodd bounced around as a restaurant manager, an office employee for a construction-equipment company, and a chauffeur. Over the years, his daydreams often drifted 3,000 miles to Boston. And now, the Standells, who reunited after all those years and perform from time to time, have played twice for Fenway fans.

Dodd was stunned by the odds-defying popularity in Boston of a song that peaked at No. 11 on the pop charts back in 1966. "When you get to be my age, you get a little choked up by this," Dodd said.

Dodd said he began following the Red Sox in the mid-1980s. But he was unaware the team had adopted "Dirty Water" until the day he heard the distinctive chords pulsating around Fenway Park at the end of an ESPN telecast of a Red Sox game. They were playing his song. "The crowd was singing every word," Dodd said, shaking his head in amazement.

Some four decades after the song's release, Dodd was still surprised that "Dirty Water" became a hit in the first place. None of the four Standells had been to Boston before creating the song. The band recorded "Dirty Water" only at the prodding of their producer, the late Ed Cobb, who wrote the hit after a visit to Boston, during which he was mugged on the Massachusetts Avenue Bridge over the Charles River, Dodd said.

Dodd and the Standells were invited by the Red Sox to perform "Dirty Water" as a Fenway Park surprise before Game 2 of the 2004 World Series. It was a dream come true for Dodd.

"Nobody knew we were going to be there, number one. And I don't care who you are, you're going to get nervous with Fenway Park sold out," Dodd said. "Then everyone went freaking crazy, and right at that moment, when I knew I wasn't singing it alone, it was just unbelievable. God, I just wanted to hug everybody."

When the Red Sox searched in 1997 for a theme to celebrate each home victory, General Manager Dan Duquette and Manager Jimy Williams chose the down-and-dirty sound of the Standells. And even though the team ownership changed, the Red Sox are committed to the song as their victory music.

RIGHT: Red Sox co-owner Tom Werner strolled with the ALCS trophy outside Fenway Park before the 2004 World Series.

LEFT: Sox co-owner John Henry (center) played guitar with members of the Standells at a playoff rally in October 2007.

4-2, in Game 6. Then Derek Lowe starved the hosts in the finale and Damon crushed them with a second-inning grand slam. "How many times can you honestly say you have a chance to shock the world?" crowed Millar after the 10-3 knockout that put Boston into the World Series for the first time since 1986.

This time the opponents were the Cardinals, who'd beaten the Red Sox in the 1946 and 1967 World Series and who boasted the season's best record. Once again the Sox, who became the first team in 56 years to start a pure knuckleballer in a Series game, won in a most unorthodox fashion, surviving a blown 7-2 lead and four errors to win, 11-9, on Mark Bellhorn's two-run homer off Pesky's Pole in the eighth.

Despite making another four errors the next night, the Sox won again, 6-2, behind the sore-ankled but irrepressible Schilling. Fate seemed to be turning in their favor after decades of disappointment. And when Martinez stifled St. Louis, 4-1, at Busch Stadium to win Game 3, the Sox fans who'd made the trip to St. Louis sensed the end of an 86-year drought. "One more game," they chanted behind the visiting dugout. "One more game."

Boston won it easily, with Lowe shutting out the Cardinals, 3-0, and closer Keith Foulke flipping the ball to Mientkiewicz for the final out that sent thousands into the streets around Fenway to celebrate. "This is like an alternate reality," said Henry, as the players—now an infamous band of self-proclaimed Idiots—sprayed each other and Johnny Pesky with champagne. "All of our fans waited their entire lives for this."

When the Sox next took the Fenway diamond on April 11, 2005, it was as champions. What made the Opening Day celebration even sweeter for their long-tormented fans was that the Yankees had to watch the proceedings from the opposite dugout. "I think everybody was curious to see just what the Red Sox would do on the day they got their World Series rings," said New York Manager Joe Torre, whose players clapped politely throughout.

The ceremonies, the first on the premises since 1919, were on the scale normally reserved for coronations. After five flowing red banners commemorating the 1903, 1912, 1915, 1916, and 1918 World Series victories had been draped along the Wall, they were eclipsed by one for 2004 that stretched from end to end. "We had some grown men on our bench about to cry," Damon said.

Damon and his teammates received regal diamond and ruby rings while franchise icons Pesky and Carl

TRIUMPH AND TRAGEDY

On the night the Red Sox completed their historic comeback in the 2004 American League Championship Series at Yankee Stadium, Boston police fired pepper-pellet guns into an unruly crowd outside Fenway Park, killing Victoria Snelgrove, a 21-year-old Emerson College student, and wounding two other people. In 2005, the City of Boston reached a $5 million settlement with the Snelgrove family, the largest wrongful death settlement in city history.

In 2007, Boston Police Commissioner Ed Davis announced that the type of pellet gun blamed in the death of Snelgrove, who was struck in the eye, would never again be used by Boston police. An independent panel concluded in 2005 that Snelgrove's death was an avoidable tragedy that was caused by poor planning and "serious errors in judgment" by Boston police officers and commanders. Two officers were suspended for 45 days and other officers received demotions and written reprimands.

The Snelgrove family also reached an undisclosed settlement in a suit against FN Herstal, the maker of the weapon. Shortly after their daughter's death, Richard and Dianne Snelgrove established a memorial fund that has funded children's playgrounds in and around her hometown of East Bridgewater and scholarships at East Bridgewater High School and Emerson College.

"Why do [the Red Sox] draw two million people? Why do they get 30,000 people at the end of the season, even when they're not in it? People come to see the ballpark, to see the Green Monster, to be close to the players. Boston must balance development growth with the preservation of what makes our city so livable—our historic character, scale, and charm. We are distinct from other American cities because we view our buildings as resources, not liabilities."

—Thomas M. Menino, mayor of Boston

Yastrzemski hoisted the championship flag atop the flagpole in left-center field. Then it was back to work. Boston began its title defense in style with an 8-1 triumph. But anyone with a sense of history and drama knew that when New York returned for the final weekend, the season likely would be on the line.

Despite losing Martinez to the Mets and Foulke to knee surgery and missing Schilling for nearly half the campaign after off-season ankle repair, the Sox remained in first place from late June until the final 10 days of September. But New York, which had been seven games under .500 in May, returned for the decisive series at Fenway a game ahead in the division.

It was God's plan, Damon reckoned, that the two blood rivals would go head-to-head for the title. After a split of the first two games gave New York the AL East crown, Boston needed either a Sunday victory or a Cleveland loss to the White Sox to avoid a one-game Fenway playoff with the Indians for the wild-card spot. The clubhouse message board was bluntly optimistic: "TOMORROW. PACK FOR 3 DAY TRIP."

"Our goal was to get into the postseason and our goal in the postseason is to win the World Series," said Schilling, after Cleveland's loss mooted his teammates' 10-1 triumph and earned them a trip to Chicago for the divisional series. "We got Step One done."

Step Two, though, proved a stumbling block as the White Sox, who hadn't won a home playoff game in 46 years, claimed the first two games by counts of 14-2 (Boston's worst October loss by run margin) and 5-4 (after trailing, 4-0) to send their scarlet counterparts home for an elimination game. "Our backs are truly against the wall," acknowledged Epstein. "It's the personality of this team not to do things easily."

The White Sox finished things off with a 5-3 decision in Fenway and went on to sweep Houston to win their first World Series since 1917, ending a drought that had been a year longer than Boston's. "No one can ever take away what we did last year," said Kevin Millar. "This year we fought. We just weren't the better team."

Fans soon found out there was fighting going on behind the scenes, too. On Halloween night, Epstein walked out of Fenway wearing a gorilla suit to avoid reporters' questions about why he'd just turned down a contract extension. When he returned (in street clothes) in January, he had a new contract and nothing but good things to say about Sox CEO Larry Lucchino.

Front-office drama aside, multiple additions and deletions were inevitable during the off-season. Pitcher Josh Beckett and third baseman Mike Lowell, who had both won rings with the Marlins, arrived in a seven-player deal. Departing free agents included Damon (to the Yankees),

PEOPLE *of the* PARK

REMDAWG'S LONG RUN

In February 1988, former Boston second baseman Jerry Remy was named analyst for Red Sox games on New England Sports Network. Little did he know at the time that his tenure in front of the camera would stretch nearly three times longer than his playing career did.

Play-by-play partners have included local legend Ned Martin, Sean McDonough, Bob Kurtz, and Don Orsillo, with whom Remy has worked the past 11 seasons. Perhaps owing in part to Remy's local roots and his clear-cut, concise game analysis, his popularity soared—he gained a nickname ("RemDawg"), a website called the Remy Report, and even a couple of restaurants that bear his name.

Remy was chosen from among five finalists in 1988 to succeed Bob Montgomery on NESN. The other candidates were also former Sox players: Dick Radatz, Rick Miller, Jim Lonborg, and Mike Andrews. Montgomery, a former Sox catcher who began as a TV analyst in 1982, continued in that role on Channel 38 through 1995.

In July 2010, Remy and NESN agreed to a multiyear contract extension. This followed a three-and-a-half-month absence from the booth during the 2009 season while he recuperated from lung cancer surgery, along with a post-surgery infection and bout with depression. Just before his return to the booth in August 2009, he said he'd received so much support from fans that he felt guilty about not coming back sooner.

"I have boxes and boxes of cards, letters, prayers, tweets, e-mails," said Remy. "But I was crying reading them. . . . In a way, you feel like you've done something right for these people." Returning to the TV booth, he realized, was the way to thank them.

Jerry Remy acknowledged the fans upon returning to the NESN broadcast booth with Don Orsillo in August 2009, following Remy's surgery for lung cancer.

ABOVE: The Red Sox and Yankees lined up for the national anthem as the first Red Sox pennant in 86 years flew over Fenway Park on Opening Day 2005.

LEFT: War veterans escorted the World Series trophy and rings.

BELOW: Red Sox legend Johnny Pesky (6) finally received a World Series ring, along with congratulations from team executives (left to right) John Henry, Tom Werner, and Larry Lucchino.

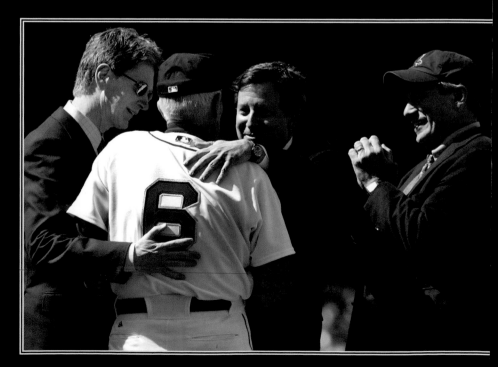

Mueller (Dodgers), and Millar (Orioles).

The sight of Damon, clean-shaven and pinstripe-crisp, unleashed a cascade of boos when he made his return the following season to Fenway, where a "JUDAS DAMON" sign hung from a balcony. "People around here are born to hate the Yankees," Damon shrugged. "That's what they are booing, the uniform."

Damon came back to torment his former supporters in August when New York tore the Sox to shreds with a five-game sweep that was even worse than the infamous Boston Massacre that sent the 1978 Sox into a tailspin. The carnage began with a Friday doubleheader that produced 12-4 and 14-11 defeats. The doubleheader consumed 8 hours and 40 minutes, with the nightcap establishing a mark as the longest nine-inning game ever at 4 hours and 45 minutes. It didn't end until 1:22 a.m., after most of the faithful had departed.

Much of the damage was done by Damon, who was 6 for 12 with two homers, a triple, and seven RBI. But Saturday's loss, a 13-5 pratfall in which Beckett walked nine batters and conceded nine earned runs, was even more unsightly. "Never happened before, to get beat up this bad," concluded Ortiz after Boston had allowed a dozen or more runs in three consecutive games for the first time in franchise history. "Doesn't matter where we were, we're going in the wrong direction."

After 8-5 and 2-1 losses completed the club's first five-game sweep since 1954, the Sox had fallen six-and-a-half

---

Before a game with Kansas City on August 2, 2005, Manny Ramirez showed off a sign that he had stashed inside the scoreboard of the Green Monster.

MONKEY BUSINESS

It was a Monday night in October 2005, and Theo Epstein had just rejected a contract offer, seemingly ending his brilliant tenure as the 11th general manager in Red Sox history after just three years. In their basement offices, Epstein and members of his baseball operations staff saw camera crews gathering outside to capture him leaving Fenway Park. How could they get Epstein out of the building without facing the camera crush?

It happened to be Halloween, and someone had a gorilla costume handy. Epstein slipped into the suit and walked out of Gate D, past the cameras with a smile on his concealed face. Three months later, after Epstein had discussed working for the Dodgers and Sox CEO Larry Lucchino had talked with Jim Beattie about replacing Epstein, their feud was over. Theo was back in the fold, and his gorilla suit was being auctioned off at the annual benefit concert, Hot Stove, Cool Music—for $11,000.

After those negotiations became something of a spectacle in 2005 (Epstein called it "far too public"), he vowed that he would not reveal the end date of any future contract. Lucchino later said, "Walls have crumbled, perceptions of one another have changed, and appreciation of one another has grown."

"I regret that it came to that and I wish we all could have handled it differently—me included," said Epstein in 2007. "I'm not in this job to be recognizable or 'famous' on the local scene. I'm in this job because I want the Red Sox to have a chance to win the World Series every year and I like contributing at this level."

With an unprecedented five playoff teams in his first six seasons as Sox GM, Epstein was not just another guy in a suit.

Bobby Doerr acknowledged the fans on August 2, 2007—"Bobby Doerr Day" at Fenway Park. Doerr's No. 1 had previously been retired by the Red Sox in 1988. The number is displayed on the façade in right field behind Doerr.

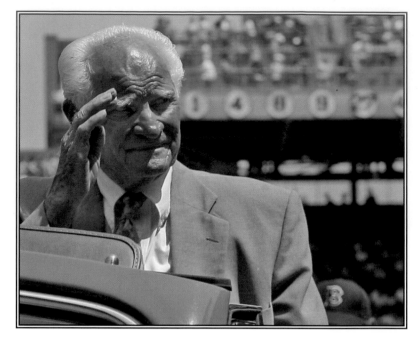

games behind New York. Boston ended the season 11 back in third place, their lowest finish in the division since 1997. It was, Epstein concluded, "an imperfect year" but it was followed by an extraordinary season that restored Boston to the top of the baseball heap.

Fenway denizens received an early hint that a remarkable season had arrived in 2007 when the Sox swept their first home encounter with New York in April, coming from at least two runs down to win all three games. After trailing by four in the eighth inning of the opener, Boston won, 7-6, when Coco Crisp knocked in two with a triple and Alex Cora singled him home with the winner. Then Ortiz knocked in four runs to spur his mates to a 7-5 triumph, and the Sox finished off the Yankees with four consecutive homers (from Ramirez, J. D. Drew, Lowell, and Varitek) off rookie left-hander Chase Wright in the finale.

"I haven't been part of anything like that, not even in Little League," marveled Lowell after the Sox had prevailed, 7-6, to sweep New York at home for the first time since 1990.

For the rest of the season, the Red Sox had the Yankees and everyone else in their rearview mirror, boosting their divisional lead to 11½ games on July 5 by sweeping Tampa Bay at home. The difference was a convenient convergence of inspired pitching and a couple of precocious rookies in second baseman Dustin Pedroia and center fielder Jacoby Ellsbury, the products of a beefed-up farm system.

The most intriguing newcomer, though, was Daisuke "Dice-K" Matsuzaka. The Sox lured the Japanese right-hander from the Seibu Lions with a $50 million contract after spending approximately that much for the privilege of chatting with him over sushi. Matsuzaka, known as "The Monster" back home, won 15 games to go along with 20 by Beckett and 17 by Wakefield. Jonathan Papelbon, a starter turned cold-hearted closer, chipped in 37 saves.

It was so dominant a staff that rookie Clay Buchholz, who pitched a no-hitter in September at Fenway in his second career start, didn't make the postseason roster. For a pleasant change, reaching the playoffs wasn't an arduous enterprise. Boston clinched a postseason berth with seven games to play and ended up with the best record in baseball (96-66) for the first time since 1946. More significant was the first divisional crown in a dozen years, which the Sox won in their clubhouse on the final weekend when the Orioles beat New York in extra innings after Matsuzaka had mastered the Twins.

The divisional series against the Angels went smoothly. First Beckett shut them out, 4-0, in the Fenway opener, and then Ramirez pushed the visitors to the brink with a three-run homer in Game 2, his first walk-off shot in a Boston uniform. "My train doesn't stop," declared Ramirez, echoing bash brother Ortiz after the 6-3 victory. The Angels had been rendered earthbound and the Sox finished them off two days later in Anaheim. "We didn't come out of spring training to win the first round," Lowell observed after Boston had scored seven runs in the eighth inning of a 9-1 smackdown. "We want to win the world championship."

But getting to the Series proved more difficult than he and his comrades might have estimated in the wake of clobbering the Indians, 10-3, in the ALCS opener at Fenway. The tide turned dramatically the next night as Cleveland scored seven in the 11th inning, with old friend Trot Nixon sending home the winner in a 13-6 bust-up that lasted five hours and 14 minutes.

The Indians then won the next two games at The Jake by 4-2 and 7-3 counts, forcing Beckett to save the season with a 7-1 gem in Game 5. But once the Sox returned to Yawkey Way, they dispatched the Tribe with baffling ease. Drew's first-inning grand slam fueled a 12-2 giggler to even the series, and the Sox scored six runs in the eighth inning of the seventh game on their way to an 11-2 win and trip to their second Fall Classic in four years.

The Rockies, who'd been up in the ozone while winning 21 of 22 games and powering past the Phillies and Diamondbacks to win their first National League pennant, were immediately brought to ground in the Series opener at Fenway, where they ran into hot Boston bats and icy pitching from Beckett. "You can't make any mistakes," sighed Colorado starter Jeff Francis after Pedroia had hit

CRIME OF THE CENTURY

It was June 2007, and Dave Roberts was joking that the signature play of his career gets closer with each viewing.

"As I watch the footage from three years ago to two years ago to when I just saw it in the clubhouse, it gets closer and closer every single time," said Roberts. "I hope five, 10, 20 years down the road that [umpire] Joe West doesn't change his mind and call me out."

On the basis of a three-second dash to second base in the ninth inning of Game 4 of the 2004 American League Championship Series, Roberts made himself into a Boston folk hero. Kevin Millar drew the walk, and Roberts ran for him. Bill Mueller got the single that drove Roberts in from second. Three people were involved in the manufacture of the run that saved the season and set the forces in motion for the greatest postseason comeback in baseball history, but somehow, Roberts's star shines brightest in the telling.

"When I was with the Dodgers," said Roberts, "Maury Wills once told me that there will come a point in my career when everyone in the ballpark will know that I have to steal a base, and I will steal that base. When I got out there, I knew that was what Maury Wills was talking about."

Roberts was a 32-year-old outfielder acquired from the Dodgers about 10 minutes before the trading deadline (for minor leaguer Henri Stanley), on the same day Nomar Garciaparra was dealt to the Cubs. Roberts was strictly fine-print material.

"That whole team, from the moment I got there, had this undeniable belief that something special was going to happen," said Roberts. When the time came, he was ready. "I was scared, excited," he says. "I can't tell you how many emotions went through me. He threw over once, and that was good because it helped settle me. He threw over again, and he almost picked me off. He threw over again, and now I was completely relaxed. I knew that after three throws they weren't going to pitch out. I got a great jump. It was close, but, thank God, Joe West called me safe."

"[Jorge] Posada made a great throw," said Giants manager Bruce Bochy, recalling the play. "It was bang-bang. It just goes to show you what a thin line there is between winning and losing. Another few inches, and he's out. And Boston's done."

Mueller's single tied the game, and then David Ortiz delivered a game-winning, series-extending homer in the 12th inning.

Almost forgotten is the postscript: Game 5 at Fenway, eighth inning, 3-2, Yankees. Millar walks. Guess who pinch runs. Pitcher Tom Gordon is so obsessed with Roberts that he goes down 3-0 to Trot Nixon, who singles Roberts to third. Jason Varitek brings him home with the tying run on a sacrifice fly, and again, the Sox win in extra innings.

Roberts never again played for the Red Sox. Not in Game 6 or Game 7 of the ALCS, or in the World Series.

Roberts's playing career was rather pedestrian. He was a .266 career hitter with 243 stolen bases in 10 seasons. He was a good teammate who could steal a base, slap a key hit, and play good defense in the outfield.

And in 2006, he was inducted into the Red Sox Hall of Fame.

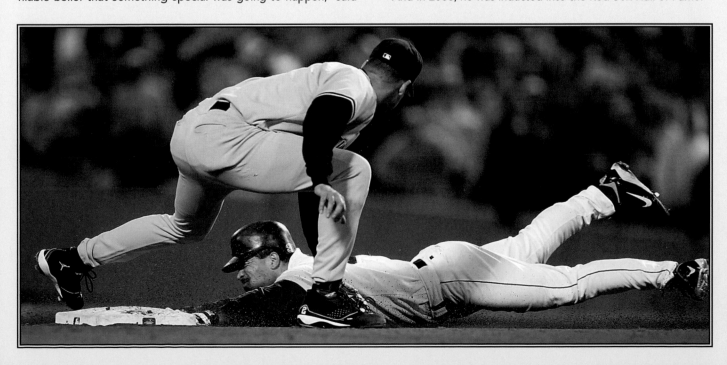

his second offering over the left-field wall to begin a 13-1 rout, a record margin for a Series opener.

When Schilling shut them down, 2-1, in Game 2—helped by Papelbon's killer eighth-inning pickoff of Matt Holliday, the first of his career—the Rockies were facing a steep climb.

The Sox adapted quickly to Denver's thin air, scoring six runs in the third inning of Game 3 without a homer and three more in the eighth for a 10-5 decision that put them on the verge of joining the Yankees and Reds as the only clubs to sweep World Series in consecutive appearances. Still, they were taking nothing for granted. "We don't want to eat the cake first before your birthday," cautioned Ramirez.

The celebration came the next day with two unlikely heroes blowing out the candles. Jon Lester, the young gun who'd begun the season in Single A and wasn't on the initial playoff roster, pitched flawlessly and pinch hitter Bobby Kielty, who'd been released by the Athletics at the end of July, smacked what turned out to be the game-winning homer in a 4-3 victory with his only swing of the Series. "I felt like I was running on clouds," said Kielty, who never played another game in a Boston uniform.

Despite the high-altitude giddiness, Sox management was quick to tamp down talk of a dynasty only three years after an 86-year curse had been lifted. "Baseball will hum-

ble you in a hurry," observed Epstein. "Just when you think you have something, it turns on you."

The odds were against Boston retaining its crown in 2008—only the Yankees had managed back-to-back World Series titles since 1993. Even repeating as division champions proved impossible as Tampa Bay, which had never had a winning season, finished two games in front. For most of the spring the Sox had been the front-runners, inspired by Lester's 7-0 no-hitter against Kansas City on May 19, less than 21 months after he'd been diagnosed with lymphoma.

But the Rays, who lost the first seven meetings at Fenway by a 45-16 aggregate, gradually made up ground and left a calling card in September when they won the final two games there, taking the finale on Carlos Pena's three-run homer in the 14th inning off Mike Timlin. With the Yankees missing the playoffs for the first time since 1994, it seemed inevitable that Boston and Tampa Bay would meet in October.

First was the customary date with the Angels in the divi-

Fans got a shower of champagne from Curt Schilling, who climbed on the dugout to celebrate after the Red Sox clinched the 2007 AL East Championship.

NO LOAVES, JUST FISHES

BY KEVIN PAUL DUPONT

October 13, 2007—As the Red Sox opened the 2007 American League Championship Series with Cleveland, the weather was unpredictable. For Fenway Park director of grounds Dave Mellor and his crew, that was hardly unusual.

"Weather dictates so much of what we do," said the 43-year-old Mellor, who became Fenway's lawn doctor when longtime director of grounds Joe Mooney handed over the rake just prior to the 2001 season.

When Mellor took the job at Fenway, on the recommendation of Mooney, a man he calls his mentor, the new man had to be schooled on the many different ways rain could foul up Fenway. Day No. 1 on the job, the two men sat in the stands, and Mooney told Mellor that heavy rains often flooded the dugouts.

"Not really a problem," said Mellor. "I saw plenty of that at County Stadium [in Milwaukee]."

Heavier rain, Mooney told him, would blow the drain covers off beneath the stands on the third-base side, and water would shoot up, geyser-like, from the ground.

Right there, with that bit of Old Faithful imagery, Mooney had the new hire's attention. Gushing water. Something he had never seen in Milwaukee.

But wait, Mooney warned, there was more.

"He tells me, 'And when it really, really, really rains, the camera pit over on first base will flood,'" recalled Mellor. "And then he says, 'And fish will swim out on the field.' Hey, I'm new here, right? I didn't challenge him. All I said was, 'OK, Joe, yeah, got that.'"

Fast-forward to Opening Day 2001, with the Yankees in town. It rained and rained, to the point that the tarp cradled two-and-a-half inches of water. Making his appointed rounds, Mellor swung by first base, and there it was, just as Mooney warned—a fish.

"I kid you not . . . I couldn't believe it," said Mellor. "A fish! I looked all around, figuring they had some camera in the stands or something, and I was on *Candid Camera*. But then I looked over to second base, and there was more. From the camera pit to second base, a total of eight fish. I only wish I had taken a picture. In fact, I should have kept one and had it mounted."

According to Mellor, when contractors ripped out the old field after the 2004 World Series, sure enough, they found a drain line that acted as the conduit that made Fenway the fish-friendliest ballpark in North America.

"Next time I saw Joe," recalled Mellor, "I said to him, 'Oh my gosh, Joe, tell me anything and I'll believe you.'"

sional series. This one, though, proved decidedly more stressful. Though the Sox won the first two games in Anaheim to run their unbeaten playoff streak against the Angels to 11, they needed a two-run homer from Drew in the ninth to win the second encounter, 7-5, after frittering away a 5-1 lead.

When the scene shifted to Fenway, the Angels were determined to make a fight of it after having been swept in the previous two postseason showdowns between the clubs. It took 12 innings, and 5 hours and 19 minutes, but the visitors managed to stay alive when Erick Aybar dropped a single in front of Crisp to score Mike Napoli from second for a 5-4 triumph.

Just in case they couldn't close things out the following night the hosts packed their bags for the West Coast. But with the score tied in the ninth, Jason Bay, who'd been acquired from the Pirates in a trade that sent Manny Ramirez to the Dodgers, hit a ground-rule double into the right-field stands, and then came home on rookie Jed Lowrie's single. "When he hit that ball I was going to score," said Bay, who'd stumbled rounding third and needed to sweep the plate with his hand to produce the run that clinched the 3-2 win. "There was no question. I was gone."

After their champagne shower, Bay and his teammates headed for Florida and a championship-series date with the Rays, who'd taken down the White Sox. While Tropicana Field had been a hothouse of horrors for Boston, which had lost eight of its nine meetings there during the season, the visitors very nearly took the first two games.

First, Matsuzaka shut out the Rays, 2-0, in the opener. Then the Sox led their next meeting three times before Tampa Bay prevailed, 9-8, in the 11th on three walks and a sacrifice fly. "We're not frustrated," insisted reliever Mike Timlin, who took the loss after not having pitched in nearly two weeks. "You come down to somebody else's place and you split, we're still looking pretty good."

But the club looked marked for death after two staggering losses on Yawkey Way pushed it to the brink. The Sox, who hadn't dropped more than two home dates to the Rays in six seasons, lost that many in consecutive nights. The visitors scored 22 runs in six-and-a-half hours of play in by far the worst consecutive postseason defeats Boston had ever suffered.

The hosts could shrug off the 9-1 battering in Game 3 as an aberration. But the 13-4 loss in Game 4, ignited by back-to-back, first-inning homers off Wakefield by Pena and Evan Longoria, left the Sox reeling. "We're down 3-1 and if we lose we're going home," said Pedroia. "Hit the panic button."

His colleagues, who'd escaped from 3-1 deficits in three previous championship series, responded with the greatest

WORLD SERIES 20

playoff comeback in franchise history two nights later, coming from seven runs down in the seventh to win, 8-7. "I've never seen a group so happy to get on a plane at 1:30 in the morning," Francona noted.

When the Sox won Game 6 by a 4-2 count at The Trop on a blinding performance by Beckett and a winning homer from Jason Varitek, who'd been 0 for 14 in the series, they were only one game from their third World Series appearance in five years. But Boston couldn't solve Matt Garza in the finale and its most improbable resurrection ended there. "We played as hard as we could," Pedroia said after the Rays had won, 3-1, and earned a World Series date with the Phillies. "We just ran out of magic."

Tampa Bay, crushed by the Phillies in the Series, proved a one-hit wonder.

A century's worth of experience had taught Boston that its perennial rival hadn't changed. "Year after year," Henry had said, "the Yankees are Halliburton." So they were again in 2009, even though the Sox won their first eight meetings with New York and led the division at the All-Star break.

The season essentially came undone in a bizarre Fenway series in late August. After New York had won the opener in a 20-11 bashfest and Boston had responded with a 14-1 blowout, the visitors took the Sunday finale, 8-4, crashing five homers off Beckett. "Right now, they're definitely better than we are," conceded Bay after the Yankees had grabbed a seven-and-a-half-game lead.

Though Francona's club finished eight games behind, it still earned its sixth playoff appearance in seven years during a month that fans had come to regard as Soxtober. As usual, Boston's dancing partner was the Angels.

This meeting, though, was unlike the others because Boston was forced to operate with a discombobulated rotation. The Sox, who hadn't lost a playoff game in Anaheim since 1986, dropped the first two as haloed aces John Lackey and Jered Weaver held the visitors to a total of one run. "I don't think it's the way we scripted it before we got here," observed Lowell after Boston had been stifled, 5-0 and 4-1. "We've definitely dug a pretty good hole for ourselves."

Boston, which had won nine of 11 elimination games under Francona and lost only one at Fenway since 1999, figured that it could make a last stand at home. Leading, 6-4, in the ninth inning of Game 3, the Sox seemed secure. But Papelbon, who hadn't allowed an earned run in 26 playoff innings, came unglued.

After allowing two inherited runners to score in the eighth, the star closer was one strike away from victory three times in the ninth, but conceded a single, a walk, and a double before Vlad Guerrero smacked a fatal two-run single to center. "The season doesn't wind down," remarked Francona after his club had absorbed a shocking 7-6 loss that left the faithful sitting stupefied in the stands. "It just comes to a crashing halt."

The 2010 season never got started, as the Red Sox lost nine of their first 13 games and were in first place for only

one day—after beating the Yankees on Opening Day. Storm warnings were evident as early as Patriots Day weekend, when the Sox were swept at home by Tampa Bay, dropping the final two games by a combined 15-3. "When you don't show up to play, you're going to get beat," Pedroia said after he and his mates had fallen into fourth place, six games off the pace. "Doesn't matter if you play the Rays or Brookline High School."

The club made an encouraging mid-June run when the National Leaguers came to town, taking eight of nine from the Phillies, Diamondbacks, and Dodgers to climb within a game of the division lead. One of the visitors was particularly familiar as Manny Ramirez returned for the first time since being traded to Los Angeles and was given a decidedly mixed reception from fans, who continued to appreciate his role in two Series triumphs even as they disdained his lackadaisical approach. "There's no reason I should have behaved that way in Boston," Ramirez admitted to a Spanish network announcer.

Yet "Mannywood" wasn't behaving much differently in L.A., and so he was wearing a White Sox uniform by September. By then his former Boston teammates were stuck in third place and out of contention after both their lineup and rotation had been shredded by injuries, with 19 players spending time on the disabled list for a total of 1,013 man-games lost to injury.

Leadoff hitter Jacoby Ellsbury played only 18 games after fracturing his ribs. Pedroia missed the final three

The Red Sox found a way to top their 2004 world title, literally. The 2007 banner was hung on Opening Day 2008, and the flags of 62 nations were also displayed, to represent the reach of Red Sox Nation. The Sox had opened the season in Japan, then played in California and Canada before their home debut.

months after breaking a foot and Kevin Youkilis was sidelined for the season after tearing a thumb muscle. Marco Scutaro injured his rotator cuff and was switched from shortstop to second base. Josh Beckett spent two months on the DL, where Daisuke Matsuzaka was placed twice.

"It's disappointing in that we didn't get where we want to go, but there's still a lot to be proud of," Epstein said on the season's final weekend, as the Sox finished below second place for the first time in 13 years. "I'd like to rewind and start over and do 162 again and see how it turns out."

As they had during the first six years after the ballpark had opened, the Fenway faithful had become accustomed to Soxtober—watching the hometown team playing for a championship—and Sox President Larry Lucchino had promised them "the constant, unwavering commitment to winning." So as Mike Lowell, Victor Martinez, and Adrian Beltre departed, the front office moved boldly to sign stars Adrian Gonzalez from San Diego and Carl Crawford from Tampa Bay for 2011.

With a $161 million payroll and 15 All-Stars on the roster, the club was widely touted as the likely champion in spring training. "We have a lot of work to do but I can see

ABOVE: A Fenway Park concession-stand worker watched Red Sox-Yankees action on a television monitor in mid-September 2007.

BELOW: Fenway Franks made their way through the park concourse before a game against the Toronto Blue Jays in July 2011.

why people are talking about going back to the World Series," acknowledged rightfielder J.D. Drew. "On paper, we have that kind of team."

But the fact that the opener at Texas was played on April Fool's Day might have been an omen about the historic pratfall that was to follow. Boston lost its first six games to the Rangers and Indians; it was the team's worst start since 1945 when most of its top players were wearing Uncle Sam's uniform. "It can't get any worse than this," third baseman Kevin Youkilis declared after the Sox lost 1-0 at Cleveland on a squeeze bunt in the eighth inning to go 0-6.

The 100th opening day at Fenway brought a delightful turnaround as the hosts drilled the Yankees 9-6. "I've never seen a team so happy to be 1-6," observed Francona. The upward ascent took time, though. It wasn't until May 16 that the club had a winning record and not until May 27 that it climbed past New York into first place.

Boston still was there at the beginning of September but an unsightly 10-0 home loss to Texas was the first misstep in a fatal tumble. Though the Sox still had a comfortable

Just two years after battling cancer, left-hander Jon Lester threw the 18th no-hitter in Red Sox history—and the team's fourth of the 2000s—beating the Kansas City Royals, 7-0, at Fenway Park on May 19, 2008. Jason Varitek was behind the plate, setting a major-league record by catching the fourth no-hitter of his career.

nine-game lead over Tampa Bay in the wild-card race, they soon went into free fall en route to the worst September swoon (7-20) in major-league history.

"It's crazy," proclaimed designated hitter David Ortiz after the players were hooted off the diamond for losing the Fenway finale to the last-place Orioles. "I've never seen anything like that around here as long as I've been here. If you would have told me in August this would happen in September, I would have laughed at you."

Going into the final six games at New York and Baltimore, Boston still had a two and a half game edge over the Rays for the wild-card spot. But the tailspin continued as the visitors lost two of three in the Bronx,

THRILLS, CHILLS, SPILLS

For years it had been easy to forget New England's hockey roots. In the first decade of the new century, the Bruins got lost in the championship seasons of the Red Sox, Patriots, and Celtics. But on New Year's Day 2010, Boston reminded North America that the Hub is still a hockey town. (And, 18 months later, they would finally bring home the Stanley Cup.)

In the third NHL Winter Classic, 38,112 stoic souls stood in the cold at Fenway Park for three hours before they were rewarded with a 2-1 Bruins victory over the Philadelphia Flyers on a tip-in goal by Marco Sturm in the second minute of extra time.

"It's the perfect day for hockey in Boston," said Bruins legend Bobby Orr, who skated to center ice for a ceremonial pregame handshake with Flyer nemesis Bobby Clarke after leading the Black and Gold onto the infield ice. "It's a thrill to see all these pros turn into kids again for one day. This is how we all started playing hockey—outdoors. And this day, here at Fenway Park, truly is a classic."

It was a day that could scarcely have been imagined when Fenway opened in 1912, a dozen years before the Bruins would take the ice for the first time.

The postcard-perfect afternoon lacked the Currier & Ives snowfall that marked the previous day's photogenic practice session, but everything else worked out the way it was sketched on the NHL blueprint.

Late in the third period, comedian Lenny Clarke came out to lead the singing of "Sweet Caroline," and the Red Sox magic took over. Mark Recchi scored a power-play goal with 2:18 remaining, and then Sturm potted the OT winner. It was time to cue up "Dirty Water." No one wanted to leave on the day Fenway put on its snow pants and we all came home to hockey.

"It's Fenway Park. It's history. It's something you're going to remember the rest of your life," said the Bruins' Patrice Bergeron. "You want to be on the good side of the outcome. You want to win."

One day later, they played the AT&T Legends Classic for charity, and 33,000 fans showed up to watch former Bruins, including Cam Neely, Brad Park, and Terry O'Reilly, skate with celebrities such as Tim Robbins, Denis Leary, Bobby Farrelly, and Kiefer Sutherland.

"I don't know how many people can actually say they skated in front of 33,000 people," said Sutherland afterward. "In the middle of a snowstorm, they stayed. I've never seen fans like that. It was pretty awesome." The game raised $200,000 apiece for the Bruins and Red Sox charitable foundations, and for a third charity, Hockey Fights Cancer.

Before they took the boards down a week later, Boston University and Boston College clashed in the college version of the Winter Classic—with BU winning, 3-2, in a battle of the previous two NCAA hockey champions before 38,472 fans.

Hockey fans in Boston were treated to a wondrous sight: a rink set up in front of the Green Monster at Fenway Park, where the Bruins and Philadelphia Flyers squared off in the NHL Winter Classic on New Year's Day 2010. Even better, team and regional icon Bobby Orr led the B's onto the ice for the start of the game, and his counterpart was longtime rival Bobby Clarke of the Flyers. The Bruins prevailed on this day, 2-1, on an overtime goal by Marco Sturm.

WHO'S OUR DADDY?

When Pedro Martinez's name came up in early 2010, nobody seemed to know what the former Red Sox pitching great was up to. He wasn't at spring training. He wasn't working on a deal to join a team at mid-season, as he had done with the Phillies the previous year. Some wondered whether he might be found under that mango tree in the Dominican Republic where he said he planned to spend his time after retirement.

But no, fittingly enough, Martinez made his first appearance of the year when he emerged from a tent in the left-field corner at Fenway to throw out the ceremonial first pitch on Opening Night vs. the Yankees. Wearing his familiar Red Sox No. 45 and blowing kisses and making hugging gestures to the fans, he strolled in from the outfield and back—at least fleetingly—into the Red Sox-Yankees rivalry that he was such a major part of. We remember his 17-strikeout effort vs. New York in 1999, when he allowed just one hit. We remember the duel in 2000 against the Yankees' Roger Clemens when Trot Nixon homered to complete a 1-0 Sox win. We remember his throwdown of Don Zimmer in Game 3 of the ALCS in 2003. We remember, too, the eighth inning of Game 7 of the 2003 ALCS when Martinez, leading, 5-2, was left in too long by Grady Little in what became one of the historic meltdowns in playoff history. We remember Pedro after a victory in 2001 snarling, "I don't believe in damn curses. Wake up the Bambino and have me face him. Maybe I'll drill him in the ass."

We remember him saying, after a loss late in the 2004 season, "I just have to tip my hat to the Yankees and call them my daddy." That comment resulted in a crescendo of "Who's your daddy?" chants from the New York faithful in his next outing there, in the 2004 ALCS. But the Red Sox busted the curse in that series, and Pedro ended his seven-year tenure with the Red Sox with a 117-37 record, a 2.52 ERA, two Cy Young Awards, and almost certain election to the Baseball Hall of Fame five years after he retires.

needing Jacoby Ellsbury's three-run homer in the 14th to salvage the finale.

After the Sox split the first two in Baltimore the season came down to the 162nd game, and for seven innings everything was breaking Boston's way, with the Sox leading 3-2 in the seventh and the Yankees drubbing the Rays 7-0. Then the skies opened in Baltimore and, during the 86-minute rain delay, the players sat in the clubhouse watching Tampa come back from the dead to even the score and send that game into extra innings.

Still, a Boston victory would mean at least a one-game playoff with the Rays and with two out in the ninth, nobody on base and closer Jonathan Papelbon on the mound, victory seemed assured. But two doubles and Robert Andino's looping liner to left that Crawford couldn't glove gave Baltimore a 4-3 triumph. By the time the Sox made it from the dugout to the clubhouse Evan Longoria had cranked a walkoff homer in the 12th to put the Rays into the divisional series.

"We can't sugarcoat this," Epstein conceded after Boston had missed the post-season in consecutive years for the first time since 2002. "This is awful. We did it to ourselves and we put ourselves in position for a crazy night like this to end our season." That crazy night ended not only a season but also an era. Francona, who'd concluded that the front office wouldn't extend his contract, resigned two days later after eight years as skipper, frustrated that he couldn't get through to veterans who had a "sense of entitlement." Epstein soon followed him out the door to take on the challenge of rebuilding another ballclub that played in a storied park and that hadn't won a World Series for even longer—the Chicago Cubs.

Amid the upheaval and uncertainty, Sox owner John Henry made an impromptu and impassioned appearance on a local sports radio talk show to assure the public that stability and success would return. "We're going to be back as an organization," he vowed. "We're going to have a top-class manager and general manager and we're going to have a great team next year."

Whether or not the calendar included a Soxtober every year, management was continuing its mission to preserve Fenway for the next generation. Tiger Stadium, which had opened on the same day as Fenway in 1912, had gone under the wrecking ball in 2009. So had The House That Ruth Built, replaced by a $2 billion pinstriped pleasure dome across the street.

Boston, though, traditionally has been reluctant to toss

its architectural treasures into the trash bin. A city that still has its original 18th-century State House and 19th-century City Hall has seen no reason to dismantle a 20th-century playground that still attracts more than three million ticket holders a year and has sold out every game since early in the 2003 season.

Fenway has undergone annual makeovers in recent years, with ownership spending $40 million in enhancements before the 2011 season—including the addition of three high-definition video screens. The total tab was 60 times more than the $650,000 that John I. Taylor had spent to build the ballpark a century earlier.

Over the past decade, John Henry and his colleagues have underwritten $285 million in improvements—from Monster seats atop the left-field wall to expanded concourses to a new playing surface—designed to carry the "lyric little bandbox" comfortably into the middle of the 21st century. Yet for all of the updating, America's Most Beloved Ballpark remains essentially as it was in 1912. If Duffy Lewis were to return today, hunting for his misplaced glove, he wouldn't need to ask directions to left field. ⚾

Game announcements and updates were made through a megaphone when the Red Sox played the Chicago Cubs on May 21, 2011—one feature of a series that marked the first meeting of the two teams at Fenway Park since the 1918 World Series. To commemorate the occasion, both teams wore throwback uniforms.

POP CULTURE

OK, so maybe the ballpark isn't always the star. But it has certainly been a major player in movies and popular culture for much of its history.

Kevin Costner's character saw old-time player Moonlight Graham's name and hometown flash on the Fenway Park message board in the ultimate baseball movie *Field of Dreams* (1989), when he attended a game with Terrance Mann, played by James Earl Jones.

Drew Barrymore as Lindsey dropped from the center-field bleachers and sprinted toward boyfriend Jimmy Fallon in the box seats as hapless security personnel pursued her in *Fever Pitch* (2005), which required a last-minute revamp when the Red Sox confounded the scriptwriters and won it all in 2004.

Ben Affleck and his homeboys stole millions in receipts from a just-concluded Sox-Yankees series in *The Town* (2010), with final scenes filmed just inside Gate D of the park. In *Moneyball* (2011), Brad Pitt as Oakland A's general manager Billy Beane discusses a job offer from the Sox on location at Fenway. The park also had cameos in *A Civil Action* (1998), *Blown Away* (1994), *Little Big League* (1994), *Major League II* (1994), and numerous documentaries.

In July 2011, New Hampshire native Adam Sandler built a replica of the Green Monster on a Cape Cod Little League field to be used in filming a comedy due out in 2012 and tentatively titled, *I Hate You, Dad*. Several ballparks and Wiffle-ball fields throughout New England pay homage to Fenway, and another replica park, dubbed "Little Fenway," hosts the Bucky Dent Baseball School (how dare he?) in Delray Beach, Florida.

On the small screen, in addition to being woven into the fabric of *Cheers*, Fenway occasionally played a part in Boston-bred producer David E. Kelley's *Ally McBeal* and *The Practice*. It was also the setting for comedy sketches by Jimmy Fallon and Rachel Dratch, as Sully and Denise, on *Saturday Night Live*.

Novelist and Sox diehard Stephen King came up with the plotline for his novel *The Girl Who Loved Tom Gordon* while at Fenway. A young girl lost for days in the Maine woods keeps up her hopes by tuning in Sox games on a Walkman.

Longtime Boston musician Jonathan Richman released a song in 2005, "As We Walk to Fenway Park in Boston Town," that appeared in *Fever Pitch*. Other music associated with Fenway and its team includes the victory song "Dirty Water" by the Standells, Neil Diamond's eighth-inning staple "Sweet Caroline," "Tessie"—the Royal Rooters' anthem that was resurrected by the Dropkick Murphys in 2004, "The Red Sox Are Winning" by Earth Opera, "Losing" by Pondering Judd, and the "Hot Stove Cool Music" series of benefit concerts spearheaded by Peter Gammons and Theo Epstein.

FENWAY PARK

2000

SEPTEMBER 4
Carlton Fisk's No. 27 is retired by the Red Sox.

OCTOBER 6
CEO John Harrington announces the team is up for sale after plans to build a new park collapse.

NOVEMBER 13
Pedro Martinez earns his third Cy Young Award.

DECEMBER 11
Manny Ramirez signs with the Red Sox in an eight-year, $160 million deal.

2001

PRESEASON
A John Hancock sign is installed above the scoreboard as the Red Sox celebrate the 100th anniversary of the team's membership in the American League.

APRIL 4
In Baltimore, newly acquired Hideo Nomo pitches a no-hitter against the Orioles—the first no-hitter in the 21st century, and the first by a Boston pitcher in 36 years.

AUGUST 16
Manager Jimy Williams is fired and replaced by Joe Kerrigan.

DECEMBER 20
The Sox are sold to a group led by John Henry, Tom Werner, and Larry Lucchino.

DECEMBER 21
Johnny Damon is signed by the Red Sox to a four-year, $31 million contract.

2002

FEBRUARY 27
Workers at Fenway begin adding nearly 400 seats for the upcoming season.

MARCH 1-5
Red Sox General Manager Dan Duquette is fired; Mike Port becomes interim GM. Manager Joe Kerrigan is fired and replaced by Grady Little.

APRIL 27
Derek Lowe pitches a no-hitter at Fenway against the Devil Rays.

JULY 5
Ted Williams dies.

JULY 22
A ceremony in honor of Ted Williams is held at Fenway. On his way home from the event, longtime team broadcaster Ned Martin dies after a heart attack.

SEPTEMBER 5
Yawkey Way Concourse and Gate A are expanded.

NOVEMBER 25
Theo Epstein takes over as Red Sox general manager from Mike Port. At 28, he is the youngest GM in MLB history.

Top of page (l-r): New staircase to bleachers, 2004; David Ortiz's rescuing of the 2004 ALCS; Boston Celtics captain Paul Pierce hamming it up, 2008.
Timeline: Bruce Springsteen in concert, 2003; unveiling the new Green Monster, 2003; Casey Fossum and Tim Wakefield in the bullpen, 2002.

Playoffs04

Marathon man

PRESEASON
The 23-foot net that once protected Lansdowne businesses from home runs comes down so Green Monster seats can be added. Two rows of seats will also be added behind home plate and Fenway will begin offering year-round tours for the first time.

SEPTEMBER 6-7
Bruce Springsteen and the E Street Band becomes the first A-list rock act to perform at Fenway, with two sold-out shows.

OCTOBER 8-16
The Sox lose the American League Championship Series against the Yankees in seven games. Afterward, manager Grady Little, faulted for not replacing Pedro Martinez during the eighth inning of Game 7, is fired.

PRESEASON
Seats are added to the right-field roof, above the grandstand.

APRIL 16
Statue of Ted Williams unveiled outside Gate B, with Johnny Pesky and Bobby Doerr on hand.

JULY 31
Nomar Garciaparra is traded to the Chicago Cubs in a complicated four-team deal that brings Orlando Cabrera and Doug Mientkiewicz to the Red Sox.

OCTOBER 10-12
Jimmy Buffett and his Coral Reefer Band play two Fenway concerts.

OCTOBER 23-24
Boston wins two World Series games at Fenway against the St. Louis Cardinals.

OCTOBER 27
The Red Sox finish a sweep of the Cardinals in St. Louis, clinching the team's first World Series victory since 1918. Church bells ring out all over New England.

PRESEASON
Major renovations of Fenway Park are undertaken. They include the installation of a new drainage system to better manage the field during rainstorms and the expansion of the clubhouse.

MARCH 23
Led by John Henry, the Red Sox team owners announce their formal commitment to stay at Fenway.

APRIL 6
Fenway hosts the premiere of the movie *Fever Pitch*, which was partially filmed at the park.

2003

2004

2005

NOVEMBER 28
Curt Schilling is acquired by the Red Sox from the Diamondbacks. He signs a two-year, $25.5-million contract extension for 2005 and 2006, with a $13 million mutual option to remain with Boston in 2007.

DECEMBER 4
Terry "Tito" Francona is hired as manager.

OCTOBER 17
With the Red Sox about to be swept by the Yankees in the ALCS, Dave Roberts scores the tying run and David Ortiz hits a home run to right field in the bottom of the 12th inning for a 6-4 Boston victory.

OCTOBER 18
Ortiz wins Game 5 at Fenway with a single in the 14th inning.

OCTOBER 20
The Sox complete an unlikely comeback from down 3-0 to the Yankees in the ALCS in New York. During the celebration in Boston, 21-year-old bystander Victoria Snelgrove is killed by a police-fired pellet bullet.

OCTOBER 30
A victory "rolling rally" with Red Sox players and management on "duck" boats begins at Fenway Park. It wends through Boston and includes a foray on the Charles River before ending at City Hall Plaza.

AUGUST 21-23
The Rolling Stones play Fenway Park.

OCTOBER 31
Theo Epstein temporarily resigns as Red Sox GM and leaves Fenway Park in a gorilla suit to avoid detection.

DECEMBER 20
Johnny Damon signs a four-year, $52 million contract with the Yankees.

FENWAY PARK

JANUARY 19
Theo Epstein returns to the Red Sox.

PRESEASON
Glass that separated patrons from the field is removed from the .406 club, which is renovated and reopened as an open seating area featuring the EMC Club. Another 1,300 seats are added with additional concession stands and restrooms.

SEPTEMBER 27
The right-field foul pole is officially christened "Pesky's Pole."

SEPTEMBER 28
Johnny Pesky's No. 6 is retired in a ceremony at Fenway.

DECEMBER 14
The Red Sox win the bidding war for Japanese pitcher Daisuke Matsuzaka, who signs a six-year, $52 million contract.

SEPTEMBER 1
Clay Buchholz pitches a no-hitter in his second career start.

OCTOBER 24-25
Boston wins the first two games of the World Series against the Colorado Rockies at Fenway.

OCTOBER 28
The Red Sox complete a sweep of the Rockies at Coors Field in Denver to win their second World Series in four years. Fans dance in the streets of New England, again.

OCTOBER 30
Another "rolling rally" is held in Boston, starting at Fenway, with a kilt-clad Jonathan Papelbon dancing a jig to the sounds of "I'm Shipping Up to Boston" by the Dropkick Murphys.

PRESEASON
Temporary luxury boxes installed for the 1999 All-Star Game are removed and permanent ones added to the State Street Pavilion level. The State Street Pavilion renovations extend to left field.

APRIL 9
After years of self-exile, Bill Buckner finally returns to Fenway and throws out the first pitch of a Red Sox game, nearly 22 years after the fielding gaffe that some say lost the World Series in 1986 against the Mets.

2006   2007   2008

MAY 19
Jon Lester pitches a no-hitter against the Kansas City Royals.

JULY 31
Manny Ramirez is traded to the Los Angeles Dodgers in a three-team deal in which the Red Sox get Jason Bay from the Pittsburgh Pirates.

NOVEMBER 18
Dustin Pedroia wins the American League MVP, the eighth player in AL history to earn MVP, Gold Glove, and Silver Slugger honors in the same season.

MAY 29-31
The Dave Matthews Band and Phish play concerts at Fenway.

JUNE 17
Fenway hosts its 500th consecutive Red Sox sellout.

AUGUST 5-6
Former Beatle Paul McCartney performs at Fenway.

SEPTEMBER 29
The Red Sox clinch the wild-card, but are later swept by the Angels in the ALDS.

JANUARY 1
The Boston Bruins beat the Philadelphia Flyers in the NHL Winter Classic at Fenway.

APRIL 5
Pedro Martinez returns to throw out the first pitch on Opening Day against the Yankees at Fenway. Neil Diamond leads the crowd in the ballpark's traditional eighth-inning sing-along of "Sweet Caroline."

MAY 5
Nomar Garciaparra Day is held at Fenway.

JULY 21
Soccer returns to Fenway after 40 years with a match between Celtic F.C. and Sporting Clube de Portugal.

AUGUST 14
Aerosmith and the J. Geils Band perform at Fenway.

SEPTEMBER 14
More than 5,000 new citizens are sworn in during a massive naturalization ceremony. The premiere of *The Town* is held later that night.

DECEMBER 6 & 11
The Red Sox acquire first baseman Adrian Gonzalez and left fielder Carl Crawford.

PRESEASON
Three new high-definition video display systems are added to Fenway as part of the park's latest series of upgrades and renovations.

MAY 20-22
The Chicago Cubs return to Fenway for the first time in 93 years.

JUNE 19
The Boston Bruins descend on the field to show off their newly acquired Stanley Cup.

2009   2010   2011

SEPTEMBER 28
The Red Sox go 7-20 in September, including a season-ending 4-3 loss to the Orioles in Baltimore, to cap the biggest collapse in MLB history. They finish 90-72, one game behind Tampa Bay for the wild card.

SEPTEMBER 30
Terry Francona resigns after two world titles in eight years as Red Sox manager. Weeks later, general manager Theo Epstein leaves the Red Sox to take the same role with the Chicago Cubs.

Top of page (l-r): Unveiling a statue of legends Ted Williams, Bobby Doerr, Johnny Pesky, and Dom DiMaggio, 2010; Red Sox General Manager Theo Epstein (right) jamming with Bill Janovitz during the 2007 Hot Stove Cool Music event at Fenway; jumping off to a fast start at Fenway's Run to Home Base fundraiser, 2011. Timeline: "Red Auerbach Day," 2007; Jason Varitek tallying the fourth Red Sox home run in a game with the Yankees, 2007; Lisbon vs. Celtic FC at Fenway, 2010; Neil Diamond singing "Sweet Caroline" on Opening Day, 2010.

PHOTOGRAPHY CREDITS

THE *BOSTON GLOBE*:

Back cover(bottom): David L. Ryan/Globe Staff
1: *Globe* file photo
2-3: Jonathan Wiggs/*Globe* staff
4-5: David L. Ryan/*Globe* staff
6: Jim Davis/*Globe* staff
7-9: David L. Ryan/*Globe* staff
10-11: *Globe* file photo
12: David L. Ryan/*Globe* staff
20: *Globe* file photo
22-23: Stan Grossfeld/*Globe* staff
27: *Globe* file photo
29: *Globe* file photo
31 (bottom): *Globe* file photo
32 (top): *Globe* file photo
35-37: *Globe* file photos
40: *Globe* file photo
51-52: *Globe* file photos
67 (top): *Globe* file photo
70: *Globe* file photo
74-75: *Globe* file photos
80-81: *Globe* file photos
84-85: *Globe* file photos
87: Stan Grossfeld/*Globe* staff
89 (top center): *Globe* file photo
93: *Globe* file photo
95-97: *Globe* file photos
103: Stan Grossfeld/*Globe* staff
104: *Globe* file photo
106-109: *Globe* file photos
111: *Globe* file photos
113: *Globe* file photo
115: *Globe* file photo
117 *Globe* file photo
118: *Globe* file photo
123: Louis Russo/*Globe* staff
125: Charles Dixon/*Globe* staff
129 (bottom): *Globe* file photo
134: *Globe* file photo
135 (top): *Globe* file photo
144: *Globe* file photo
146: *Globe* file photo
150 (top): Harry Brett for the *Globe*
150 (bottom): Jack Sheehan/*Globe* staff
151 (left): Gilbert E. Friedberg/*Globe* staff
151 (right): Dan Goshtigian/ *Globe* staff
152: *Globe* file photos
155 (top): *Globe* file photo
155 (bottom): John Tlumacki/*Globe* staff
158: Dan Goshtigian/*Globe* staff
159: Ted Dully/*Globe* staff
162: Dan Goshtigian/*Globe* staff
163: *Globe* file photos
164: Ted Dully/*Globe* staff
165: Charles B. Carey/*Globe* staff
166 (center): *Globe* file photo
167 (top left): Frank O'Brien/*Globe* staff
167 (top right): Tom Landers/*Globe* staff
167 (bottom left and right): Dan Goshtigian/*Globe* staff
170: Dan Goshtigian/*Globe* staff
171: George Rizer/*Globe* staff
172: Don Preston/*Globe* staff
173: Dan Goshtigian/*Globe* staff
175: Dan Goshtigian/*Globe* staff
176: George Rizer/*Globe* staff
177 (top): Dan Sheehan/*Globe* staff
177 (bottom): Paul Connell/*Globe* staff
178 (left): Frank O'Brien/*Globe* staff
178 (right): David L. Ryan/*Globe* staff
187 (top): David L. Ryan/*Globe* staff

187 (bottom): Jack O'Connell/*Globe* staff
188: Frank O'Brien/*Globe* staff
190: Ulrike Welsch/*Globe* staff
191 (left): *Globe* file photo
191 (right): George Rizer/*Globe* staff
192: David L. Ryan/*Globe* staff
193: Don Preston/*Globe* staff
194 (top): Frank O'Brien/*Globe* staff
194 (bottom): *Globe* file photo
195 (top center): Frank O'Brien/*Globe* staff
195 (top right): George Rizer/*Globe* staff
195 (bottom): Janet Knott/*Globe* staff
198: John Blanding/*Globe* staff
199 (top): David L. Ryan/*Globe* staff
199 (bottom): Frank O'Brien/*Globe* staff
200: Ted Gartland/*Globe* staff
201: *Globe* file photo
202-203: Jim Wilson/*Globe* staff
204: Stan Grossfeld/*Globe* staff
206: Joanne Rathe/*Globe* staff
207: George Rizer/*Globe* staff
208: John Blanding/*Globe* staff
209 (top): Suzanne Kreiter/*Globe* staff
209 (bottom): George Rizer/*Globe* staff
210: Stan Grossfeld/*Globe* staff
211: Jim Davis/*Globe* staff
212: Stan Grossfeld/*Globe* staff
213: David Molnar for the *Globe*
214: Bill Brett/*Globe* staff
215: Tom Herde/*Globe* staff
216 (top): Mark Cardwell/*Globe* staff
217 (top left and right): Bill Greene/*Globe* staff
217 (bottom left): John Blanding/*Globe* staff
217 (bottom right): Suzanne Kreiter/*Globe* staff
218: Jim Davis/*Globe* staff
221: Pat Greenhouse/*Globe* staff
223-224: Jim Davis/*Globe* staff
225: Stan Grossfeld/*Globe* staff
226: John Tlumacki/*Globe* staff
227: Stan Grossfeld/*Globe* staff
228: Jim Davis/*Globe* staff
229: Barry Chin/*Globe* staff
230: Stan Grossfeld/*Globe* staff
231 (top): Dominic Chavez/*Globe* staff
231 (bottom): Bill Greene/*Globe* staff
232-233: Stan Grossfeld/*Globe* staff
234: Max Becherer/*Globe* staff
235: Barry Chin/*Globe* staff
236 (bottom): Barry Chin/*Globe* staff
237 (top left): George Rizer/*Globe* staff
237 (top center): Jim Davis/*Globe* staff
237 (top right): Mark Wilson/*Globe* staff
237 (bottom): Barry Chin/*Globe* staff
238: Jim Davis/*Globe* staff
240: Wendy Maeda/*Globe* staff
241: David L. Ryan/*Globe* staff
242: John Tlumacki/*Globe* staff
243: Jim Davis/*Globe* staff
244: David L. Ryan/*Globe* staff
245 (bottom): Jim Davis/*Globe* staff
246: Barry Chin/*Globe* staff
247: Bill Greene/*Globe* staff
248 (top): Stan Grossfeld/*Globe* staff
248 (bottom): Yoon S. Byun/*Globe* staff
249 (top): Barry Chin/*Globe* staff
249 (center and bottom): Jim Davis/*Globe* staff
250 (bottom): Jim Davis/*Globe* staff
251: Stan Grossfeld/*Globe* staff
253: John Tlumacki/*Globe* staff
254: Stan Grossfeld/*Globe* staff

255: Jim Davis/*Globe* staff
256 (top): Bill Greene/*Globe* staff
256 (left): Stan Grossfeld/*Globe* staff
256 (right): Jim Davis/*Globe* staff
257-258: Jim Davis/*Globe* staff
259: Stan Grossfeld/*Globe* staff
260: Jim Davis/*Globe* staff
262-263: Jim Davis/*Globe* staff
264: Yoon S Byun/*Globe* staff
265-268: Jim Davis/*Globe* staff
269: Barry Chin/*Globe* staff
271 (top left, bottom left): Stan Grossfeld/*Globe* staff
271 (top right): Barry Chin/*Globe* staff
272 (top): Stan Grossfeld/*Globe* staff
272 (bottom): Jim Davis/*Globe* staff
273 (top left): David L. Ryan/*Globe* staff
273 (top center): Bill Brett/*Globe* staff
273 (top right): Aram Boghosian for the *Globe*
273 (center left): Stan Grossfeld/*Globe* staff
273 (center right): Jim Davis/*Globe* staff
273 (bottom): Barry Chin/*Globe* staff
278: David L. Ryan/*Globe* staff

ADDITIONAL PHOTOS BY:

WERNER H. KUNZ
Front Cover

BOSTON PUBLIC LIBRARY
13, 24, 45 (top and bottom), 48-49, 50 (Norman B. Leventhal Map Center), 54, 57, 66 (top left and bottom right), 67 (top right), 67 (center and bottom), 68, 78, 82, 88 (top), 89 (top left and right, center, and bottom left and right), 92, 105, 114, 117 (center), 122 (top and bottom), 127

ASSOCIATED PRESS
Back cover(top), 14, 59, 72-73, 79, 86, 90, 98-99, 101, 108-109, 116 (top and bottom), 117 (top left), 118, 120-121, 124, 126, 128-129 (top), 130-131 (bottom), 132-133, 135-136 (top and bottom), 147, 153-154, 156-157, 166 (left and bottom), 168,175, 180-186, 195 (top left), 196, 216 (bottom), 220, 222, 236 (top), 245, 250 (top), 252, 259 (top), 267 (top), 270

COURTESY OF BASEBALLFEVER.COM
33-34, 42, 50-51 (top left and right), 58, 60 (bottom left), 67 (top center)

LIBRARY OF CONGRESS
38-39

JOSHUA MCDONNELL
p8–9

JOHN F. KENNEDY LIBRARY
31 (top)

NATIONAL BASEBALL HALL OF FAME
145

NATIONAL BASEBALL LIBRARY
43

NORTHEASTERN UNIVERSITY
32 (bottom)

MARK RUCKER/TRANSCENDENTAL GRAPHICS, GETTY IMAGES
64

CORBIS
65

INDEX